9th Workshop on Innovative Use of NLP for Building Educational Applications 2014

Held at ACL 2014

Baltimore, Maryland, USA
26 June 2014

ISBN: 978-1-63439-198-6

Printed from e-media with permission by:

Curran Associates, Inc.
57 Morehouse Lane
Red Hook, NY 12571

Some format issues inherent in the e-media version may also appear in this print version.

Printed by Curran Associates, Inc. (2014)

For permission requests, please contact the Association for Computational Linguistics at the address below.

Association for Computational Linguistics
209 N. Eighth Street
Stroudsburg, Pennsylvania 18360

Phone: 1-570-476-8006
Fax: 1-570-476-0860

acl@aclweb.org

Additional copies of this publication are available from:

Curran Associates, Inc.
57 Morehouse Lane
Red Hook, NY 12571 USA
Phone: 845-758-0400
Fax: 845-758-2634
Email: curran@proceedings.com
Web: www.proceedings.com

Introduction

The field of NLP and education has matured dramatically since the first workshop in 1997, where the primary focus was on grammatical error detection and correction. As a community we have continued to improve existing capabilities and to identify and generate innovative and creative methods. Automated writing evaluation systems are now commercially viable, and are used to score millions of test-taker essays on high-stakes assessments. The educational and assessment landscape, especially in the United States, continues to foster a strong interest and high demand that furthers the state-of-the-art in automated writing evaluation capabilities, expanding the analysis of written responses to writing genres beyond those typicallyfound on standardized assessments. Much of the current demand for creative new educational applications results from the development of the Common Core State Standards Initiative (CCSSI). The goal of CCSSI is to ensure college- and workplace-readiness. The CCSSI describes what K-12 students should be learning with regard to reading, writing, speaking, listening, and media and technology.

Major advances in speech technology have made it possible to include speech in both assessment and Intelligent Tutoring Systems (ITS). These advances have made it possible for spoken constructed responses are now being evaluated. Consistent with this, there is also a renewed interest in spoken dialog for instruction and assessment. Relative to continued innovation, the explosive growth of mobile applications has increased interest in game-based assessment.

In the past few years, the use of NLP in educational applications gained visibility outside of the Computational Linguistics (CL) community. First, the Hewlett Foundation reached out to public and private sectors by sponsoring two competitions (both inspired by the CCSSI): one for automated essay scoring, and one for scoring of short response items. The motivation driving these competitions was to engage the larger scientific community in this enterprise. Massive Open Online Courses (MOOCs) are now also beginning to incorporate automated writing scoring systems to manage the thousands of writing assignments that can be generated in a single MOOC course. Another breakthrough for educational applications within the CL community is the large number of shared task competitions in the last few years. There have been four shared tasks on grammatical error correction, with the most recent edition hosted at CoNLL 2014. In 2013, there was a SemEval Shared Task on Student Response Analysis and one on Native Language Identification (hosted at the 2013 edition of this workshop). All of these competitions increased the visibility of the research space for using NLP to build educational applications.

As a community, we continue to improve existing capabilities and to identify and generate innovative ways to use NLP in applications for writing, reading, speaking, critical thinking, curriculum development, and assessment. Steady growth in the development of NLP-based applications for education has prompted an increased number of workshops, typically focusing on a single subfield. In this workshop, we present papers from all subfields: tools for scoring of text and speech, dialogue and intelligent tutoring, language corpora, and grammatical error detection.

We received 35 submissions and accepted six oral presentations and 14 poster presentations. Each paper was reviewed by three members of the Program Committee who were a good fit for each paper. We continue to have a strong policy concerning conflicts of interest. First, we make a concerted effort to not assign papers to reviewers if the paper had an author from their institution. Second, members of the organizing committee recuse themselves if there was a conflict of interest.

This workshop offers an opportunity to present and publish work that is highly relevant to the ACL, but is also highly specialized, and so this workshop is often a more appropriate venue for such work. The Poster session offers more breadth in terms of topics related to NLP and education, and maintains the original concept of a workshop. We believe that the workshop framework designed to introduce work in progress and new ideas needs to be revived, and we hope that we have achieved this with the breadth and variety of research accepted for this workshop. The total number of acceptances represents a 57% acceptance rate across oral and poster presentations.

While the field is growing, we do recognize that there is a core group of institutions and researchers who work in this area. With a higher acceptance rate, we were able to include papers from a wider variety of topics and institutions. The papers accepted to this workshop were selected on the basis of several factors, including the relevance to a core educational problem space, the novelty of the approach or domain, and the strength of the research.

The workshop is pleased to have an invited speaker this year, Dr. Norbert Elliot, Professor of English at New Jersey Institute of Technology, who will discuss his multi-disciplinary work, spanning across writing studies and innovation related to the design of NLP applications for educational purposes.

The accepted papers fall under five main themes:

Automatic Writing Assessment Measures: Four papers focus on assessment of student writing. Somasundraran and Chodorow investigate scoring short-text vocabulary items and Leeman-Munk et al investigate scoring short-text items that contain spelling errors. Kharkwal and Muresan investigate using sentence processing complexity as a feature for scoring essays. Zhang and Litman study the process of student essay revision.

Readability: Two papers investigate text difficulty of reading passages. Salesky and Shen on the passage level and Dell'Orletta, et al on the sentence level.

Assessing Speech: We have six papers on automatically assessing speech. Three papers target two novel populations: Cheng et al and Metallinou and Cheng investigate automatic speech scoring of young English language learners and Zechner et al describe an end-to-end system for assessing the spoken responses in a language assessment for EFL teachers who are non-native English speakers. Evanini and Wang present work on detecting plagiarized responses and Yoon and Xie present work on detecting non-scorable responses. Finally, Loukina et al investigate whether the ROUGE method can be used to automatically evaluate the content coverage of spoken summaries.

Automatic Item Generation: Swanson et al's paper discusses data-driven methods for automatic generation of language education exercises. Zesch and Melamud describe a method that uses context-sensitive lexical inference rules to automatically generate challenging distractors for multiple-choice gap-fill items.

Grammatical Errors: There are two papers on grammatical errors made by language learners. Madnani and Cahill give a proof-of-concept for giving feedback about preposition errors to English language learners. Rytting et al describe a corpus of word-level listening errors for learners of Arabic.

MOOCs and Collaborative Learning: Ramesh, et al use machine learning to investigate discussion forums in MOOC contexts; this work is critical to progress in data mining of MOOCs. Peer-review is a prominent topic in education, especially as it is currently widely used in MOOC contexts for evaluating constructed responses. Nguyen and Litman's paper aims to automatically predict whether peer feedback is of high quality. In the context of collaborative learning, Ahrenberg and Tarvi discuss a method of teacher-student computer-based collaboration in the context of a translation class.

We wish to thank everyone who showed interest and submitted a paper, all of the authors for their contributions, the members of the Program Committee for their thoughtful reviews, and everyone who attends this workshop. We would especially like to thank our six sponsors: American Institutes for Research, CTB/McGraw-Hill, Educational Testing Service, edX, LightSide and Pearson, whose contributions have supported an invited speaker, student workshop dinner subsidy, and workshop Tshirts! In addition, we would like to thank Emilie Bennett-Kjenstad and Joya Tetreault for creating the T-shirt design.

Joel Tetreault, Yahoo! Labs
Jill Burstein, Educational Testing Service
Claudia Leacock, CTB/McGraw-Hill

Organizers:

Joel Tetreault, Yahoo! Labs
Jill Burstein, Educational Testing Service
Claudia Leacock, CTB/McGraw-Hill

Program Committee:

Andrea Abel, EURAC, Italy
Oistein Andersen, University of Cambridge, UK
Sumit Basu, Microsoft Research, USA
Timo Baumann, University of Hamburg, Germany
Lee Becker, Hapara, USA
Delphine Bernhard, Université de Strasbourg, France
Jared Bernstein, Pearson, USA
Kristy Boyer, North Carolina State University, USA
Chris Brew, Nuance Communications, Inc., USA
Ted Briscoe, University of Cambridge, UK
Chris Brockett, Microsoft Research, USA
Julian Brooke, University of Toronto, USA
Aoife Cahill, Educational Testing Service, USA
Min Chi, North Carolina State University, USA
Martin Chodorow, Hunter College, CUNY, USA
Mark Core, University of Southern California, USA
Daniel Dahlmeier, SAP, Singapore
Barbara Di Eugenio, University of Illinois at Chicago, USA
Markus Dickinson, Indiana University, USA
Bill Dolan, Microsoft Research, USA
Myrosia Dzikovska, University of Edinburgh, UK
Yo Ehara, Miyao Lab., National Institute of Informatics, Japan
Maxine Eskenazi, Carnegie Mellon University, USA
Keelan Evanini, ETS, USA
Michael Flor, ETS, USA
Peter Foltz, Pearson Knowledge Technologies, USA
Jennifer Foster, Dublin City University, Ireland
Thomas Francois, UC Louvain, Belgium
Anette Frank, University of Heidelberg, Germany
Michael Gamon, Microsoft Research, USA
Caroline Gasperin, Swiftkey, UK
Kallirroi Georgila, University of Southern California
Iryna Gurevych, University of Darmstadt, Germany
Na-Rae Han, University of Pittsburgh, USA
Trude Heift, Simon Frasier University, Canada
Michael Heilman, ETS, USA
Derrick Higgins, ETS, USA
Rebecca Hwa, University of Pittsburgh, USA
Radu Ionescu, University of Bucharest, Romania
Ross Israel, Indiana University, USA
Pamela Jordan, University of Pittsburgh, USA

Levi King, Indiana University, USA
Ola Knutsson, Stockholm University, Sweden
Ekaterina Kochmar, University of Cambridge, UK
Mamoru Komachi, Tokyo Metropolitan University, Japan
John Lee, City University of Hong Kong
Baoli Li, Henan University of Technology, China
Diane Litman, University of Pittsburgh, USA
Annie Louis, University of Edinburgh, UK
Xiaofei Lu, Penn State University, USA
Nitin Madnani, ETS, USA
Montse Maritxalar, University of the Basque Country, Spain
Mourad Mars, University of Monastir, Tunisia
James Martin, University of Colorado, USA
Aurélien Max, LIMSI-CNRS, France
Julie Medero, University of Washington, USA
Detmar Meurers, University of Tubingen, Germany
Lisa Michaud, Merrimack College, USA
Rada Mihalcea, University of Michigan, USA
Michael Mohler, Language Computer Corporation, USA
Jack Mostow, Carnegie Mellon University, USA
Smaranda Muresan, Columbia University, USA
Ani Nenkova, University of Pennsylvania, USA
Hwee Tou Ng, National University of Singapore, Singapore
Rodney Nielsen, University of Colorado, USA
Mari Ostendorf, University of Washington, USA
Ted Pedersen, University of Minnesota, USA
Heather Pon-Barry, Arizona State University, USA
Matt Post, Johns Hopkins University, USA
Patti Price, PPRICE Speech and Language Technology, USA
Marti Quixal, University of Texas at Austin, USA
Carolyn Rosé, Carnegie Mellon University, USA
Andrew Rosenberg, Queens College, CUNY, USA
Mihai Rotaru, TextKernel, the Netherlands
Alla Rozovskaya, Columbia University, USA
Keisuku Sakaguchi, Johns Hopkins University, USA
Mathias Schulze, University of Waterloo, Canada
Serge Sharoff, University of Leeds, UK
Swapna Somasundaran, ETS, USA
Richard Sproat, Google, USA
Helmer Strik, Radboug University Nijmegen, the Netherlands
Nai-Lung Tsao, National Central University, Taiwan
Lucy Vanderwende, Microsoft Research, USA
Giulia Venturi, Institute of Computational Linguistics "Antonio Zampolli" (ILC-CNR), Italy
Carl Vogel, Trinity College, Ireland
Elena Volodina, University of Gothenburg, Sweden
Monica Ward, Dublin City University, Ireland
Pete Whitelock, Oxford University Press, UK
Magdalena Wolska, University of Tubingen, Germany
Peter Wood, University of Saskatchewan in Saskatoon, Canada
Wenting Xiong, University of Pittsburgh, USA
Huichao Xue, University of Pittsburgh, USA

Helen Yannakoudakis, University of Cambridge, UK
Marcos Zampieri, Saarland University, Germany
Klaus Zechner, ETS, USA
Torsten Zesch, University of Duisburg-Essen, Germany

Invited Speaker:

Dr. Norbert Elliot
Professor of English, New Jersey Institute of Technology
Writing Studies and Innovation in Designing NLP Educational Applications: A Multidisciplinary Perspective

Table of Contents

Conference Program

Thursday, June 26, 2014

8:45–9:00 Load Presentations

9:00–9:15 Opening Remarks

9:15–9:40 *Automated Measures of Specific Vocabulary Knowledge from Constructed Responses ('Use These Words to Write a Sentence Based on this Picture')*
Swapna Somasundaran and Martin Chodorow

9:40–10:05 *Automatic Assessment of the Speech of Young English Learners*
Jian Cheng, Yuan Zhao D'Antilio, Xin Chen and Jared Bernstein

10:05–10:25 *Automatic detection of plagiarized spoken responses*
Keelan Evanini and Xinhao Wang

10:30–11:00 Break

11:00–11:20 *Understanding MOOC Discussion Forums using Seeded LDA*
Arti Ramesh, Dan Goldwasser, Bert Huang, Hal Daume and Lise Getoor

11:20–12:30 Invited Speaker: Norbert Elliot

12:20–2:00 Lunch

2:00–3:30 Posters and Demos

Translation Class Instruction as Collaboration in the Act of Translation
Lars Ahrenberg and Ljuba Tarvi

The pragmatics of margin comments: An empirical study
Debora Field, Stephen Pulman and Denise Whitelock

Surprisal as a Predictor of Essay Quality
Gaurav Kharkwal and Smaranda Muresan

Towards Domain-Independent Assessment of Elementary Students' Science Competency using Soft Cardinality
Samuel Leeman-Munk, Angela Shelton, Eric Wiebe and James Lester

Thursday, June 26, 2014 (continued)

Automatic evaluation of spoken summaries: the case of language assessment
Anastassia Loukina, Klaus Zechner and Lei Chen

An Explicit Feedback System for Preposition Errors based on Wikipedia Revisions
Nitin Madnani and Aoife Cahill

Syllable and language model based features for detecting non-scorable tests in spoken language proficiency assessment applications
Angeliki Metallinou and Jian Cheng

Improving Peer Feedback Prediction: The Sentence Level is Right
Huy Nguyen and Diane Litman

ArCADE: An Arabic Corpus of Auditory Dictation Errors
C. Anton Rytting, Paul Rodrigues, Tim Buckwalter, Valerie Novak, Aric Bills, Noah H. Silbert and Mohini Madgavkar

Similarity-Based Non-Scorable Response Detection for Automated Speech Scoring
Su-Youn Yoon and Shasha Xie

Natural Language Generation with Vocabulary Constraints
Ben Swanson, Elif Yamangil and Eugene Charniak

Automated scoring of speaking items in an assessment for teachers of English as a Foreign Language
Klaus Zechner, Keelan Evanini, Su-Youn Yoon, Lawrence Davis, Xinhao Wang, Lei Chen, Chong Min Lee and Chee Wee Leong

Automatic Generation of Challenging Distractors Using Context-Sensitive Inference Rules
Torsten Zesch and Oren Melamud

Sentence-level Rewriting Detection
Fan Zhang and Diane Litman

3:30–4:00 Break

4:00–4:25 *Exploiting Morphological, Grammatical, and Semantic Correlates for Improved Text Difficulty Assessment*
Elizabeth Salesky and Wade Shen

4:25–4:50 *Assessing the Readability of Sentences: Which Corpora and Features?*
Felice Dell'Orletta, Martijn Wieling, Giulia Venturi, Andrea Cimino and Simonetta Montemagni

Thursday, June 26, 2014 (continued)

4:50–5:15	*Rule-based and machine learning approaches for second language sentence-level readability* Ildikó Pilán, Elena Volodina and Richard Johansson
5:15–5:30	Closing Remarks

Automated Measures of Specific Vocabulary Knowledge from Constructed Responses ("Use These Words to Write a Sentence Based on this Picture")

Swapna Somasundaran
Educational Testing Services
660 Rosedale Road,
Princeton, NJ 08541, USA
ssomasundaran@ets.org

Martin Chodorow
Hunter College and the Graduate Center
City University of New York,
New York, NY 10065, USA
martin.chodorow@hunter.cuny.edu

Abstract

We describe a system for automatically scoring a vocabulary item type that asks test-takers to use two specific words in writing a sentence based on a picture. The system consists of a rule-based component and a machine learned statistical model which uses a variety of construct-relevant features. Specifically, in constructing the statistical model, we investigate if grammar, usage, and mechanics features developed for scoring essays can be applied to short answers, as in our task. We also explore new features reflecting the quality of the collocations in the response, as well as features measuring the consistency of the response to the picture. System accuracy in scoring is 15 percentage points greater than the majority class baseline and 10 percentage points less than human performance.

1 Introduction

It is often said that the best way to see if a person knows the meaning of a word is to have that person use the word in a sentence. Despite this widespread view, most vocabulary testing continues to rely on multiple choice items (e.g. (Lawless et al., 2012; Lawrence et al., 2012)). In fact, few assessments use constructed sentence responses to measure vocabulary knowledge, in part because of the considerable time and cost required to score such responses manually. While much progress has been made in automatically scoring writing quality in essays (Attali and Burstein, 2006; Leacock et al., 2014; Dale et al., 2012), the essay scoring engines do not measure proficiency in the use of specific words, except perhaps for some frequently confused homophones (e.g., its/it's, there/their/they're, affect/effect).

In this paper we present a system for automated scoring of targeted vocabulary knowledge based on short constructed responses in a picture description task. Specifically, we develop a system for scoring a vocabulary item type that is in operational use in English proficiency tests for non-native speakers. Each task prompt in this item type consists of two target key words, for which the vocabulary proficiency is tested, and a picture that provides the context for the sentence construction. The task is to generate a single sentence, incorporating both key words, consistent with the picture. Presumably, a test-taker with competent knowledge of the key words will be able to use them in a well-formed grammatical sentence in the context of the picture.

Picture description tasks have been employed in a number of areas of study ranging from second language acquisition to Alzheimer's disease (Ellis, 2000; Forbes-McKay and Venneri, 2005). Pictures and picture-based story narration have also been used to study referring expressions (Lee et al., 2012) and to analyze child narratives in order to predict language impairment (Hassanali et al., 2013). Evanini et al. (2014) employ a series of pictures and elicit (oral) story narration to test English language proficiency. In our task, the picture is used as a constraining factor to limit the type and content of sentences that can be generated using the given key words.

In the course of developing our system, we examined existing features that have been developed for essay scoring, such as detectors of errors in grammar, usage and mechanics, as well as collocation features, to see if they can be re-used for scoring short responses. We also developed new features for assessing the quality of sentence construction using Pointwise Mutual Information (PMI). As our task requires responses to describe the prompt pictures, we manually constructed detailed textual descriptions of the pictures, and de-

Proceedings of the Ninth Workshop on Innovative Use of NLP for Building Educational Applications , pages 1–11,
Baltimore, Maryland USA, June 26, 2014.

veloped features that measure the overlap between the content of the responses and the textual description. Our automated scoring system is partly based on deterministic scoring criteria and partly statistical. Overall, it achieves an accuracy of 76%, which is a 15 percentage point improvement over a simple majority class baseline.

The organization of this paper is as follows: Section 2 describes the picture description task and the scoring guide that is used to manually score the picture description responses operationally. It also considers which aspects of scoring may be handled best by deterministic procedures and which are more amenable to statistical modeling. Section 3 details the construction of a reference corpus of text describing each picture, and Section 4 presents the features used in scoring. Section 5 describes our system architecture and presents our experiments and results. Detailed analysis is presented in Section 6, followed by related work in Section 7 and a summary with directions for future research in Section 8.

2 Task Description and Data

The picture description task is an item type that is in actual operational use as part of a test of English. It consists of a picture, along with two key words, one or both of which may be in an inflected form. Test-takers are required to use the two words in one sentence to describe the picture. They may change the inflections of the words as appropriate to the context of their sentence, but they must use some form of both words in one sentence. Requiring them to produce a response based on the picture constrains the variety of sentences and words that they are likely to generate.

Trained human scorers evaluate the responses based on appropriate use of grammar and the relevance of the sentence to the picture. The operational scoring guide is as follows:

score = 3 The response consists of ONE sentence that: (a) has no grammatical errors, (b) contains forms of both key words used appropriately, AND (c) is consistent with the picture.

score = 2 The response consists of one or more sentences that: (a) have one or more grammatical errors that do not obscure the meaning, (b) contain BOTH key words, (but they may not be in the same sentence and the form of the word(s) may not be accurate), AND (c) are consistent with the picture.

score = 1 The response: (a) has errors that interfere with meaning, (b) omits one or both key words, OR (c) is not consistent with the picture.

score = 0 The response is blank, written in a foreign language, or consists of keystroke characters.

Our decisions about scoring system design are based on the scoring guide and its criteria. Some aspects of the scoring can be handled by simple pattern matching or lookup, while others require machine learning. For example, score 0 is assigned to responses that are blank or are not in English. This can be detected and scored in a straightforward way. On the other hand, the determination of grammaticality for the score points 3, 2 and 1 depends on the presence and severity of grammatical errors. A wide variety of such errors appear in responses, including errors of punctuation, subject-verb agreement, preposition usage and article usage. The severity of an error depends on how problematic the error is, and the system will have to learn this from the behavior of the trained human scorer(s), making this aspect of the scoring more amenable to statistical modeling.

Similarly, statistical modeling is more suitable for determining the consistency of the response with respect to the picture. According to the scoring guide, a response gets a score of 0 or 1 if it is not consistent with the picture, and gets a score of 2 or 3 if it is consistent. Thus, this aspect cannot solely determine the score of a response – it influences the score in conjunction with other language proficiency factors. Further, measures of how relevant a response is to a picture are likely to fall on a continuous scale, making a statistical modeling approach appropriate.

Finally, although there are some aspects of the scoring guide, such as the number of sentences and the presence of the key words, that can be measured trivially, they do not act as sole determinants of the score. For example, having more than one sentence can result in the response receiving a score of 2 or 1. The number of sentences works in conjunction with other factors such as severity of grammar errors and relevance to the picture. Hence its contribution to the final score is best modeled statistically.

As a result of the heterogeneous nature of the problem, our system is made up of a statistical learning component as well as a non-statistical component.

2.1 Data

The data set consists of about 58K responses to 434 picture prompts. The mean response length was 11.26 words with a standard deviation of 5.10. The data was split into 2 development sets (consisting of a total of about 2K responses) and a final train-test set (consisting of the remaining 56K responses) used for evaluation. All 58K responses were human scored using the scoring rubric discussed in Section 2. About 17K responses were double annotated. The inter-annotator agreement, using quadratic weighted kappa (QWK), was 0.83. Score point 3, the most frequent class, was assigned to 61% of the responses, followed by score point 2 (31%), score point 1 (7.6%) and score point 0 (0.4%).

3 Reference Picture Descriptions

The pictures in our task vary in their complexity. A typical prompt picture might be a photograph of an outdoor marketplace, the inside of an airport terminal, a grocery store, a restaurant or a store room. Because consistency with respect to the picture is a crucial component in our task, we needed a reliable and exhaustive textual representation of each picture. Therefore, we manually constructed a *reference text corpus* for each of our 434 picture prompts. We chose to use manual creation of the reference corpus instead of trying automated image recognition because automated methods of image recognition are error prone and would result in a noisy reference corpus. Additionally, automated approaches would, at best, give us a (noisy) list of items that are present in the picture, but not the overall scene or event depicted.

Two annotators employed by a company that specializes in annotation created the reference corpora of picture descriptions. The protocol used for creating the reference corpus is shown below:

Part-1: List the items, setting, and events in the picture.
List, one by one, all the items and events you see in the picture. These may be animate objects (e.g. man), inanimate objects (e.g. table) or events (e.g. dinner). Try to capture both the overall setting (restaurant), as well as the objects that make up the picture (e.g. man, table, food). These are generally (but not necessarily) nouns and noun phrases. Some pictures can have many items, while some have only a few. The goal is to list 10-15 items and to capture as many items as possible, *starting with the most obvious ones*.
If the picture is too sparse, and you are not able to list at least 10 items, please indicate this as a comment.

Part:2 Describe the picture
Describe the scene unfolding in the picture. The scene in the picture may be greater than the sum of its parts (many of which you will list in part-1). For example, the objects in a picture could be "shoe" "man" "chair", but the scene in the picture could be that of a shoe purchase. The description tries to recreate the scene (or parts of the scene) depicted in the picture.
Generate a paragraph of 5-7 sentences describing the picture. Some of these sentences will address what is going on, while some may address relations between items. The proportions of these will differ, based on the picture. Make sure that you generate at least one sentence containing the two key words.
If the picture is too simple, and you are not able to generate at least 5 sentences, please indicate this as a comment.

The human annotator was given the picture and the two key words. The protocol for creating each reference corpus asked the annotator to first exhaustively list all the items (animate and inanimate) in the picture. Then, the annotator was asked to describe the scene in the picture. We used this two step process in order to capture, as much as possible, all objects, relationships between objects, settings and events depicted in the pictures.

The size of the reference corpus for each prompt is much larger than the single sentence test-taker response. This is intentional as the goal is to make the reference corpus as exhaustive as possible. We used a single annotator for each prompt. Double annotation using a secondary annotator was done in cases where we felt that the coverage of the corpus created by the primary annotator was insufficient[1].

In order to test coverage, we used a small development set of essays from each prompt and compared the coverage of the generated reference corpus over the development essays. If the coverage (proportion of content words in the responses that were found in the reference corpus) was less than 50% (this was the case for about 20% of the prompts), we asked the secondary annotator to create a new reference corpus for the prompt. The two reference corpora for the prompt were then simply combined to form a single reference corpus.

4 Features for automated scoring

Because the score points in the scoring guide conflate, to some degree, syntactic, semantic, and other weaknesses in the response, we carried out a scoring study on a second small development set (comprising of a total of 80 responses from 4 prompts, picked randomly) to gather insight into the general problems in English language proficiency exhibited in the responses. For the study, it was necessary to have test-taker responses rescored by an annotator using an analytic scheme which makes the types and locations of problems explicit. This exercise revealed that, in addition to the factors stated explicitly in the scoring guide, there is another factor that results in low comprehension (readability) of the sentence and that reflects lower English proficiency. Specifically, the annotator tagged many sentences as being "awkward". This awkwardness was due to poor choice of words or to poor construction of the sentence. For example, in the sentence "The man is putting some food in bags while he is recording for the payment", "recording for the payment" was marked as an awkward phrase. Based on our annotation of the scores and on the descriptions in the scoring guide, we selected features designed to capture grammar, picture relevance and awkward usage. We discuss each of our feature sets in the following subsections.

4.1 Features for Grammatical Error Detection

Essay scoring engines such as e-rater® (Attali and Burstein, 2006) typically use a number of grammar, usage and mechanics features that detect and quantify different types of English usage errors in essays. Examples of some of these error types are: *Run-on Sentences*, *Subject Verb Agreement Errors*, *Pronoun Errors*, *Missing Possessive Errors*, *Wrong Article Errors*, *Missing Article Errors*, *Preposition Errors*, *Non-standard Verb or Word Form Errors*, *Double Negative Errors*, *Fragment or Missing Comma Errors*, *Ill-formed Verb Errors*, *Wrong Form of Word Errors*, *Spelling Errors*, *Wrong Part of Speech Errors*, and *Missing Punctuation Errors* .

In addition to these, essay scoring engines often also use as features the Number of Sentences that are Short, the Number of Sentences that are Long, the Number of Passive Sentences, and other features that are relevant only for longer texts such as essays. Accordingly, we selected, from e-rater 113 grammar, word usage, mechanics and lexical complexity features that could be applied to our short response task. This forms our *grammar* feature set.

4.2 Features for Measuring Content Relevance

We generated a set of features that measure the content overlap between a given response and the corresponding reference corpus for the prompt. For this, first the keywords and the stop words were removed from the response and the reference corpus, and then the proportion of overlap was calculated between the lemmatized content words of the response and the lemmatized version of the corresponding reference corpus, as follows:

$$\frac{|Response \cap Corpus|}{|Response|}$$

It is not always necessary for the test-taker to use exactly the same words found in the reference corpus. For example, the annotator might have referred to a person in the picture as a "lady", while a response may refer to the same person as a "woman" or "girl" or even just "person". Thus, we needed to go beyond simple lexical match. In order to account for synonyms, we expanded the content words in the reference corpus by adding their synonyms, as provided in Lin's thesaurus (Lin, 1998) and then compared the expanded reference to each response. Along the same lines, we also used expansions from WordNet synonyms, WordNet hypernyms and WordNet hyponyms. The following is the list of our content

[1]We do not conduct inter-annotator agreement studies as the goal of the double annotation was to create a diverse description.

relevance features. Each measures the proportion of overlap as described by the equation above between the lemmatized response and

1. **lemmas:** the lemmatized reference corpus.
2. **cov-lin:** the reference corpus expanded using Lin's thesaurus.
3. **cov-wn-syns:** the reference corpus expanded using WordNet Synonyms.
4. **cov-wn-hyper:** the reference corpus expanded using WordNet Hypernyms.
5. **cov-wn-hypo:** the reference corpus expanded using WordNet Hyponyms.
6. **cov-all:** the reference corpus expanded using all of the above methods.

Mean proportions of overlap ranged from 0.65 for lemmas to 0.97 for cov-all.

The 6 features listed above, along with the prompt id give a total of 7 features that form our *relevance* feature set. We use prompt id as a feature because the extent of overlap can depend on the prompt. Some pictures are very sparse, so, the description of the picture in the response will be short, and will not vary much from the reference corpus. For these, a good amount of overlap between the response and reference corpus is expected. Other pictures are very dense with a large number of objects and items shown. In this case, any single response may describe just a small subset of the items and satisfy the consistency criteria, and consequently, even a small overlap between the response and the reference corpus may be sufficient.

4.3 Features for Awkward Word Usage

In order to measure awkward word usage, we explored PMI-based features, and also investigated whether some features developed for essay scoring can be used effectively for this purpose.

4.3.1 PMI-based ngram features

Non-native writing is often characterized by inappropriate combinations of words, indicating the writer's lack of knowledge of collocations. For example, "recording for the payment" might be better expressed as "entering the price in the cash register". As "recording for the payment" is an inappropriate construction, it is not likely to be common, for example, in a large web corpus. We use this intuition in constructing our PMI-based features.

We find the PMI of all adjacent word pairs (bigrams), as well as all adjacent word triples (trigrams) in the Google 1T web corpus (Brants and Franz, 2006) using the TrendStream database (Flor, 2013).

PMI between word pairs (bigram AB) is defined as:

$$\log_2 \frac{p(AB)}{p(A).p(B)}$$

and between word triples (trigram ABC) as

$$\log_2 \frac{p(ABC)}{p(A).p(B).p(C)}$$

The higher the value of the PMI, the more common is the collocation for the word pair/triple in well formed texts. On the other hand, negative values of PMI indicate that the given word pair (or triple) is less likely than chance to occur together. We hypothesized that this would be a good indicator of awkward usage, as suggested in (Chodorow and Leacock, 2000).

The PMI values for adjacent words obtained over the entire response are then assigned to bins, with 8 bins for word pairs and another 8 for word triples. Each bin represents a range for PMI p taking real values $\mathbb{R}$ as follows:

$$bin_1 = \{p \in \mathbb{R} \mid p > 20\}$$
$$bin_2 = \{p \in \mathbb{R} \mid 10 < p \leq 20\}$$
$$bin_3 = \{p \in \mathbb{R} \mid 1 < p \leq 10\}$$
$$bin_4 = \{p \in \mathbb{R} \mid 0 < p \leq 1\}$$
$$bin_5 = \{p \in \mathbb{R} \mid -1 < p \leq 0\}$$
$$bin_6 = \{p \in \mathbb{R} \mid -10 < p \leq -1\}$$
$$bin_7 = \{p \in \mathbb{R} \mid -20 < p \leq -10\}$$
$$bin_8 = \{p \in \mathbb{R} \mid p \leq -20\}$$

Once the PMI values for the adjacent word pairs in the response are generated, we generate two sets of features. The first set is based on the counts of word pairs falling into each bin (for example, *Number of pairs falling into* bin_1, *Number of pairs falling into* bin_2 and so on). The second set of features are based on percentages (for example *Percentage of pairs falling into* bin_1, *Percentage of pairs falling into* bin_2 etc.). These two sets result in a total of 16 features. We similarly generate 16 more features for adjacent word triples. We use percentages in addition to raw counts to account for the length of the response. For example, it is possible for a long sentence to have phrases that are awkward as well as well formed, giving the same counts of phrases in the high-PMI value bins as that of a short sentence that is entirely well formed.

In addition to binning, we also encode as features the maximum, minimum and median PMI value obtained over all word pairs. The first two features capture the best and the worst word collocations in a response. The median PMI value captures the overall general quality of the response in a single number. For example, if this is a low number, then the response generally has many bad phrasal collocations. Finally a *null-PMI* feature is used to count the number of pairs that had zero entries in the database. This feature is an indicator that the given words or word collocations were not found even once in the database. Given the size of the underlying database, this usually happens in cases when words are misspelled, or when the words never occur together.

All features created for bigrams are also created for trigrams. We thus have a total of 40 features, called the *pmi* feature set.

4.3.2 Features from essay scoring

A number of measures of collocation quality have been proposed and implemented (e.g. (Futagi et al., 2008; Dahlmeier and Ng, 2011)). We use e-rater's measure of the density of 'good' collocations found in the response. Another source of difficulty for non-native writers is the selection of appropriate prepositions. We use the mean probability assigned by e-rater to the prepositions in the response. These two measures, one for the quality of collocations and the other for the quality of prepositions, are combined in our *colprep* feature set.

4.4 Scoring Rubric-based Features

As seen in Section 2, some of the criteria for scoring are quite straightforward (e.g. "omits one or both key words"). While these are not sole determinants of a score, they are certainly strong influences. Thus, we encode four criteria from the scoring guide. These form our final feature set, *rubric*, and are binary values, answering the questions: Is the first key word from the prompt present in the response? Is the second key word from the prompt present in the response? Are both key words from the prompt present in the response? Is there more than one sentence in the response?

Table 1 provides a list of feature types and the corresponding number of features of each type.

Feature set type	Number of Features
grammar	113
relevance	7
pmi	40
colprep	2
rubric	4

Table 1: Feature sets and the counts of features in each set

5 System and Evaluation

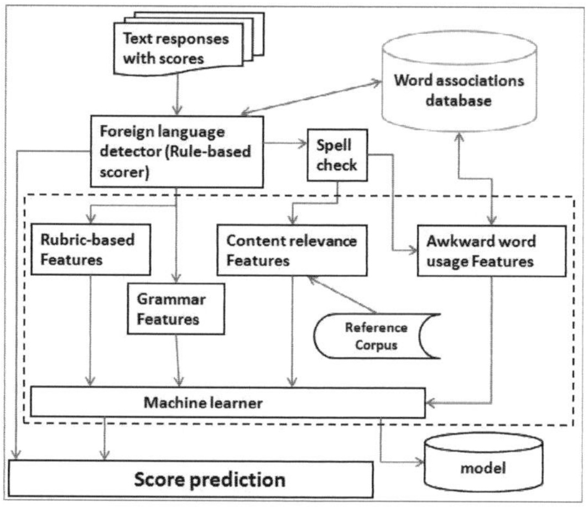

Figure 1: System Architecture

As noted earlier, the system is partly rule-based and partly statistical. Figure 1 illustrates the system architecture. The rule-based part captures the straightforward deterministic scoring criteria while the machine learning component encodes features described in Section 4 and learns how to weight the features for scoring based on human-scored responses.

As described in Section 2, detection of conditions that result in a score of zero are straightforward. Our rule-based scorer (shown as "Foreign Language Detector" in Figure 1) assigns a zero score to a response if it is blank or non-English. The system determines if the response is non-English based on the average of PMI bigram scores over the response. If the average score is less than a threshold value, the system tags it as a non-English sentence. The threshold was determined by manually inspecting the PMI values obtained for sentences belonging to English and non-English news texts. Responses given zero scores by this module are filtered out and do not go to the next stage.

Responses that pass the rule-based scorer are then sent to the statistical scorer. Here, we encode the features discussed in Section 4. Spell checking and correction are carried out before features for content relevance and PMI-based awkward word usage are computed. This is done in order to prevent misspellings from affecting the reference corpus match or database search. The original text is sent to the Grammar feature generator as it creates features based on misspellings and other word form errors. Finally, we use all the features to train a Logistic Regression model using sklearn. Note that the statistical system predicts all 4 scores (0 through 3). This is because the rule-based system is not perfect; that is, it might miss some responses that should receive zero scores, and pass them over to the next stage.

5.1 Metrics

We report our results using overall accuracy, quadratic weighted kappa (QWK) and score-level precision, recall and f-measure. The precision P of the system is calculated for each score point i as

$$P_i = \frac{|S_i \cap H_i|}{|S_i|}$$

where $|S_i|$ is the number of responses given a score of i by the system, and $|S_i \cap H_i|$ is the number of responses given a score of i by the system as well as the human rater.

Similarly, recall, R is calculated for each score point i as

$$R_i = \frac{|S_i \cap H_i|}{|H_i|}$$

F-measure F_i is calculated as the harmonic mean of the precision P_i and recall R_i at each score point i. Accuracy is the ratio of the number of responses correctly classified over the total number of responses.

5.2 Results

All of the responses in the train-test set were passed through the rule-based zero-scorer. A total of 210 responses had been scored as zero by the human scorer. The rule-based system scored 222 responses as zeros, of which 184 were correct.

The precision P^{rule} of the rule-based system is calculated as

$$P_0^{rule} = \frac{184}{222} = 82.9\%$$

Similarly, Recall is calculated as

$$R_0^{rule} = \frac{184}{210} = 87.6\%$$

The corresponding F-measure is 85.2%

The remaining responses pass to the next stage where machine learning is employed. We performed 10 fold cross-validation experiments using Logistic Regression as well as Random Forest learners. As the results are comparable, we only report those from logistic regression.

	Accuracy in %	Agreement (QWK)
Baseline	61.00	-
System	76.23	0.63
Human	86.00	0.83

Table 2: Overall system and human accuracy (in percentage) and agreement (using Quadratic Weighted Kappa)

Table 2 reports the results. The system achieves an accuracy of 76.23%, which is more than a 15 percentage point improvement over the majority class baseline of 61%. The majority class baseline always predicts a score of 3. Compared to human performance, system performance is 10 percentage points lower (human-human agreement is 86%). Quadratic weighted kappa for system-human agreement is also lower (0.63) than for human-human agreement (0.83).

Table 3 reports the precision, recall and F-measure of the system for each of the score points.

Score point	Precision	Recall	F-measure
0	84.2	68.3	72.9
1	78.4	67.5	72.6
2	70.6	50.4	58.8
3	77.8	90.5	83.6

Table 3: Overall system performance at each score point using all features

6 Analysis

In order to understand the usefulness of each feature set in scoring the responses, we constructed systems using first the individual features alone, and then using feature combinations. Table 4 reports the accuracy of the learner using individual features alone. We see that, individually, each feature set performs much below the performance of the full system (that has an accuracy of 76.23%), which is expected, as each feature set represents a particular aspect of the construct. However, in general, each of the feature-sets (except *colprep*) shows improvement over baseline, indicating that they contribute towards performance improvement in the automated system.

Grammar features are the best of the individual feature sets at 70% accuracy, indicating that grammatical error features developed for longer texts can be applied to single sentences. The PMI-based feature set is the second best performer, indicating its effectiveness in capturing word usage issues. While *colprep* and *pmi* both capture awkward usage, *pmi* alone shows better performance (67.44%) than *colprep* alone (61.26%). Also, when *rubric* is used alone, the resulting system produces a four percentage point improvement over the baseline, with 65% accuracy, indicating the presence of responses where the test-takers are not able to incorporate one or both words in a single sentence. The relevance feature set by itself does not show substantial improvement over the baseline. This is not surprising, as according to the scoring guide, a response gets a score of 0 or 1 if it does not describe the picture, and gets a score of 2 or 3 if it is relevant to the picture. Hence, this feature cannot solely and accurately determine the score.

Feature Set	Accuracy in %
grammar	70.30
pmi	67.44
rubric	65.00
relevance	62.50
colprep	61.26

Table 4: System performance for individual features

Table 5 reports accuracies of systems built using feature set combinations. The first feature set combination, *grammar + colprep*, is a set of all features obtained from essay scoring. Here we see that addition of *colprep* does not improve the performance over that obtained by grammar features alone. Further, when *colprep* is combined with *pmi* (*colprep+pmi*, row 2), there is a slight drop in performance as compared to using pmi-based features alone. These results indicate that *colprep*, while being useful for larger texts, does not transfer well to the simple single sentence responses in our task.

Further, in Table 5 we see that the system using a combination of the pmi feature set and the relevance feature set (*pmi+relevance*) achieves an accuracy of 69%. Thus, this feature combination is able to improve performance over that using either feature set alone, indicating that while content relevance features by themselves do not create an impact, they can improve performance when added to other features. Finally, the feature combination of all new features developed for this task (*pmi + relevance+ rubric*) yields 73% accuracy, which is again better than each individual feature set's performance, indicating that they can be synergistically combined to improve system performance.

Feature Set	Accuracy in %
(i) grammar + colprep	70.31
(ii) colprep + pmi	67.42
(iii) pmi + relevance	69.05
(iv) pmi + relevance + rubric	73.21

Table 5: System performance for feature combinations (i) typically used in essay scoring, (ii) that measure awkwardness, (iii) newly proposed here, (iv) newly proposed plus rubric-specific criteria

7 Related Work

Most work in automated scoring and learner language analysis has focused on detecting grammar and usage errors (Leacock et al., 2014; Dale et al., 2012; Dale and Narroway, 2012; Gamon, 2010; Chodorow et al., 2007; Lu, 2010). This is done either by means of handcrafted rules or with statistical classifiers using a variety of information. In the case of the latter, the emphasis has been on representing the contexts of function words, such as articles and prepositions. This work is relevant inasmuch as errors in using content words, such as nouns and verbs, are often reflected in the functional elements which accompany them, for example, articles that indicate the definiteness or countability of nouns, and prepositions that mark the cases of the arguments of verbs.

Previous work (Bergsma et al., 2009; Bergsma et al., 2010; Xu et al., 2011) has shown that models which rely on large web-scale n-gram counts can be effective for the task of context-sensitive spelling correction. Measures of ngram association such as PMI, log likelihood, chi-square, and t have a long history of use for detecting collocations and measuring their quality (see (Manning and Schütze, 1999) and (Leacock et al., 2014) for reviews). Our application of a large n-gram database and PMI is to detect inappropriate word usage.

Our task also differs from work focusing on evaluating content (e.g. (Meurers et al., 2011; Sukkarieh and Blackmore, 2009; Leacock and Chodorow, 2003)) in that, although we are looking for usage of certain content words, we focus primarily on measuring knowledge of vocabulary.

Recent work on assessment measures of depth of vocabulary knowledge (Lawless et al., 2012; Lawrence et al., 2012), has argued that knowledge of specific words can range from superficial (idiomatic associations built up through word co-occurrence) to topical (meaning-related associations between words) to deep (definitional knowledge). Some of our features (e.g. awkward word usage) capture some of this information (e.g., idiomatic associations between words), but assigning the depth of knowledge of the key words is not the focus of our task.

Work that is closely related to ours is that of King and Dickinson (2013). They parse picture descriptions from interactive learner sentences, classify sentences into syntactic types and extract the logical subject, verb and object in order to recover simple semantic representations of the descriptions. We do not explicitly model the semantic representations of the pictures, but rather our goal in this work is to ascertain if a response is relevant to the picture and to measure other factors that reflect vocabulary proficiency.

We employ human annotators and use word similarity measures to obtain alternative forms of description because the proprietary nature of our data prevents us from releasing our pictures to the public. However, crowd sourcing has been used by other researchers to collect human labels for images and videos. For example, Rashtchian et al. (2010) use Amazon Mechanical Turk and Von Ahn and Dabbish (2004) create games to entice players to correctly label images. Chen and Dolan (2011) use crowd sourcing to collect multiple paraphrased descriptions of videos to create a paraphrasing corpus.

In a vast body of related work, automated methods have been explored for the generation of descriptions of images (Kulkarni et al., 2013; Kuznetsova et al., 2012; Li et al., 2011; Yao et al., 2010; Feng and Lapata, 2010a; Feng and Lapata, 2010b; Leong et al., 2010; Mitchell et al., 2012). There is also work in the opposite direction, of finding or generating pictures for a given narration. Joshi et al. (2006) found the best set of images from an image database to match the keywords in a story. Coyne and Sproat (2001) developed a natural language understanding system which converts English text into three-dimensional scenes that represent the text. For a high-stakes assessment, it would be highly undesirable to have any noise in the gold-standard reference picture descriptions. Hence we chose to use manual description for creating our reference corpus.

8 Summary and Future Directions

We investigated different types of features for automatically scoring a vocabulary item type which requires the test-taker to use two words in writing a sentence based on a picture. We generated a corpus of picture descriptions for measuring the relevance of responses, and as a foundation for feature development, we performed preliminary fine-grained annotations of responses. The features used in the resulting automated scoring system include newly developed statistical measures of word usage and response relevance, as well as features that are currently found in essay scoring engines. System performance shows an overall accuracy in scoring that is 15 percentage points above the majority class baseline and 10 percentage points below human performance.

There are a number of avenues open for future exploration. The automated scoring system might be improved by extending the relevance feature to include overlap with previously collected high-scoring responses. The reference corpus could also be expanded and diversified by using a large number of annotators, at least some of whom are speakers of the languages that are most prominently represented in the population of test-takers. Finally, one particular avenue we would like to explore is the use of our features to provide feedback in low stakes practice environments.

References

Yigal Attali and Jill Burstein. 2006. Automated essay scoring with e-rater v. 2.0. *Journal of Technology, Learning, and Assessment*, 4:3.

Shane Bergsma, Dekang Lin, and Randy Goebel. 2009. Web-scale n-gram models for lexical disambiguation. In *IJCAI*.

Shane Bergsma, Emily Pitler, and Dekang Lin. 2010. Creating robust supervised classifiers via web-scale n-gram data. In *Proceedings of the 48th Annual Meeting of the Association for Computational Linguistics*, pages 865–874. Association for Computational Linguistics.

Thorsten Brants and Alex Franz. 2006. Web 1T 5-gram Version 1. In *Linguistic Data Consortium, Philadelphia*.

David L Chen and William B Dolan. 2011. Collecting highly parallel data for paraphrase evaluation. In *Proceedings of the 49th Annual Meeting of the Association for Computational Linguistics: Human Language Technologies-Volume 1*, pages 190–200. Association for Computational Linguistics.

Martin Chodorow and Claudia Leacock. 2000. An unsupervised method for detecting grammatical errors. In *Proceedings of the Conference of the North American Chapter of the Association of Computational Linguistics (NAACL)*, pages 140–147.

Martin Chodorow, Joel R Tetreault, and Na-Rae Han. 2007. Detection of grammatical errors involving prepositions. In *Proceedings of the fourth ACL-SIGSEM workshop on prepositions*, pages 25–30. Association for Computational Linguistics.

Bob Coyne and Richard Sproat. 2001. Wordseye: an automatic text-to-scene conversion system. In *Proceedings of the 28th annual conference on Computer graphics and interactive techniques*, pages 487–496. ACM.

Daniel Dahlmeier and Hwee Tou Ng. 2011. Correcting semantic collocation errors with L1 induced paraphrases. In *Proceedings of the Conference on Empirical Methods in Natural Language Processing*, EMNLP '11, pages 107–117, Stroudsburg, PA, USA. Association for Computational Linguistics.

Robert Dale and George Narroway. 2012. A framework for evaluating text correction. In *LREC*, pages 3015–3018.

Robert Dale, Ilya Anisimoff, and George Narroway. 2012. HOO 2012: A report on the preposition and determiner error correction shared task. In *Proceedings of the Seventh Workshop on Building Educational Applications Using NLP*, pages 54–62. Association for Computational Linguistics.

Rod Ellis. 2000. Task-based research and language pedagogy. *Language teaching research*, 4(3):193–220.

Keelan Evanini, Michael Heilman, Xinhao Wang, and Daniel Blanchard. 2014. Automated scoring for TOEFL Junior comprehensive writing and speaking. Technical report, ETS, Princeton, NJ.

Yansong Feng and Mirella Lapata. 2010a. How many words is a picture worth? Automatic caption generation for news images. In *Proceedings of the 48th Annual Meeting of the Association for Computational Linguistics*, ACL '10, pages 1239–1249, Stroudsburg, PA, USA. Association for Computational Linguistics.

Yansong Feng and Mirella Lapata. 2010b. Topic models for image annotation and text illustration. In *Human Language Technologies: The 2010 Annual Conference of the North American Chapter of the Association for Computational Linguistics*, HLT '10, pages 831–839, Stroudsburg, PA, USA. Association for Computational Linguistics.

Michael Flor. 2013. A fast and flexible architecture for very large word n-gram datasets. *Natural Language Engineering*, 19(1):61–93.

KE Forbes-McKay and Annalena Venneri. 2005. Detecting subtle spontaneous language decline in early Alzheimers disease with a picture description task. *Neurological sciences*, 26(4):243–254.

Yoko Futagi, Paul Deane, Martin Chodorow, and Joel Tetreault. 2008. A computational approach to detecting collocation errors in the writing of non-native speakers of English. *Computer Assisted Language Learning*, 21(4):353–367.

Michael Gamon. 2010. Using mostly native data to correct errors in learners' writing: A meta-classifier approach. In *Human Language Technologies: The 2010 Annual Conference of the North American Chapter of the Association for Computational Linguistics*, pages 163–171. Association for Computational Linguistics.

Khairun-nisa Hassanali, Yang Liu, and Thamar Solorio. 2013. Using Latent Dirichlet Allocation for child narrative analysis. *ACL 2013*, page 111.

Dhiraj Joshi, James Z. Wang, and Jia Li. 2006. The story picturing engine—a system for automatic text illustration. *ACM Trans. Multimedia Comput. Commun. Appl.*, 2(1):68–89, February.

Levi King and Markus Dickinson. 2013. Shallow semantic analysis of interactive learner sentences. In *Proceedings of the Eighth Workshop on Innovative Use of NLP for Building Educational Applications*, pages 11–21, Atlanta, Georgia, June. Association for Computational Linguistics.

Girish Kulkarni, Visruth Premraj, Vicente Ordonez, Sagnik Dhar, Siming Li, Yejin Choi, Alexander C. Berg, and Tamara L. Berg. 2013. Babytalk: Understanding and generating simple image descriptions. *IEEE Transactions on Pattern Analysis and Machine Intelligence*, 99(PrePrints):1.

Polina Kuznetsova, Vicente Ordonez, Alexander C Berg, Tamara L Berg, and Yejin Choi. 2012. Collective generation of natural image descriptions. In *Proceedings of the 50th Annual Meeting of the Association for Computational Linguistics: Long Papers-Volume 1*, pages 359–368. Association for Computational Linguistics.

René Lawless, John Sabatini, and Paul Deane. 2012. Approaches to assessing partial vocabulary knowledge and supporting word learning: Assessing vocabulary depth. In *Annual Meeting of the American Educational Research Association, April 13-17, 2012, Vancouver, CA.*

Joshua Lawrence, Elizabeth Pare-Blagoev, René Lawless, and Chen Deane, Paul andLi. 2012. General vocabulary, academic vocabulary, and vocabulary depth: Examiningpredictors of adolescent reading comprehension. In *Annual Meeting of the American Educational Research Association.*

Claudia Leacock and Martin Chodorow. 2003. C-rater: Automated scoring of short-answer questions. *Computers and the Humanities*, 37(4):389–405.

Claudia Leacock, Martin Chodorow, Michael Gamon, and Joel Tetreault. 2014. *Automated Grammatical Error Detection for Language Learners*. Synthesis Lectures on Human Language Technologies. Morgan & Claypool.

Choonkyu Lee, Smaranda Muresan, and Karin Stromswold. 2012. Computational analysis of referring expressions in narratives of picture books. *NAACL-HLT 2012*, page 1.

Chee Wee Leong, Rada Mihalcea, and Samer Hassan. 2010. Text mining for automatic image tagging. In *Proceedings of the 23rd International Conference on Computational Linguistics: Posters*, pages 647–655. Association for Computational Linguistics.

Siming Li, Girish Kulkarni, Tamara L Berg, Alexander C Berg, and Yejin Choi. 2011. Composing simple image descriptions using web-scale n-grams. In *Proceedings of the Fifteenth Conference on Computational Natural Language Learning*, pages 220–228. Association for Computational Linguistics.

Dekang Lin. 1998. Automatic retrieval and clustering of similar words. In *Proceedings of the 17th international conference on Computational linguistics-Volume 2*, pages 768–774. Association for Computational Linguistics.

Xiaofei Lu. 2010. Automatic analysis of syntactic complexity in second language writing. *International Journal of Corpus Linguistics*, 15(4).

Christopher D. Manning and Hinrich Schütze. 1999. *Foundations of Statistical Natural Language Processing*. MIT Press.

Detmar Meurers, Ramon Ziai, Niels Ott, and Stacey M Bailey. 2011. Integrating parallel analysis modules to evaluate the meaning of answers to reading comprehension questions. *International Journal of Continuing Engineering Education and Life Long Learning*, 21(4):355–369.

Margaret Mitchell, Xufeng Han, Jesse Dodge, Alyssa Mensch, Amit Goyal, Alex Berg, Kota Yamaguchi, Tamara Berg, Karl Stratos, and Hal Daumé III. 2012. Midge: Generating image descriptions from computer vision detections. In *Proceedings of the 13th Conference of the European Chapter of the Association for Computational Linguistics*, pages 747–756. Association for Computational Linguistics.

Cyrus Rashtchian, Peter Young, Micah Hodosh, and Julia Hockenmaier. 2010. Collecting image annotations using Amazon's Mechanical Turk. In *Proceedings of the NAACL HLT 2010 Workshop on Creating Speech and Language Data with Amazon's Mechanical Turk*, pages 139–147. Association for Computational Linguistics.

Jana Zuheir Sukkarieh and John Blackmore. 2009. C-rater: Automatic content scoring for short constructed responses. In *FLAIRS Conference*.

Luis Von Ahn and Laura Dabbish. 2004. Labeling images with a computer game. In *Proceedings of the SIGCHI conference on Human factors in computing systems*, pages 319–326. ACM.

Wei Xu, Joel Tetreault, Martin Chodorow, Ralph Grishman, and Le Zhao. 2011. Exploiting syntactic and distributional information for spelling correction with web-scale n-gram models. In *Proceedings of the Conference on Empirical Methods in Natural Language Processing*, pages 1291–1300. Association for Computational Linguistics.

Benjamin Z Yao, Xiong Yang, Liang Lin, Mun Wai Lee, and Song-Chun Zhu. 2010. I2t: Image parsing to text description. *Proceedings of the IEEE*, 98(8):1485–1508.

Automatic Assessment of the Speech of Young English Learners

Jian Cheng[1], **Yuan Zhao D'Antilio**[1], **Xin Chen**[1], **Jared Bernstein**[2]

[1]Knowledge Technologies, Pearson, Menlo Park, California, USA
[2]Tasso Partners LLC, Palo Alto, California, USA
jian.cheng@pearson.com

Abstract

This paper introduces some of the research behind automatic scoring of the speaking part of the *Arizona English Language Learner Assessment*, a large-scale test now operational for students in Arizona. Approximately 70% of the students tested are in the range 4-11 years old. We cover the methods used to assess spoken responses automatically, considering both what the student says and the way in which the student speaks. We also provide evidence for the validity of machine scores. The assessments include 10 open-ended item types. For 9 of the 10 open item types, machine scoring performed at a similar level or better than human scoring at the item-type level. At the participant level, correlation coefficients between machine overall scores and average human overall scores were: Kindergarten: 0.88; Grades 1-2: 0.90; Grades 3-5: 0.94; Grades 6-8: 0.95; Grades 9-12: 0.93. The average correlation coefficient was 0.92. We include a note on implementing a detector to catch problematic test performances.

1 Introduction

Arizona English Language Learner Assessment (AZELLA) (Arizona Department of Education, 2014) is a test administered in the state of Arizona to all students from kindergarten up to grade 12 (K-12) who had been previously identified as English learners (ELs). AZELLA is used to place EL students into an appropriate level of instructional and to reassess EL students on an annual basis to monitor their progress. AZELLA was originally a fully human-delivered paper-pencil test covering four domains: listening, speaking, reading and writing. The Arizona Department of Education chose to automate the delivery and scoring of the speaking parts of the test, and further decided that test delivery via speakerphone would be the most efficient and universally accessible mode of administration. During the first field test (Nov. 7 - Dec. 2, 2011) over 31,000 tests were administered to 1st to 12th graders on speakerphones in Arizona schools. A second field test in April 2012 delivered over 13,000 AZELLA tests to kindergarten students. This paper reports research results based on analysis of data sets from the 44,000 students tested in these two administrations.

2 AZELLA speaking tests

AZELLA speaking tests are published in five *stages* (Table 1), one for each of five grade ranges or student levels. Each stage has four fixed test forms. Table 1 presents the total number of field tests delivered for each stage, or level.

Table 1: Stages, grades, and number of field tests

Stage	I	II	III	IV	V
Grade	K	1-2	3-5	6-8	9-12
N	13184	10646	9369	6439	5231

Fourteen different speaking exercises (item-types) were included in the various level-specific forms of the test. Some item-types were accompanied by images; some only had audio prompts. Note, however, that before the change to automatic administration and scoring, test forms had only included speaking item-types from a set of thirteen different types, of which ten were not designed to constrain the spoken responses. On the contrary, these ten item-types were designed to elicit relatively open-ended displays of speaking ability, and most test forms included one or two items of most types. A *Repeat Sentence* item type was added to the test designs (10 Repeat items per test form at every level), yielding test forms with around

Proceedings of the Ninth Workshop on Innovative Use of NLP for Building Educational Applications , pages 12–21,
Baltimore, Maryland USA, June 26, 2014. ©2014 Association for Computational Linguistics

27 items total, including Repeats. Table 2 lists all the speaking item types that are presented in one AZELLA test form for Stage III (Grades 3-5). Some items such as *Questions on Image*, *Similarities & Differences*, *Ask Qs about a Statement*, and *Detailed Response to Topic* are presented as a sequence of two related questions and the two responses are human-rated together to produce one holistic score.

Table 2: Stage III (Grades 3-5) items.

Descriptions	items/test	Score-Points
Repeat Sentence	10	0-4
Read-by-Syllables	3	0-1
Read-Three-Words	3	0-1
Questions on Image	3	0-4
Similarities & Differences	2	0-4
Give Directions from Map	1	0-4
Ask Qs about a Statement	1	0-4
Give Instructions	1	0-4
Open Question on Topic	1	0-4
Detailed Response to Topic	1	0-4

Table 3: Item types used in AZELLA speaking field tests.

Description (restriction)	Score-Points
Naming (Stage I)	0-1
Short Response (Stage I)	0-2
Open Question (Stage I)	0-2
Read-by-Syllables	0-1
Read-Three-Words	0-1 or 0-3
Repeat Sentence	0-4
Questions on Image	0-4
Similarities & Differences (III)	0-4
Give Directions from Map	0-4
Ask Qs about a Thing (II)	0-2
Ask Qs about a Statement (III)	0-4
Give Instructions	0-4
Open Questions on Topic	0-4
Detailed Response to Topic	0-4

All the speaking item-types used at any level in the AZELLA field tests are listed in Table 3. Item-types used at only one stage (level) are noted. From Table 3 we can see that, except for *Naming*, *Repeat Sentence*, *Read-by-Syllables*, and *Read-Three-Words*, all the items are fairly unconstrained questions. Engineering considerations did not guide the design of these items to make them be more suitable for machine learning and automatic scoring, and they were, indeed, a challenge to score.

By tradition and by design, human scoring of AZELLA responses is limited to a single holistic score, guided by sets of Score-Point rubrics defining scores at 2, 3, 4, or 5 levels. The column *Score-Points* specifies the number of categories used in holistic scoring. One set of five abbreviated holistic rubrics for assigning points by human rating is presented below in Table 4. For the *Repeat Sentence* items only, separate human ratings were collected under a pronunciation rubric and a fluency rubric.

Table 4: Example AZELLA abbreviated holistic rubric (5 Score-Points).

Points	Descriptors
4	*Correct understandable English using two or more sentences.* 1. Complete declarative or interrogative sentences. 2. Grammar (or syntax) errors are not evident and do not impede communication. 3. Clear and correct pronunciation. 4. Correct syntax.
3	*Understandable English using two or more sentences.* 1. Complete declarative or interrogative sentences. 2. Minor grammatical (or syntax) errors. 3. Clear and correct pronunciation.
2	*An intelligible English response.* 1. Less than two complete declarative or interrogative sentences. 2. Errors in grammar (or syntax). 3. Attempt to respond with clear and correct pronunciation.
1	*Erroneous responses.* 1. Not complete declarative or interrogative sentences. 2. Significant errors in grammar (or syntax). 3. Not clear and correct pronunciation.
0	Non-English or silence.

3 Development and validation data

From the data in the first field test (Stages II, III, IV, V), for each AZELLA Stage, we randomly sampled 300 tests (75 tests/form x 4 forms) as a validation set and $1,200$ tests as a development set. For the data in the second field test (Stage I), we randomly sampled 167 tests from the four forms as the validation set and $1,200$ tests as the development set. No validation data was used for model training.

3.1 Human transcriptions and scoring

In the development sets, we needed from 100 to 300 responses per item to be transcribed, depending on the complexity of the item type. In the validation sets, all responses were fully transcribed. Depending on the item type, we got single or double transcriptions, as necessary.

All responses from the tests were scored by trained professional raters according to predefined rubrics (Arizona Department of Education, 2012), such as those in Table 4. Departing from usual practice in production settings, we used the average score from different raters as the final score during machine learning. The responses in each validation set were double rated (producing two final scores) for use in validation. Note that five of the 1,367 tests in the validation sets had no human transcriptions and ratings, and so were excluded from the final validation results.

4 Machine scoring methods

Previous research on automatic assessment of spoken responses can be found in Bernstein et al. (2000; 2010), Cheng (2011) and Higgins et al. (2011). Past work on automatic assessment of children's oral reading fluency has been reported at the passage-level (Cheng and Shen, 2010; Downey et al., 2011) and at the word-level (Tepperman et al., 2007). A comprehensive review of spoken language technologies for education can be found in Eskanazi (2009). The following subsections summarize the methods we have used for scoring AZELLA tests. Those methods with citations have been previously discussed in research papers. Other methods described are novel modifications or extensions of known methods.

Both the linguistic content and the manner of speaking are scored. Our machine scoring methods include a combination of automatic speech recognition (ASR), speech processing, statistical modeling, linguistics, word vectors, and machine learning. The speech processing technology was built to handle the different rhythms and varied pronunciations used by a range of natives and learners. In addition to recognizing the words spoken, the system also aligns the speech signal, i.e., it locates the part of the signal containing relevant segments, syllables, and words, allowing the system to assign independent scores based on the content of what is spoken and the manner in which it is said. Thus, we derive scores based on the words used, as well as the pace, fluency, and pronunciation of those words in phrases and sentences. For each response, base measures are then derived from the linguistic units (segments, syllables, words), with reference to statistical models built from the spoken performances of natives and learners. Except for the Repeat items, the system produces only one holistic score per item from a combination of base measures.

4.1 Acoustic models

We tried various sets of recorded responses to train GMM-HMM acoustic models as implemented in HTK (Young et al., 2000). Performance improved by training acoustic models on larger sets of recordings, including material from students out of the age range being tested. For example, training acoustic models using only the Stage II transcriptions to recognize other Stage II responses was significantly improved by using more data from outside the Stage II data set, such as other AZELLA field data. We observed that the more child speech data, the better the automatic scoring. The final acoustic models used for recognition were trained on all transcribed AZELLA field data, except the data in the validation sets, plus data from an unrelated set of children's oral reading of passages (Cheng and Shen, 2010), and the data collected during the construction of the Versant Junior English tests for use by young children in Asia (Bernstein and Cheng, 2007). Thus, the acoustic models were built using any and all relevant data available: totaling about 380 hours of data (or around $176,000$ responses). The word error rate (WER) over all the validation sets using the final acoustic models is around 35%.

For machine scoring (after recognition and alignment), native acoustic models are used to compute native likelihoods of producing the observed base measures. Human listeners classified student recordings from Stage II (grades 1-2) as native or non-native. For example, in Stage II data, 287 subjects were identified as native and the recordings from these 287 subjects plus the native recordings from the Versant Junior English tests were used to build native acoustic models for grading. (approximately 66 hours of speech data, or $39,000$ responses).

4.2 Language models

Item-specific bigram language models were built using the human transcription of the development-set as described in Section 3.1.

4.3 Content modeling

"Content" refers to the linguistic material (words, phrases, and semantic elements) in the spoken response. Appropriate response content reflects the speaker's productive control of English vocabulary and also indicates how well the test-taker understood the prompt. Previous work on scoring linguistic content in the speech domain includes Bernstein et al. (2010) and Xie et al. (2012).

Except for the four relatively closed-response-form items (*Naming, Repeat, Read-by-Syllables* and *Read-Three-Words*), we produced a $word\_vector$ score for each response (Bernstein et al., 2010). The value of the $word\_vector$ score is calculated by scaling the weighted sum of the occurrence of a large set of expected words and word sequences available in an item-specific response scoring model. An automatic process assigned weights to the expected words and word sequences according to their semantic relation to known good responses using a method similar to latent semantic analysis (Landauer et al., 1998). The $word\_vector$ score is generally the most powerful feature used to predict the final human scores.

Note that a recent competition to develop accurate scoring algorithms for student-written short-answer responses (Kaggle, 2012) focused on a similar problem to the content scoring task for AZELLA open-ended responses. We assume that the methods used by the prize-winning teams, for example Tandalla (2012) and Zbontar (2012), should work well for the AZELLA open-ended material too, although we did not try these methods.

For the responses to *Naming*, *Read-by-Syllables*, and *Read-Three-Words* items, the machine scoring makes binary decisions based on the occurrence of a correct sequence of syllables or words ($keywords$). In Stage II forms, for first and second grade students, the responses to *Read-Three-Words* items were human-rated in four categories. For this stage, the machine counted the number of words read correctly.

For the responses to Repeat items, the recognized string is compared to the word string recited in the prompt, and the number of word errors ($word\_errors$) is calculated as the minimum number of substitutions, deletions, and/or insertions required to find a best string match in the response. This matching algorithm ignores hesitations and filled or unfilled pauses, as well as any leading or trailing material in the response (Bernstein et al., 2010). A verbatim repetition would have zero word errors. For Repeat responses, the percentage of words repeated correctly ($percent\_correct$) was used as an additional feature.

4.4 Duration modeling

Phone-level duration statistics contribute to machine scores of test-takers' pronunciation and fluency. Native-speakers segment duration statistics from Versant Junior English tests (Bernstein and Cheng, 2007) were used to compute the log-likelihood of phone durations produced by test-takers. No data from AZELLA tests contributed to the duration models. We calculated the phoneme duration log-likelihood: log_seg_prob and the inter-word silence duration log-likelihood: $iw\_log\_seg\_prob$ (Cheng, 2011).

Assume in a recognized response that the sequence of phonemes and their corresponding durations are p_i and D_i, $i = 1...N$, then the log likelihood segmental probability for phonemes (log_seg_prob) was computed as:

$$log\_seg\_prob = \frac{1}{N-2}\sum_{i=2}^{N-1}\log(\Pr(D_i)), \quad (1)$$

where $\Pr(D_i)$ was the probability that a native would produce phoneme p_i with the observed duration D_i in the context found. The first and last phonemes in the response were not used for the calculation of the log_seg_prob because durations of these phonemes as determined by the ASR were more likely to be incorrect. The log likelihood segmental probability for inter-word silence durations, $iw\_log\_seg\_prob$, was calculated the same way (Cheng, 2011).

4.5 Spectral modeling

To construct scoring models for pronunciation and fluency, we computed several spectral likelihood features with reference to native and learner segment-specific models applied to the recognition alignment, computing the phone-level posterior probabilities given the acoustic observation X

that is recognized as p_i:

$$P(p_i|X) = \frac{P(X|p_i)P(p_i)}{\sum_{k=1}^{m} P(X|p_k)P(p_k)} \quad (2)$$

where k runs over all the potential phonemes. In a real-world ASR system, it is extremely difficult to estimate $\sum_{k=1}^{m} P(X|p_k)P(p_k)$ precisely. So approximations are used, such as substituting a maximum for the summation, etc. Formula 2 is the general framework for pronunciation diagnosis (Witt and Young, 1997; Franco et al., 1999; Witt and Young, 2000) and pronunciation assessment (Witt and Young, 2000; Franco et al., 1997; Neumeyer et al., 1999; Bernstein et al., 2010). Various authors use different approximations to suit the particulars of their data and their applications.

In the AZELLA spectral scoring, we approximated Formula 2 with the following procedure. After the learner acoustic models produce a recognition result, we force-align the utterance on the recognized word string, but using the native monophone acoustic models, producing acoustic log-likelihood, duration and time boundaries for every phone. For each such phone, again using the native monophone time alignment, we perform an all-phone recognition using the native monophone acoustic models. The recognizer calculates a log-likelihood for every phone and picks the best match from all possible phones over that time frame. For each phone-of-interest in a response, we calculated the average spectral score difference as:

$$spectral\_1 = \frac{1}{N} \sum_{i=1}^{N} \frac{lp_i^{fa} - lp_i^{ap}}{d_i} \quad (3)$$

where the variables are:

- lp_i^{fa} is the log-likelihood corresponding to the i-th phoneme by using the forced alignment method;
- lp_i^{ap} is the log-likelihood by using the all-phone recognition method;
- d_i is its duration;
- N is the number of phonemes of interest in a response.

In calculating $spectral\_1$, all possible phonemes are included. We define another variable, $spectral\_2$, that only accumulates the log-likelihood for a target set of phonemes that learners often have difficulty with. We call the percentage of phones from the all-phone recognition that match the phones from the forced alignment the *percent phone match*, or *ppm*. We take Formula 3 as the average log of the approximate posterior probabilities that phones were produced by a native.

4.6 Confidence modeling

After finishing speech recognition, we can assign speech confidence scores to words and phonemes (Cheng and Shen, 2011). Then for every response, we can compute the average confidence, the percentage of words or phonemes whose confidences are lower than a threshold value as features to predict test-takers' performance.

4.7 Final models

AZELLA holistic score rubrics (Arizona Department of Education, 2012), such as those shown in Table 4, consider both the answer content and the manner of speaking used in the response. The automatic scoring should consider both too. Features $word\_vector$, $keywords$, $word\_errors$, $percent\_correct$ can represent content scores based on what is spoken. Features log_seg_prob, $iw\_log\_seg\_prob$, $spectral\_1$, $spectral\_2$, ppm can represent both the rhythmic and segmental aspects of the performance as native likelihoods of producing the observed base measures. By feeding these features to models, we can effectively predict human holistic scores, as well as human pronunciation and fluency ratings, although we did not model grammar errors in the way they are specifically described in the rubrics, e.g. in Table 4.

For each item, a specific combination of base scores was selected. So, on an item-by-item basis, we tried two methods of combination: (i) multiple linear regression and (ii) neural networks with one hidden layer trained by back propagation. Then we selected the one that was more accurate for that item. For almost all items, the neural network model worked better.

4.8 Unscorable test detection

Many factors can render a test unscorable: poor sound quality (recording noise, mouth too close to the microphone, too soft, etc.), gibberish (nonsense words, noise, or a foreign language), off-topic (off topic, but intelligible English), unintelligible English (e.g. a good-faith attempt to respond in English, but is so unintelligible and/or disfluent that it cannot be understood confidently).

There have been several approaches to dealing with this issue (Cheng and Shen, 2011; Chen and Mostow, 2011; Yoon et al., 2011). Some unscorable tests can be identified easily by a human listener, and we reported research on a specified unscorable category (off-topic) before (Cheng and Shen, 2011). Dealing with a specified category could be significantly easier than dealing with wide-open items as in AZELLA. Also, because we did not collect human "unscorable" ratings for this data, we worked on predicting the absolute overall difference between human and machine scores; which is like predicting outliers. If the difference is expected to exceed a threshold, the test should be sent for human grading.

Many problems were due to low volume recordings made by shy kids, so we identified features to deal with low-volume tests. These included maximum energy, the number of frames with fundamental frequency, etc., using many features mentioned in Cheng and Shen (2011). The method used to detect off-topic responses did not work well here, but features based on lattice confidence seemed to work fairly well. If we define an unscorable test as one with an overall difference between human and machine scores greater than or equal to 3 (within the score range 0-14), our final unscorable test detector achieves an equal-error rate of 16.5% in validation sets; or when fixing the false rejection rate at 6%, the false acceptance rate is 44%. We are actively investigating better methods to achieve acceptable performance for use in real tests.

5 Experimental results

All results presented in this section used the validation data sets, while the recognition and scoring models were built from completely separate material. The participant-level speaking scores were designed not to consider the scores from *Read-by-Syllables* and *Read-Three-Words*. For each test, the system produced holistic scores for Repeat items and for non-Repeat items. For every Repeat item, the machine generated pronunciation, fluency and accuracy scores mapped into the 0 to 4 score-point range. Both human and machine holistic scores for a Repeat response are equal to: $50\% \cdot Accuracy + 25\% \cdot Pronunciation + 25\% \cdot Fluency$. Accuracy scores were scaled as $percent\_correct$ times four. Human accuracy scores were based on human transcriptions instead of ASR transcriptions. Holistic scores for Repeat items at the participant level were the simple average of the corresponding item-level scores.

For every non-Repeat item, we generated one holistic score that considered pronunciation, fluency and content together. The non-Repeat holistic scores at the participant level were the simple average of the corresponding item level scores after normalizing them to the same scale. The final generated holistic scores for Repeats were scaled to a $0-4$ range and non-Repeat holistic scores were scaled to a $0-10$ range to satisfy an AZELLA design requirement that Repeat items count for 4 points and non-Repeats count for 10 points. The overall participant level scores are the sum of the Repeat holistic scores and the non-Repeat holistic scores (maximum 14). All machine-generated scores are continuous values. In the following tables, H-H r stands for the human-human correlation and M-H r stands for the correlation between machine-generated scores and average human scores.

Table 5: Human rating reliabilities and Machine-human correlations by item type. Third column gives mean and standard deviation of words per response.

S	Item types	Words/response $\mu \pm \sigma$	H-H r	M-H r
I	Naming	2.5 ± 2.5	0.83	0.67
I	Short Response	5.7 ± 3.8	0.71	0.73
I	Open Question	8.7 ± 7.9	0.70	0.76
I	Repeat Sentence	5.0 ± 2.5	0.91	0.83
II	Questions on Image	14.0 ± 10.8	0.87	0.86
II	Give Directions from Map	10.9 ± 9.7	0.82	0.84
II	Ask Qs about a Thing	6.8 ± 5.9	0.83	0.64
II	Open Question on Topic	11.6 ± 10.6	0.75	0.72
II	Give Instructions	11.5 ± 10.0	0.83	0.80
II	Repeat Sentence	6.1 ± 2.9	0.95	0.85
III	Questions on Image	14.5 ± 10.2	0.87	0.77
III	Similarities & Differences	19.5 ± 11.6	0.75	0.75
III	Give Directions from Map	16.3 ± 11.2	0.74	0.85
III	Ask Qs about a Statement	16.7 ± 13.4	0.79	0.82
III	Give Instructions	17.0 ± 12.8	0.77	0.81
III	Open Question on Topic	13.9 ± 11.1	0.85	0.85
III	Detailed Response to Topic	13.8 ± 10.5	0.81	0.80
III	Repeat Sentence	6.4 ± 3.2	0.97	0.88
IV	Questions on Image	13.9 ± 11.8	0.84	0.84
IV	Give Directions from Map	13.7 ± 13.3	0.84	0.90
IV	Open Question on Topic	17.2 ± 15.2	0.82	0.82
IV	Detailed Response to Topic	13.9 ± 11.4	0.85	0.87
IV	Give Instructions	16.5 ± 15.7	0.87	0.90
IV	Repeat Sentence	6.9 ± 3.2	0.96	0.89
V	Questions on Image	17.3 ± 12.0	0.80	0.76
V	Open Question on Topic	18.7 ± 14.9	0.84	0.82
V	Detailed Response to Topic	17.7 ± 15.2	0.88	0.87
V	Give Instructions	17.2 ± 16.6	0.90	0.90
V	Give Directions from Map	22.4 ± 16.8	0.86	0.85
V	Repeat Sentence	6.4 ± 3.5	0.95	0.89

We summarize the psychometric properties of different item types that contribute to the final scores in Table 5. For each item-type and each stage, the third column in Table 5 presents the mean and standard deviation of the words-per-response produced by students, showing that older students generally produce more spoken material. We found that the number of words spoken is a better measure than speech signal duration to represent the amount of material produced, because young English learners often emit long silences while speaking. The difference between the two measures in columns 4 and 5 is statistically significant (two-tailed, $p < 0.05$) for item types *Naming (Stage I)*, *Ask Qs about a Thing (Stage II)*, *Questions on Image (Stage III)*, and *Repeat Sentence (all Stages)*, in which machine scoring does not match human; and for item types *Give Directions from Map (Stage III, IV)*, in which machine is better than a single human score. For almost all open-ended items, machine scoring is similar to or better than human scoring. We noticed that machine scoring of one open-ended item type, *Ask Qs about a Thing* used in Stage II test forms, was significantly worse than human scoring, leading us to identify problems specific to the item type itself, both in the human rating rubric and in the machine grading approach. Arizona is not using this item type in operational tests.

Figures 1, 2, 3, 4, 5 present scatter plots of overall scores at the participant level comparing human and machine scores for test in each AZELLA stage. Figure 6 shows the averaged human holistic score distribution for participants in the validation set for Stage V. The human holistic score distributions for participants in other AZELLA stages are similar to those in Figure 6, except the means shift somewhat.

We identified several participants for whom the difference between human and machine scores is bigger than 4 in Figures 1, 2, 3, 4, 5. Listening to the recordings of these tests, we concluded that the most important factor was low Signal-to-Noise Ratio (SNR). Either the background noise was very high (in 6 of 1,362 tests in the validation set), or speech volume was low (in 3 of 1,362 tests in the validation set). Either condition can make recognition difficult. With very low voice amplitude and high background noise levels, the SNR of some outlier response recordings is so low that human raters refuse to affirm that they understand the

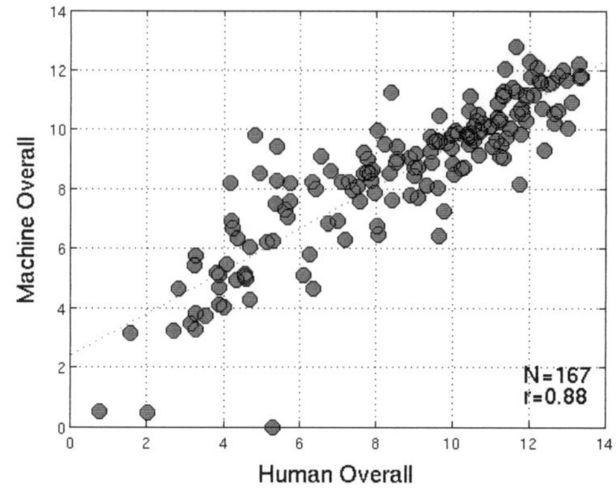

Figure 1: Overall human vs. machine scores at the participant level for Stage I (Grade K). Mean and standard deviation for human scores: $(8.74, 3.1)$.

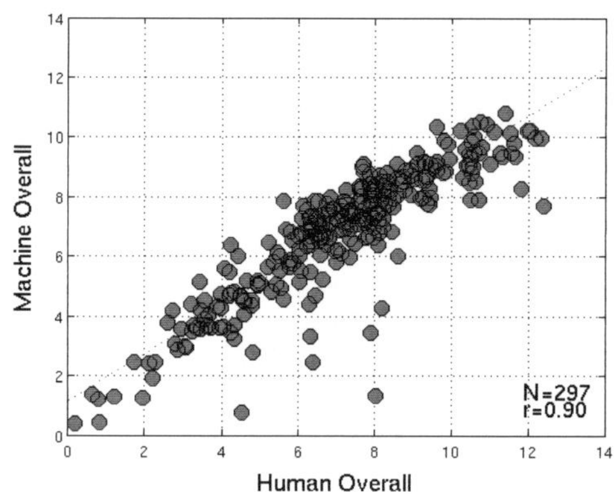

Figure 2: Overall human vs. machine scores at the participant level for Stage II (Grades 1-2). Mean and standard deviation for human scores: $(7.1, 2.5)$.

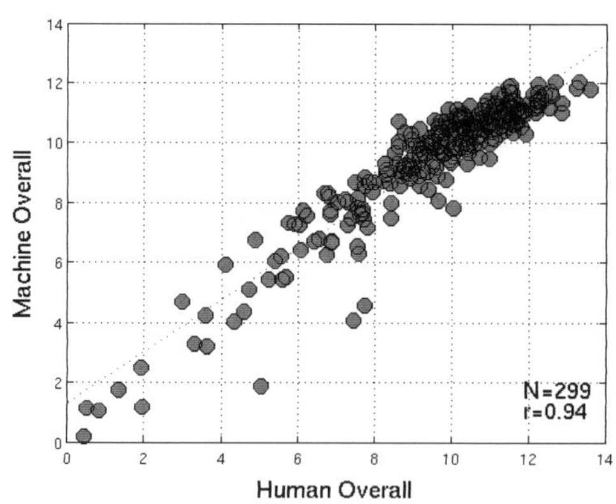

Figure 3: Overall human vs. machine scores at the participant level for Stage III (Grades 3-5). Mean and standard deviation for human scores: $(9.6, 2.3)$.

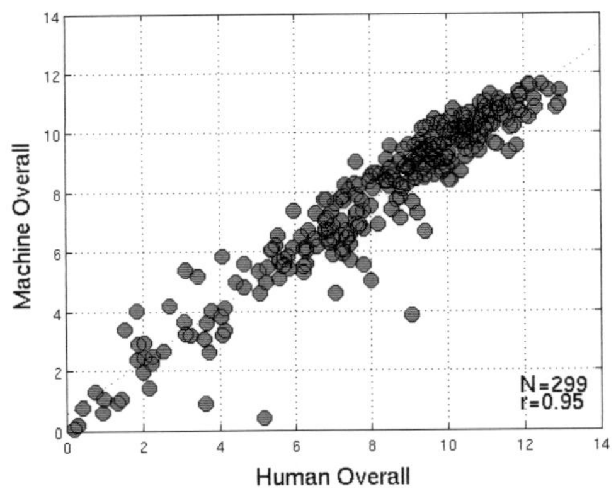

Figure 4: Overall human vs. machine scores at the participant level for Stage IV (Grades 6-8). Mean and standard deviation for human scores: $(8.3, 2.9)$.

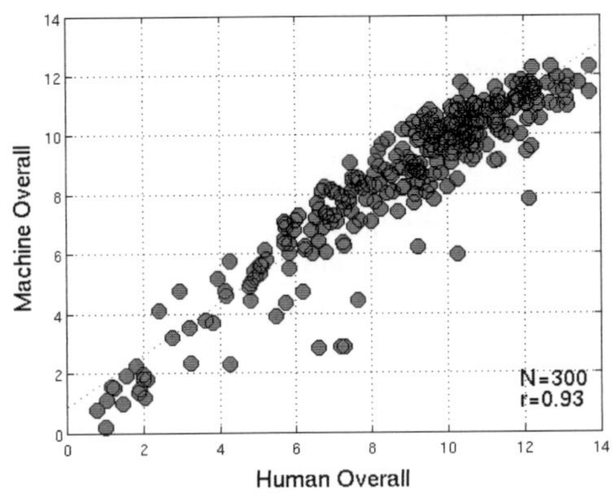

Figure 5: Overall human vs. machine scores at the participant level for Stage V (Grades 9-12). Mean and standard deviation for human scores: $(8.9, 2.9)$.

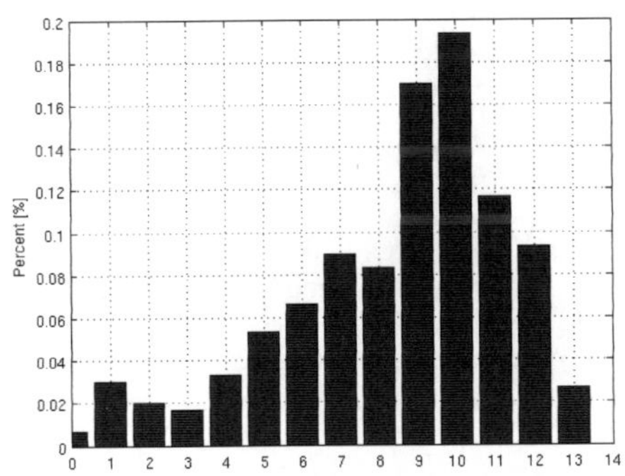

Figure 6: Distribution of average human holistic score for participants in the validation set for Stage V (Grades 9-12).

content of the response or rate its pronunciation. Since many young children in kindergarten and early elementary school speak softly, the youngest children's speech is substantially harder to recognize (Li and Russell, 2002; Lee et al., 1999). This probably contributes to the lower reliabilities in Stage I and II. When setting the total rejection rate at 6%, our unscorable test detector identifies only 7 of the 13 outlier tests.

Table 6: Reliability of human scores and Human-Machine correlations of overall test scores by stage.

Stage	H-H r	M-H r
I	0.91	0.88
II	0.96	0.90
III	0.97	0.94
IV	0.98	0.95
V	0.98	0.93
Average	0.96	0.92

Table 6 summarizes the reliabilities of the tests in different stages. At the participant level, the average inter-rater reliability coefficient across the five stages was 0.96, suggesting that the well-trained human raters agree with each other with high consistency when ratings are combined over all the material in all the responses in a whole test; the average correlation coefficient between machine-generated overall scores and average human overall scores was 0.92. This suggests that the machine grading may be sufficiently reliable for most purposes.

Table 7: Test reliability by stage, separating non-Repeat holistic scores and Repeat holistic scores.

Stage	H-H r NonRptH	M-H r NonRptH	H-H r RptH	M-H r RptH
I	0.85	0.83	0.99	0.94
II	0.93	0.89	0.99	0.90
III	0.95	0.92	0.99	0.92
IV	0.96	0.95	0.99	0.94
V	0.96	0.91	0.99	0.93
Average	0.93	0.90	0.99	0.93

Table 7 summarizes the reliabilities of test scores in the different stages considering the non-Repeat holistic scores and Repeat holistic scores separately to check the effect of adding the Repeat items. Repeat items improve the machine reliability in Stage I significantly, but not so much for other stages. This difference may relate to the difficulty in eliciting sufficient speech samples in non-Repeat items from the young EL students in Stage I. Eliciting spoken materials in Repeat items is more straightforward. Consideration of Table 7 suggests that using only open-ended item-types can also achieve sufficiently reliable results.

6 Discussion and future work

We believe that we can improve this system further by scoring Repeat items using a partial credit Rasch model (Masters, 1982) instead of the average of $percent\_correct$, which should improve the reliability of the Repeat item type. We may also be able to train a better native acoustic model by using a larger sample of native data from AZELLA, if we are given access to the test-taker demographic information.

The original item selection and assignment of items to forms was quite simple and had room for improvement. Currently in the AZELLA testing program, test forms go through a post-pilot revision, so that the operational tests only include good items in the final test forms. This post-pilot selection and arrangement of items into forms should improve human-machine correlations beyond the values reported here. If we effectively address the problem of shy-kids-talking-softly, the scoring performance will definitely improve even more. Getting young students to talk louder is probably something that can be best done at the testing site (by instruction or by example); and it may solve several problems. We are happy to report that the first operational AZELLA test with automatic speech scoring took place between January 14 and February 26, 2013, with approximately 140,700 tests delivered.

Recent progress in machine learning has applied deep neural networks (DNNs) to many long-standing pattern recognition and classification problems. Many groups have now applied DNNs to the task of building better acoustic models for speech recognition (Hinton et al., 2012). DNNs have repeatedly been shown to work better than Gaussian mixture models (GMMs) for ASR acoustic modeling (Hinton et al., 2012; Dahl et al., 2012). We are actively exploring the use of DNNs for use in recognition of children's speech. We expect that DNN acoustic models can overcome some of the recognition difficulties mentioned in this paper (e.g. low SNR in responses and short response item types like *Naming*) and boost the final assessment accuracy significantly.

7 Conclusions

We have reported an evaluation of the automatic methods that are currently used to assess spoken responses to test tasks that occur in Arizona's AZELLA test for young English learners. The methods score both the content of the responses and the quality of the speech produced in the responses. Although most of the speaking item types in the AZELLA tests are unconstrained and open-ended, machine scoring accuracy is similar to or better than human scoring for most item types. We presented basic validity evidence for machine-generated scores, including an average correlation coefficient between machine-generated overall scores and human overall scores derived from subscores that are based on multiple human ratings. Further, we described the design, implementation and evaluation of a detector to catch problematic, unscorable tests. We believe that near-term re-optimization of some scoring process elements may further improve machine scoring accuracy.

References

Arizona Department of Education. 2012. AZELLA update. `http://www.azed.gov/standards-development-assessment/files/2012/12/12-12-12-update-v5.pdf`. [Accessed 19-March-2014].

Arizona Department of Education. 2014. Arizona English Language Learner Assessment (AZELLA). `http://www.azed.gov/standards-development-assessment/arizona-english-language-learner-assessment-azella`. [Accessed 19-March-2014].

J. Bernstein and J. Cheng. 2007. Logic and validation of a fully automatic spoken English test. In V. M. Holland and F. P. Fisher, editors, *The Path of Speech Technologies in Computer Assisted Language Learning*, pages 174–194. Routledge, New York.

J. Bernstein, J. De Jong, D. Pisoni, and B. Townshend. 2000. Two experiments on automatic scoring of spoken language proficiency. In *Proc. of STIL (Integrating Speech Technology in Learning)*, pages 57–61.

J. Bernstein, A. Van Moere, and J. Cheng. 2010. Validating automated speaking tests. *Language Testing*, 27(3):355–377.

W. Chen and J. Mostow. 2011. A tale of two tasks: Detecting children's off-task speech in a reading tutor. In *Interspeech 2011*, pages 1621–1624.

J. Cheng and J. Shen. 2010. Towards accurate recognition for children's oral reading fluency. In *IEEE-SLT 2010*, pages 91–96.

J. Cheng and J. Shen. 2011. Off-topic detection in automated speech assessment applications. In *Interspeech 2011*, pages 1597–1600.

J. Cheng. 2011. Automatic assessment of prosody in high-stakes English tests. In *Interspeech 2011*, pages 1589–1592.

G. Dahl, D. Yu, L. Deng, and A. Acero. 2012. Context-dependent pretrained deep neural networks for large vocabulary speech recognition. *IEEE Transactions on Speech and Audio Processing, Special Issue on Deep Learning for Speech and Lang. Processing*, 20(1):30–42.

R. Downey, D. Rubin, J. Cheng, and J. Bernstein. 2011. Performance of automated scoring for children's oral reading. In *Proceedings of the Sixth Workshop on Innovative Use of NLP for Building Educational Applications*, pages 46–55.

M. Eskanazi. 2009. An overview of spoken language technology for education. *Speech Communication*, 51:832–844.

H. Franco, L. Neumeyer, Y. Kim, and O. Ronen. 1997. Automatic pronunciation scoring for language instruction. In *ICASSP 1997*, pages 1471–1474.

H. Franco, L. Neumeyer, M. Ramos, and H. Bratt. 1999. Automatic detection of phone-level mispronunciation for language learning. In *Eurospeech 1999*, pages 851–854.

D. Higgins, X. Xi, K. Zechner, and D. Williamson. 2011. A three-stage approach to the automated scoring of spontaneous spoken responses. *Computer Speech and Language*, 25:282–306.

G. Hinton, L. Deng, Y. Dong, G. Dahl, A. Mohamed, N. Jaitly, A. Senior, V. Vanhoucke, P. Nguyen, T. Sainath, and B. Kingsbury. 2012. Deep neural networks for acoustic modeling in speech recognition: The shared views of four research groups. *IEEE Signal Processing Magazine*, 29(6):82–97.

Kaggle. 2012. The Hewlett Foundation: Short answer scoring. `http://www.kaggle.com/c/asap-sas;http://www.kaggle.com/c/asap-sas/details/winners`. [Accessed 20-April-2014].

T. K. Landauer, P. W. Foltz, and D. Laham. 1998. Introduction to latent semantic analysis. *Discourse Processes*, 25:259–284.

S. Lee, A. Potamianos, and S. Narayanan. 1999. Acoustics of children's speech: developmental changes of temporal and spectral parameters. *Journal of Acoustics Society of American*, 105:1455–1468.

Q. Li and M. Russell. 2002. An analysis of the causes of increased error rates in children's speech recognition. In *ICSLP 2002*, pages 2337–2340.

G. N. Masters. 1982. A Rasch model for partial credit scoring. *Psychometrika*, 47(2):149–174.

L. Neumeyer, H. Franco, V. Digalakis, and M. Weintraub. 1999. Automatic scoring of pronunciation quality. *Speech Communication*, 30:83–93.

L. Tandalla. 2012. ASAP Short Answer Scoring Competition System Description: Scoring short answer essays. `https://kaggle2.blob.core.windows.net/competitions/kaggle/2959/media/TechnicalMethodsPaper.pdf`. [Accessed 20-April-2014].

J. Tepperman, M. Black, P. Price, S. Lee, A. Kazemzadeh, M. Gerosa, M. Heritage, A. Alwan, and S. Narayanan. 2007. A Bayesian network classifier for word-level reading assessment. In *Interspeech 2007*, pages 2185–2188.

S. M. Witt and S. J. Young. 1997. Language learning based on non-native speech recognition. In *Eurospeech 1997*, pages 633–636.

S. M. Witt and S. J. Young. 2000. Phone-level pronunciation scoring and assessment for interactive language learning. *Speech Communication*, 30:95–108.

S. Xie, K. Evanini, and K. Zechner. 2012. Exploring content features for automated speech scoring. In *Proceedings of the 2012 Conference of the North American Chapter of the Association for Computational Linguistics: Human Language Technologies*, pages 103–111.

S.-Y. Yoon, K. Evanini, and K. Zechner. 2011. Non-scorable response detection for automated speaking proficiency assessment. In *Proceedings of the Sixth Workshop on Innovative Use of NLP for Building Educational Applications*, pages 152–160.

S. J. Young, D. Kershaw, J. Odell, D. Ollason, V. Valtchev, and P. Woodland. 2000. *The HTK Book Version 3.0*. Cambridge University, Cambridge, England.

J. Zbontar. 2012. ASAP Short Answer Scoring Competition System Description: Short answer scoring by stacking. `https://kaggle2.blob.core.windows.net/competitions/kaggle/2959/media/jzbontar.pdf`. [Accessed 20-April-2014].

Automatic detection of plagiarized spoken responses

Keelan Evanini and Xinhao Wang
Educational Testing Service
660 Rosedale Road, Princeton, NJ, USA
{kevanini,xwang002}@ets.org

Abstract

This paper addresses the task of automatically detecting plagiarized responses in the context of a test of spoken English proficiency for non-native speakers. A corpus of spoken responses containing plagiarized content was collected from a high-stakes assessment of English proficiency for non-native speakers, and several text-to-text similarity metrics were implemented to compare these responses to a set of materials that were identified as likely sources for the plagiarized content. Finally, a classifier was trained using these similarity metrics to predict whether a given spoken response is plagiarized or not. The classifier was evaluated on a data set containing the responses with plagiarized content and non-plagiarized control responses and achieved accuracies of 92.0% using transcriptions and 87.1% using ASR output (with a baseline accuracy of 50.0%).

1 Introduction

The automated detection of plagiarism has been widely studied in the domain of written student essays, and several online services exist for this purpose.[1] In addition, there has been a series of shared tasks using common data sets of written language to compare the performance of a variety of approaches to plagiarism detection (Potthast et al., 2013). In contrast, the automated detection of plagiarized spoken responses has received little attention from both the NLP and assessment communities, mostly due to the limited application of automated speech scoring for the types of spoken responses that could be affected by plagiarism. Due to a variety of factors, though, this is likely to change in the near future, and the automated detection of plagiarism in spoken language will become an increasingly important application.

First of all, English continues its spread as the global language of education and commerce, and there is a need to assess the communicative compentance of high volumes of highly proficient non-native speakers. In order to provide a valid evaluation of the complex linguistic skills that are necessary for these speakers, the assessment must contain test items that elicit spontaneous speech, such as the Independent and Integrated Speaking items in the TOEFL iBT test (ETS, 2012), the Retell Lecture item in the Pearson Test of English Academic (Longman, 2010), and the oral interview in the IELTS Academic assessment (Cullen et al., 2014). However, with the increased emphasis on complex linguistic skills in assessments of non-native speech, there is an increased chance that test takers will prepare canned answers using test preparation materials prior to the examination. Therefore, research should also be conducted on detecting spoken plagiarized responses in order to prevent this type of cheating strategy.

In addition, there will also likely be an increase in spoken language assessments for native speakers in the K-12 domain in the near future. Curriculum developers and assessment designers are recognizing that the assessment of spoken communication skills is important for determining a student's college readiness. For example, the Common Core State Standards include Speaking & Listening English Language Arts standards for each grade that pertain to a student's ability to communicate information and ideas using spoken language.[2] In order to assess these standards, it

[1]For example, http://turnitin.com/en_us/features/originalitycheck, http://www.grammarly.com/plagiarism-checker/, and http://www.paperrater.com/plagiarism_checker.

[2]http://www.corestandards.org/ELA-Literacy/SL/

Proceedings of the Ninth Workshop on Innovative Use of NLP for Building Educational Applications , pages 22–27,
Baltimore, Maryland USA, June 26, 2014. ©2014 Association for Computational Linguistics

will be necessary to develop standardized assessments for the K-12 domain that contain items eliciting spontaneous speech from the student, such as presentations, group discussions, etc. Again, with the introduction of these types of tasks, there is a risk that a test taker's spoken response will contain prepared material drawn from an external source, and there will be a need to automatically detect this type of plagiarism on a large scale, in order to provide fair and valid assessments.

In this paper, we present an initial study of automated plagiarism detection on spoken responses containing spontaneous non-native speech. A data set of actual plagiarized responses was collected, and text-to-text similarity metrics were applied to the task of classifying responses as plagiarized or non-plagiarized.

2 Previous Work

A wide variety of techniques have been employed in previous studies for the task of detecting plagiarized written documents, including n-gram overlap (Lyon et al., 2006), document fingerprinting (Brin et al., 1995), word frequency statistics (Shivakumar and Garcia-Molina, 1995), Information Retrieval-based metrics (Hoad and Zobel, 2003), text summarization evaluation metrics (Chen et al., 2010), WordNet-based features (Nahnsen et al., 2005), and features based on shared syntactic patterns (Uzuner et al., 2005). This task is also related to the widely studied task of paraphrase recognition, which benefits from similar types of features (Finch et al., 2005; Madnani et al., 2012). The current study adopts several of these features that are designed to be robust to the presence of word-level modifications between the source and the plagiarized text; since this study focuses on spoken responses that are reproduced from memory and subsequently processed by a speech recognizer, metrics that rely on exact matches are likely to perform sub-optimally. To our knowledge, no previous work has been reported on automatically detecting similar spoken documents, although research in the field of Spoken Document Retrieval (Haputmann, 2006) is relevant.

Due to the difficulties involved in collecting corpora of actual plagiarized material, nearly all published results of approaches to the task of plagiarism detection have relied on either simulated plagiarism (i.e., plagiarized texts generated by experimental human participants in a controlled environment) or artificial plagiarism (i.e., plagiarized texts generated by algorithmically modifying a source text) (Potthast et al., 2010). These results, however, may not reflect actual performance in a deployed setting, since the characteristics of the plagiarized material may differ from actual plagiarized responses. To overcome this limitation, the current study is based on a set of actual plagiarized responses drawn from a large-scale assessment.

3 Data

The data used in this study was drawn from the TOEFL® Internet-based test (TOEFL® iBT), a large-scale, high-stakes assessment of English for non-native speakers, which assesses English communication skills for academic purposes. The Speaking section of TOEFL iBT contains six tasks, each of which requires the test taker to provide an extended response containing spontaneous speech. Two of the tasks are referred to as Independent tasks; these tasks cover topics that are familiar to test takers and ask test takers to draw upon their own ideas, opinions, and experiences in a 45-second spoken response (ETS, 2012). Since these two Independent tasks ask questions that are not based on any stimulus materials that were provided to the test taker (such as a reading passage, figure, etc.), the test takers can provide responses that contain a wide variety of specific examples.

In some cases, test takers may attempt to game the assessment by memorizing canned material from an external source and adapting it to a question that is asked in one of the Independent tasks. This type of plagiarism can affect the validity of a test taker's speaking score; however, it is often difficult even for trained human raters to recognize plagiarized spoken responses, due to the large number and variety of external sources that are available from online test preparation sites.

In order to better understand the strategies used by test takers who incorporated material from external sources into their spoken responses and to develop a capability for automated plagiarism detection for speaking items, a data set of operational spoken responses containing potentially plagiarized material was collected. This data set contains responses that were flagged by human raters as potentially containing plagiarized material and then subsequently reviewed by rater supervisors. In the review process, the responses were transcribed and compared to external source materials obtained through manual internet searches; if it was determined that the presence of plagiarized material made it impossible to provide a valid assessment of the test taker's performance on the task, the response was assigned a score of 0. This study investigates a set of 719 responses that were flagged as potentially plagiarized between October 2010 and December 2011; in this set, 239 responses were assigned a score of 0 due to the presence of a significant amount of plagiarized content from an identified source. This set of 239 responses is used in the experiments described below.

During the process of reviewing potentially plagiarized responses, the raters also collected a data set of external sources that appeared to have been used by test takers in their responses. In some cases, the test taker's spoken response was nearly identical to an identified source; in other cases, several sentences or phrases were clearly drawn from a particular source, although some modifications were apparent. Table 1 presents a sample source that was identified for several of the 239 responses in the data set.[3] Many of the plagiarized responses contained extended sequences of words that directly match idiosyncratic features of this source, such as the phrases "how romantic it can ever be" and "just relax yourself on the beach."

In total, 49 different source materials were identified for all of the potentially plagiarized responses in the corpus.[4] In addition to the source materials and the plagiarized responses, a set of non-plagiarized control responses was also obtained in order to conduct classification experiments between plagiarized and non-plagiarized responses. Since the plagiarized responses were collected over the course of more than one year, they were drawn from many different TOEFL iBT test forms; in total, the 239 plagiarized responses comprise 103 distinct Independent test questions. Therefore, it was not practical to obtain control data from all of the test items that were represented in the plagiarized set; rather, approximately 300 responses were extracted from each of the four test items that were most frequently represented in the set of plagiarized responses. Table 2 provides a summary of the three data sets used in the study, along with summary statistics about the length of the responses in each set.

Well, the place I enjoy the most is a small town located in France. I like this small town because it has very charming ocean view. I mean the sky there is so blue and the beach is always full of sunshine. You know how romantic it can ever be, just relax yourself on the beach, when the sun is setting down, when the ocean breeze is blowing and the seabirds are singing. Of course I like this small French town also because there are many great French restaurants. They offer the best seafood in the world like lobsters and tuna fishes. The most important, I have been benefited a lot from this trip to France because I made friends with some gorgeous French girls. One of them even gave me a little watch as a souvenir of our friendship.

Table 1: Sample source passage used in plagiarized responses

Data Set	N	Number of Words	
		Mean	Std. Dev.
Sources	49	122.5	36.5
Plagiarized	239	109.1	18.9
Control	1196	84.9	24.1

Table 2: Summary of the data sets

As Table 2 shows, the plagiarized responses are on average a little longer than the control responses. This is likely due to the fact that the plagiarized responses contain a large percentage of memorized material, which the test takers are able to produce using a fast rate of speech, since they had likely rehearsed the content several times before taking the assessment.

4 Methodology

The general approach taken in this study for determining whether a spoken response is plagiarized or not was to compare its content to the content of each of the source materials that had been identified for the responses in this corpus. Given a test response, a comparison was made with each

[3]This source is available from several online test preparation websites, for example http://www.mhdenglish.com/eoenglish_article_view_1195.html.

[4]A total of 39 sources were identified for the set of 239 responses in the Plagiarized set; however, all 49 identified sources were used in the experiments in order to make the experimental design more similar to an operational set-up in which the exact set of source texts that will be represented in a given set of plagiarized responses is not known.

of the 49 reference sources using the following 9 text-to-text similarity metrics: 1) Word Error Rate (WER), or edit distance between the response and the source; 2) TER, similar to WER, but allowing shifts of words within the text at a low edit cost (Snover et al., 2006); 3) TER-Plus, an extension of TER that includes matching based on paraphrases, stemming, and synonym substitution (Snover et al., 2008); 4) a WordNet similarity metric based on presence in the same synset;[5] 5) a WordNet similarity metric based on the shortest path between two words in the *is-a* taxonomy; 6) a WordNet similarity metric similar to (5) that also takes into account the maximum depth of the taxonomy in which the words occur (Leacock and Chodorow, 1998); 7) a WordNet similarity metric based on the depth of the Least Common Subsumer of the two words (Wu and Palmer, 1994); 8) Latent Semantic Analysis, using a model trained on the British National Corpus (BNC, 2007); 9) BLEU (Papineni et al., 2002). Most of these similarity metrics (with the exception of WER and TER) are expected to be robust to modifications between the source text and the plagiarized response, since they do not rely on exact string matches.

Each similarity metric was used to compute 4 different features comparing the test response to each of the 49 source texts: 1) the document-level similarity between the test response and the source text; 2) the single maximum similarity value from a sentence-by-sentence comparison between the test response and the source text; 3) the average of the similarity values for all sentence-by-sentence comparisons between the test response and the source text; 4) the average of the maximum similarity values for each sentence in the test response, where the maximum similarity of a sentence is obtained by comparing it with each sentence in the source text. The intuition behind using the features that compare sentence-to-sentence similarity as opposed to only the document-level similarity feature is that test responses may contain a combination of both passages that were memorized from a source text and novel content. Depending on the amount of the response that was plagiarized, these types of responses may also receive a score of 0; so, in order to also detect these responses as plagiarized, a sentence-by-sentence comparison approach may be more effective.

The experiments described below were conducted using both human transcriptions of the spoken responses as well as the output from an automated speech recognition (ASR) system. The ASR system was trained on approximately 800 hours of TOEFL iBT responses; the system's WER on the data used in this study was 0.411 for the Plagiarized set and 0.362 for the Control set. Since the ASR output does not contain sentence boundaries, these were obtained using a Maximum Entropy sentence boundary detection system based on lexical features (Chen and Yoon, 2011). Before calculating the similarity features, all of the texts were preprocessed to normalize case, segment the text into sentences, and remove disfluencies, including filled pauses (such as *uh* and *um*) and repeated words. No stemming was performed on the words in the texts for this study.

5 Results

As described in Section 4, 36 similarity features were calculated between each spoken response and each of the 49 source texts. In order to examine the performance of these features in discriminating between plagiarized and non-plagiarized responses, classification experiments were conducted on balanced sets of Plagiarized and Control responses, and the results were averaged using 1000 random subsets of 239 responses from the Control set.[6] In addition, the following different feature sets were compared: All (all 36 features), Doc (the 9 document-level features), and Sent (the 27 features based on sentence-level comparisons). The J48 decision tree model from the Weka toolkit (with the default parameter settings) was used for classification, and 10-fold cross-validation was performed using both transcriptions and ASR output. Table 3 presents the results of these experiments, including the means (and standard deviations) of the accuracy and kappa (κ) values (for all experiments, the baseline accuracy is 50%).

6 Discussion and Future Work

As Table 3 shows, the classifier achieved a higher accuracy when using the 9 document-level similarity features compared to using the 27 sentence-

[5] For the WordNet-based similarity metrics, the similarity scores for pairs of words were combined to obtain document- and sentence-level similarity scores by taking the average maximum pairwise similarity values, similar to the sentence-level similarity feature defined in (4) below.

[6] Experiments were also conducted using the full Control set, and the results showed a similar relative performance of the feature sets.

Text	Features	Accuracy	κ
Trans.	All	0.903 (0.01)	0.807 (0.02)
	Doc	0.920 (0.01)	0.839 (0.02)
	Sent	0.847 (0.01)	0.693 (0.03)
ASR	All	0.852 (0.02)	0.703 (0.03)
	Doc	0.871 (0.01)	0.742 (0.03)
	Sent	0.735 (0.02)	0.470 (0.04)

Table 3: Mean Accuracy and κ values (and standard deviations) for classification results using the 239 responses in the Plagiarized set and 1000 random subsets of 239 responses from the Control set

level similarity features. In addition, the combined set of 36 features resulted in a slightly lower performance than when only the 9 document-level features were used. This suggests that the sentence level features are not as robust as the document-level features, probably due to the increased likelihood of chance similarities between sentences in the response and a source text. Despite the fact that the plagiarized spoken responses in this data set may contain some original content (in particular, introductory material provided by the test taker in an attempt to make the plagiarized content seem more relevant to the specific test question), it appears that the document-level features are most effective. Table 3 also indicates that the performance of the classifier decreases by approximately 5% - 10% when ASR output is used. This indicates that the similarity metrics are reasonably robust to the presence of speech recognition errors in the text, and that the approach is viable in an operational setting in which transcriptions of the spoken responses are not available.

A more detailed error analysis indicates that the precision of the classifier, with respect to the Plagiarized class, is higher than the recall: on the transcriptions, the average precision using the Doc features was 0.948 (s.d.= 0.01), whereas the average recall was 0.888 (s.d.=0.01); for the ASR set, the average precision was 0.904 (s.d.=0.02), whereas the average recall was 0.831 (s.d.=0.02). This means that the rate of false positives produced by this classifier is somewhat lower than the rate of false negatives. In an operational scenario, an automated plagiarized spoken response detection system such as this one would likely be deployed in tandem with human raters to review the results and provide a final decision about whether a given spoken response was plagiarized or not. In that case, it may be desirable to tune the classifier parameters to increase the recall so that fewer cases of plagiarism would go undetected, assuming that there are suffient human reviewers available to process the increased number of false positives that would result from this approach. Improving the classifier's recall is also important for practical applications of this approach, since the distribution of actual responses is heavily imbalanced in favor of the non-plagiarized class. The current set of experiments only used a relatively small Control set of 1196 responses for which transcriptions could be obtained in a cost effective manner in order to be able to compare the system's performance using transcriptions and ASR output. Since there was only a minor degradation in performance when ASR output was used, future experiments will be conducted using a much larger Control set in order to approximate the distribution of categories that would be observed in practice.

One drawback of the method described in this study is that it requires matching source texts in order to detect a plagiarized spoken response. This means that plagiarized spoken responses based on a given source text will not be detected by the system until the appropriate source text has been identified, thus limiting the system's recall. Besides attempting to obtain additional source texts (either manually, as was done for this study, or by automated means), this could also be addressed by comparing a test response to all previously collected spoken responses for a given population of test takers in order to flag pairs of similar responses. While this method would likely produce a high number of false positives when the ASR output was used, due to chance similarities between two responses in a large pool of test taker responses resulting from imperfect ASR, performance could be improved by considering additional information from the speech recognizer when computing the similarity metrics, such as the N-best list. Additional sources of information that could be used for detecting plagiarized responses include stylistic patterns and prosodic features; for example, spoken responses that are reproduced from memory likely contain fewer filled pauses and have a faster rate of speech than non-plagiarized responses; these types of non-lexical features should also be investigated in future research into the detection of plagiarized spoken responses.

Acknowledgments

We would like to thank Beata Beigman Klebanov, Dan Blanchard, Nitin Madnani, and three anonymous BEA-9 reviewers for their helpful comments.

References

BNC. 2007. The British National Corpus, version 3. Distributed by Oxford University Computing Services on behalf of the BNC Consortium, http://www.natcorp.ox.ac.uk/.

Sergey Brin, James Davis, and Hector Garcia-Molina. 1995. Copy detection mechanisms for digital documents. In *Proceedings of the ACM SIGMOD Annual Conference*, pages 398–409.

Lei Chen and Su-Youn Yoon. 2011. Detecting structural events for assessing non-native speech. In *Proceedings of the 6th Workshop on Innovative Use of NLP for Building Educational Applications, NAACL-HLT*, pages 38–45, Portland, OR. Association for Computational Linguistics.

Chien-Ying Chen, Jen-Yuan Yeh, and Hao-Ren Ke. 2010. Plagiarism detection using ROUGE and WordNet. *Journal of Computing*, 2(3):34–44.

Pauline Cullen, Amanda French, and Vanessa Jakeman. 2014. *The Official Cambridge Guide to IELTS*. Cambridge University Press.

ETS. 2012. *The Official Guide to the TOEFL® Test, Fourth Edition*. McGraw-Hill.

Andrew Finch, Young-Sook Hwang, and Eiichiro Sumita. 2005. Using machine translation evaluation techniques to determine sentence-level semantic equivalence. In *Proceedings of the Third International Workshop on Paraphrasing*, pages 17–24.

Alexander Haputmann. 2006. Automatic spoken document retrieval. In Ketih Brown, editor, *Encylclopedia of Language and Linguistics (Second Edition)*, pages 95–103. Elsevier Science.

Timothy C. Hoad and Justin Zobel. 2003. Methods for identifying versioned and plagiarised documents. *Journal of the American Society for Information Science and Technology*, 54:203–215.

Claudia Leacock and Martin Chodorow. 1998. Combining local context and WordNet similarity for word sense identification. In Christiane Fellbaum, editor, *WordNet: An Electronic Lexical Database*, pages 305–332. MIT Press.

Pearson Longman. 2010. *The Official Guide to Pearson Test of English Academic*. Pearson Education ESL.

Caroline Lyon, Ruth Barrett, and James Malcolm. 2006. Plagiarism is easy, but also easy to detect. *Plagiary*, 1:57–65.

Nitin Madnani, Joel Tetreault, and Martin Chodorow. 2012. Re-examining machine translation metrics for paraphrase identification. In *Proceedings of the 2012 Conference of the North American Chapter of the Association for Computational Linguistics: Human Language Technologies*, pages 182–190, Montréal, Canada, June. Association for Computational Linguistics.

Thade Nahnsen, Özlem Uzuner, and Boris Katz. 2005. Lexical chains and sliding locality windows in content-based text similarity detection. CSAIL Technical Report, MIT-CSAIL-TR-2005-034.

Kishore Papineni, Salim Roukos, Todd Ward, and Wei-Jing Zhu. 2002. BLEU: A method for automatic evaluation of machine translation. In *Proceedings of the 40th Annual Meeting of the Association for Computational Linguistics*.

Martin Potthast, Benno Stein, Alberto Barrón-Cedeño, and Paolo Rosso. 2010. An evaluation framework for plagiarism detection. In *Proceedings of the 23rd International Conference on Computational Linguistics*.

Martin Potthast, Matthias Hagen, Tim Gollub, Martin Tippmann, Johannes Kiesel, Paolo Rosso, Efstathios Stamatatos, and Benno Stein. 2013. Overview of the 5th International Competition on Plagiarism Detection. In Pamela Forner, Roberto Navigli, and Dan Tufis, editors, *CLEF 2013 Evaluation Labs and Workshop – Working Notes Papers*.

Narayanan Shivakumar and Hector Garcia-Molina. 1995. SCAM: A copy detection mechanism for digital documents. In *Proceedings of the Second Annual Conference on the Theory and Practice of Digital Libraries*.

Matthew Snover, Bonnie Dorr, Richard Schwartz, Linnea Micciulla, and John Makhoul. 2006. A study of translation edit rate with targeted human annotation. In *Proceedings of Association for Machine Translation in the Americas*, pages 223–231.

Matt Snover, Nitin Madnani, Bonnie Dorr, and Richard Schwartz. 2008. TERp: A system description. In *Proceedings of the First NIST Metrics for Machine Translation Challenge (MetricsMATR)*, Waikiki, Hawaii, October.

Özlem Uzuner, Boris Katz, and Thade Nahnsen. 2005. Using syntactic information to identify plagiarism. In *Proceedings of the 2nd Workshop on Building Educational Applications using NLP. Ann Arbor*.

Zhibiao Wu and Martha Palmer. 1994. Verb semantics and lexical selection. In *Proceedings of the 32nd Annual Mmeeting of the Association for Computational Linguistics (ACL)*.

Understanding MOOC Discussion Forums using Seeded LDA

[1]Arti Ramesh, [1]Dan Goldwasser, [1]Bert Huang, [1]Hal Daumé III, [2]Lise Getoor
[1]University of Maryland, College Park [2]University of California, Santa Cruz
{artir, bert, hal}@cs.umd.edu, goldwas1@umiacs.umd.edu, getoor@soe.ucsc.edu

Abstract

Discussion forums serve as a platform for student discussions in massive open online courses (MOOCs). Analyzing content in these forums can uncover useful information for improving student retention and help in initiating instructor intervention. In this work, we explore the use of topic models, particularly *seeded topic models* toward this goal. We demonstrate that features derived from topic analysis help in predicting *student survival*.

1 Introduction

This paper highlights the importance of understanding MOOC discussion forum content, and shows that capturing discussion forum content can help uncover students' intentions and motivation and provide useful information in predicting course completion.

MOOC discussion forums provide a platform for exchange of ideas, course administration and logistics questions, reporting errors in lectures, and discussion about course material. Unlike classroom settings, where there is face-to-face interaction between the instructor and the students and among the students, MOOC forums are the primary means of interaction in MOOCs. However, due to the large number of students and the large volume of posts generated by them, MOOC forums are not monitored completely. Forums can include student posts expressing difficulties in course-work, grading errors, dissatisfaction in the course, which are possible precursors to students dropping out.

Previous work analyzing discussion forum content tried manually labeling posts by categories of interest (Stump et al., 2013). Unfortunately, the effort involved in manually annotating the large amounts of posts prevents using such solutions on a large scale. Instead, we suggest using natural language processing tools for identifying relevant aspects of forum content automatically. Specifically, we explore *SeededLDA* (Jagarlamudi et al., 2012), a recent extension of topic models which can utilize a lexical seed set to bias the topics according to relevant domain knowledge.

Exploring data from three MOOCs, we find that forum posts usually belong to these three categories—a) course content, which include discussions about course material (COURSE), b) meta-level discussions about the course, including feedback and course logistics (LOGISTICS), and c) other general discussions, which include student introductions, discussions about online courses (GENERAL). In order to capture these categories automatically we provide seed words for each category. For example, we extract seed words for the COURSE topic from each course's syllabus. In addition to the automatic topic assignment, we capture the sentiment polarity using *Opinionfinder* (Wilson et al., 2005). We use features derived from topic assignments and sentiment to predict student course completion *(student survival)*. We measure course completion by examining if the student attempted the final exam/ last few assignments in the course. We follow the observation that LOGISTICS posts contain feedback about the course. Finding high-confidence LOGISTICS posts can give a better understanding of student opinion about the course. Similarly, posting in COURSE topic and receiving good feedback (i.e., votes) is an indicator of student success and might contribute to survival. We show that modeling these intuitions using topic assignments together with sentiment scores, helps in predicting student survival. In addition, we examine the topic assignment and sentiment patterns of some users and show that topic assignments help in understanding student concerns better.

Proceedings of the Ninth Workshop on Innovative Use of NLP for Building Educational Applications , pages 28–33,
Baltimore, Maryland USA, June 26, 2014. ©2014 Association for Computational Linguistics

2 Modeling Student Survival

Our work builds on work by Ramesh et al. (2013) and (2014) on modeling student survival using Probabilistic Soft Logic (PSL). The authors included behavioral features, such as lecture views, posting/voting/viewing discussion forum content, linguistic features, such as sentiment and subjectivity of posts, and social interaction features derived from forum interaction. The authors looked at indication of sentiment without modeling the context in which the sentiment was expressed: positive sentiment implying survival and negative sentiment implying drop-out. In this work, we tackle this problem by adding topics, enabling reasoning about specific types of posts. While sentiment of posts can indicate general dissatisfaction, we expect this to be more pronounced in LOGISTICS posts as posts in this category correspond to issues and feedback about the course. In contrast, sentiment in posts about course material may signal a particular topic of discussion in a course and may not indicate attitude of the student toward the course. In Section 4.3, we show some examples of course-related posts and their sentiment, and we illustrate that they are not suggestive of student survival. For example, in *Women and the Civil Rights Movement* course, the post—*"I think our values are shaped by past generations in our family as well, sometimes negatively."*—indicates an attitude towards an issue discussed as part of the course. Hence, identifying posts that fall under LOGISTICS can improve the value of sentiment in posts. In Section 3, we show how these are translated into rules in our model.

2.1 Probabilistic Soft Logic

We briefly overview the some technical details behind Probabilistic Soft Logic (PSL). For brevity, we omit many specifics, and we refer the reader to (Broecheler et al., 2010; Bach et al., 2013) for more details. PSL is a framework for collective, probabilistic reasoning in relational domains. Like other statistical relational learning methods (Getoor and Taskar, 2007), PSL uses weighted rules to model dependencies in a domain. However, one distinguishing aspect is that PSL uses continuous variables to represent truth values, relaxing Boolean truth values to the interval [0,1].

Table 1 lists some PSL rules from our model. The predicate *posts* captures the relationship between a post and the user who posted it. Predicate *polarity(P)* represents sentiment via its truth value in $[0, 1]$, where 1.0 signifies positive sentiment, and 0.0 signifies negative sentiment. *upvote(P)* is 1.0 if the post has positive feedback and 0.0 if the post had negative or no feedback. *U* and *P* refer to *user* and *post* respectively. These features can be combined to produce rules in Table 1. For example, the first rule captures the idea that posts with positive sentiment imply student survival.

- $posts(U, P) \wedge polarity(P) \rightarrow survival(U)$
- $posts(U, P) \wedge \neg polarity(P) \rightarrow \neg survival(U)$
- $posts(U, P) \wedge upvote(P) \rightarrow survival(U)$

Table 1: Example rules in PSL

3 Enhancing Student Survival Models with Topic Modeling

Discussion forums in online courses are organized into threads to facilitate grouping of posts into topics. For example, a thread titled *errata, grading issues* is likely a place for discussing course logistics and a thread titled *week 1, lecture 1* is likely a place for discussing course content. But a more precise examination of such threads reveals that these heuristics do not always hold. We have observed that *course content* threads often house *logistic content* and vice-versa. This demands the necessity of using computational linguistics methods to classify the content in discussion forums.

In this work, we—1) use topic models to map posts to topics in an unsupervised way, and 2) employ background knowledge from the course syllabus and manual inspection of discussion forum posts to seed topic models to get better separated topics. We use data from three Coursera MOOCs: *Surviving Disruptive Technologies*, *Women and the Civil Rights Movement*, and *Gene and the Human Condition* for our analysis. In discussion below, we refer to these courses as DISR-TECH, WOMEN, and GENE, respectively.

3.1 Latent Dirichlet Allocation

Table 2 gives the topics given by *latent Dirichlet allocation* (LDA) on discussion forum posts. The words that are likely to fall under LOGISTICS are underlined in the table. It can be observed that these words are spread across more than one topic. Since we are especially interested in posts that are on LOGISTICS, we use *SeededLDA* (Jagarlamudi et al., 2012), which allows one to specify *seed* words that can influence the discovered topics toward our desired three categories.

topic 1:	kodak, management, great, innovation, post, agree, film, understand, something, problem, businesses, changes, needs
topic 2:	good, change, publishing, brand, companies, publishers, history, marketing, traditional, believe, authors
topic 3:	think, work, technologies, newspaper, content, paper, model, business, disruptive, information, survive, print, media, course, assignment
topic 4:	digital, kodak, company, camera, market, quality, phone, development, future, failed, high, right, old,
topic 5:	amazon, books, netflix, blockbuster, stores, online, experience, products, apple, nook, strategy, video, service
topic 6:	time, grading, different, class, course, major, focus, product, like, years
topic 7:	companies, interesting, class, thanks, going, printing, far, wonder, article, sure

Table 2: Topics identified by LDA

topic 1:	thank, professor, lectures, assignments, concept, love, thanks, learned, enjoyed, forums, subject, question, hard, time, grading, peer, lower, low
topic 2:	learning, education, moocs, courses, students, online, university, classroom, teaching, coursera

Table 3: Seed words in LOGISTICS and GENERAL for DISR-TECH, WOMEN and GENE courses

topic 3a:	disruptive, technology, innovation, survival, digital, disruption, survivor
topic 3b:	women, civil, rights, movement, american, black, struggle, political, protests, organizations, events, historians, african, status, citizenship
topic 3c:	genomics, genome, egg, living, processes, ancestors, genes, nature, epigenitics, behavior, genetic, engineering, biotechnology

Table 4: Seed words for COURSE topic for DISR-TECH, WOMEN and GENE courses

topic 1:	time, thanks, one, low, hard, question, course, love, professor, lectures, lower, another, concept, agree, peer, point, never
topic 2:	online, education, coursera, students, university, courses, classroom, moocs, teaching, video
topic 3:	digital, survival, management, disruption, technology, development, market, business, innovation
topic 4:	publishing, publisher, traditional, companies, money, history, brand
topic 5:	companies, social, internet, work, example
topic 6:	business, company, products, services, post, consumer, market, phone, changes, apple
topic 7:	amazon, book, nook, readers, strategy, print, noble, barnes

Table 5: Topics identified by SeededLDA for DISR-TECH

topic 1:	time, thanks, one, hard, question, course, love, professor, lectures, forums, help, essays, problem, thread, concept, subject
topic 2:	online, education, coursera, students, university, courses, classroom, moocs, teaching, video, work, english, interested, everyone
topic 3:	women, rights, black, civil, movement, african, struggle, social, citizenship, community, lynching, class, freedom, racial, segregation
topic 4:	violence, public, people, one, justice, school,s state, vote, make, system, laws
topic 5:	idea, believe, women, world, today, family, group, rights
topic 6:	one, years, family, school, history, person, men, children, king, church, mother, story, young
topic 7:	lynching, books, mississippi, march, media, youtube, death, google, woman, watch, mrs, south, article, film

Table 6: Topics identified by SeededLDA for WOMEN

topic 1:	time, thanks, one, answer, hard, question, course, love, professor, lectures, brian, lever, another, concept, agree, peer, material, interesting
topic 2:	online, education, coursera, students, university, courses, classroom, moocs, teaching, video, knowledge, school
topic 3:	genes, genome, nature, dna, gene, living, behavior, chromosomes, mutation, processes
topic 4:	genetic, biotechnology, engineering, cancer, science, research, function, rna
topic 5:	reproduce, animals, vitamin, correct, term, summary, read, steps
topic 6:	food, body, cells, alleles blood, less, area, present, gmo, crops, population, stop
topic 7:	something, group, dna, certain, type, early, large, cause, less, cells

Table 7: Topics identified by SeededLDA for GENE

3.2 Seeded LDA

We experiment by providing seed words for topics that fall into the three categories. The seed words for the three courses are listed in tables 3 and 4. The seed words for LOGISTICS and GENERAL are common across all the three courses. The seed words for the COURSE topic are chosen from the course-syllabus of the courses. This construction of seed words enables the model to be applied to new courses easily. Topics *3a*, *3b*, and *3c* denote the course specific seed words for DISR-TECH, WOMEN, and GENE courses respectively. Since the syllabus is only an outline of the class, it does not contain all the terms that will be used in class discussions. To capture other finer course content discussions as separate topics, we include k more topics when we run the SeededLDA. We notice that not including more topics here, only including the seeded topics (i.e., run SeededLDA with exactly three topics) results in some words from course content discussions, which were not specified in the course-seed words, appearing in the LOGISTICS or GENERAL topics. Thus, the k extra topics help represent COURSE topics that do not directly correspond to the course seeds. Note that these *extra* topics are not seeded. We experimented with different values of k on our experiments and found by manual inspection that the topic-terms produced by our model were well separated for $k = 3$. Thus, we run *SeededLDA* with 7 total topics. Tables 5, 6, and 7 give the topics identified for DISR-TECH, WOMEN and GENE by *SeededLDA*. The topic assignments so obtained are used as input features to the PSL model—the predicate for the first topic is LOGISTICS, the second one is GENERAL and the rest are summed up to get the topic assignment for COURSE.

3.3 Using topic assignments in PSL

We construct two models—a) DIRECT model, including all features except features from topic

survival = 0.0	polarity = 0.25	logistics = 0.657 general = 0.028 course = 0.314	JSTOR allowed 3 items (texts/writings) on my 'shelf' for 14 days. But, I read the items and wish to return them, but cannot, until 14 days has expired. It is difficult then, to do the extra readings in the "Exploring Further" section of Week 1 reading list in a timely manner. Does anyone have any ideas for surmounting this issue?
survival = 0.0	polarity = 0.0	logistics = 0.643 general = 0.071 course = 0.285	There are some mistakes on quiz 2. Questions 3, 5, and 15 mark you wrong for answers that are correct.
survival = 0.0	polarity = 0.25	logistics = 0.652 general = 0.043 course = 0.304	I see week 5 quiz is due April 1(by midnight 3/31/13).I am concerned about this due date being on Easter, some of us will be traveling, such as myself. Can the due date be later in the week? Thank you

Table 8: Logistics posts containing negative sentiment for dropped-out students

survival = 1.0	polarity = 0.0	logistics = 0.67 general = 0.067 course = 0.267	I was just looking at the topics for the second essay assignments. The thing is I dont see what the question choices are. I have the option of Weeks and I have no idea what that even means. Can someone help me out here and tell me what the questions for the second essay assignment are I think my computer isnt allowing me to see the whole assignment! Someone please help me out and let me know that the options are.
survival = 1.0	polarity = 0.25	logistics = 0.769 general = 0.051 course = 0.179	I'd appreciate someone looks into the following: Lecture slides for the videos (week 5) don't open (at all) (irrespective of the used browser). Some required reading material for week 5 won't open either (error message). I also have a sense that there should be more material posted for the week (optional readings, more videos, etc). Thanks. — I am not seeing a quiz posted for Week 5.
survival = 1.0	polarity = 0.78	logistics = 0.67 general = 0.067 course = 0.267	Hopefully the Terrell reading and the Lecture PowerPoints now open for you. Thanks for reporting this.

Table 9: Example of change in sentiment in a course logistic thread

survival = 1.0	polarity = 0.25	logistics = 0.372 general = 0.163 course = 0.465	I've got very interested in the dynamic of segregation in terms of space and body pointed by Professor Brown and found a document written by GerShun Avilez called "Housing the Black Body: Value, Domestic Space,and Segregation Narratives".
survival = 1.0	polarity = 0.9	logistics = 0.202 general = 0.025 course = 0.772	I think that you hit it on the head, the whole idea of Emancipation came as a result not so much of rights but of the need to get the Transcontinental Railroad through the mid-west and the north did not want the wealth of the southern slave owners to overshadow the available shares. There are many brilliant people "good will hunting", and their brilliance either dies with them or dies while they are alive due to intolerance. Many things have happened in my life to cause me to be tolerant to others and see what their debate is, Many very evil social ills and stereotypes are a result of ignorance. It would be awesome if the brilliant minds could all come together for reform and change.
survival = 1.0	polarity = 0.167	logistics = 0.052 general = 0.104 course = 0.844	I think our values are shaped by past generations in our family as well – sometimes negatively. In Bliss, Michigan where I come from, 5 families settled when the government kicked out the residents – Ottowa Tribe Native Americans. I am descended from the 5 families. All of the cultural influences in Bliss were white Christian – the Native American population had never been welcomed back or invited to stay as they had in Cross Village just down the beach. My family moved to the city for 4 years during my childhood, and I had African American, Asian, and Hispanic classmates and friends. When we moved back to the country I was confronted with the racism and generational wrong-doings of my ancestors. At the tender age of 10 my awareness had been raised! Was I ever pissed off when the full awareness of the situation hit me! I still am.

Table 10: Posts talking about COURSE content

DIRECT	DIRECT+TOPIC
$posts(U,P) \wedge polarity(P) \rightarrow survival(U)$	$posts(U,P) \wedge topic(P, \text{LOGISTICS}) \wedge \neg polarity(P) \rightarrow survival(U)$
$posts(U,P) \wedge \neg polarity(P) \rightarrow \neg survival(U)$	$posts(U,P) \wedge topic(P, \text{LOGISTICS}) \wedge \neg polarity(P) \rightarrow survival(U)$
$posts(U,P) \rightarrow survival(U)$	$posts(U,P) \wedge topic(P, \text{GENERAL}) \rightarrow \neg survival(U)$
$posts(U,P) \wedge upvote(P) \rightarrow survival(U)$	$posts(U,P) \wedge topic(P, \text{COURSE}) \wedge upvote(P) \rightarrow survival(U)$
	$posts(U_1,P) \wedge posts(U_2,P) \wedge topic(P, \text{COURSE}) \wedge survival(U_1) \rightarrow survival(U_2)$

Table 11: Rules modified to include topic features

modeling, and b) DIRECT+TOPIC model, including the topic assignments as features in the model. Our DIRECT model is borrowed from Ramesh (2014). We refer the reader to (Ramesh et al., 2013) and (Ramesh et al., 2014) for a complete list of features and rules in this model.

Table 11 contains examples of rules in the DIRECT model and the corresponding rules including topic assignments in DIRECT+TOPIC model. The first and second rules containing polarity are changed to include LOGISTICS topic feature, following our observation that polarity matters in *meta-course* posts. While the DIRECT model regards posting in forums as an indication of survival, in the DIRECT+TOPIC model, this rule is changed to capture that students that post a lot of *general* stuff *only* on the forums do not necessarily participate in course-related discussions. The fourth rule containing *upvote* predicate, which signifies posts that received positive feedback in the form of votes, is changed to include the topic-feature COURSE. This captures the significance of posting *course-related* content that gets positive feedback as opposed to *logistics* or *general* content in the forums. This rule helps us discern posts in general/logistic category that can get a lot of positive votes (*upvote*), but do not necessarily indicate student survival. For example, some introduction threads have a lot of positive votes, but do not necessarily signify student survival.

4 Empirical Evaluation

We conducted experiments to answer the following question—how much do the topic assignments from *SeededLDA* help in predicting student survival? We also perform a qualitative analysis of topic assignments, the sentiment of posts, and their correspondence with student survival.

COURSE	MODEL	AUC-PR POS.	AUC-PR NEG.	AUC-ROC
DISR-TECH	DIRECT	0.764	0.628	0.688
	DIRECT+TOPIC	**0.794**	0.638	**0.708**
WOMEN	DIRECT	0.654	0.899	0.820
	DIRECT+TOPIC	**0.674**	0.900	**0.834**
GENE	DIRECT	0.874	0.780	0.860
	DIRECT+TOPIC	**0.894**	**0.791**	**0.873**

Table 12: Performance of DIRECT and DIRECT+TOPIC models in predicting student survival. Statistically significant scores typed in bold.

4.1 Datasets and Experimental Setup

We evaluate our models on three Coursera MOOCs: DISR-TECH, WOMEN-CIVIL, and GENE, respectively. Our data consists of anonymized student records, grades, and online behavior recorded during the seven week duration of each course. We label students as *survival = 1.0* if they take the final exam/quiz and *survival = 0.0* otherwise. In our experiments, we only consider students that completed at least *one* quiz/assignment. We evaluate our models using area under precision-recall curve for positive and negative *survival* labels and area under ROC curve. We use ten-fold cross-validation on each of the courses, leaving out 10% of users for testing and revealing the rest of the users for training the model weights. We evaluate statistical significance using a paired t-test with a rejection threshold of *0.05*.

4.2 Survival Prediction using topic features

Table 12 shows the prediction performance of the DIRECT and DIRECT+TOPIC model. The inclusion of the topic-features improves student survival prediction in all the three courses.

4.3 Discussion topic analysis using topic features

Table 8 shows some posts by users that did not survive the class. All these posts have negative sentiment scores by *Opinionfinder* and belong to LOGISTICS. Also, in the forum, all these posts were not answered. This suggests that students might drop out if their *course-logistics* questions are not answered. Table 9 gives examples of student posts that also have a negative sentiment. But the sentiment of the thread changes when the issue is resolved (last row in the table). We observe that these two students survive the course and a timely answer to their posts might have been a reason influencing these students to complete the course.

Tables 8 and 9 show how student survival may depend on forum interaction and responses they receive. Our approach can help discover potential points of contention in the forums, identifying potential drop outs that can be avoided by intervention.

Table 10 shows posts flagged as COURSE by the *SeededLDA*. The polarity scores in the COURSE posts indicate opinions and attitude toward course specific material. For example, post #3 in Table 10 indicates opinion towards human rights. While the post's polarity is negative, it is clear that this polarity value is not directed at the course and should not be used to predict student survival. In fact, all these users survive the course. We find that participation in course related discussion is a sign of survival. These examples demonstrate that analysis on COURSE posts can mislead survival and justify our using topic predictions to focus sentiment analysis on LOGISTICS posts.

5 Discussion

In this paper, we have taken a step toward understanding discussion content in massive open online courses. Our topic analysis is coarse-grained, grouping posts into three categories. In our analysis, all the meta-content—course logistics and course feedback—were grouped under the same topic category. Instead, a finer-grained topic model could be seeded with different components of meta-content as separate topics. The same applies for course-related posts too, where a finer-grained analysis could help identify difficult topics that may cause student frustration and dropout.

Acknowledgements We thank the instructors for letting us use data from their course. This work is supported by National Science Foundation under Grant No. CCF0937094. Any opinions, findings, and conclusions or recommendations expressed in this material are those of the author(s) and do not necessarily reflect the views of the National Science Foundation.

References

Stephen H. Bach, Bert Huang, Ben London, and Lise Getoor. 2013. Hinge-loss Markov random fields: Convex inference for structured prediction. In *Uncertainty in Artificial Intelligence*.

Matthias Broecheler, Lilyana Mihalkova, and Lise Getoor. 2010. Probabilistic similarity logic. In *Uncertainty in Artificial Intelligence (UAI)*.

Lise Getoor and Ben Taskar. 2007. *Introduction to Statistical Relational Learning (Adaptive Computation and Machine Learning)*. The MIT Press.

Jagadeesh Jagarlamudi, Hal Daumé, III, and Raghavendra Udupa. 2012. Incorporating lexical priors into topic models. In *Proceedings of the 13th Conference of the European Chapter of the Association for Computational Linguistics*, EACL '12, pages 204–213, Stroudsburg, PA, USA. Association for Computational Linguistics.

Angelika Kimmig, Stephen H. Bach, Matthias Broecheler, Bert Huang, and Lise Getoor. 2012. A short introduction to probabilistic soft logic. In *NIPS Workshop on Probabilistic Programming: Foundations and Applications*.

Arti Ramesh, Dan Goldwasser, Bert Huang, Hal Daume III, and Lise Getoor. 2013. Modeling learner engagement in MOOCs using probabilistic soft logic. In *NIPS Workshop on Data Driven Education*.

Arti Ramesh, Dan Goldwasser, Bert Huang, Hal Daume III, and Lise Getoor. 2014. Learning latent engagement patterns of students in online courses. In *Proceedings of the Twenty-Eighth AAAI Conference on Artificial Intelligence*.

Glenda S. Stump, Jennifer DeBoer, Jonathan Whittinghill, and Lori Breslow. 2013. Development of a framework to classify mooc discussion forum posts: Methodology and challenges. In *NIPS Workshop on Data Driven Education*.

Theresa Wilson, Paul Hoffmann, Swapna Somasundaran, Jason Kessler, Janyce Wiebe, Yejin Choi, Claire Cardie, Ellen Riloff, and Siddharth Patwardhan. 2005. OpinionFinder: A system for subjectivity analysis. In *Proceedings of HLT/EMNLP on Interactive Demonstrations*.

Translation Class Instruction as Collaboration in the Act of Translation

Lars Ahrenberg
Department of Computer and Information Science,
Linköping University
lars.ahrenberg@liu.se

Ljuba Tarvi
University of Helsinki
Helsinki, Finland
ljuba.tarvi@welho.com

Abstract

The paper offers an effective way of teacher-student computer-based collaboration in translation class. We show how a quantitative-qualitative method of analysis supported by word alignment technology can be applied to student translations for use in the classroom. The combined use of natural-language processing and manual techniques enables students to 'co-emerge' during highly motivated collaborative sessions. Within the advocated approach, students are proactive seekers for a better translation (grade) in a teacher-centered computer-based peer-assisted translation class.

1 Introduction

Tools for computer-assisted translation (CAT), including translation memories, term banks, and more, are nowadays standard tools for translators. The proper use of such tools and resources are also increasingly becoming obligatory parts of translator training. Yet we believe that translation technology has more to offer translator training, in particular as a support for classroom interaction. Our proposal includes a quantitative analysis of translations, supported by word alignment technology, to enable joint presentation, discussion, and assessment of individual student translation in class. For comparisons with related work, see section 4.

From the pedagogical point of view, the suggested procedure embraces at least four types of evaluation: students' implied self-evaluation, a preliminary computer evaluation, teacher's evaluation after manually correcting the imperfect computer alignment and assessment, and peer evaluation during the collaborative team work in class, when the versions produced by the students are simultaneously displayed, discussed and corrected if necessary.

Theoretically, translations are viewed here as mappings between two languages through emergent conceptual spaces based on an intermediate level of representation (e.g., Honkela et. al., 2010). In terms of praxis, the basic approach is rooted in the idea (Vinay & Darbelnet, 1958) of consecutive numbering of the tokens (words) in the original text. This simple technique enables - finding and labeling, in accordance with a chosen set of rules, certain isomorphic correspondences between the source and target tokens. Finding such correspondences is what current machine translation approaches attempt to achieve by statistical means in the training phase.

The quantitative-qualitative technique we use here is the Token Equivalence Method (TEM) (Tarvi 2004). The use of the TEM in translation teaching originated as an argument (involving the second author) in a teacher-student debate over the relevance of a grade. The considerable time spent on the manual preparation of texts for translation using the TEM proved to be fairly well compensated for by the evident objectivity of the grades - the argument that, say, only 65% of the original text has been retained in a translation is difficult to brush aside. Later, the method was applied in research. Tarvi (2004) compared the classical Russian novel in verse by A. Pushkin *Eugene Onegin* (1837) with its nineteen English translations. Figures calculated manually on 10% of the text of the novel showed an excellent fit with the results on the same material obtained elsewhere by conventional comparative methods. Thus, we believe that characterizations of relations between source and target texts in ob-

Proceedings of the Ninth Workshop on Innovative Use of NLP for Building Educational Applications , pages 34–42,
Baltimore, Maryland USA, June 26, 2014.

jective terms is a good thing for translation evaluation.

1.1 The TEM: Basics and Example

Methodologically, the TEM focuses not on translation 'shifts' but on what has been kept in translation. The basic frame for analysis in the TEM is the Token Frame (2.2.1), which accounts for the number of the original tokens retained in translations. The other four frames (2.2.2-3, 2.3.1-2), although useful in gauging the comparative merits of the translations and the individual strategies, are optional.

To concisely illustrate the method, one sentence will be used – the famous 13-token opening sentence of Leo Tolstoy's *Anna Karenina*: *Vse schastlivye semyi pohozhi drug na druga, kazhdaya neschastlivaya semya neschastliva po svoemu.* (All happy families resemble one another, every unhappy family is unhappy in its own way.)

Eight English translations of this sentence (2.1) will be used for analysis.

The source text and all its translations are tokenized and analyzed linguistically in different ways. NLP tools such as lemmatizers, part-of-speech taggers and parsers can be applied. Most importantly, however, to support the computation of the Token Frames (2.2.1), they must be word-aligned with the source text (2.6). The teacher or the students are expected to review the alignments and correct them if they are not acceptable. Given the corrected alignments, the aligned data can be used by the teacher and the students in the classroom.

After this introduction of the basics of the theoretical approach and relevant automatic methods for their implementation, the paper is built around the basic structural foci of any instruction unit: before class (2), in class (3), and outside class (4).

2 Before class

This section describes the techniques of processing Source Texts (ST) and Target Texts (TT) by teachers and students.

2.1 Token Numbering and Labeling

The procedure starts with consecutive numbering of the original tokens:

(1)Vse (2)schastlivye (3)semyi (4)pohozhi (5)drug (6)na (7)druga, (8)kazhdaya (9)neschastlivaya (10)semya (11)neschastliva (12)po (13)svoemu.

The second step is establishing, via the procedure of (corrected) alignment, the correspondences between the Source tokens (St) and Target tokens (Tt). As a result, every corresponding TT token (Tt), if found, is designated with the number of its source counterpart (St). Besides, since no Tt may remain unlabeled, two types of Tts which have no counterparts in the ST are labeled as Extra tokens (2.3.1) and Formal tokens (2.3.2). Here are the eight translations of the example sentence:

Leo Wiener: (1899):
(1)All (2)happy (3)families (4)resemble (5-6-7)one another; (8)every (9)unhappy (10)family (Ft)is (11)unhappy (12)in (Ft)its (13)own way.

Constance Garnett (1901):
(2)Happy (3)families (Ft)are (1)all (4)alike; (8)every (9)unhappy (10)family (Ft)is (11)unhappy (12)in (Ft)its (13)own way.

Rochelle S. Townsend (1912):
(1)All (2)happy (3)families (Ft)are (Et)more (Et)or (Et)less (4)like (5-6-7)one another; (8)every (9)unhappy (10)family (Ft)is (11)unhappy (12)in (Ft)its (13)own (Et)particular way.

Aylmer & Louise Maude (1918):
(1)All (2)happy (3)families (4)resemble (5-6-7)one another, (Et)but (8)each (9)unhappy (10)family (Ft)is (11)unhappy (12)in (Ft)its (13)own way.

Rosemary Edmonds (1954):
(1)All (2)happy (3)families (Ft)are (4)alike; (Et)but (Ft)an (9)unhappy (10)family (Ft)is (11)unhappy (12)after (Ft)its (13)own fashion.

Joel Carmichael (1960):
(2)Happy (3)families (Ft)are (1)all (4)alike; (8)every (9)unhappy (10)family (Ft)is (11)unhappy (12)in (Ft)its (13)own way.

David Magarschack (1961):
(1)All (2)happy (3)families (Ft)are (4)like (5-6-7)one another; (8)each (9)unhappy (10)family (Ft)is (11)unhappy (12)in (Ft)its (13)own way.

Richard Pevear & Larisa Volokhonsky (2000):
(1)All (2)happy (3)families (Ft)are (4)alike; (8)each (9)unhappy (10)family (Ft)is (11)unhappy (12)in (Ft)its (13)own way.

As is seen, two of the versions are clones (Carmichael, Pevear-Volokhonsky), one translation (Garnett) differs from the original only by the choice of the adjective (St 8), while the remaining five versions are more diverse. Note the mode of denoting Tts suggested here: only the meaningful denotative tokens get labeled, e.g., *are (4)alike*, or *is (11)unhappy*; if not one Tt but a group of tokens is used as an isomorph to a single St, the whole group is underlined, e.g., *(13)own way*, or *(13)own fashion*.

Although St 4 has been rendered as *are alike* (Edmonds, Pevear-Volokhonsky, Garnett, Carmichael), *are like* (Townsend, Magarschack), and *resemble* (Wiener, the Maudes), all these rendering are viewed as retaining the denotative meaning of the original token. Or, for instance, St 12, whether rendered as *after* (Edmonds) or *in* (all the rest), is also viewed as retained in translation. The connotative shades of meaning most suitable for the outlined goals can be discussed in class (3.2).

This mode of displaying the isomorphisms can be converted to the style of representation used in word alignment systems such as Giza++ (Och and Ney, 2003) as follows: Extra tokens and Formal tokens give rise to null links. Groups of tokens that correspond yield groups of links. Thus, the analysis for Wiener's translation would come out as below:

1-1 2-2 3-3 4-4 5-5 5-6 6-5 6-6 7-5 7-6 8-7 9-8 10-9 0-10 11-11 12-12 0-13 13-14 13-15.

In gauging the content, two types of basic and optional analytical frames, content and formal, are used. Based on the way of calculating the results, the analytical frames will be considered here in two sections, percentage frames (2.2) and count frames (2.3).

2.2 The TEM: Percentage Frames

The results in these frames are calculated as percentages of the ST information retained in translations.

2.2.1 Basic Content Frame (Token Frame)

After finding the isomorphic counterparts, the percentages of the retained tokens are presented in Table 1 (column I). As one can see, Wiener, the Maudes, Magarschack and Townsend translated all thirteen tokens and, hence, scored 100% each; Garnett, Carmichael and Pevear-Volokhonsky omitted Sts 5-6-7 and thus scored 76%, while Edmonds left out four tokens, Sts 5-6-7-8, thus retaining 69% of the original.

2.2.2 Optional Formal Frame 1 (Morphology Frame)

In this frame, if a token is rendered with the same part of speech as in the original, the Tt in question gets a count. As can be seen in Table 1 (column II), only two translators, Wiener and the Maudes, kept the same type of predicate 1 (St 4) as in the original – *resemble* – while in the remaining six translations the type of predicate 1 has been changed into a compound one: *are alike* (Edmonds, Pevear-Volokhonsky, Garnett, Carmichael), and *are like* (Townsend, Magarschack). Therefore, in this frame, Wiener and the Maudes get a 100% each; Edmonds, with her two changed parts of speech, gets 84%, while the remaining five translators, who changed one part of speech each, score 92%.

2.2.3 Optional Formal Frame 2 (Syntax)

Another possible way of gauging the 'presence' of the original in its translation is monitoring the syntactic changes. If at least two tokens are rendered in the same sequence as in the original and preserve the same syntactic functions, they are considered syntactically kept. Non-translated Sts are viewed as non-kept syntactic positions. Table 1 (column III) shows that Edmonds, who lost four syntactic positions, scores 76%, Garnett, Magarschack and Townsend get 92% each, the rest translators score a 100%.

2.2.4 The Translation Quotient (TQ)

As a result of either manual or computer-assisted translation processing, the teacher gets a tabulated picture (Table 1) of the three analyzed frames (columns I, II, III).

In an attempt to combine the obtained figures in a meaningful whole, the Translation Quotient parameter (TQ, column IV) is used: it is the arithmetic mean of the percentages in the monitored frames. If one adds up the percentage results in all three frames and divides the obtained figure by the number of frames, one gets a TQ, measured in percentage points (pp), which reflects a general quantitative picture of the content-form rendering of the original. This cumulative parameter has shown a perfect fit with the results obtained by other methods of comparative assessment (Tarvi 2004). Table 1 shows four groups of TQ results, from 100% (2 versions) through 97% (2) through 86% (3) to 74% (1).

2.3 The TEM: Count Frames

To further differentiate the translations in their closeness to the original, pure counts of some quantitative parameters can be added to the picture in Table 1: column V (extra tokens, Ets) and VI (formal Tokens, Fts).

2.3.1 Optional Content Frame 1

This frame is a useful tool of assessment, as it shows what has been added to the translation, i.e., the Tts that have no counterparts in the original, labeled as extra Tokens (Et). Table 1 (column V) shows that Wiener, Magarschack, Garnett, Carmachael, and Pevear-Volokhonsky added no extra Tokens (Ets), the Maudes and Edmonds added by one Et each, while Townsend – four.

2.3.2 Optional Formal Frame 3

In this frame, the center of attention is formal Tokens (Fts) – articles, tense markers, etc. Table 1 (column VI) shows that Fts are employed in different quantities: Wiener and the Maudes used two Fts each, Edmonds used four, the rest translators – three Fts each.

2.4 TEM Results: the 13-Token Sentence

The table below gives a cumulative picture of the results in each of the five frames considered:

Table 1. Cumulative Overall Table (13 tokens): Rank Order

I TF (2.2.1) (%)	II MF (2.2.2) (%)	III SF (2.2.3) (%)	IV TQ (2.2.4) (pp)	V Et (2.2.5) (count)	VI Ft (2.2.6) (count)
Leo Wiener (1899)					
100	100	100	100	0	2
Aylmer & Louise Maude (1918)					
100	100	100	100	1	2
David Magarschack (1961)					
100	92	100	97	0	3
Rochelle S. Townsend (1912)					
100	92	100	97	4	3
Constance Garnett (1901)					
76	92	92	86	0	3
Joel Carmichael (1960)					
76	92	92	86	0	3
Pevear & Volokhonsky (2000)					
76	92	92	86	0	3
Rosemary Edmonds (1954)					
69	84	69	74	1	4

As is seen, there are four groups of the TQ results. In the 100% group, Wiener has a slight advantage (in terms of isomorphism) over the Maudes, since he introduced no extra tokens. In the 97% group, Townsends's translation inferiority (in terms of closeness) is expressed in four extra tokens as compared to no extra tokens in Magarschack's version. In the 86% block, no distinctions can be made because they are word-for-word clones, except for Pevear-Volokhonsky's use of 'each' instead of 'every' (St 8). Edmonds' version (TQ = 74%) has a record (for this sample) number of formal tokens, four. It does not imply that the translation is bad – this kind of judgment can arise only after a discussion in classroom (3.3).

The one-sentence example, used here pedagogically to explain the TEM techniques, cannot be considered to be fairly representative of the quantitative parameters and their qualitative implications of translated texts. Therefore, we offer the results obtained for a much bigger sample from *Anna Karenina*.

2.4.1 TEM Results: the 405-Token Excerpt

Sheldon (1997) performs a detailed conventional comparative analysis of the four 'focal points' of the novel: the opening sentence considered above (13 tokens), the ball scene (73 tokens), the seduction scene (103 tokens) and the suicide scene (216 tokens). He analyzed the seven translations considered here, except for the version by Pevear and Volokhonsky, which was published three years later. Sheldon concluded that it was Carmichael who showed the best fit with the original.

Here are the quantitative results obtained with the TEM applied to the same excerpts.

Table 2. Cumulative Overall Table (405 tokes): Rank Order

Lost tokens (count)	Kept tokens (count)	TQ (%)	Ft used (count)	Et used (count)
David Magarshack (1961)				
9	396	97,7	96	14
Joe Carmichael (1960)				
18	387	95,5	95	15
Constance Garnett (1901)				
20	385	95,0	90	8
Aylmer & Louise Maude (1918)				
30	375	92,5	91	17
Rosemary Edmonds (1954)				
34	371	91,6	87	14
Leo Wiener (1899)				
57	348	85,9	74	20
Rochelle S. Townsend (1912)				
69	336	82,9	79	42

As is seen, the TQs range from 97,7% to 82,9%. Since the TEM does not cover all aspects of Sheldon's analysis, it favors Magarshack's version, with Carmichael's translation lauded by Sheldon following it closely.

2.5 Language pair independence

In our example with translation from Russian to English, there is an asymmetry in that formal tokens are largely to be seen only on the target side. However, the TEM frames can equally be applied in the reverse direction or to any language pair. Whether or not we choose to exclude some formal tokens from the counting, the frames are applied in the same way to all translations and their relative differences will be revealed.

2.6 Computational analysis

It has been suggested before that virtual learning environments are useful for translation teaching (e.g., Fictumova (2007)). Our point here is that fine-grained quantitative methods, such as the TEM, can be put to use given support from computational linguistic tools. The proposed environment consists of a central server and a number of client systems for the students. Communication between them is handled as in any e-learning environment, where exercises, grades and other course materials can be stored and accessed. The server includes several modules for monolingual text analysis, such as sentence segmentation, tokenization, lemmatization and PoS-tagging. A parser may also be included to support the computation of the syntax frame. More importantly, there are modules for sentence and word alignments, since this is what is required to support the TEM analysis. In addition, there are modules for reviewing and correcting outputs from all analyzers.

2.6.1 Tokenization

In principle, tokenization, numbering and labeling of tokens (2.1), are processes that computers can handle with ease. It is important, though, that the tokenization is done in a way that supports the purpose to which it will be used. In this case, a tokenization module that only looks at spaces and separators will not be optimal, as the primary unit of TEM is semantic, and may span several text words. Moreover, punctuation marks are not treated as separate tokens in the TEM. This problem could be overcome by tokenizing in two steps. In the first step punctuation marks are removed, lexical tokens are identified using word lists and then formatted as character strings that have no internal spaces. In the second stage spaces are used to identify and number the tokens. Formal tokens can to a large extent be identified as part of this process, using word lists, but extra tokens cannot be identified until after the word alignment.

2.6.2 Sentence alignment

In some cases the translation task may require students not to change sentence boundaries and a one-to-one correspondence between source sentences and sentences of the translations can be assumed to hold when translations are delivered. If not, a sentence alignment tool such as hunalign (Varga et al., 2005) can be used.

2.6.3 Word alignment

The accuracy of word alignment systems are quite far from 100%. The best performing systems are either statistical, such as Giza++ (Och & Ney, 2003), or hybrid (Moore et al., 2006) and require vast amounts of text to perform well. In the translation class context, the source text will be fairly short, perhaps a few thousand words as a maximum. Even with, say, 20 student translations, the total bitext, consisting of the source text repeated once for each student translation and sentence-aligned with it, will be too short for a statistical aligner to work well. For this reason, a hybrid system that relies on a combination of bilingual resources and statistics for the word alignment seems to be the best choice (cf. Ahrenberg & Tarvi, 2013).

An advantage of having a short source text is that the teacher can develop a dictionary for it in advance to be used by the word aligner. While a teacher cannot predict all possible translations that a student may come up with, this is a resource that can be re-used and extended over several semesters and student groups.

Table 3. Alignment performance on an excerpt from Anna Karenina using different combinations of statistical alignment and lexical resources.

	Prec	Recall	F-score
Giza++	0.499	0.497	0.498
Wordlist based	0.881	0.366	0.517
Combination	0.657	0.610	0.633
Comb + filters	0.820	0.508	0.628

Table 3 shows some results for the Russian-English 405-token excerpt discussed above with different combinations of Giza++-output and lexicon-based alignments. Standard tokenization was used except that punctuation marks were deleted. The source then consists of eight iterations of the excerpt, altogether 3304 tokens[1] and the target text consisting of eight different translations has 4205 tokens. The files were lemmatized before alignment.

The bilingual resources used are a word list of English function words such as articles and possessives that are likely to have no formal counterpart in the source and a bilingual word list created by looking up content words in Google

[1] Standard tokenization does not recognize multitoken units.

Translate. Not all translations suggested by Google have been included. The mean number of translations per Russian lemma is 1.5. In the combinations priority has been given to the alignments proposed by the word lists as they are deemed to have a higher precision.[2] So, the third row means that Giza++ alignments have been replaced by null links and lexical links induced by the word lists in all cases where there was a contradiction. The fourth row is the result of applying a set of filters based on word frequencies in the corpus and alignment topology to the previous combination.

Obviously, if a complete alignment is called for it is clear that the output of the system must be reviewed and hand-aligned afterwards. There are several interactive word-alignment tools that can be used for this purpose (Tiedemann, 2011), but it will still be time-consuming. However, the burden can be shared between teacher and students, and efforts may be focused on a part of the text only.

2.7 Workflow

After selection of a ST to be used for a translation exercise, the system will have it segmented into sentences, tokenized, and numbered. Then the teacher checks the outcome and corrects it if necessary. The files are then sent to the students. Within the suggested approach, the students are asked to use the client version of the system for translation and then upload their translations to their teacher by a set date before class, or to bring them to class on memory sticks.

When a student translation is in place in the server system, it can be aligned and graded automatically. Of course, the significance of the grades depends on the accuracy of the alignment, but both the student and the teacher can contribute to the reviewing. For instance, the teacher might have marked some words and phrases as especially significant and the student can review the alignments for them in the system for his or her particular translation.

3 In Class

When translations and their alignments are in place in the server system, they can be used as input to various visualization tools. This we see as a further advantage of our approach which will stimulate discussion and reflections among the students. Students' translations can be displayed individually or collectively, on a sentence basis or a phrase basis. Using again the opening sentence of *Anna Karenina* as our example, the outcome for one sentence can look as in Figure 1, where also some of the token frames described above are automatically computed from the alignment.[3] Within this format, the teacher is acting as a post-editing human agent who can combine both manners of assessment – computer-assisted and manual.

Since the method combines human and computer resources, it might raise the effectiveness of translation class instruction manifold (Lengyel 2006: 286). The TEM also depersonalizes the problem of grading.

Figure 1. Alignment screenshot for Segment 1 of Translation 1 (Joel Carmichael, 1960) with metrics.

Sentence 1

Src tokens	Trl tokens	Correspondences
[1] все	Happy	2
[2] счастливые	families	3
[3] семьи	are	0
[4] похожи	all	1
[5] друг	alike	4
[6] на	every	8
[7] друга	unhappy	9
[8] каждая	family	10
[9] несчастливая	is	0
[10] семья	unhappy	11
[11] несчастлива	in	12
[12] по-	its	0
[13] своему	own	13
	way	13
	Null aligned	5,6,7

Metrics:

Basic Content Frame:	76.9
Optional Content Frame:	0
Basic Formal Frame:	3
Optional Formal Frame 1:	...

3.1 From Translation Quotients to Grades

As has been demonstrated, the TEM allows one to get a certain 'cline of fidelity' from the most faithful translation to the freest version. Based on these relative assessments, one can convert the cumulative figures obtained on a number of quantitative parameters to grades. It should be remembered that although the analytical ad-

[2] The fact that precision is not 100% for wordlist based alignment has two major causes. First, some content words appear two or three times in a sentence and the system does not manage to pick the right occurrence. Also, some common English prepositions get aligned when they shouldn't.

[3] Alignments of the excerpts from Anna Karenina can be accessed at http://www.ida.liu.se/~lah/AnnaK/

vantage of the frames is that they are minimally subjective, the step from TQ to grades is neither context- nor value-free but depends heavily on the translation task.

Table 4. From TQs to Grades

	TQ	Rank	Grade
Magarshack	**97,7**	1	Excellent
Carmichael	**95,5**	2	Good
Garnett	**95,0**	3	Good
The Maudes	**92,5**	4	Good -
Edmonds	**91,6**	5	Good -
Wiener	**85,9**	6	Satisfactory
Townsend	**82,9**	7	Satisfactory -

3.2 Gauging Quality

The highlight of the approach is class team work, in the course of which students are expected to have a chance to insert meaningful corrections into their translations and thus improve their 'home' grades by the end of class. Because the tokens are numbered, the teacher can easily bring any St, or a group of Sts, on the screen together with all the versions of its or their translations.

It is at this stage that the qualitative side of the TEM comes into play with the aim of improving the final quantitative grade. Let us, for instance, consider the way a group of two tokens from the sentence-example has been rendered. As can be seen here in the manual (Table 5) and computer (Figure 2) versions, this pair of source tokens has been rendered in three different ways. In a computer-equipped class, the required changes can be immediately introduced into the translated texts under discussion.

3.3 Final Grading

As was mentioned in Section 1, the suggested procedure embraces the four basic types of translation evaluation. The method generates absolute score (overall estimates) based on relative scores in separate frames (Table 1).

The first monitoring gives a quantitative estimate of students' homework. After class discussion, which is supposed, like any post-editing, to change the home translations for the better, one more monitoring is carried out, using the same frames. If the system is made incremental, the final grade, which is an arithmetic mean of the home and class grades, can be registered automatically. If, at the end of class, the final grades are exhibited on screen in their ranking order, it might be the best possible motivation for students to work diligently both at home and in class.

Table 5. Renderings of Source tokens 12-13

LW:	(12)in (Ft)its (13)own way.
CG:	(12)in (Ft)its (13)own way.
ALM:	(12)in (Ft)its (13)own way.
JC:	(12)in (Ft)its (13)own way.
DM:	(12)in (Ft)its (13)own way.
RPLV:	(12)in (Ft)its (13)own way.
RE:	(12)after (Ft)its (13)own fashion.
RT:	(12)in (Ft)its (13)own (Et)particular way.

Figure 2. Renderings of Source tokens 12-13 (computed alignments)

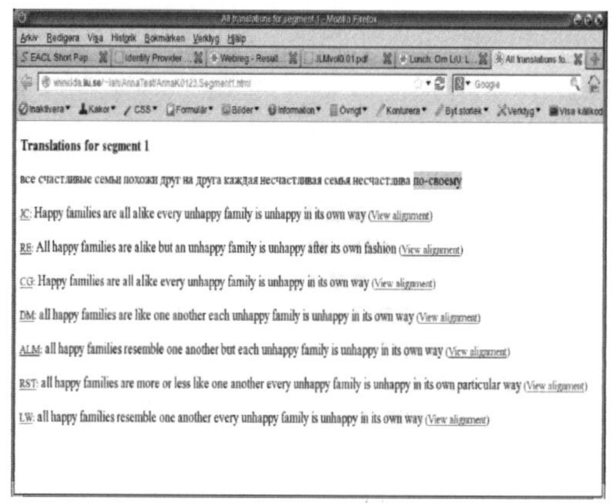

4 Outside Class

Within machine translation research, work has been going on for several years, and is still very active, for the search of metrics that assess the similarity of a system translation with human reference translations. Metrics, such as BLEU (Papineni et al.. 2002), TER (Snover et al.. 2006), and Meteor (Lavie and Denkowski: 2009), could also be included in the proposed environment. Published translations or translations that the teacher recognizes as particularly good can be used as reference translations. However, the scores of these metrics do not give as much qualitative information as the TEM frames.

The role of corpora in translation and translation training is a topic of some interest (e.g. Zanettin et al.: 2003). In translator training, the corpora are mostly seen as resources for the student to use when practicing translation (Lopez-

Rodriguez and Tercedor-Sanchez: 2008). This is orthogonal to what we are proposing here, i.e., enabling immediate comparisons and assessments of students' translations as a class-based activity. A system with a similar purpose is reported in Shei and Pain (2002: 323) who describe it as an "intelligent tutoring system designed to help student translators learn to appreciate the distinction between literal and liberal translation". Their system allows students to compare their own translations with reference translations and have them classified in terms of categories such as literal, semantic, and communicative. The comparisons are made one sentence at a time, using the Dice coefficient, i.e., by treating the sentences as bags of words. Our proposal, in contrast, uses more advanced computational linguistics tools and provides text level assessment based on word alignment.

Michaud and McCoy (2013) describe a system and a study where the goal, as in our proposal, is to develop automatic support for translator training. They focus on the inverted TERp metric (Snover et al., 2009) for evaluation of student translations. TERp requires a reference translation but can represent the difference between a given translation and the reference in terms of editing operations such as insertion, deletion, change of word order and matches of different kinds. A weak positive correlation with instructor-based grades (using Pearson's r) could be demonstrated in the study and the authors argue that TERp is sufficiently reliable to provide feed-back to students in a tutoring environment.

The main difference between their proposal and ours is that we start with a metric that has been developed for the task of grading human translations, while TERp is originally an MT metric. Thus, TEM does not require reference translations, but on the other hand its computation has not been automated and so, that is where our current efforts are focused. It should be emphasized that the teacher's load within this approach remains quite heavy but the reviewing work may be shared between teachers and students.

Both the TEM and TERp provide quantitative measurements that can lay the foundation for qualitative discussions and feedback to students but as the TEM does not require a reference it gives the students more freedom in improving their work.

As a more or less objective way of measuring the quantity with allowances made for quality, the method can also be used by teachers at exams, by editors for choosing a translation, by managers recruiting new in-house translators, by translators for self-monitoring, etc. The computer-generated figures are obtained right on the spot – they may not be exactly accurate but they give a rough general picture at the level of content-form 'presence' of the original in its translations.

Acknowledgement

We are grateful to the anonymous reviewers who provided useful comments and additional references.

References

Ahrenberg, Lars and Tarvi, Ljuba. 2013. Natural language processing for the translation class. Proceedings of the second workshop on NLP for computer-assisted language learning at NODALIDA 2013 (May 22, Oslo). NEALT Proceedings Series 17 / Linköping Electronic Conference Proceedings 86: 1–10.

Carmichael, Joel. 1960. *Anna Karenina*, by Lev Tolstoy. New York: Bantam Books, 1980.

Edmonds, Rosemary. 1954. *Anna Karenina*, by Lev Tolstoy. London: The Folio Society, 1975.

Garnett, Constance. 1901. *Anna Karenina*, by Leo Tolstoy, with revisions by Leonard J. Kent and Nina Berberova. New York: Modern Library, 1993.

Honkela, Timo *et al.* 2010. *GIGA: Grounded Intersubjective Concept Analysis: A Method for Enhancing Mutual Understanding and Participation*, Espoo: Aalto University School of Science and Technology.

Lavie, Alon and Denkowski, Michael J. 2009. 'The Meteor metric for automatic evaluation of machine translation,' *Machine Translation*, Vol 23 (2-3) 105-115.

Lengyel, István. 2006. 'Book reviews. Ljuba Tarvi: *Comparative Translation Assessment: Quantifying Quality,' Across Languages and Cultures* 7 (2) 2006, 284-286.

Liang, Percy, Taskar, Ben, and Klein, Dan. 2006. 'Alignment by Agreement.' In *Proceedings of the Human Language Technology Conference of the North American Chapter of the Association for Computational Linguistics*, 2006, 104-111.

López-Rodríguez, Clara Inés and Tercedor-Sánchez, María Isabel. 2008. 'Corpora and Students' Autonomy in Scientific and Technical Translation training,' *Journal of Specialized Translation* (JoSTrans), Issue 09 (2008), 2-19.

Magarschack, David. 1961. *Anna Karenina*, by Lev Tolstoy. New York: The New American Library.

Maude, Louise and Maude, Aylmer. 1918. *Anna Karenina*, by Lev Tolstoy, a Norton Critical Edition, ed. George Gabian, with the Maude translation as revised by George Gibian. 2d edition. New York: Norton and Co, 1995.

Michaud, Lisa N. and McCoy, Patricia Ann. 2013. Applying Machine Translation Metrics to Student-Written Translations. *Proceedings of the Eighth Workshop on Innovative Use of NLP for Building Educational Applications (BEA8),* 2013, 306-311.

Moore, Robert C, Yih, Wen-tau, and Bode, Anders. 2006. 'Improved Discriminative Bilingual Word Alignment.' In *Proceedings of the 21st International Conference on Computational Linguistics and 44th Annual Meeting of the ACL*, 2006, 513-520.

Papineni, Kishore, Roukos, Salim, Ward, Todd, and Zhu, Wei-Jing. 2002. 'BLEU: a method for automatic evaluation of machine translation.' In *Proceedings of the 40th Annual Meeting on Association for Computational Linguistics*, 311-318.

Pevear, Richard & Volokhonsky, Larissa. 2000. *Leo Tolstoy. Anna Karenina*. Penguin Books.

Shei, Chi-Chiang and Pain, Helen. 2002. 'Computer-Assisted Teaching of Translation Methods.' *Literary & Linguistic Computing*, Vol, 17, No 3 (2002), 323-343.

Sheldon, Richard. 1997. 'Problems in the English Translation of Anna Karenina.' *Essays in the Art and Theory of Translation*, Lewiston-Queenston-Lampeter: The Edwin Mellen Press, 1997

Snover, Matthew, Dorr, Bonnie, Schwartz, Richard, Micciulla, Linnea and Makhoul, John. 2006. 'A Study of Translation Edit Rate with Targeted Human Annotation.' *Proceedings of the 7th Conference of the Association for Machine Translation in the Americas*, 223-231.

Snover, Matthew, Madnani, Nitin, Dorr, Bonnie J., and Schwartz, Richard. 2009. Fluency, adequacy, or HTER? Exploring different judgments with a tunable MT metric. *Proceedings of the EACL Fourth Workshop on Statistical Machine Translation, Athens, Greece, March 30-31, 2009*: 259-268.

Tarvi, Ljuba. 2004. *Comparative Translation Assessment: Quantifying Quality*, Helsinki: Helsinki University Press.

Tiedemann. 2011. *Bitext Alignment*. Morgan & Claypool Publishers.

Townsend, Rochelle S. 1912. *Anna Karenina*, by Count Leo Tolstoi. London & Toronto: J.M. Dent & Sons; New york: E.P. Dutton and Co, 1928.

Varga, Daniel, Németh, Laszlo, Halácsy, Peter, Kornai, Andras, Trón, Viktor, and Viktor Nagy, 2005. Parallel corpora for medium density languages. *Proceedings of RANLP 2005.*

Vinay, Jean-Paul & Darbelnet, Jean. 1995 [1958]. *Comparative Stylistics of French and English. A Methodology for Translation,* Amsterdam: John Benjamins.

Wiener, Leo. 1899. *Anna Karenina*, by Lyof N. Tolstoi, vols II-IV: *The Novels and Other Works of Lyof N. Tolstoi*. New York: Charles Scribner's Sons, 1904.

Zanettin, Federico, Bernardini, Silvia, and Stewart, Dominic (eds.). 2003. *Corpora in Translator Education*, Manchester.

The pragmatics of margin comments: An empirical study

Debora Field, Stephen Pulman
Dept Computer Science
University of Oxford
Oxford OX1 3QD, UK
firstname.lastname@cs.ox.ac.uk

Denise Whitelock
Institute of Educational Technology
The Open University
Milton Keynes MK7 6AA, UK
denise.whitelock@open.ac.uk

Abstract

This paper describes the design and rationale behind a classification scheme for English margin comments. The scheme's design was informed by pragmatics and pedagogy theory, and by observations made from a corpus of 24,387 margin comments from assessed university assignments. The purpose of the scheme is to computationally explore content and form relationships between margin comments and the passages to which they point. The process of designing the scheme resulted in the conclusion that margin comments require more work to understand than utterances do, and that they are more prone to being misunderstood.

1 Introduction

We have a collection of 24,387 real margin comments, expressed in English, which we want to exploit through machine learning in order to inform the design of an automatic margin comments generator. The corpus margin comments were added by humans to a corpus of real assessed university assignments. The assignments were argumentative essays submitted towards a Master's degree in Education.

We have designed a margin comment classification scheme which classifies natural language (NL) margin comments without reference to the essay parts to which they point. High inter-annotator agreement scores have been achieved for the scheme. We plan to use the scheme to look for relationships between the corpus comments and the essay parts to which they point.

This paper is about the classification scheme's design, including what led to the design decisions, which were informed by examination of the margin comments, the assignments corpus, and consideration of key ideas in pragmatics and pedagogy. A feature of margin comments that became clear during the design process, and that influenced the design, is that margin comments are harder to understand and are more prone to being misunderstood than conversational utterances.

2 What are the corpus comments like?

The design of the classification scheme is based on answers we sought to three core questions:

- What are the margin comments like?
- What are they 'doing'?
- How do they get their messages across?

A margin comment is a message written or typed by an assessor and positioned in the 'margin' of a piece of text produced by a learner. Most margin comments graphically point to a part of the learner text, and the message content of a margin comment typically concerns the text part to which the comment points. The margin comments in our corpus had been added to word-processed assignments using a digital commenting tool.

To gain a first impression of what the corpus margin comments were like, we carried out some frequency counts and from these derived a set of simple pattern-matching rules for clustering similar comments—143 complex regular expressions to match the start of a comment. Most of the rules invoked one or more of 13 regex groups. Each group was a disjunction of strings (*e.g.,* 29 'negative' verb disjuncts). Each comment was typed on the basis of its first sentence only, on the grounds that any subsequent sentences were most likely elaborations on the first (based on manual scrutiny of hundreds of comments.) Probable comment-initial filler words were skipped. The clustering rules assigned a type to 90.9% of the comments. The following subsections describe some of the results.

Proceedings of the Ninth Workshop on Innovative Use of NLP for Building Educational Applications , pages 43–53,
Baltimore, Maryland USA, June 26, 2014.

2.1 Positive-sounding

Expressions that are positive-sounding in general (*e.g.,* 'good', freq. 5,177) and positive with respect to essay writing (*e.g.,* 'interesting', freq. 954) were very common.[1] There were 9,272 occurrences of a positive-sounding adjective. In contrast, there were 551 occurrences of a negative-sounding adjective, the top 3 being 'difficult' (freq. 133), 'missing' (123), 'informal' (90). A large proportion of positive-sounding comments were descriptions. For example, 3,151 comments (12.9%) began with 'good'.

2.2 Missing, unnecessary, or inappropriate

3,351 comments expressed the idea that something was missing from the essay that marker M thought should have been present (1a). 574 comments expressed the idea that something was present in the essay that M thought should not have been (1b). 2,069 comments expressed the idea that something that was present in the essay that M thought should have been different in some way (1c).[2]

(1) a. Could you have developed this?
b. I would not leave a space.
c. Another long quote

2.3 Confusion and apparent uncertainty

1,119 comments expressed confusion or apparent uncertainty. Many confusion expressions concerned M's understanding. There were 1,232 expressions concerned with comprehensibility. Many uncertainty expressions concerned M's agreement or understanding. There were 1,193 expressions concerned with agreement.

2.4 Questions

4,307 comments (17.6%) ended in a question mark and 1,109 comments began with a WH question word. 1,119 comments were polar questions.

2.5 Parts of instructions

6,169 expressions looked like parts of instructions or polite suggestions, the top 3 being 'you might' (freq. 882), 'you need' (693) and 'explain' (332).

2.6 Adversative conjunctions

There were 2,237 occurrences of 'but', 283 of 'although', 127 of 'however', typically used in the corpus to present contrasting or opposing opinion.

[1]All quoted example terms are case-insensitive.

[2]All examples in the paper are real, whole comments from the corpus, apart from examples that are prefixed with a '^', which are interpretations. Punctuation, spelling, capitalisation, *etc.*in the examples are faithfully reproduced.

2.7 Non-sentential

The distribution of comment lengths is heavily skewed towards short comments (Figure 1).[3] Just under 9.5 % of comments have 11 characters or fewer. The top 3 most frequent comment lengths were 10 characters (freq. 430), 4 characters (freq. 358) and 1 character (freq. 316).

Scrutiny of many short comments revealed that non-sentential comments are the main reason for the brevity. These include elliptical comments (2a), fragments (2b), and other non-sentential expressions such as exclamations (2c) and short directives (Klein, 1985; Merchant, 2004) (2d).

(2) a. Why not?
b. Good point
c. What a good idea.
d. Reference

Very short corpus comments that are complete sentences are rare (set 3).

(3) a. Avoid jargon
b. This is unclear.

2.8 Politeness

There are 3,996 occurrences of terms typically used to soften the impact of a criticism or make an instruction sound like a suggestion (hereon 'softeners'), including 'perhaps' (freq. 863), 'rather' (422), and 'a little' (381). There are also 7,287 occurrences of conditional auxiliary verbs (including many non-modal uses of 'would'), which are typically used to make polite suggestions.

2.9 Informality

There are 3,818 contractions, including "don't" (freq. 568), "I'm" (370), "you're" (138). Filler words were also common. 444 comments began with 'ok' (a range of spellings), and 1109 comments began with 'yes' (some of these express agreement, but most are fillers).

2.10 Skills

We noticed 4 large groups of terms relating to particular skills. Table 1 shows each group, the number of occurrences of terms from that group, an example term from that group, and the number of occurrences of the example. Category 'presentation' includes matters relating to the presentation of English, such as spelling, grammar, formatting, and style.

[3]The inset in Figure 1 is the main figure presented on log-log scale axes.

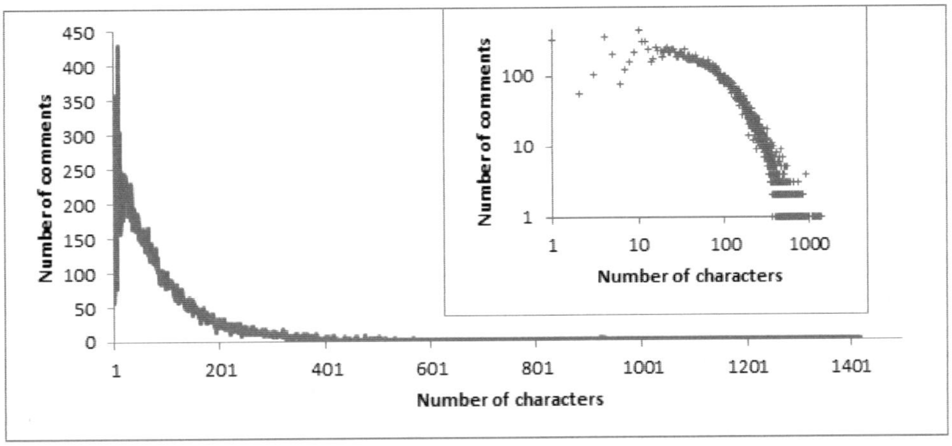

Figure 1: Distribution of comment lengths

Grouping	Freq.	Example	Freq.
Argument	14705	'argument'	817
Referencing	6657	'reference'	1322
Essay structure	5243	'section'	614
Presentation	2613	'sentence'	428

Table 1: Skills-related terms in comments corpus

2.11 Are margin comments conversation?

The corpus investigations revealed frequent use of phenomena common in speech: non-sentential expressions, contractions, politeness devices, softeners, and fillers. This led us to consider whether a dialogue act taxonomy such as DIT (Bunt, 1990) or DAMSL (Core and Allen, 1997) might be suitable for typing margin comments.

Many pedagogy papers have argued or assumed that margin comments are or are like a conversation. Straub (1996) reviewed a number of contemporary papers, including (Ziv, 1984; Danis, 1987; Lindemann, 1987; Anson, 1989) to explore the question: "what does it mean to treat teacher commentary as a dialogue?" (Straub, 1996, p. 375). Straub concluded that margin comments are not conversational utterances, either real or imaginary, and that what pedagogy scholars were referring to was the informal style of comments. Informal language was becoming popular as a result of the movement away from 'teaching product' to 'teaching process', which encouraged the expression of empathy with the learner, because it was thought this would make teacher comments more likely to be read and acted upon (Hairston, 1982).

From linguistics, Schegloff (1999), tackles the problem of whether there is such a thing as 'ordinary conversation'. He first defines 'talk-in-interaction' (p. 406), which includes speech spoken with the intention of communicating messages to some audience. Next Schegloff talks about 'speech exchange systems' (citing (Sacks et al., 1974)), which are "organizational formats for talk-in-interaction" (Schegloff, 1999, p. 407), including the lecture format, classroom discourse, courts-in-session, meetings, debates, *etc.* Margin comments arguably qualify as a speech exchange system, even though they are written, not spoken. But Schegloff's definition of 'ordinary conversation' arguably excludes margin comments on the grounds that they *don't* involve "generic aspects of talking-in-interaction such as turn-taking, sequence organization, repair organization, overall structural organization" (p. 413), and on the grounds that they *are* "subject to functionally specific or context-specific restrictions" (p. 407).

Having considered relevant literature, we concluded that margin comments are not conversation, principally on the grounds that there is no turn taking—only the marker M gets the opportunity to 'speak' and only the comment's addressee A gets the opportunity to 'hear'. Whilst there is common ground (Stalnaker, 1972; Thomason, 1990) and accommodation (Clark and Haviland, 1974; Lewis, 1979; Kamp, 1981) there is no turn taking and therefore no grounding (Clark and Schaefer, 1989). M presents utterances, and the constraints of the context demand that A must accept the evidence. Consequently, if A misunderstands M's intended message, there is no mechanism to enable M or A to discover that A has misunderstood the message; and if A is confused by M's comment, there is no opportunity for A to ask M for clarification.

We concluded that dialogue acts were an inappropriate classification scheme for margin comments, because the conditions for human-to-human dialogue do not apply.

3 What are margin comments 'doing'?

If dialogue acts are inappropriate, what kinds of things *are* NL margin comments 'doing'? Consider WH questions (4).

(4) Why bold?

When M asks a WH question in a margin comment, M is not desiring or expecting A to supply the requested information to M. The Addressee A of a NL margin comment will never take a turn in response to that comment. This is something of which A and marker M are both mutually aware before the comments are written by M, and it has important repercussions with respect to M's intentions. Consider also imperatives (5).

(5) Explain what they do.

5 looks like an instruction, but cannot be. The corpus comments were added to the final, submitted versions of assessed assignments. There was no desire or expectation on M's part that A would revise the essay in response to M's comments.

M must have been desiring *something* by these comments (otherwise there would be no comments), but that something is not what one might expect given their linguistic surface forms. This suggests that margin comments are like indirect speech acts (Searle, 1969; Searle and Vanderveken, 1985)—acts which have an *apparent* function that is distinct from what the comment is *really* 'doing' (Austin, 1962). We would argue that, for the evaluative comments in the corpus (which are the vast majority), the thing the comments are doing is this: **to communicate M's opinion to A about the essay part to which the comment pointed**.

This conclusion is not surprising. NL margin comments are doing what all margin comments are doing, it seems, including non-NL coded comment schemes. Why this conclusion *seems* surprising is that margin comments do not look like expressions of opinion about weaknesses and strengths. Instead they look like excerpts from friendly, informal conversations. The informality is, however, masking the principal messages of the comments, which are evaluative ones.

4 How do NL margin comments express whether the essay met the standard?

Having decided what NL margin comments are doing, we reasoned that M's opinion expressed by a comment must have two aspects, on the grounds that they do not just point to essay parts, they contain messages. The two aspects are: (1) ***Whether*** **or not essay part P to which a comment points attained the required standard**; (2) ***How*** **P attained (or did not attain) the required standard**. The required standard is a standard defined by some set of principles or instructions of which M and A are typically mutually aware.

We observed that the semantics of very few corpus comments communicated a message approaching 'This essay part has failed to achieved the agreed standard'. Set 6 shows two of them.

(6) a. Something's wrong or missing here...
b. Two line sentences is not enough to get the maximum 30% marks for this section

For the vast majority of comments, ***whether*** **essay part P attained the required standard was communicated implicitly by the use of certain types of words and syntactic structures**. To convey attainment or surpassing of the standard, positive-sounding adjectives were used extensively (section 2), also positive-sounding adverbs, and terms of liking, agreement, and understanding. A much wider variety of techniques was used to convey *failure* to attain the standard, including negative-sounding verbs (*e.g.*, 'contradict'), negative-sounding adjectives (*e.g.*, 'inappropriate'), lone noun phrases (*e.g.*, 'brackets'), questions, instructions, polite suggestions, notifications of marker edits, referrals to authoritative sources, and assertions of uncertainty, confusion, doubt, disagreement, and non-understanding.

Addressee A's understanding of whether essay part P had attained the required standard would therefore have depended on A's being able to correctly interpret the semantics of the comment. For non-native speakers of English, this may have presented a problem.[4] Since many corpus comments

[4]The corpus assignments were towards a distance-learning degree course, and many of the students are likely to have been non-native speakers of English.

constitute a lone modified noun phrase, and since the meanings of everyday adjectives change depending on what they are modifying, it may have been difficult for A to tell whether a comment was a criticism or a commendation (set 7).

(7) a. A very long sentence.
b. Very strong supporting quote.
c. A strong argument
d. A big assumption

Note that the way we decide whether these are criticisms or commendations is by considering the type of entity the adjective is modifying. We know quotes should be strong, so 7b must be a commendation. We know assumptions should not be big, so 7d must be a criticism. This means that, in addition to having a sensitivity to compositional semantics, the addressees of these comments would have needed to possess expert knowledge about what sentences, quotes, arguments, and assumptions should be like in order to be able to infer whether the essay part had met the standard.

Difficulties in understanding whether an essay part has met the standard are also caused by the use of non-sentential expressions (set 8).

(8) a. Reference
b. Colloquialism
c. No issues
d. No comma
e. No apostrophe

Which of the following interpretations (if any) applies to each of the set 8 comments?

(9) a. ˆ The named thing is missing
b. ˆ The spelling of the named thing is incorrect
c. ˆ The named thing is erroneously included
d. ˆ The named thing needs correcting
e. ˆ This part attains the required standard

In order to understand these comments, A has to inspect the passage to which the comment points to see whether it contains the object named by the comment. If it does, there may still be the possibility that it should be present, but that there is something wrong with it.

5 Scheme design: *Skill* targeted

We have considered what the corpus margin comments are doing, and the ways in which they express whether an essay part met the required standard. The way in which a comment conveys *h*ow the standard was or was not met is embodied by the comments classification scheme's design. The scheme has three layers, and here we consider the first. When M wrote a comment, M had in mind a good-essay-writing principle. Our classification scheme makes explicit the skill area of that essay-writing principle. Consider set 10.

(10) a. Why not?
b. Why bold?

To understand what these comments mean, we first need to know what M intended, which we have argued was to communicate to A whether and how the related essay part had reached an agreed standard. On that account, the comments (a) and (b) in 10 mean something like (a) and (b) in 11.

(11) a. ˆThe argument here would have been improved by including an explanation of why not.
b. ˆThe use of bold font here is questionable.

These are very different messages. One comment is alerting A to some missing argument, and the other is questioning A's use of different fonts. How do we know this, given that both comments have very similar syntactic structure?

Addressee A works out that these comments mean very different things by first identifying the skill area that the comment is targeting, and then considering what that skill area is *like*—in what ways it can be good or bad. To understand 10a, A needs to observe that essay part P contains a statement, and to infer that M is responding to the argument made by the statement. To understand 10b, A needs to observe that P contains some text in bold font, and to infer that M is questioning the use of the bold font. The difficulty here is that conversational-style comments do not make it explicit whether they are targeting content or form.

Concluding that the identification of a comment's target is often critical to understanding it, we defined 11categories for the scheme's 'targeted skill' layer. The corpus investigations (see 2.10) revealed four main skill areas targeted by comments:

- Referencing
  - Situating work in the relevant literature, referencing conventions
- Structuring Essays
  - Layout, scope, components
- Composing Argument
  - Content, quality, arguing techniques, comprehensibility
- Presenting English
  - Spelling, grammar, formatting, style

We made **Referencing** and **Structure** target categories in their own right. Owing to the high frequency of comments expressing confusion and comprehensibility (see 2.3) we made **Comprehensibility** a target category. Comments targeting the content of an argument, the quality of an argument (not including its comprehensibility), and arguing techniques are covered by target category **Argument**. We divide the skill area of presenting English into five subcategories: **Formatting**, **Grammar**, **Punctuation**, **Spelling**, **Style**.

An additional target category is **Context-Dependent**. This is assigned if an evaluative comment has very little information in it about what its targeted skill might be (set 12).

(12) a. Good [212 occurrances]
b. Avoid
c. Unfinished

The 11th target category, **Author**, is assigned to all comments which appear non-evaluative. These include, for example, casual observations, personal reminiscences, and expressions of gratitude.

6 Scheme design: marker's *Attitude*

Having concluded that each corpus comment was communicating M's opinion about an essay part, for the next layer in the scheme, we focused on opinion types. The investigation results revealed three common types (see section 2.2), which we named **Miss**, **Reject**, and **Condemn**. The attitudes do not involve the emotional connotations normally associated with these names in everyday communication. (Hereon we will refer to these as categories of attitude, rather than opinion.)

Having observed the large proportion of polar questions and expressions of uncertainty or doubt in the corpus (see 2.3 and 2.4), we decided to treat Miss, Reject, and Condemn as attitudes held by M with certainty, and to add another attitude **Doubt** to cover comments in which M called into question things that A had done, or in which M expressed some uncertainty or doubt.

- **Doubt**: "Why bold?"
  - M considers that something in the essay is of questionable value.

Since expressions of uncertainty are often used as softeners rather than to express actual uncertainty, it seemed inappropriate to treat apparent uncertainty as a qualifier (Bunt, 2011) of attitudes. If we treat it as a qualifier, it suggests that M was not sure about M's own opinion, rather than that the target of M's comment was questionable. Doubt is the attitude most applicable to the majority of polar questions in the corpus.

A further attitude, which is a sub-type of Condemn, is defined as **Dispute** (see section 2.6):

- **Dispute**: "Not necessarily."
  - M holds views that are in opposition to some proposition in the essay.

A further attitude **Commend** covers all comments that announce a 'strength' (see section 2.1):

- **Commend**: "Good"
  - M considers that something in the essay has attained or exceeded the required standard, or is pleasing or interesting to M.

Two further attitudes (**Refer** and **Exclaim**) are defined, which have a special characteristic.

- **Refer**: "Ditto."
  - M believes that A would benefit from reading a particular source.
- **Exclaim**: "Ah!"
  - M is surprised or shocked by something in the essay that M does not specify.

It is not possible to tell whether Refer comments are evaluative or not without reading the source to which M has referred the addressee. Similarly, it is impossible to tell whether Exclaim comments are evaluative or not, either from the comment or the essay part to which the comment points.

Two final attitudes—**Engage** and **Thank**—are reserved for non-evaluative comments, *i.e.*, comments whose target is Author.

- **Engage**: "I know how you feel."
  - M finds something about the essay or about A engaging. It appears that M has become engaged in a way that is more complex than liking or finding interesting.
- **Thank**: "Thanks"
  - M is grateful to A.

These attitudes are what we term 'solidarity' attitudes, in that we assume that they were made in order to engender positive feelings in A. Engage comments have a very wide variety of forms and topics, which we will not be attempting to analyse in the initial rounds of the machine learning trials. Thank comments are all expressions of gratitude.

7 Scheme design: *Linguistic Act*

The third layer of the categorisation scheme identifies what we are calling the 'linguistic act' of the comment. The acts are distinguished principally by surface form and do not concern the evaluative (or non-evaluative) message that the comment is attempting to communicate.

We began with the three basic English sentence types: declarative, interrogative, imperative. We divided 'interrogative' into acts **WH Question** and **Polar Question**, as they have clearly distinguishable surface forms.

We also divided declarative comments into two acts: **Assertion** and **Description**. All margin comments, including interrogatives and imperatives, are by definition assertions of M's opinions, we have argued. The scheme's act Assertion is reserved for assertions of propositions in response to argument (13a, 13b) and explicit expressions concerning understanding (13c), agreement (13d), verification or certainty. Many assertions are subjective-sounding.

(13) a. That is impossible!
b. This is true of many other organisations
c. I don't understand
d. Not sure I agree!

Act Description is assigned to a comment which is a description of a (non-propositional) object in or quality of an essay part P or of an action that has been carried out by author A and that is evidenced by part P (set 14).

(14) a. Too many references.
b. Factors clearly articulated.
c. This is a very strong assertion

Splitting declaratives into acts Description and Assertion is a small step away from categorising linguistic acts according to syntax only. The move separates declarative comments which respond directly to propositional content from all other declarative comments.

We interpreted 'imperative' as linguistic act category **Instruction**. We treat the category loosely, allowing it to include comments that do not use the imperative form but that look like guidance on what should have been done (set 15).

(15) a. You should add a citation here.
b. I would not leave a space.
c. Ditto

All Instruction comments talk in a variety of ways about things that were not done but that should have been, whereas all Description comments (set 14) talk about what was actually done. This distinction is not too dissimilar to the distinction between imperatives and declaratives. That Instruction comments do not always have the imperative form is a repercussion of the informal conversational style of the comments.

A sixth 'dummy' linguistic act category is assigned to all comments with attitude Engage, because we will not be attempting to analyse those.

The linguistic act layer, then, categorises the comment's form, while the target and attitude layers categorise its meaning. The linguistic act accounts for what the comment is *apparently* doing (see section 3). The attitude and target account for what the comment is *really* doing. A stark difference between utterances and margin comments is that, to understand an utterance, hearer H does not have to work out what speaker S was really doing (Ramsay and Field, 2008); whereas to understand a margin comment, addressee A does have to work out what marker M was really doing.

8 Evaluation

We have demonstrated that the classification scheme can be deployed with high agreement levels between independent annotators. Agreement by two annotators was calculated for 313 sample comments that were annotated by each annotator independently. Annotator A designed the scheme over several months. Annotator B spent about 50 minutes learning the scheme (from no prior exposure to it). Annotator B took a mean average of 1.1 minutes to fully annotate each comment in the sample. Annotator A took a mean average of .49 minutes to fully annotate each comment.

The corpus comprised 1,408 essays submitted for 13 different assessed university Master's modules, the official word limits of which ranged from 500 to 4,000. The essays had been marked by 20 different markers. The number of essays marked by each marker varied. The mean average number of comments per essay per marker ranged from 4.83 to 47.00. To avoid potential bias towards the more prolific markers' styles, the same number of essays were randomly sampled for each marker (where possible), and approximately the same number of comments were randomly sampled from each of those essays.

Some tutors appear to prefer very short comments, some long. For some (but not all) of the tutors who marked essays of different lengths, there was a correlation between essay length and the number of margin comments. No analysis of linguistic style similarities across comments within individual essays was carried out for this paper.

Inter-annotator agreement was calculated using Cohen's Kappa for each of the three layers of the scheme independently. 95% confidence intervals (CI) for test statistics were generated through 10,000 statistical bootstrappings of the annotated comments. The agreement coefficient for the attitude layer was 0.874 (95% CI, 0.831–0.914), for the target layer was 0.791 (0.734–0.844), and for the linguistic act layer was 0.822 (0.770–0.869). The percentage agreement across all three layers was 72.1% (67.0%–77.0%) (the percentage of comments for which both annotators were in agreement on all three layers). There were no occurrences of comments which both annotators deemed unclassifiable. One of the comments was deemed unclassifiable by one annotator.

The scheme has five attitude+target cross-layer dependencies (Engage+Author, Thank+Author, Refer+Context-Dependent, Exclaim+Context-Dependent, Dispute+Argument), and five target+act cross-layer dependencies (each of the same five pairs plus a linguistic act). We acknowledge that these might argue for a more complex agreement calculation. It is expected that some linguistic act categories are unlikely to combine with some attitude categories, though this requires empirical verification. A conservative estimate of the number of possible combinations of attitude, target, and act that we believe might be found in the corpus is 155 combinations. Additionally, some categories from a given layer appear to be more frequent than other categories from the same layer. We acknowledge, therefore, that a weighted coefficient method may be more suitable for calculating inter-annotator agreement.

9 Comparison with previous work

Now that the categorisation scheme has been described, we will discuss comparisons with previous work. Categorisation schemes have been devised or re-used in order to analyse written feedback, and discover where improvements might be made. The studies were principally interested in whether the marker was writing comments that would 'feed forward'. Measures for deciding whether a comment would feed forward tended to revolve around the power of a comment to motivate its addressee, or whether the comment contained explanatory text that would make it clear how to do things better in future. We have not found any feedback categorisation schemes primarily concerned with how opinion in comments is conveyed through the medium of NL.

Hyland (2001) designed a feedback classification scheme that was used to analyse the quality of feedback for a distance-learning language course. Hyland's scheme focused on targeted skills, affective aspects, and explicit pointers for future writing. Bales (1950) devised 12 categories for the purpose of analysing small group interactions, which were later applied to the analysis of margin comments by Whitelock *et al.* (2004). Bales' scheme focused on affective aspects (including solidarity, tension, antagonism), and pragmatics aspects (suggestions, opinions, disagreements, requests). Brown and Glover's (2006) scheme focused on skills, content, affective aspects, and feeding forward. They used their scheme to argue that the feedback in a particular corpus of comments was of limited value, because most of the comments did not aid learning or understanding (Brown et al., 2004). Nelson and Schunn (2009) wanted to identify conditions under which addressees of peer feedback might actually implement that feedback. Their categories focused on the linguistic features of comments (including summarisation, specificity, explanations) and affective issues. Perpignan (2003) viewed margin comments as part of dialogue and discussed the "intentions and interpretations of the exchange from both the teacher's and the learners' perspective" (p. 259). The work did not attempt to analyse the linguistic features of feedback.

The categorisation scheme with the strongest resemblance to ours was Ferris *et al.* (1997). The scheme viewed margin comments as having two 'phases': teacher's goal, and linguistic form (p. 163). The scheme has a very different interpretation of the intention of the marker from ours. It confuses marker intention with comment target. It implicitly recognises what we call marker attitude, but identifies only one (our Commend). It implicitly recognises the target of a comment but has only two target types ('form' and 'content').

10 Discussion

We have presented a classification scheme for margin comments which is based on observations of real data and on linguistics theory. The goal of the classification was to ultimately use machine learning to look for relationships between the margin comments and the essay parts to which they point so that we could design an automatic NL margin comments generator. The scheme therefore focuses on the linguistic aspects of margin comments: their form and meaning. It is designed to classify comments independently of the essay parts to which the comments point. This was to ensure that the comments in isolation could be classified to a useful level of agreement, and, in future work, to make it possible to investigate whether essay properties can be used to predict characteristics of margin comments. The 3-layered scheme enables the intended evaluative meanings of margin comments to be captured despite their conversational style, while also preserving linguistic information about that style (set 16).

(16) a. Could you have developed this?
  i. *Attitude:* Miss
  ii. *Target:* Argument
  iii. *Act:* Polar Question

b. Why bold?
  i. *Attitude:* Doubt
  ii. *Target:* Formatting
  iii. *Act:* WH Question

c. No issues
  i. *Attitude:* Commend
  ii. *Target:* Context-Dependent
  iii. *Act:* Assertion

The classification scheme is arguably a suitable scheme for all margin comments expressed in NL, with the proviso that the skills being targeted by the comments would need to be tailored to the document type if it were not an argumentative essay.

Details not discussed earlier include the following. (i) We use a skills precedence list to select a target for comments that are ambiguous over skill area. (ii) Prior to categorisation, each comment is segmented, and one 'principal segment' only is identified for categorisation. This is for 4 reasons. (1) Many comments begin with filler words (*e.g.,* 'yes', 'well', 'ok', 'hmm'); (2) Many begin with preambles (*e.g.,* 'minor point', 'Just one thought'); (3) Many use a commendation as a softener before delivering the main message; (4) Many contain more than one clause or sentence. We usually assume the first non-filler/non-preamble segment is the principal segment, and that any non-filler segments that follow are elaborations on the first segment. The exception to this is comments in which a commendation is used as a softener, in which case the segment that follows the softener becomes the principal segment.

High inter-annotator agreement scores have been achieved for the classification scheme. We have not yet annotated the whole corpus, but we intend to. We will also calculate inter-annotator agreement for a higher number of sampled comments, since the number of possible combinations of attitude, target, and act is so high (*circa* 155, see section 8). We may make small changes to the annotation scheme before doing any further annotation. In particular, we are considering dividing target Argument into two or three subcategories.

While designing the classification scheme, we have observed that, despite their conversational style—indeed because of it—understanding NL margin comments is harder than understanding conversational utterances. Although the essay part to which a comment points is a public object and therefore in M and A's views of the common ground, the aspect of the essay part that M is targeting usually remains unexpressed and private in M's mental state. A therefore has to do some inferencing to identify that aspect. In other words, A has to do some inferencing to fill in gaps in A's view of the common ground that do not arise in a conversation. This extra work is necessary just to understand the comment. To fully benefit from the comment by inferring the essay-writing principle M had in mind requires even more work.

The planned machine learning investigations will attempt to recognise and categorise appropriate opportunities for feedback comments by looking for associations between the categories assigned to each margin comment according to our scheme, and features of the passage in the essay to which a comment points—simple n-gram features, more complex measures of semantic similarity, and analysis of syntactic structure will be experimented with. The planned automatic feedback comment generator will be informed by the machine learning investigations. The form and style of the comments generated is yet to be decided.

Acknowledgments

This work was supported by the Engineering and Physical Sciences Research Council (grant numbers EP/J005959/1 and EP/J005231/1).

References

Chris Anson. 1989. Response styles and ways of knowing. In *Writing and Response: Theory, Practice, Research*, pages 332–366. NCTE, Urbana, IL.

J.L. Austin. 1962. *How to do things with words*. Oxford University Press, Oxford, 2nd edition.

R.F. Bales. 1950. A set of categories for the analysis of small group interactions. *American Sociological Review*, 15(2):257–263.

E. Brown and C. Glover. 2006. Evaluating written feedback. In C. Bryan and K. Clegg, editors, *Innovative assessment in higher education*, pages 81–91. Routledge, Abingdon.

E. Brown, C. Glover, V. Stevens, and S. Freake. 2004. Evaluating the effectiveness of written feedback as an element of formative assessment in science. In C. Rust, editor, *Proceedings of the 12th Improving Student Learning Symposium*. The Oxford Centre for Staff and Learning Development, Oxford Brookes University, Oxford.

Harry C. Bunt. 1990. DIT: Dynamic interpretation in text and dialogue. In *ITK research report / Institute for Language Technology and Artificial Intelligence, 15*.

Harry Bunt. 2011. The semantics of dialogue acts. In *Proceedings of the 9th International Conference on Computational Semantics*. Oxford.

H.H. Clark and S.E. Haviland. 1974. Psychological processes in linguistic explanation. In D. Cohen, editor, *Explaining linguistic phenomena*. Hemisphere Publication Corporation, Washington.

H.H. Clark and E.F. Schaefer. 1989. Contributing to discourse. *Cognitive Science*, (13):259–294.

M. G. Core and J. Allen. 1997. Coding dialogs with the DAMSL annotation scheme. In *AAAI Fall Symposium on Communicative Action in Humans and Machines*, MIT, Cambridge, MA.

M. Francine Danis. 1987. The voice in the margins: Paper-marking as conversation. *Freshman English News*, (15):18–20.

Dana R. Ferris, Susan Pezone, Cathy R. Tade, and Sharee Tinti. 1997. Teacher commentary on student writing: Descriptions and implications. *Journal of Second Language Writing*, 6(2):155–182.

Maxine Hairston. 1982. The winds of change: Thomas Kuhn and the revolution in the teaching of writing. *College Composition and Communication*, 33(1):76–88.

F. Hyland. 2001. Providing effective support: investigating feedback to distance learners. *Open Learning*, 16(3):233–247.

J.A.W. Kamp. 1981. A theory of truth and semantic representation. In J. Groenendijk, T. Janssen, and M. Stockhof, editors, *Formal methods in the study of language*, pages 177–321. Mathematical Centre Tracts, Amsterdam.

Wolfgang Klein. 1985. Ellipse, fokusgliederung und thematischer stand. In Reinhard Meyer-Hermann and Hannes Rieser, editors, *Ellipsen und fragmentarische Ausdrücke*, pages 1–24. Niemeyer, Tübingen.

D. Lewis. 1979. Scorekeeping in a language game. *Journal of Philosophical Logic*, (9):339–359.

Erika Lindemann. 1987. *A Rhetoric for Writing Teachers*. Oxford UP, New York, 2nd edition edition.

Jason Merchant. 2004. Fragments and ellipsis. *Linguistics and philosophy*, (27):661–738.

Melissa M. Nelson and Christian D. Schunn. 2009. The nature of feedback: how different types of peer feedback affect writing performance. *Instructional Science*, 37:375–401.

Hadara Perpignan. 2003. Exploring the written feedback dialogue: a research, learning and teaching practice. *Language Teaching Research*, 7(2):259–278.

Allan Ramsay and Debora Field. 2008. Speech acts, epistemic planning and Grice's maxims. *Journal of Logic and Computation*, 18:431–457.

H. Sacks, E.A. Schegloff, and G. Jefferson. 1974. A simplest systematics for the organization of turn-taking for conversation. *Language*, (50):696–735.

E.A. Schegloff. 1999. Discourse, pragmatics, conversation, analysis. *Discourse Studies*, 1(4):405–435.

J.R. Searle and D. Vanderveken. 1985. *Foundations of illocutionary logic*. Cambridge University Press, New York.

J.R. Searle. 1969. *Speech acts: An essay in the philosophy of language*. Cambridge University Press, Cambridge.

R Stalnaker. 1972. Pragmatics. In D. Davidson and G. Harman, editors, *Semantics of natural language (Synthese Library, Vol. 40)*, pages 380–397. D. Reidel, Dordrecht, Holland.

R. Straub. 1996. Teacher response as conversation: more than casual talk, an exploration. *Rhetoric Review*, 14(2):374–98.

R.H. Thomason. 1990. Accommodation, meaning, and implicature: Interdisciplinary foundations for pragmatics. In P.R. Cohen, J. Morgan, and M.E. Pollack, editors, *Intentions in communication*, pages 325–363. MIT, Cambridge, Massachusetts.

D. Whitelock, S. Watt, Y. Raw, and Moreale E. 2004. Analysing tutor feedback to students: first steps towards constructing an electronic monitoring system. *Association for Learning Technology Journal*, 11(3):31–42.

Nina Ziv. 1984. the effect of teacher comments on the writing of four college freshmen. In R. Beach and L. Bridwell, editors, *New Directions in Composition Research*, pages 362–380. Guilford, New York.

Surprisal as a Predictor of Essay Quality

Gaurav Kharkwal
Department of Psychology
Center for Cognitive Science
Rutgers University, New Brunswick
gaurav.kharkwal@gmail.com

Smaranda Muresan
Department of Computer Science
Center for Computational Learning Systems
Columbia University
smara@ccls.columbia.edu

Abstract

Modern automated essay scoring systems rely on identifying linguistically-relevant features to estimate essay quality. This paper attempts to bridge work in psycholinguistics and natural language processing by proposing sentence processing complexity as a feature for automated essay scoring, in the context of English as a Foreign Language (EFL). To quantify processing complexity we used a psycholinguistic model called *surprisal theory*. First, we investigated whether essays' average surprisal values decrease with EFL training. Preliminary results seem to support this idea. Second, we investigated whether surprisal can be effective as a predictor of essay quality. The results indicate an inverse correlation between surprisal and essay scores. Overall, the results are promising and warrant further investigation on the usability of surprisal for essay scoring.

1 Introduction

Standardized testing continues to be an integral part of modern-day education, and an important area of research in educational technologies is the development of tools and methodologies to facilitate automated evaluation of standardized tests. Unlike multiple-choice questions, automated evaluation of essays presents a particular challenge. The specific issue is the identification of a suitable evaluation rubric that can encompass the broad range of responses that may be received.

Unsurprisingly then, much emphasis has been placed on the development of Automated Essay Scoring (henceforth, AES) systems. Notable AES systems include Project Essay Grade (Page, 1966; Ajay et al., 1973), ETS's *e-rater*® (Burstein et al., 1998; Attali and Burstein, 2006), Intelligent Essay Assessor™ (Landauer et al., 2003), BETSY (Rudner and Liang, 2002), and Vantage Learning's IntelliMetric™ (Elliot, 2003). The common thread in most modern AES systems is the identification of various observable linguistic features, and the development of computational models that combine those features for essay evaluation.

One aspect of an essay's quality that almost all AES systems do not yet fully capture is sentence processing complexity. The ability to clearly and concisely convey information without requiring undue effort on the part of the reader is one hallmark of good writing. Decades of behavioral research on language comprehension has suggested that some sentence structures are harder to comprehend than others. For example, passive sentences, such as *the girl was pushed by the boy*, are known to be harder to process than semantically equivalent active sentences, such as *the boy pushed the girl* (Slobin, 1966; Forster and Olbrei, 1972; Davison and Lutz, 1985; Kharkwal and Stromswold, 2013). Thus, it is likely that the overall processing complexity of the sentence structures used in an essay could influence its perceived quality.

One reason why sentence processing complexity has not yet been fully utilized is the lack of a suitable way of quantifying it. This paper proposes the use of a psycholinguistic model of sentence comprehension called *surprisal theory* (Hale, 2001; Levy, 2008) to quantify sentence processing complexity. The rest of the paper is organized as follows. Section 2 describes the surprisal theory, and discusses its applicability in modeling sentence processing complexity. Section 3 details our investigation on whether essays' average surprisal values decrease following English as a Foreign Language training. Section 4 presents a study where we investigated whether surprisal can be effective as a predictor of essay quality. Lastly, Sec-

Proceedings of the Ninth Workshop on Innovative Use of NLP for Building Educational Applications , pages 54–60,
Baltimore, Maryland USA, June 26, 2014.

The	judge	who	angered	the	criminal	slammed	the	gavel	Mean
5.64	6.94	6.93	11.60	2.32	9.19	16.92	1.94	4.68	7.35
The	**judge**	**who**	**the**	**criminal**	**angered**	**slammed**	**the**	**gavel**	**Mean**
5.64	6.94	6.93	4.20	9.21	13.73	16.65	2.21	4.69	7.80

Table 1: Surprisal values of two example relative-clause sentences. The values were computed using a top-down parser by Roark et al. (2009) trained on the Wall Street Journal corpus.

tion 5 concludes the paper.

2 Surprisal Theory

The *surprisal theory* (Hale, 2001; Levy, 2008) estimates the word-level processing complexity as the negative log-probability of a word given the preceding context (usually, preceding syntactic context). That is:

$$\text{Complexity}(w_i) \propto -\log P(w_i|w_{1\ldots i-1}, \texttt{CONTEXT})$$

Essentially, the surprisal model measures processing complexity at a word as a function of how unexpected the word is in its context. Surprisal is minimized (i.e. approaches zero) when a word *must* appear in a given context (i.e., when $P(w_i|w_{1\ldots i-1}, \texttt{CONTEXT}) = 1$), and approaches infinity as a word becomes less and less likely. Crucially, the surprisal theory differs from n-gram based approaches by using an underlying language model which includes a lexicon and a syntactic grammar (the language model is usually a Probabilistic Context-Free Grammar, but not restricted to it).

To better understand surprisal, consider the following two example sentences:

(1) *The judge who angered the criminal slammed the gavel.*

(2) *The judge who the criminal angered slammed the gavel.*

Both sentences are center-embedded relative clause sentences that differ in whether the subject or the object is extracted from the relative clause. Critically, they both share the same words differing only in their relative order. Behavioral studies have found that object-extracted relative clause sentences (2) are harder to process than subject-extracted relative clause sentences (1) (King and Just, 1991; Gordon et al., 2001; Grodner and Gibson, 2005; Staub, 2010; Traxler et al., 2002; Stromswold et al., 1996). The surprisal values at each word position of the two example sentences are shown in Table 1.

As we can see from Table 1, the mean surprisal value is greater for the object-extracted relative clause sentence. Hence, the surprisal theory correctly predicts greater processing cost for that sentence. Furthermore, it allows for a finer-grained analysis of where the processing cost might occur, specifically at the onset of the relative clause (*the*) and the end (*angered*). Other differences, such as greatest difficulty at the main verb are shared with the subject-extracted relative clause, and are plausible because both sentences are center-embedded. These predictions are consistent with patterns observed in behavioral studies (Staub, 2010).

In addition to relative clauses, the surprisal theory has been used to model various other behavioral findings (Levy, 2008; Levy and Keller, 2012). Moreover, corpora analyses examining surprisal's effectiveness revealed a high correlation between word-level suprisal values and the corresponding reading times, which act as a proxy for processing difficulties (Demberg and Keller, 2008; Boston et al., 2008; Frank, 2009; Roark et al., 2009).

Thus, the surprisal theory presents itself as an effective means of quantifying processing complexity of sentences, and words within them. Next, we discuss a series of evaluations that we performed to determine whether surprisal values reflect quality of written essays.

3 Experiment 1

In the first experiment, we investigate whether an essay's mean surprisal value decreases after suitable English as a Foreign Language (EFL) educational training. Here, we make the assumption that EFL training improves a person's overall writing quality, and that surprisal value acts as a proxy for writing quality.

Topic	Term	Total		Syntactic		Lexical	
		Mean	SD	Mean	SD	Mean	SD
Analysis	Term 1	6.34	3.32	2.37	1.86	3.97	3.24
	Term 2	6.28	3.30	2.34	1.85	3.94	3.23
Arg.	Term 1	6.24	3.29	2.34	1.85	3.90	3.23
	Term 2	6.15	3.36	2.28	1.85	3.87	3.24

Table 2: Means and standard deviations of total surprisal, syntactic surprisal, and lexical surprisal for *Analysis* and *Argumentation* essays

3.1 Corpus

We used the Uppsala Student English corpus provided by the Department of English at Uppsala University (Axelsson, 2000). The corpus contained 1,489 essays written by 440 Swedish university students of English at three different levels. The total number of words was 1,221,265, and the average length of an essay was 820 words. The essays were written on a broad range of topics, and their lengths were limited to be between 700-800 words. The topics were divided based on student education level, with 5 essay topics written by first-term students, 8 by second-term students, and 1 by third-term students.

To facilitate comparison, we chose similar topics from the first and second-term sets. We thus had two sets of essays. The first set consisted of *Analysis* essays which are written as a causal analysis of some topic, such as "television and its impact on people." The second set consisted of *Argumentation* essays where students argue for or against a topic or viewpoint. We further imposed the restriction that only essays written by the same student in both terms were selected. That is, if a student wrote an essay on a chosen topic in the first term, but not the second, or vice-versa, their essay was not considered. This selection resulted in 38 pairs of *Analysis* essays and 20 pairs of *Argumentation* essays across the two terms, for a total of 116 essays.

3.2 Computing Surprisal

We computed the surprisal value of each word in an essay by using a broad-coverage top-down parser developed by Roark et al. (2009). The parser was trained on sections 02-24 of the Wall Street Journal corpus of the Penn Treebank (Marcus et al., 1993). Essentially, the parser computes a word's surprisal value as the negative log-probability of the word given the preceding words using prefix probabilities. Thus, the surprisal value of the ith word is calculated as:

$$\textsc{Surprisal}(w_i) = -\log \frac{\text{PrefixProb}(w_{1...i})}{\text{PrefixProb}(w_{1...i-1})}$$

Moreover, it decomposes each word's surprisal value into two components: syntactic surprisal and lexical surprisal. Syntactic surprisal measures the degree of unexpectedness of the part-of-speech category of a word given the word's sentential context. On the other hand, lexical surprisal measures the degree of unexpectedness of the word itself given its sentential context and a part-of-speech category.

For every essay, we measured the syntactic, lexical, and total (i.e., summed) surprisal values for each word. Subsequently, the averages of the three surprisal values were computed for every essay, and those means were used for further analyses. Henceforth, surprisal values for an essay refers to their mean surprisal values.

3.3 Results and Discussion

Table 2 reports the means and standard deviations of the three surprisal measures of the essays.[1] As can be seen, there seems to be a reduction in all three surprisal values across terms, and second term essays tend to have a lower mean surprisal than first term essays. To analyze these differences, we computed linear mixed-effect regression models (Baayen, 2008; Baayen et al., 2008) for the two essay categories. Each model included Term as a fixed factor and Student as a random intercept.

While our analysis shows that essays in the second term have an overall mean surprisal values less than than essays in the first term, these differences were not statistically significant. There are a number of factors that could have influenced these results. We made an assumption that only a single term of EFL training could significantly improve

[1]It is important to note here that these means and standard deviations are computed on mean surprisal values per essays and not surprisal values at individual words.

Score	Total		Syntactic		Lexical	
	Mean	SD	Mean	SD	Mean	SD
Low	6.22	0.39	2.46	0.22	3.76	0.29
Medium	6.10	0.34	2.35	0.17	3.75	0.26
High	6.09	0.28	2.27	0.14	3.82	0.24

Table 3: Means and standard deviations of total surprisal, syntactic surprisal, and lexical surprisal for the three different essay score levels

essay quality, and hence decrease overall surprisal values of essays. However, it is likely that a single term of training is insufficient, and perhaps the lack of a significant difference between surprisal values reflects no improvement in essay quality across the two terms. Unfortunately, these essays were not previously scored, and thus we were unable to assess whether essay quality improved over terms.

4 Experiment 2

In the second experiment, we directly examined whether surprisal values are related to essay quality by using a dataset of pre-scored essays.

4.1 Corpus

For this experiment, we used a corpus of essays written by non-native English speakers. These essays are a part of the Educational Testing Service's corpus which was used in the first shared task in Native Language Identification (Blanchard et al., 2013)[2] .

The corpus consisted of 12,100 essays, with a total number of 4,142,162 words, and the average length of an essay was 342 words. The essays were on 8 separate topics, which broadly asked students to argue for or against a topic or a viewpoint. Each essay was labeled with an English language proficiency level (*High*, *Medium*, or *Low*) based on the judgments of human assessment specialists. The distribution of the essays per score-category was: *Low* = 1,325; *Medium* = 6,533; and *High* = 4,172. In order to ensure an equitable comparison, and to balance each group, we decided to choose 1,325 essays per score-category, for a total of 3,975 essays.

4.2 Computing Surprisal

As in Experiment 1, for every essay we measured the syntactic, lexical, and total surprisal values for each word. We computed the averages of the three surprisal values, and used those means for further analysis.

4.3 Results and Discussion

Table 3 reports the means and standard deviations of the three surprisal values for every essay per score-category. We analyzed the differences between the means using linear mixed-effects regression models (Baayen, 2008; Baayen et al., 2008). Essay Score was treated as a fixed effect and Essay Topic was included as a random intercept. The results indicate that *Low*-scoring essays had a significantly greater mean total surprisal value than *Medium* or *High*-scoring essays. However, the difference in mean total surprisal values for *Medium* and *High*-scoring essays was not significant. On the other hand, for syntactic and lexical surprisal, the means for all three essay score levels were significantly different from one another.

We further evaluated the three surprisal values by performing a correlation test between them and the essay scores. Table 4 reports the output of the correlation tests. All three surprisal values were found to be significantly inversely correlated with essay scores. However, only syntactic surprisal obtained a correlation coefficient of a sufficiently large magnitude of 0.39.

A similar evaluation was performed by Attali and Burstein (2006) in their evaluation of the features used in ETS's *e-rater* system. Interestingly, the magnitude of the correlation coefficient for syntactic surprisal reported here is within the range of coefficients corresponding to *e-rater*'s features when they were correlated with TOEFL essay scores (see Attali and Burstein, 2006, Table 2). Granted, a direct comparison between coefficients is not recommended as the datasets used were different, such a finding is still promising. Overall, the results shed a positive light on the use of surprisal, specifically syntactic surprisal, as a feature for automated essay scoring.

Despite the promising pattern of our results,

[2]Copyright © 2014 ETS. `www.ets.org`

Dep Var	ρ	t-value	p-value
Total	-.15	-9.87	$< .001$
Syntactic	-.39	-26.53	$< .001$
Lexical	.08	5.35	$< .001$

Table 4: Pearson's R coefficients between the three surprisal values and the essay scores

they must be taken with a grain of salt. The dataset that we used did not contain the actual scores of the essays, and we had to work with broad classifications of essay scores into *Low*, *Medium*, and *High* score levels. A possible avenue of future work is to test whether these results hold when using finer-grain essays scores.

5 Conclusions and Future Work

We proposed the use of the *surprisal theory* to quantify sentence processing complexity for use as a feature in essay scoring. The results are encouraging, and warrant further evaluation of surprisal's effectiveness in determining essay quality.

One point of concern is that the relationship between mean surprisal values and essay scores is likely to vary depending on the general quality of the essays. Here, we used a corpus of essays written by non-native English speakers, and as such, these essays are bound to be of a lower overall quality than essays written by native English speakers. For example, consider the following, somewhat questionable, sentences chosen from the subset of essays having a *High* score:

(3) *Some people might think that traveling in a group led by a tour guide is a good way.*

(4) *This is possible only if person understands ideas and concept.*

(5) *It is an important decision, how to plan your syllabus.*

These examples suggest that even high-scoring essays written by non-native English speakers may not necessarily be flawless, and as such, grammatical acceptability may play a crucial role in determining their overall quality. Therefore, it is possible that for lower-quality essays, high surprisal values reflect the presence of grammatical errors. On the other hand, for better-written essays, moderate-to-high surprisal values may reflect structural variability, which arguably is preferable to monotonous essays with simpler sentence structures. Thus, it is likely that the relation between surprisal values and essay scores depends on the overall quality of the essays in general. For an equitable evaluation, further tests will need to determine surprisal's efficacy over a broader range of essays.

Another critical point is the choice of corpus used to compute surprisal. Whatever choice is made essentially dictates and constrains the grammar of the language under consideration. Here, we used the WSJ corpus and, thus, implicitly made an assumption about the underlying language model. Therefore, in our case, a good essay, i.e. one with a lower surprisal score, would be one which is stylistically closer to the WSJ corpus. Future work will need to investigate the role played by the underlying language model, with special emphasis on evaluating language models that are specific to the task at hand. In other words, it would be interesting to compare a surprisal model that is built using a collection of previous essays with a surprisal model that uses a broader language model.

Lastly, our evaluations were aimed at determining whether surprisal can be an effective predictor of essay quality. Further tests will need to evaluate how well the measure contributes to essay score predictions when compared to related approaches that rely on non-syntactic language models, such as n-grams. Moreover, future work will need to determine whether adding mean surprisal values to an AES system results in a performance improvement.

Acknowledgments

We are indebted to ETS for sharing their data with us, and supporting us through this project. This work would not be possible without their help. We are also thankful to the reviewers for their helpful and encouraging comments. The opinions set forth in this publication are those of the author(s) and not ETS.

References

Helen B. Ajay, P. I. Tillett, and Ellis B. Page. 1973. Analysis of essays by computer (AEC-II). *Final*

Report to the National Center for Educational Research and Development for Project, (8-0101).

Yigal Attali and Jill Burstein. 2006. Automated essay scoring with e-rater® v. 2. *The Journal of Technology, Learning and Assessment*, 4(3).

Margareta W. Axelsson. 2000. USE – the Uppsala Student English corpus: An instrument for needs analysis. *ICAME Journal*, 24:155–157.

Harald R. Baayen, Douglas J. Davidson, and Douglas M. Bates. 2008. Mixed-effects modeling with crossed random effects for subjects and items. *Journal of memory and language*, 59(4):390–412.

Harald R. Baayen. 2008. *Analyzing linguistic data: A practical introduction to statistics using R*. Cambridge University Press.

Daniel Blanchard, Joel Tetreault, Derrick Higgins, Aoife Cahill, and Martin Chodorow. 2013. TOEFL11: A corpus of non-native english. *Educational Testing Service*.

Marisa Boston, John Hale, Reinhold Kliegl, Umesh Patil, and Shravan Vasishth. 2008. Parsing costs as predictors of reading difficulty: An evaluation using the potsdam sentence corpus. *Journal of Eye Movement Research*, 2(1):1–12.

Jill Burstein, Karen Kukich, Susanne Wolff, Chi Lu, and Martin Chodorow. 1998. Enriching automated essay scoring using discourse marking. In *Proceedings of the Workshop on Discourse Relations and Discourse Marking*, pages 206–210.

Alice Davison and Richard Lutz. 1985. Measuring syntactic complexity relative to discourse context. In David R. Dowty, Lauri Karttunen, and Arnold M. Zwicky, editors, *Natural language parsing: Psychological, computational, and theoretical perspectives*, pages 26–66. Cambridge: Cambridge University Press.

Vera Demberg and Frank Keller. 2008. Data from eye-tracking corpora as evidence for theories of syntactic processing complexity. *Cognition*, 109:193–210.

Scott Elliot, 2003. *Automated essay scoring: a cross disciplinary approach*, chapter IntelliMetric: From here to validity, pages 71–86. Lawrence Erlbaum Associates, Mahwah, NJ.

Kenneth Forster and Ilmar Olbrei. 1972. Semantic heuristics and syntactic analysis. *Cognition*, 2(3):319–347.

Stefan L Frank. 2009. Surprisal-based comparison between a symbolic and a connectionist model of sentence processing. In *Proceedings of the 31st annual conference of the cognitive science society*, pages 1139–1144. Cognitive Science Society Austin, TX.

Peter C. Gordon, Randall Hendrick, and Marcus Johnson. 2001. Memory interference during language processing. *Journal of Experimental Psychology: Learning, Memory and Cognition*, 27:1411–1423.

Daniel Grodner and Edward Gibson. 2005. Consequences of the serial nature of linguistic input for sentenial complexity. *Cognitive Science*, 29(2):261–290.

John Hale. 2001. A probabilistic Earley parser as a psycholinguistic model. In *Proceedings of the 2nd Conference of the North American Chapter of the Association for Computational Linguistics*, volume 2, pages 159–166, Pittsburgh, PA.

Gaurav Kharkwal and Karin Stromswold. 2013. Good-enough language processing: Evidence from sentence-video matching. *Journal of psycholinguistic research*, 43(1):1–17.

Jonathan King and Marcel A. Just. 1991. Individual differences in sentence processing: The role of working memory. *Journal of Memory and Language*, 30:580–602.

Thomas K. Landauer, Darrell Laham, and Peter W. Foltz, 2003. *Automated essay scoring: a cross disciplinary approach*, chapter Automated scoring and annotation of essays with the Iintelligent Essay Assessor, pages 87–112. Lawrence Erlbaum Associates, Mahwah, NJ.

Roger Levy and Frank Keller. 2012. Expectation and locality effects in german verb-final structures. *Journal of Memory and Language*.

Roger Levy. 2008. Expectation-based syntactic comprehension. *Cognition*, 106(3):1126–1177.

Mitchell P. Marcus, Mary Ann Marcinkiewicz, and Beatrice Santorini. 1993. Building a large annotated corpus of English: The Penn Treebank. *Computational linguistics*, 19(2):313–330.

Ellis B. Page. 1966. The imminence of grading essays by computer. *Phi Delta Kappan*, 47(5):238–243.

Brian Roark, Asaf Bachrach, Carlos Cardenas, and Christophe Pallier. 2009. Deriving lexical and syntactic expectation-based measures for psycholinguistic modeling via incremental top-down parsing. In *Proceedings of the 2009 Conference on Empirical Methods in Natural Language Processing: Volume 1-Volume 1*, pages 324–333. Association for Computational Linguistics.

Lawrence M. Rudner and Tahung Liang. 2002. Automated essay scoring using Bayes' theorem. *The Journal of Technology, Learning and Assessment*, 1(2).

Dan Slobin. 1966. Grammatical transformations and sentence comprehension in childhood and adulthood. *Journal of Verbal Learning and Verbal Behavior*, 5(3):219–227.

Adrian Staub. 2010. Eye movements and processing difficulty in object relative clauses. *Cognition*, 116(1):71–86.

Karin Stromswold, David Caplan, Nathaniel Alpert, and Scott Rauch. 1996. Localization of syntactic comprehension by position emission tomography. *Brain and Language*, 52:452–473.

Matthew J. Traxler, Robin K. Morris, and Rachel E. Seely. 2002. Processing subject and object relative clauses: Evidence from eye movements. *Journal of Memory and Language*, 47:69–90.

Towards Domain-Independent Assessment of Elementary Students' Science Competency using Soft Cardinality

Samuel P. Leeman-Munk, Angela Shelton, Eric N. Wiebe, James C. Lester
North Carolina State University
Raleigh, North Carolina 27695
{ spleeman, anshelto, wiebe, lester } @ ncsu.edu

Abstract

Automated assessment of student learning has become the subject of increasing attention. Students' textual responses to short answer questions offer a rich source of data for assessment. However, automatically analyzing textual constructed responses poses significant computational challenges, exacerbated by the disfluencies that occur prominently in elementary students' writing. With robust text analytics, there is the potential to analyze a student's text responses and accurately predict his or her future success. In this paper, we propose applying soft cardinality, a technique that has shown success grading less disfluent student answers, on a corpus of fourth-grade responses to constructed response questions. Based on decomposition of words into their constituent character substrings, soft cardinality's evaluations of responses written by fourth graders correlates with summative analyses of their content knowledge.

1 Introduction

As a tool for automated assessment, short answer questions reveal cognitive processes and states in students that are difficult to uncover in multiple-choice equivalents (Nicol, 2007). Even when it seems that items could be designed to address the same cognitive construct, success in devising multiple-choice and short answer items that behave with psychometric equivalence has proven to be limited (Kuechler & Simkin, 2010). Because standards-based STEM education in the United States explicitly promotes the development of writing skills for which constructed response items are ideally suited (NGSS Lead States, 2013; Porter, McMaken, Hwang, & Yang, 2011; Southavilay, Yacef, Reimann, & Calvo, 2013), the prospect of designing text analytics techniques for automatically assessing students' textual responses has become even more appealing (Graesser, 2000; Jordan & Butcher, 2013; Labeke, Whitelock, & Field, 2013).

An important family of short answer questions is the constructed response question. A constructed response question is designed to elicit a response of no more than a few sentences and features a relatively clear distinction between incorrect, partially correct, and correct answers. Ideally, a system designed for *constructed response analysis* (CRA) would be machine-learned from examples that include both graded student answers and expert-constructed "reference" answers (Dzikovska, Nielsen, & Brew, 2012).

The challenges of creating an accurate machine-learning-based CRA system stem from the variety of ways in which a student can express a given concept. In addition to lexical and syntactic variety, students often compose ill-formed text replete with ungrammatical phrasings and misspellings, which significantly complicate analysis. The task of automated grading also becomes increasingly difficult as the material graded comes from questions and domains more and more distant from that of human graded responses on which the system is trained, leading to interest in domain-independent CRA systems designed to deal with this challenge (Dzikovska et al., 2013).

In this paper we explore the applications of soft cardinality (Jimenez, Becerra, & Gelbukh, 2013), an approach to constructed response analysis that has shown prior success in domain-independent CRA. We investigate whether soft cardinality is robust to the disfluency common among elementary students and whether its analyses of a student's work as she progresses through a problem-solving session can be used to roughly predict the content knowledge she will have at the end.

Because like other bag of words techniques, soft cardinality is independent of word order, it is robust to grammatical disfluencies. What distinguishes soft cardinality, however, is its character-overlap technique, which allows it to evaluate word similarity across misspellings. We evaluate soft cardinality on a dataset of textual responses to short-text science questions collected in a

Proceedings of the Ninth Workshop on Innovative Use of NLP for Building Educational Applications , pages 61–67,
Baltimore, Maryland USA, June 26, 2014. ©2014 Association for Computational Linguistics

study conducted at elementary schools in two states. Responders were in fourth grade and generally aged between nine and ten. We train our system on student responses to circuits questions and test it on two domains in the physical sciences—circuits and magnetism. The results indicate that, soft cardinality shows promise as a first step for predicting a student's future success with similar content even grading unseen domains in the presence of high disfluency.

This paper is structured as follows. Section 2 provides related work as a context for our research. Section 3 introduces the corpus, collected on tablet-based digital science notebook software from elementary students. Section 4 describes soft cardinality and an evaluation thereof. Section 6 discusses the findings and explores how soft cardinality may serve as the basis for future approaches to real-time formative assessment.

2 Related Work

Short answer assessment is a much-studied area that has received increased attention in recent years. Disfluency and domain-independence have been the beneficiaries of some of this attention, but cutting edge systems seem to be designed first for correctly spelled in-domain text, and then have domain-independence and disfluency management added afterwards.

For example, one system from Educational Testing Services (ETS) uses an approach to domain independence called "domain adaptation" (Heilman & Madnani, 2013). Domain adaptation generates a copy of a given feature for grading answers to seen questions, answers to unseen questions in seen domain, and answers to questions in unseen domains, and each of these has a separate weight. An item represented in the training data uses all three of these feature copies, and an item from another domain will only use the latter, "generic" feature copy.

Spell correction is also often treated as a separate issue, handled in the data-cleaning step of a CRA system. The common approach at this step is to mark words as misspelled if they do not appear in a dictionary and replace them with their most likely alternative. This technique only corrects non-word spelling errors (Leacock & Chodorow, 2003). Another approach is to use *Soundex hashes* that translate every word into a normalized form based on its pronunciation (Ott, Ziai, Hahn, & Meurers, 2013). This second approach is generally featured alongside a more traditional direct comparison.

The primary limitation of CRA for elementary school education is that evaluations of state-of-the-art systems on raw elementary student response data are limited. C-rater provides a small evaluation on fourth-grade student math responses, but most evaluation is on seventh, eighth and eleventh grade students (Leacock & Chodorow, 2003; Sukkarieh & Blackmore, 2009). Furthermore, the two datasets presented in SemEval's shared task (Dzikovska et al., 2013) for testing and training featured relatively few spelling errors. The BEETLE corpus was drawn from undergraduate volunteers with a relatively strong command of the English language, and the SciEntsBank corpus, which was drawn from 3-6th graders, was originally intended for speech and as such was manually spell-corrected. The Hewlett Foundation's automated student assessment prize (ASAP) shared task for short answer scoring was drawn entirely from tenth grade students (Hewlett, 2012).

3 Corpus

We have been exploring constructed response assessment in the context of science education for upper elementary students with the LEONARDO CYBERPAD (Leeman-Munk, Wiebe, & Lester, 2014). Under development in our laboratory for three years, the CYBERPAD is a digital science notebook that runs on tablet and web based computing platforms. The CYBERPAD integrates intelligent tutoring systems technologies into a digital science notebook that enables students to model science phenomena graphically. With a focus on the physical and earth sciences, the LEONARDO PADMATE, a pedagogical agent, supports students' learning with real-time problem-solving advice. The CYBERPAD's curriculum is based on that of the Full Option Science System (Foss Project, 2013). As students progress through the curriculum, they utilize LEONARDO's virtual notebook, complete virtual labs, and write responses to constructed response questions. To date, the LEONARDO CYBERPAD has been implemented in over 60 classrooms around the United States.

The short answer and pre/post-test data used in this investigation were gathered from fourth grade students during implementations of The CYBERPAD in public schools in California and North Carolina. The data collection for each class took place over a minimum of five class periods with students completing one or more new investigations each day. Students completed investigations in one or both of two modules, "Energy and Circuits," and "Magnetism." Most questions included "starter text" that students were expected to complete. Students were able to modify the starter text in any way including deleting or replacing it entirely, although most students simply added to the starter text. Example answers can be found in a previous work on the same dataset (Leeman-Munk et al., 2014).

Two human graders scored students' responses from the circuits module on a science score rubric with three categories: *incorrect*, *partially correct*, and *correct*. The graders graded one class of data and then conferred on disagreeing results. They then graded other classes. On a sample of 10% of the responses of the classes graded after conferring, graders achieved a Cohen's Kappa of 0.72.

The graders dealt with considerable disfluency in the student responses in the LEONARDO corpus. An analysis of constructed responses in the Energy and Circuits module reveals that 4.7% of tokens in all of student answers combined are not found in a dictionary. This number is higher in the Magnetism module, 7.8%. This is in contrast to other similar datasets, such as the BEETLE corpus of undergraduate text answers to science questions, which features a 0.8% rate of out-of-dictionary words (Dzikovska, Nielsen, & Brew, 2012). In each case, the numbers underestimate overall spelling errors. Misspellings such as 'batter' for 'battery', are not counted as missing in a dictionary test. These *real-word spelling errors* nevertheless misrepresent a student's meaning and complicate analysis. We describe how soft cardinality addresses these issues in Section 4.

4 Methodology and Evaluation

Soft cardinality (Jimenez, Becerra, & Gelbukh, 2013) uses decompositions of words into character sequences, known as *q-grams*, to gauge similarity between two words. We use it here to bridge the gap between misspellings of the same word. Considering "dcells" in an example answer, "mor dcells," and "D-cells" in the reference answer, we can find overlaps in "ce," "el," "ll," "ls," "ell," "lls," and so on up to and including "cells." This technique functions equally well for real-word spelling errors such as if the student had forgotten the "d" and typed only "cells." Such overlaps signify a close match for both of these words. We evaluated the soft cardinality implementation of a generic short answer grading framework that we developed, WRITEEVAL, based on an answer grading system described in an earlier work (Leeman-Munk et al., 2014). We used 100-fold cross-validation on the "Energy and Circuits" module. We compare WRITEEVAL using soft cardinality to the majority class baseline and to WRITEEVAL using Precedent Feature Collection (PFC), a latent semantic analysis technique that performs competitively with the second highest-scoring system in Semeval Task 7 on unseen answers on the SciEntsBank corpus (Dzikovska et al., 2013). Using a Kruskal-Wallis test over one hundred folds, both systems significantly outperform the baseline ($p<.001$), which achieved an accuracy score of .61. We could not evaluate the scores directly on the Magnetism dataset as we did not have any human-graded gold standard for comparison.

To evaluate soft cardinality's robustness to disfluency, we created a duplicate of the Energy and Circuits dataset and manually spell-corrected it. Table 1 and Figures 1 and 2 show our results. Using the Kruskal-Wallis Test, on the uncorrected data PFC's accuracy suffered with marginal significance ($p = .054$) while macro-averaged precision and recall both suffered significantly ($p < .01$). Soft cardinality suffered much less, with a marginally significant decrease in performance ($p=.075$) only in recall. The decreases in accuracy and precision had $p=.88$ and $p=.25$ respectively.

To determine the usefulness of automatic grading of science content in predicting the overall trajectory of a student's performance, we computed a running average of the grades given by soft cardinality (converted to '1', '2', and '3' for incorrect, partially correct, correct) on students' answers as they progressed through the Energy and Circuits module and the Magnetism module. Because we would intend to be able to use this technique in a classroom on entirely new questions and student answers, we use running average instead of a regression, which would require prior data on the questions to determine the weights.

Students completed a multiple-choice test before and after their interaction with the CYBERPAD. The Energy and Circuits module and the Magnetism module each had different tests – there were ten questions on the Energy and Circuits test and twenty on the Magnetism test. We calculated the correlation of our running average of formative assessments against the student's score on the final test.

A critical assumption underlying the running average is that students answered each question in order. Although WRITEEVAL does not prevent students from answering questions out of order, it is organized to strongly encourage linear progression.

We excluded empty responses from the running average because we did not want an artificial boost from simply noting what questions students did and did not answer. Data from students who did not take the pre or post-test was excluded, and students missing responses to more than twenty out of twenty-nine questions in Magnetism or fifteen out of twenty questions in Energy and Circuits were excluded from consideration. After cleaning, our results include 85 students in Energy and Circuits and 61 in Magnetism.

Sp.Cr.	System	Accuracy	Precision	Recall
Yes	SoftCr	.68	.55	.54
No	SoftCr	.68	.52	.50*
Yes	PFC	.78	.61	.58
No	PFC	.74*	.54**	.52**

Table 1. Accuracy and Macro-Averaged Precision and Recall for Soft-Cardinality and PFC on spell-corrected and uncorrected versions of the LEONARDO Energy and Circuits module.
*marginally significant decrease from spell-checked
**significant decrease from spell-checked

Figure 1 depicts the correlation between the running average of automatic scoring by WRITEEVAL soft cardinality, PFC, and human scores with post-test score on the responses in the Energy and Circuits module. When spell-corrected, the correlation, as shown in Figure 2, surprisingly becomes worse. We discuss a possible reason for this in the discussion section.

Figure 3 shows correlation of the running average of Magnetism's automatic scores with post-test. For soft cardinality, significant correlation starts five questions in and stays for the rest of the 29. As it relies heavily on relevant training data, PFC is less stable and does not achieve nearly as high a correlation.

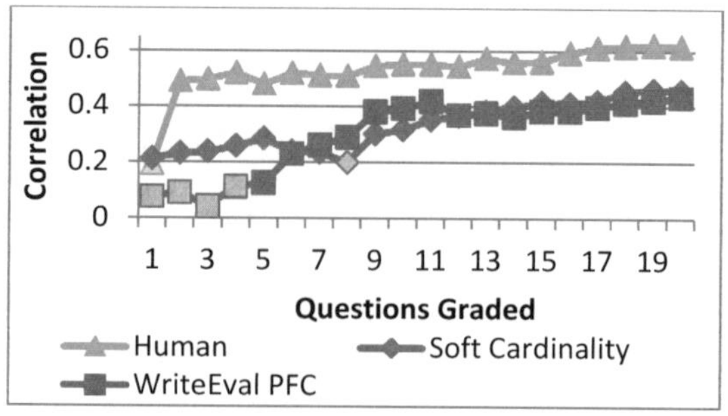

Figure 1. Correlation of grading systems on Energy and Circuits with post-test score. Dark-colored points indicate significant correlation (p<.05)

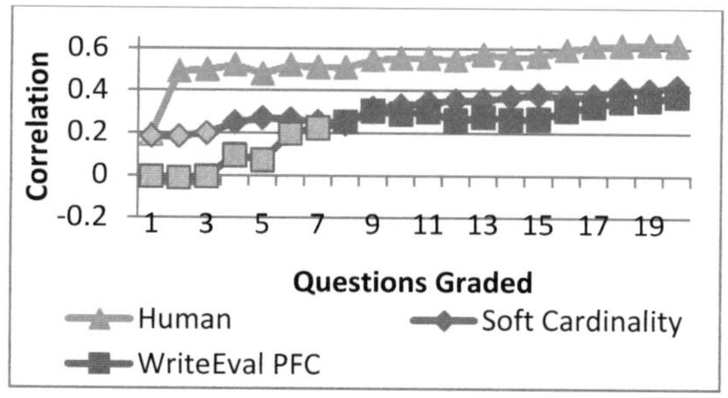

Figure 2. Correlation of grading systems on spell-corrected Energy and Circuits with post-test score. Dark-colored points indicate significant correlation (p<.05)

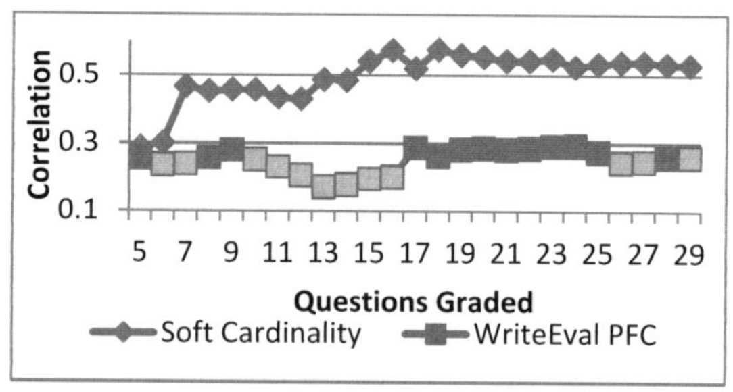

Figure 3. Correlation of the Running Average of WRITEEVAL with soft cardinality with post-test Scores on the Magnetism module of the LEONARDO corpus. Dark-colored points indicate significant correlation (p<.05)

5 Discussion

The evaluation suggests that a relatively simple technique such as soft cardinality, despite performing less well than a domain specific technique in the presence of relevant training data, is more robust to spelling errors and can be far more effective at grading questions and domains not present in the training data.

Soft cardinality is representative of the potential of domain independent, disfluency-robust CRA systems.

The improvement against the gold standard on spell-corrected data but loss of correlation against the post-test scores suggests that poor spelling is a predictor of poor post-test knowledge at the end of a task. This could be because the students were less able to learn the material due to their poor language skills, they were less able to complete the test effectively despite knowing the material again due to poor language skills, or it could be a latent factor that affects both the students use of language and their eventual circuits knowledge such as engagement. This result shows the challenge of separating different skills in evaluating students.

The significance of soft cardinality's correlation over the running average for all but the eighth question as well as the generally high significant correlation achieved in the magnetism evaluation indicates the predictive potential of soft cardinality. Soft cardinality's performance in Magnetism suggests that with only a relatively limited breadth of training examples it can effectively evaluate answers to questions in some unseen domains. It is important to note that Energy and Circuits and Magnetism are both subjects in the physical sciences, and the questions and reference answers themselves were authored by the same individuals. As such this result should not be overstated, but is still a promising first step towards the goal of domain-independence in constructed response analysis.

6 Conclusion

This paper presents a novel application of the soft cardinality text analytics method to support assessment of highly disfluent elementary school text. Using q-gram overlap to evaluate word similarity across nonstandard spellings, soft cardinality was evaluated on highly disfluent constructed response texts composed by fourth grade students interacting with a tablet-based digital science notebook. The evaluation included an in-domain training corpus and another out-of-domain corpus. The results of the evaluation suggest that soft cardinality generates assessments that are predictive of students' post-test performance even in highly disfluent out-of-domain corpora. It offers the potential to produce assessments in real-time that may serve as early warning indicators to help teachers support student learning.

Soft cardinality's current performance levels suggest several promising directions for future work. First, it will be important to develop techniques to deal with widely varying student responses without relying directly on training data. These techniques will take inspiration in part from bag-of-words techniques such as soft cardinality and Precedent Feature Collection, but will themselves likely take word order into account as there is a sizeable subset of answers whose meaning is dependent on word order. The use of distributional semantics will also be of help in resolving similarities between different words. Secondly, work should be done to consider answers in more detail than simple assessment of correctness. More detailed rubrics such as Task 7's 5-way rubric (Dzikovska et al., 2013) would allow for more detailed feedback from tutors. Further, detailed analysis of individual understandings and misconceptions within answers would be even more helpful, and will be the focus of future work. Third, it will be instructive to incorporate the WRITEEVAL framework into the LEONARDO CYBERPAD digital science notebook to investigate techniques for classroom-based formative assessment that artfully utilize both intelligent support by the PADMATE onboard intelligent tutor and personalized support by the teacher. Finally, it will be important to to investigate additional techniques to evaluate student answers more accurately using less training data from more distant domains.

Reliable analysis of constructed response items not only provides additional summative analysis of writing ability in science, but also gives the teacher a powerful formative assessment tool that can be used to guide instructional strategies at either the individual student or whole class level. Given that time for science instruction is limited at the elementary level, the use of real-time assessment to address student misconceptions or missing knowledge immediately can be an invaluable classroom tool.

7 Acknowledgements

The authors wish to thank our colleagues on the LEONARDO team for their contributions to the design, development, and classroom implementations of LEONARDO: Courtney Behrle, Mike Carter, Bradford Mott, Peter Andrew Smith, and Robert Taylor. This material is based upon work supported by the National Science Foundation under Grant No. DRL1020229. Any opinions, findings, and conclusions or recommendations expressed in this material are those of the authors and do not necessarily reflect the views of the National Science Foundation.

References

Dzikovska, M., Brew, C., Clark, P., Nielsen, R. D., Leacock, C., Mcgraw-hill, C. T. B., & Bentivogli, L. (2013). SemEval-2013 Task 7 : The joint student response analysis and 8th recognizing textual entailment challenge. In *Second Joint Conference on Lexical and Computational Semantics (*SEM), Volume 2: Proceedings of the Seventh International Workshop on Semantic Evaluation (SemEval 2013)* (Vol. 2, pp. 263–274).

Dzikovska, M., Nielsen, R., & Brew, C. (2012). Towards effective tutorial feedback for explanation questions: A dataset and baselines. In *Proceedings of the 2012 Conference of the North American Chapter of the Association for Computational Linguistics: Human Language Technologies* (pp. 200–210). Montreal, Canada. Retrieved from http://dl.acm.org/citation.cfm?id=2382057

Foss Project. (2013). Welcome to FossWeb. Retrieved October 20, 2013, from http://www.fossweb.com/

Graesser, A. (2000). Using latent semantic analysis to evaluate the contributions of students in AutoTutor. *Interactive Learning Environments*, *8*(2), 1–33. Retrieved from http://www.tandfonline.com/doi/full/10.1076/1049-4820(200008)8%3A2%3B1-B%3BFT129

Heilman, M., & Madnani, N. (2013). ETS : Domain adaptation and stacking for short answer scoring. In *Second Joint Conference on Lexical and Computational Semantics (*SEM), Volume 2: Proceedings of the Seventh International Workshop on Semantic Evaluation (SemEval 2013)* (Vol. 1, pp. 96–102).

Hewlett, W. (2012). The Hewlett Foundation: Short answer scoring. Retrieved March 16, 2014, from https://www.kaggle.com/c/asap-sas/data?Data_Set_Descriptions.zip

Jimenez, S., Becerra, C., & Gelbukh, A. (2013). SOFTCARDINALITY: hierarchical text overlap for student response analysis. In *Second Joint Conference on Lexical and Computational Semantics (*SEM), Volume 2: Proceedings of the Seventh International Workshop on Semantic Evaluation (SemEval 2013)* (Vol. 2, pp. 280–284). Retrieved from http://www.gelbukh.com/CV/Publications/2013/SOFTCARDINALITY Hierarchical Text Overlap for Student Response Analysis.pdf

Jordan, S., & Butcher, P. (2013). Does the Sun orbit the Earth ? Challenges in using short free-text computer-marked questions . In *Proceedings of HEA STEM Annual Learning and Teaching Conference 2013: Where Practice and Pedagogy Meet*. Birmingham, UK.

Kuechler, W., & Simkin, M. (2010). Why is performance on multiple-choice tests and constructed-response tests not more closely related? Theory and an empirical test. *Decision Sciences Journal of Innovative Education*, *8*(1), 55–73. Retrieved from http://onlinelibrary.wiley.com/doi/10.1111/j.1540-4609.2009.00243.x/full

Labeke, N. Van, Whitelock, D., & Field, D. (2013). OpenEssayist: extractive summarisation and formative assessment of free-text essays. In *First International Workshop on Discourse-Centric Learning Analytics*. Leuven, Belgium. Retrieved from http://oro.open.ac.uk/37548/

Leacock, C., & Chodorow, M. (2003). C-rater: Automated scoring of short-answer questions. *Computers and the Humanities*, *37*(4), 389–405. Retrieved from http://link.springer.com/article/10.1023/A%3A1025779619903

Leeman-Munk, S. P., Wiebe, E. N., & Lester, J. C. (2014). Assessing Elementary Students' Science Competency with Text Analytics. In *Proceedings of the Fourth International Conference on Learning Analytics & Knowledge*. Indianapolis, Indiana.

NGSS Lead States. (2013). *Next Generation Science Standards: For States, By States*. Washington DC: National Academic Press.

Nicol, D. (2007). E-assessment by design: Using multiple-choice tests to good effect. *Journal of Further and Higher Education*, *31*(1), 53–64. Retrieved from http://www.tandfonline.com/doi/abs/10.1080/03098770601167922

Ott, N., Ziai, R., Hahn, M., & Meurers, D. (2013). CoMeT : Integrating different levels of linguistic modeling for meaning assessment. In *Second Joint Conference on Lexical and Computational Semantics (*SEM), Volume 2: Proceedings of the Seventh International Workshop on Semantic Evaluation (SemEval 2013)* (Vol. 2, pp. 608–616).

Porter, A., McMaken, J., Hwang, J., & Yang, R. (2011). Common core standards the new US intended curriculum. *Educational Researcher, 40*(3), 103–116. Retrieved from http://edr.sagepub.com/content/40/3/103.short

Southavilay, V., Yacef, K., Reimann, P., & Calvo, R. A. (2013). Analysis of collaborative writing processes using revision maps and probabilistic topic models. In *Proceedings of the Third International Conference on Learning Analytics and Knowledge - LAK '13* (pp. 38–47). New York, New York, USA: ACM Press. doi:10.1145/2460296.2460307

Sukkarieh, J., & Blackmore, J. (2009). C-rater: Automatic content scoring for short constructed responses. *Proceedings of the 22nd International FLAIRS Conference*, 290–295. Retrieved from http://www.aaai.org/ocs/index.php/FLAIRS/2009/paper/download/122/302

Automatic evaluation of spoken summaries: the case of language assessment

Anastassia Loukina, Klaus Zechner, Lei Chen
Educational Testing Service (ETS)
Princeton, NJ 08541, USA
aloukina@ets.org, kzechner@ets.org, lchen@ets.org

Abstract

This paper investigates whether ROUGE, a popular metric for the evaluation of automated written summaries, can be applied to the assessment of spoken summaries produced by non-native speakers of English. We demonstrate that ROUGE, with its emphasis on the recall of information, is particularly suited to the assessment of the summarization quality of non-native speakers' responses. A standard baseline implementation of ROUGE-1 computed over the output of the automated speech recognizer has a Spearman correlation of $\rho = 0.55$ with experts' scores of speakers' proficiency ($\rho = 0.51$ for a content-vector baseline). Further increases in agreement with experts' scores can be achieved by using types instead of tokens for the computation of word frequencies for both candidate and reference summaries, as well as by using multiple reference summaries instead of a single one. These modifications increase the correlation with experts' scores to a Spearman correlation of $\rho = 0.65$. Furthermore, we found that the choice of reference summaries does not have any impact on performance, and that the adjusted metric is also robust to errors introduced by automated speech recognition ($\rho = 0.67$ for human transcriptions vs. $\rho = 0.65$ for speech recognition output).

1 Introduction

In this paper we explore whether metrics commonly used for the automated evaluation of written summaries can be used to evaluate spoken summaries in the context of language assessment.

The performance of automatic summarization systems is routinely evaluated using content metrics such as ROUGE (Lin and Rey, 2004), which measures the *n*-gram overlap between the candidate summary and a set of reference summaries (see also Rankel et al. (2013) for historical background). ROUGE is a recall-oriented metric inspired by its precision-oriented counterpart BLEU, developed to evaluate machine translations (Papineni et al., 2002). Recent research in this area has been focused on identifying the most reliable variants of ROUGE and best practices in the application of the metric (Owczarzak et al., 2012; Rankel et al., 2013). These studies (reviewed in more detail in Section 2.1) showed that less commonly used variants of ROUGE may in fact be more consistent with human judgments, at least in the context of automatic summary evaluation.

Beyond the research in automatic summarization systems, ROUGE has also been used to evaluate written summaries in the context of educational assessment. Madnani et al. (2013) showed that one of the variants of ROUGE, in combination with other metrics, performed consistently well for the automated scoring of written responses to summary tasks produced by middle- and high-school students. They did not investigate the effect of using other variants of ROUGE.

In this paper, we explore whether ROUGE can be used to automatically evaluate the content coverage of spoken summaries produced by non-native speakers in the context of language assessment. As in case of automatic text summaries, the human raters who score these responses are asked to assess whether the summary accurately conveys the information contained in the stimulus. While the length of the spoken responses is more loosely constrained than in case of automatic text summaries, human raters do not penalize for extraneously irrelevant language. Therefore recall-oriented ROUGE is an attractive evaluation metric for this task.

At the same time, unlike automatic text sum-

Proceedings of the Ninth Workshop on Innovative Use of NLP for Building Educational Applications , pages 68–78,
Baltimore, Maryland USA, June 26, 2014. ©2014 Association for Computational Linguistics

maries, spoken summaries are abstractive and often contain ungrammatical sequences, repetitions, repairs, and other disfluencies. Further 'noise' is introduced by transcription errors generated by the automated speech recognition system. In this study, we assess whether (a) ROUGE is robust against this type of noise; (b) how many reference summaries are necessary to obtain reliable evaluation; and (c) how the choice of specific reference summaries affects the performance of the metric (Section 4.1). We also assess which variants of ROUGE have the most agreement with human judgments on this type of summary and what adjustments can be made to mitigate the effects of disfluencies and errors introduced by automated speech recognition (Section 4.2). Finally, we test how well our adjusted variant of ROUGE can predict the human scores on unseen data (Section 4.3).

2 Related work

2.1 The application of ROUGE to evaluation of automatic text summarization

There exist various versions of ROUGE which differ in terms of the length of their n-grams, the use of skip-bigrams, the application of stemming, and the exclusion of stop-words. Several studies have compared these variants to identify those most consistent with human judgments. In earlier work, Lin (2004) reported that variants based on unigrams and skip-bigrams (ROUGE-SU4) or bigrams alone (ROUGE-2) performed best. ROUGE-2 was also identified as the best variant more recently by Owczarzak et al. (2012). Rankel et al. (2013) found that linear combinations of these metrics with ROUGE based on longer n-grams are more accurate in finding significantly different systems.

Previous work also explored various methods of text pre-processing prior to the computation of ROUGE, including stemming and the removal of stop-words, neither of which had any substantial effect on the performance of ROUGE (Lin and Rey, 2004; Owczarzak et al., 2012). Owczarzak et al. (2012) reported that the agreement with human judgments was, in fact, higher if the stop-words were retained.

All applications discussed so far used ROUGE to evaluate the textual summarization of written texts. There have also been attempts to apply this metric to text summaries of speech data with mixed results (see Nenkova and McKeown (2011) for a review). ROUGE performed reasonably well for the evaluation of text summaries of spoken presentations (Hirohata et al., 2005), but was not correlated with the summary accuracy of summaries of meetings or conversations (although see (Penn and Zhu, 2008)).

Most of this work was performed on extractive summaries produced by summarization systems that used multiple summaries to evaluate each system. In this study, we explore the application of ROUGE to the evaluation of abstractive summaries produced by students in a language assessment context with an aim of producing a separate evaluation for each summary. Furthermore, the fact that these are spoken responses adds an extra layer of complexity to the analysis, therefore the results of previous studies cannot directly be applied to this new context.

2.2 Previous approaches to the content evaluation of spoken summaries for assessment purposes

The research on the automated scoring of content accuracy in a language assessment has primarily focused on the evaluation of written essays. Most previous approaches in this area have used so-called "bag-of-words"-based models, gleaned from the discipline of information retrieval. The basic idea is that an essay is considered to be highly content relevant to a given topic when it contains words that are similar to those seen in previously collected essays with high human-rater scores. For instance, Attali and Burstein (2006) used a vector-space model to compute the cosine similarities between word vectors found in an essay to be automatically scored and word vectors comprising previously scored essays with the same human-rater score. In a similar vein, Foltz et al. (1999) computed a compressed vector space based on singular value decomposition for a set of document-word vectors, called latent semantic analysis, and then computed similarity scores for essays based on this more compact representation.

It should be noted, though, that since all of these models do not take word sequences into account, they must be considered knowledge-poor in that they cannot distinguish between syntactic roles or a list of random words versus a well-formed sentence. In operational systems, such bag-of-words similarity features are combined with features which evaluate grammar and other aspects of language use; therefore a random list of content words is unlikely to lead to a high overall score. However, finer-grained distinctions such as negations or subject-object relationships between words are often lost.

Applications of these methods to spontaneous speech in spoken-language assessments have been conducted much more recently as this domain of language assessment relies on the output of Automatic Speech Recognition systems (ASR) that typically have a fairly high word-error rate. These errors can negatively affect the accuracy of the methods developed for written responses. Furthermore, spoken responses differ in many properties from written ones (Biber et al., 2004) and the validity of existing methods for assessing speech needs to be established before they can be used for operational scoring.

Xie et al. (2012) presented experiments using content features on spontaneous-speech data based on vector-space models, latent semantic analysis, as well as point-wise mutual information. Some of these content features showed higher correlations with human scores than features measuring other aspects of speaking proficiency, such as fluency or pronunciation. Chen and Zechner (2012) also used a vector space model for the scoring of spontaneous speech, but extended it by using the ontological information contained in WordNet. Finally, Xiong et al. (2013) used a variety of approaches to capture the content of spontaneous responses from the same corpus that we are investigating in this paper. Approaches varied from computing the overlap between key words in the stimuli and responses to a more traditional vector space model based on content vector analysis.

While these approaches have good correlations with human scores, they have a number of shortcomings. The best performing method suggested by Xiong et al. (2013) requires the manual annotation of the relevant key words for each prompt before the computation of the metric. Vector space models do not have this limitation, but they require a substantial number of reference summaries to achieve consistent results. Supporting this point, Chen (2013) showed that at least 50 reference responses were necessary to obtain moderate agreement between the cosine similarity measure and human judgments, with further improvement in agreement as the number of reference responses is increased to 200. These limitations pose practical difficulties when new items are added to the tests: the computation of content metrics for each new item requires either a manual annotation or a relatively large number of reference responses.

ROUGE appears promising in this context since it does not have either of these limitations. First, the computation of ROUGE does not require manual annotation. Second, research on the evaluation of written summaries suggests that relatively few reference summaries may be necessary to obtain reliable results, e.g., only four references were used for the summary evaluation at the Text Analysis Conference (Rankel et al., 2013). In addition, the recall-based nature of ROUGE is well-aligned with the evaluation criteria for these responses. Therefore in this paper, we explore whether any of the variants of ROUGE can be successfully applied to the content scoring of spoken summaries and what modifications may be necessary to achieve optimal performance.

3 Data and methodology

3.1 Description of the corpus

The study is based on a corpus of responses collected during the pilot administration of the TOEFL®Junior™Comprehensive test, an international assessment of English proficiency targeted at middle-school students aged from 11 to 15 (see also Xiong et al. (2013) who used a subset of this corpus).

The corpus used in this study included 5,934 spoken responses produced by 1,611 speakers; all learners of English as a foreign language residing in different countries. In addition to a read-aloud task that was not relevant for this paper, the speakers were presented with four other tasks. First, the speakers were asked to describe a sequence of six pictures. For the remaining three taks, the speakers listened to one announcement and two fragments from a lecture and were then asked to summarize the content of what they heard. The students were provided with a list of concepts that test takers were expected to cover in their responses.

For example, a student may have listened to a teacher giving an assignment in history class.[1] This assignment required the class to go to the library, look up information about the water supply in old and modern cities, answer the questions on their worksheet, and write a short paragraph about

[1] http://toefljr.caltesting.org/sampletest/s-historylesson.html

their findings. The students were then asked to respond to the following prompt:

> *Imagine that your classmate was not in class today. Tell your classmate about what the history teacher asked the students to do. Be sure to talk about the following:*
> *- the library*
> *- the worksheet*
> *- the homework*

The corpus contained responses to 24 different prompts with 6 different sets of prompts. Each speaker only answered one set of prompts giving 4 responses per speaker. The recording time for each response was limited to 60 seconds. The actual number of words varied between participants with an average 72 words per response (σ = 29).

From the originally recorded 6,444 responses, we excluded from further analysis 510 responses (about 8%), which contained either no speech or where the quality of the recording was too low for further analysis. All remaining 5,934 responses were scored on a scale of 1-4 by two expert human raters on a holistic scale that reflects all aspects of speaking proficiency, including pronunciation, grammar, and content coverage.[2] For content coverage, the raters were asked to consider whether the key information contained in the prompt was conveyed accurately or, in case of the picture description prompt, whether the story was complete. When the difference in the scores assigned by the two raters was greater than 1, the final score was assigned by an adjudicator.

The corpus was divided into non-overlapping training and testing partitions. The training partition contained 3,337 responses from 915 speakers and the test partition contained 2,597 spoken responses from 696 speakers. Both partitions included responses for the same prompts but there was no speaker overlap.

All responses were converted to text using a state-of-the-art automatic speech recognizer (ASR) with constrained vocabulary (see Evanini and Wang (2013) for further details). To evaluate the effect of the errors that may have been introduced by the ASR system, all responses were transcribed manually by professional human transcribers. Comparison with the human transcription showed that the ASR word error rate for this corpus was 26.5% for picture narration tasks and 29.4% for the summarization tasks.

[2]see http://www.ets.org/s/toefl_junior/pdf/toefl_junior_comprehensive_speaking_scoring_guides.pdf for the scoring rubrics

3.2 Computation of the metrics

Evaluation metrics. ROUGE was computed using equation (1) as an *n*-gram (gr_n) overlap between candidate summary and each summary (*S*) from the set of reference summaries (*RS*).

$$ROUGE_N = \frac{\sum\limits_{S \in RS} \sum\limits_{gr_n \in S} Count_{overlap}(gr_n)}{\sum\limits_{S \in RS} \sum\limits_{gr_n \in S} Count(gr_n)} \quad (1)$$

We used *n*-grams whereby *n* was in a range from 1 to 4 (ROUGE 1-4) and a combination of unigrams with skip-bigrams with maximum step of four words (ROUGE-SU1-4). Finally, we also computed a combined measure ROUGE-ALL which is the geometrical mean of ROUGE-1–ROUGE-4, computed by using the same smoothing procedure as for BLEU (Papineni et al., 2002).

We used the cosine distance (CVA) between the response and reference summaries as a baseline metric as this metric is commonly used for evaluating document similarity in the context of language assessment. CVA was computed as the cosine distance between candidate responses and the same reference responses as used for the computation of ROUGE. All term frequencies were weighted using *tf-idf* where tf is the frequency of a term in a given response and idf is the inverse document frequency. idf frequencies were computed based on all of the responses in the corpus.

Reference summaries. The reference summaries were selected from responses with the highest human rater final score (4). This approach is similar to using system outputs as pseudo-models for the evaluation of machine-translation or automatic-summarization systems (cf. Louis and Nenkova (2013)). It has also been successfully applied to the content assessment of written answers by Madnani et al. (2013) who used one randomly selected highly scored summary as a reference summary.

Since previous work on summarization evaluation showed that multiple summaries increase the reliability of evaluations (Louis and Nenkova, 2013; Nenkova and McKeown, 2011), we tested how many summaries were necessary to achieve consistent results. We therefore computed ROUGE for each response using up to 10 randomly selected responses with final score of 4. To investigate the effect that different choices of reference summaries may have on the metrics, we repeated the analysis for 20 randomly selected sets of reference responses.

The corpus did not contain a sufficient number of responses with the maximum score for each prompt. Therefore, this part of the analysis was based on a subset of 1,784 responses selected from the training partition. This set included only 12 prompts for which human raters assigned a score of 4 to more than 11 responses.

Text preprocessing. For the evaluation of written summaries, ROUGE is usually computed using the raw counts of all of the terms. In addition to using this classical approach using unstemmed terms (*'all'*), we also computed ROUGE using three other approaches: (1) excluding all stop-words (*'Non-stop'*); (2) setting the frequency of all n-grams within each summary to 1, that is, counting types instead of tokens (*'Types'*); (3) excluding all stop-words and counting types only (*'Non-stop types'*). Finally, we computed all of these ROUGE variants using raw text as well as lemmatized text. As a result, we computed 72 different variants of ROUGE for each response and each combination of reference summaries: nine different types of ROUGE (eight different n-gram lengths and ROUGE-ALL) computed using four different methods of text processing and two possible approaches to lemmatization. All of the computations were done both on ASR and manual transcriptions.

3.3 Evaluation

We computed the Spearman's rank correlation between the metric and the holistic score assigned by the first rater to identify the best method of computing ROUGE and the optimal number of references. Performance of the metric may be affected by properties of the prompt (cf. (Nenkova and Louis, 2008)), therefore we first analyzed each prompt separately and then selected the variants that achieved the highest performance across all of the prompts. Since correlation coefficients are not normally distributed, we used several non-parametric methods to identify significant differences including non-parametric bootstrapping and non-parametric ANOVAs. These analyses were done using the data from the training partition of the corpus.

We then evaluated how well the selected variants of ROUGE predicted human scores using a linear regression model trained on all of the data from the training partition using pooled data from all of the prompts. The model was tested on an unseen test partition that had not been used for any of the analyses.

Finally, we tested whether the new metrics improved the performance of the automated scoring engine for spoken responses. The current system assigns scores based on the linear combination of features with empirical weights obtained by training scoring models on scores assigned by expert raters (Zechner et al., 2009; Higgins et al., 2011). Current features measure various aspects of speaking proficiency such as fluency, pronunciation, and grammar usage. The performance of the system is evaluated with correlations and quadratic kappas between the scores assigned by the human raters and rounded predicted scores.

4 Results

All analyses were performed twice: each for metrics computed using ASR and manual transcriptions. We found that although the exact values of the correlation coefficients differed across these two transcriptions, the overall pattern of results remained the same. There was also a high correlation in metric values between the two types of transcription (Pearson's r for different types of ROUGE varied between 0.81 for ROUGE-4 and 0.9 for ROUGE-1). Since automated scoring relies on the output of automatic speech recognition, all numerical results reported in the main text of this section are based on ASR output. The tables report the numbers for both ASR and manual transcriptions.

4.1 Number and choice of reference responses

Number of references. To identify the optimal number of references for each prompt and metrics, we first found N_{best}, which had the highest correlation with human scores and then identified the lowest number of reference summaries for which the correlation coefficient was not significantly lower than the correlation coefficient for N_{best}.

Comparisons between different correlations

were performed using the general method suggested by Zou (2007) for comparing overlapping correlations as implemented by Baguley (2012, p.224) but we used bootstrapped confidence intervals (Wilcox, 2009). Confidence intervals for each correlation coefficient were constructed using pigeonhole bootstrapping (Owen, 2007) with 1,000 samples. For each N reference, we pooled the values computed for 20 randomly selected sets of different reference summaries. We then independently sampled responses and sets of references and selected values at each bootstrap repetition at the intersection of the two samples. The confidence intervals were constructed using the adjusted percentile method (Davison and Hinkley, 1997, p. 203-213). Since this analysis is more sensitive to Type II errors ('false negatives'), we set the significance threshold at $\alpha = 0.15$.

The optimal number of references varied between prompts, metrics, and methods of computation, but never exceeded 8. On average, optimal performance was achieved with 3 references. More references were required to achieve optimal performance for ROUGE based on longer n-grams (using the Kruskal-Wallis test, a non-parametric analysis of variance, $p < 2.2 \times 10^{-16}$). For example, two references on average were required to achieve reliable results for ROUGE-1, but for ROUGE-4 this number was four references. The required number of references was also significantly dependent on the prompt (Kruskal-Wallis test, $p < 2.2 \times 10^{-16}$) with averages varying between two and four. When the number of references was equal to or greater than the optimal number, there were no significant differences in the correlation coefficients across the different reference models.

For the analysis in the following section each of the 72 variants of ROUGE for each prompt was computed using the optimal N references identified for this variant and prompt.

4.2 Types of ROUGE and different methods of computation

The correlation coefficients between the summarization metrics and human ratings depended on the length of n-grams (Kruskal-Wallis test $p < 2.2 \times 10^{-16}$). While all types of ROUGE were positively correlated with human ratings, the correlation coefficients were the highest for ROUGE-1 and ROUGE-SU2-4, which performed significantly better than ROUGE-3-4 and the combined measures ROUGE-ALL (post-hoc Tukey HSD test on ranked observations, p varied from $p < 1 \times 10^{-10}$ to 2.804×10^{-4}). The average correlations across the different types of text pre-processing for ASR and manual transcriptions are shown in Table 1.

Metrics	ASR output	Manual
ROUGE-1	0.616	0.637
ROUGE-SU4	0.592	0.608
ROUGE-SU3	0.595	0.609
ROUGE-SU2	0.594	0.613
ROUGE-SU1	0.598	0.619
ROUGE-ALL	0.523	0.527
ROUGE-2	0.553	0.560
ROUGE-3	0.468	0.461
ROUGE-4	0.366	0.357

Table 1: Average correlation coefficient with human scores (Spearman's ρ) across different methods of computation for ROUGE based on n-grams of different lengths. The table shows the results for metrics computed based on ASR and manual transcriptions.

The effect of text pre-processing differed across the metrics: for metrics that relied on consecutive n-grams with $n>2$, the removal of stop-words led to further drops in performance (Kruskal-Wallis test $p = 4.4 \times 10^{-5}$). For ROUGE based on unigrams and skip-bigrams, counting only type frequencies led to a significant improvement in performance (Kruskal-Wallis test, $p = 0.00017$). Correlations for the different types of pre-processing for the measures that performed the best are given in Table 2. Lemmatization did not make a significant difference to metric performance.

Pre-processing	ASR ouput	Manual
All	0.573	0.606
Non-stop	0.585	0.600
Non-stop types	0.601	0.617
Types	0.622	0.634

Table 2: Average correlation coefficient with human proficiency score (Spearman's ρ) across ROUGE-1 and ROUGE-SU1-4 for different methods of text processing. The table shows the results for metrics computed based on ASR output and manual transcriptions.

Finally, a summarization metric performed better on tasks that required the test takers to summarize an announcement or lecture (average $\bar{\rho} = 0.653$ for ROUGE-1 and ROUGE-SU1-4) rather than on tasks that required them to describe a picture sequence (average $\bar{\rho} = 0.437$, Mann-Whitney-Wilcox test, a non-parametric test for comparing two independent samples, $p < 2.2 \times 10^{-16}$).

4.3 Evaluation of the final model

Analysis by prompt showed that the variants of ROUGE that included unigram counts (ROUGE and ROUGE-SU1-4) had the best correlations with human scores across all prompts. Further improvement in their performance was obtained by counting type frequencies only and by using several reference summaries. The optimal *N* references for these variants of ROUGE varied between prompts, but never exceeded four which was therefore selected as the optimal *N* references for this corpus.

Based on these results we computed ROUGE-1 metrics for all responses in the original training partition using four randomly selected, highly scored responses for each prompt and *'types'* method of pre-processing. We then compared it with two baselines: (1) cosine distance (CVA) computed using type frequencies only and the same four references, and (2) naïve implementation of ROUGE-1 computed using one randomly selected reference summary and raw frequencies (tokens). The newly adjusted version of ROUGE-1 metrics performed significantly above the baselines (using Zou's method for the comparison of overlapping correlations with confidence intervals constructed at $\alpha = 0.001$). The correlation coefficients are shown in Table 3.

Metric	ASR output	Manual
New ROUGE-1	0.652	0.673
Base ROUGE-1	0.55	0.589
CVA	0.508	0.451

Table 3: Correlation coefficients with human scores (Spearman's ρ) for the entire training partition for the newly adjusted version of ROUGE and the baseline metrics. The table shows the results for metrics computed based on ASR and manual transcriptions.

We then trained a standard linear regression model using the human scores as the dependent variables and summarization metrics as independent variables. The accuracy of prediction was evaluated using two metrics as suggested, for example, by Williamson et al. (2012): quadratic weighted kappa (κ) and Pearson's correlation coefficient (r) between the observed and predicted scores. For computation of κ, the predicted scores were trimmed to the range of human scores and rounded to the nearest integer.

Repeated 10-fold cross-validation on the training partition showed that a model based on ROUGE-1 produced averages of $\bar{r} = 0.65$ ($\sigma = 0.031$) and $\bar{\kappa} = 0.54$ ($\sigma = 0.036$). The model based on a linear combination of several ROUGE variants using longer n-grams and a recursive feature elimination (Kuhn and Johnson, 2013, p. 480) did not show any improvement in the performance as compared to a model based on a single ROUGE-1.

Finally, we tested the performance of the metrics on an unseen test set that had not been used for any previous analyses. We tested both the model based solely on the content metric as well as on the performance of the content metrics in combination with 11 other features used for the automated scoring of spoken responses that measure pronunciation accuracy, prosody, fluency, and grammar. These results are presented in Table 4. Note that the performance of the content-only model based on the new ROUGE-1 was in line with the estimates obtained on the training set. Zou's method for comparing overlapping correlations showed that in all cases, the difference between the model based on an adjusted ROUGE and the baselines was significant at $\alpha = 0.001$. In line with previous results, the models based on manual transcriptions showed better agreement with human scores than the models based on ASR output.

Table 4 shows that the addition of content metrics lead to relatively small increase in the performance of the integrated models. This is due to the fact that for most speakers different aspects of proficiency tend to be correlated. For example, more fluent speakers also achieve higher ROUGE scores (the correlation between ROUGE and pronunciation accuracy (Chen et al., 2009) is $r = 0.62$). As a result, a model which measures only one aspect of performance such as fluency may sometimes reach near optimal performance and adding further predictors leads to a relatively small gain. When interpreting these results, it is important to bear in mind that empirical performance is only

Model	ASR		Manual	
	r	κ	r	κ
Content only				
CVA	0.492	0.340	0.469	0.303
Base ROUGE	0.587	0.440	0.632	0.489
New ROUGE	0.655	0.540	0.700	0.590
Integrated model				
No content	0.678	0.565	0.678	0.565
CVA	0.691	0.600	0.698	0.602
Base ROUGE	0.700	0.597	0.719	0.610
New ROUGE	0.715	0.617	0.738	0.652

Table 4: Performance of the linear regression model based on one content metric and an 'integrated' model based on 11 features that measure pronunciation, fluency, and grammar before and after the addition of 'Base ROUGE,' 'CVA' or 'New ROUGE.' The table shows the correlation coefficients (Pearson's r) and quadratic weighted kappa kappas (κ) between the predicted scores and human ratings for the unseen test set. The agreement between the two expert raters on this dataset is $\kappa = 0.69$.

one aspect of evaluation of automated scoring systems. In addition to high agreement with human scores, operational automatic scoring systems also need to show good construct representation by covering different aspects of speaker performance (Williamson et al., 2012). This requirement ensures the validity of automated scores and prevents future test-takers from fine-tuning their performance to one particular feature measured by the scoring system. Therefore the addition of ROUGE to the automated scoring model serves both goals: it improves the agreement with human raters and also expands the construct coverage of the model.

5 Discussion

Summarization metrics can be successfully used to evaluate spoken summaries in the context of language assessment. Although the naïve implementation of ROUGE had good agreement with the scores assigned by human raters, several modifications led to a further increase in the performance.

Some of our findings show common patterns with what has previously been reported for written summaries. ROUGE-1, ROUGE-SU4 and ROUGE-2 are the three variants of ROUGE most commonly used for the evaluation of automatic text summaries. Our results showed that the first two of these measures (ROUGE-1 and ROUGE-SU4) were also most suitable for content assessment of spoken responses. We note that both of these measures include unigram counts. More recently, Rankel et al. (2013) and Owczarzak et al. (2012) reported that metrics based on longer consecutive n-grams or linear combinations of different variants are more accurate. We did not find this for our data. Since our data represents abstractive summaries, poor performances of longer n-grams is not surprising. Finally, as in the case of written summaries, there was no effect of lemmatization while the removal of stop-words sometimes led to a decrease in performance.

Similar to written summaries, the use of more than one reference summary improved the performance. We found that the optimal number of reference summaries varied between prompts and metrics. For ROUGE-1, this number never exceeded four across all prompts in our corpus. Furthermore, we found that the choice of reference summaries from the pool of highly scored responses had no significant effect on the performance of the metric.

In addition to good agreement with human scores, metrics used for automated scoring also need to match the construct of interest, as defined by the assessment program (Williamson et al., 2012). The scoring guidelines for the tasks used in this paper ask raters to judge whether the key information contained in the prompt has been conveyed accurately. A notable difference between ROUGE and previously used metrics is that as a recall measure, ROUGE does not penalize for the lack of precision. Our results suggest that a recall-oriented approach has better agreement with human judgments than cosine distance which combines both precision and recall.

Recall-based approaches are sensitive to the length of candidate responses. In the case of automatic summary evaluation, the length of the summaries is limited to a predefined number of words. In this data, the length of the responses is limited more loosely by the time available to record the response and the actual number of words varied between the responses. Therefore, a recall-based approach may produce inflated scores by assigning higher metric values to a response which contains multiple repetitions of the same n-gram as long as the n-gram occurs several times in the reference response. The common occurrence of repairs and repetitions in spoken speech further aggravates this problem further. We addressed this issue by only counting type frequencies, which also improved agreement with human judgments.

The adjusted metric had better agreement with human judgments than other "bag-of-words" approaches such as the cosine-based measure commonly used for content scoring that requires a much larger set of model responses than ROUGE. It also performed equally well on human and ASR transcriptions and did not require any manual annotation of the data. We also found that the performance of ROUGE depended on the task: we obtained better agreement for tasks that required the student to summarize a stimulus rather than tasks that required the student to describe a sequence of pictures. While in both cases the students produced short summary-like texts, the picture description task allowed for greater variability between the responses than the summarization task and, therefore, recall-oriented comparisons with highly-scored responses showed less agreement with human scores.

As a "bag-of-words" approach, ROUGE-1 has the same shortcomings as other methods discussed in Section 2.2 in that it doesn't distinguish between syntactic roles. While variants based on longer *n*-grams could in theory address this, our results showed that neither a linear nor a geometric combination of these variants with ROUGE-1 improved agreement with human scores. This issue has also been acknowledged in the context of non-extractive text summarization and new metrics such as AutoSummEng (Giannakopoulos and Karkaletsis, 2011) have been developed to address it. Future research will include the conceptualization and development of metrics that can address the content accuracy of spoken summaries beyond the 'bag-of-words' approach.

6 Conclusion

In this paper we applied ROUGE, a recall-based metrics for evaluation of written summaries to the automatic assessment of spoken summaries produced by non-native speakers of English. We performed a thorough evaluation of different types of ROUGE by varying the length of *n*-grams, various methods of frequency computation, and text-preprocessing. We also explored the effect of the number of reference summaries. We found that the standard baseline implementation of ROUGE-1 computed over the output of the automated speech recognizer showed good agreement with expert ratings and performed better than the cosine similarity measure commonly used for the evaluation content of spoken responses. A further increase in agreement with human ratings could be achieved by using types instead of tokens for the frequency computation of both candidate and reference summaries. We also found that the use of several reference summaries improves the performance of the metric, but only four reference summaries were necessary to achieve reliable results.

Acknowledgments

We would like to thank Keelan Evanini, Nitin Madnani, Xinhao Wang, Derrick Higgins and three anonymous reviewers for their helpful comments and suggestions and René Lawless for editing assistance.

References

Yigal Attali and Jill Burstein. 2006. Automated essay scoring with e-rater V. 2. *The Journal of Technology, Learning and Assessment*, 4(3):1–30.

Thomas Baguley. 2012. *Serious Stats: A guide to advanced statistics for the behavioral sciences*. Palgrave Macmillan.

Douglas Biber, Susan M. Conrad, Randi Reppen, Pat Byrd, Marie Helt, Victoria Clark, Viviana Cortes, Eniko Csomay, and Alfredo Urzua. 2004. *Representing language use in the university: analysis of TOEFL 2000 Spoken and Written academic language corpus*. Educational Testing Service, Princeton.

Miao Chen and Klaus Zechner. 2012. Using an ontology for improved automated content scoring of spontaneous non-native speech. In *Proceedings of the 7th Workshop on Building Educational Applications Using NLP*, pages 86–94, Stroudsburg, PA. Association for Computational Linguistics.

Lei Chen, Klaus Zechner, and Xiaoming Xi. 2009. Improved pronunciation features for construct-driven assessment of non-native spontaneous speech. In *Proceedings of Human Language Technologies: The 2009 Annual Conference of the North American Chapter of the Association for Computational Linguistics*, NAACL '09, pages 442–449, Stroudsburg, PA, USA. Association for Computational Linguistics.

Lei Chen. 2013. Applying unsupervised learning to support vector space model based speaking assessment. *Proceedings of the 8th Workshop on Innovative Use of NLP for Building Educational Applications, Atlanta, Georgia*, pages 58–62.

Anthony C. Davison and David V. Hinkley. 1997. *Bootstrap Methods and their Application (Cambridge Series in Statistical and Probabilistic Mathematics)*. Cambridge University Press.

Keelan Evanini and Xinhao Wang. 2013. Automated speech scoring for non-native middle school students with multiple task types. *Proceedings of Interspeech 2013, Lyon, France*, pages 2435–2439.

Peter W. Foltz, Darrell Laham, and Thomas K. Landauer. 1999. Automated essay scoring: applications to educational technology. In B. Collis and R. Oliver, editors, *Proceedings of World Conference on Educational Multimedia, Hypermedia and Telecommunications 1999*, pages 939–944.

George Giannakopoulos and Vangelis Karkaletsis. 2011. AutoSummENG and MeMoG in Evaluating Guided Summaries. In *TAC 2011 Workshop*, Gaithersburg, MD, USA. NIST.

Derrick Higgins, Xiaoming Xi, Klaus Zechner, and David Williamson. 2011. A three-stage approach to the automated scoring of spontaneous spoken responses. *Computer Speech & Language*, 25(2):282–306, April.

Makoto Hirohata, Yousuke Shinnaka, Koji Iwano, and Sadaoke Furui. 2005. Sentence extraction-based presentation summarization techniques and evaluation metrics. In *Acoustics, Speech, and Signal Processing, 2005. Proceedings. (ICASSP '05). IEEE International Conference on*, volume 1, pages 1065–1068.

Max Kuhn and Kjell Johnson. 2013. *Applied Predictive Modeling*. Springer.

Chin-Yew Lin and Marina Rey. 2004. ROUGE: A package for automatic evaluation of summaries. In Stan Szpakowicz Marie-Francine Moens, editor, *Text Summarization Branches Out: Proceedings of the ACL-04 Workshop*, pages 74–81, Barcelona, Spain. Association for Computational Linguistics.

Chin-Yew Lin. 2004. Looking for a few good metrics: Automatic summarization evaluation - how many samples are enough. In *Proceedings of the NTCIR Workshop*, pages 1765–1776, Tokyo.

Annie Louis and A Nenkova. 2013. Automatically assessing machine summary content without a gold standard. *Computational Linguistics*, 39(2):267–300.

Nitin Madnani, Jill Burstein, John Sabatini, and Tenaha O'Reilly. 2013. Automated scoring of a summary-writing task designed to measure reading comprehension. In *Proceedings of the 8th Workshop on Innovative Use of NLP for Building Educational Applications*, pages 163–168, Atlanta, Georgia. Association for Computational Linguistics.

Ani Nenkova and Annie Louis. 2008. Can you summarize this? Identifying correlates of input difficulty for generic multi-document summarization. In *Proceedings of the ACL-08: HLT*, pages 825–833. Association for Computational Linguistics.

Ani Nenkova and Kathleen McKeown. 2011. Automatic summarization. *Foundations and Trends in Information Retrieval*, 5(2-3):103–233.

Karolina Owczarzak, John M. Conroy, Hoa Trang Dang, and Ani Nenkova. 2012. An assessment of the accuracy of automatic evaluation in summarization. In *Proceedings of workshop on evaluation metrics and system comparison for automatic summarization.*, pages 1–9, Stroudsburg, PA. Association for Computational Linguistics.

Art B. Owen. 2007. The pigeonhole bootstrap. *The Annals of Applied Statistics*, 1(2):386–411.

Kishore Papineni, Salim Roukos, Todd Ward, and Wei-jing Zhu. 2002. BLEU : a Method for Automatic Evaluation of Machine Translation. In *Proceedings of the 40th Annual Meeting of the ACL*, pages 311–318, Philadelphia, PA. Association for Computational Linguistics.

Gerald Penn and Xiaodan Zhu. 2008. A Critical Reassessment of Evaluation Baselines for Speech Summarization. In *in Proceedings of RANLP workshop on Crossing Barriers in Text Summarization Research*, number June, pages 470–478, Columbus, Ohio, June. Association for Computational Linguistics.

Peter A. Rankel, John. M. Conroy, Hoa Trang Dang, and Ani Nenkova. 2013. A decade of automatic content evaluation of news summaries: reassessing the state of the art. In *Proceedings of the 51st Annual Meeting of the Association for Computational Linguistics, Sofia, Bulgaria, August 4-9, 2013*, pages 131–136, Sofia. Association for Computational Linguistics.

Rand R. Wilcox. 2009. Comparing Pearson correlations: dealing with heteroscedasticity and nonnormality. *Communications in Statistics - Simulation and Computation*, 38(10):2220–2234.

David M. Williamson, Xiaoming Xi, and F. Jay Breyer. 2012. A framework for evaluation and use of automated scoring. *Educational measurement: issues and practice*, 31(1):2–13.

Shasha Xie, Keelan Evanini, and Klaus Zechner. 2012. Exploring content features for automated speech scoring. In *NAACL HLT '12 Proceedings of the 2012 Conference of the North American Chapter of the Association for Computational Linguistics: Human Language Technologies*, pages 103–111.

Wenting Xiong, Keelan Evanini, Klaus Zechner, and Lei Chen. 2013. Automated content scoring of spoken responses containing multiple parts with factual information. In Pierre Badin, Thomas Hueber, Gérard Bailly, Didier Demolin, and Françoise Raby, editors, *Proceedings of SLaTE 2013, Grenoble, France*, pages 137–142, Grenoble.

Klaus Zechner, Derrick Higgins, Xiaoming Xi, and David M. Williamson. 2009. Automatic scoring of non-native spontaneous speech in tests of spoken English. *Speech Communication*, 51(10):883–895.

Guang Yong Zou. 2007. Toward using confidence intervals to compare correlations. *Psychological methods*, 12(4):399–413.

An Explicit Feedback System for Preposition Errors based on Wikipedia Revisions

Nitin Madnani and **Aoife Cahill**
Educational Testing Service
660 Rosedale Road
Princeton, NJ 08541, USA
{nmadnani,acahill}@ets.org

Abstract

This paper presents a proof-of-concept tool for providing automated explicit feedback to language learners based on data mined from Wikipedia revisions. The tool takes a sentence with a grammatical error as input and displays a ranked list of corrections for that error along with evidence to support each correction choice. We use lexical and part-of-speech contexts, as well as query expansion with a thesaurus to automatically match the error with evidence from the Wikipedia revisions. We demonstrate that the tool works well for the task of preposition selection errors, evaluating against a publicly available corpus.

1 Introduction

A core feature of learning to write is receiving feedback and making revisions based on that feedback (Biber et al., 2011; Lipnevich and Smith, 2008; Truscott, 2007; Rock, 2007). In the field of second language acquisition, the main focus has been on *explicit* or *direct* feedback vs. *implicit* or *indirect* feedback. In writing, explicit or direct feedback involves a clear indication of the location of an error as well as the correction itself, or, more recently, a meta-linguistic explanation (of the underlying grammatical rule). Implicit or indirect written feedback indicates that an error has been made at a location, but it does not provide a correction.

The work in this paper describes a novel tool for presenting language learners with explicit feedback based on human-authored revisions in Wikipedia. Here we describe the proof-of-concept tool that provides explicit feedback on one specific category of grammatical errors, preposition selection. We restrict the scope of the tool in order to be able to carry out a focused study, but expect that our findings presented here will also generalize to other error types. The task of preposition selection errors has been well studied (Tetreault and Chodorow, 2008; De Felice and Pulman, 2009; Tetreault et al., 2010; Rozovskaya and Roth, 2010; Dahlmeier and Ng, 2011; Seo et al., 2012; Cahill et al., 2013), and the availability of public, annotated corpora containing such errors provides easy access to evaluation data.

Our tool takes a sentence with a grammatical error as input, and returns a *ranked* list of possible corrections. The tool makes use of frequency of correction in edits to Wikipedia articles (as recorded in the Wikipedia revision history) to calculate the rank order. In addition to the ranked list of suggestions, the tool also provides evidence for each correction based on the actual changes made between different versions of Wikipedia articles. The tool uses the notion of "context similarity" to determine whether a particular edit to a Wikipedia article can provide evidence of a correction in a given context.

Specifically, this paper makes the following contributions:

1. We build a tool to provide explicit feedback for preposition selection errors in the form of ranked lists of suggested corrections.
2. We use evidence from human-authored corrections for each suggested correction on a list.
3. We conduct a detailed examination of how the performance of the tool is affected by varying the type and size of contextual information and by the use of query expansion.

The remainder of this paper is organized as follows: §2 describes related work and §3 outlines potential approaches for using Wikipedia revision data in a feedback tool. §4 outlines the core system

Proceedings of the Ninth Workshop on Innovative Use of NLP for Building Educational Applications , pages 79–88,
Baltimore, Maryland USA, June 26, 2014.

for generating feedback and §5 presents an empirical evaluation of this system. In §6 we describe a method for enhancing the system using query expansions. We discuss our findings and some future work in §7 and, finally, conclude in §8.

2 Related Work

Attali (2004) examines the general effect of feedback in the Criterion system (Burstein et al., 2003) and finds that students presented with feedback are able to improve the overall quality of their writing, as measured by an automated scoring system. This study does not investigate different kinds of feedback, but rather looks at the issue of whether feedback in general is useful for students. Shermis et al. (2004) look at groups of students who used Criterion and students who did not and compare their writing performance as measured by high-stakes state assessment. They found that, in general, the students who made use of Criterion and its feedback improved their writing skills. They analyze the distributions of the individual grammar and style error types and found that Criterion helped reduce the number of repeated errors, particularly for mechanics (e.g. spelling and punctuation errors). Chodorow et al. (2010) describe a small study in which Criterion provided feedback about article errors to students writing an essay for a college-level course. They find, similarly to Attali (2004), that the number of article errors was reduced in the final revised version of the essay.

Gamon et al. (2009) describe *ESL Assistant* — a web-based proofreading tool designed for language learners who are native speakers of East-Asian languages. They used a decision-tree approach to detect and offer suggestions for potential article and preposition errors. They also allowed the user to compare the various suggestions by showing results of corresponding web searches. Chodorow et al. (2010) also describe a small study where *ESL Assistant* was used to offer suggestions for potential grammatical errors to web users while they were composing email messages. They reported that users were able to make effective use of the explicit feedback for that task. The tool had been offered as a web service but has since been discontinued.

Our tool is similar to *ESL Assistant* in that both produce a list of possible corrections. The main difference between the tools is that ours automatically derives the ranked list of correction suggestions from a very large corpus of annotated errors, rather than performing a web search on all possible alternatives in the context. The advantage of using an error-annotated corpus is that it contains implicit information about frequent confusion pairs (e.g. "at" instead of "in") that are independent of the frequency of the preposition and the current context.

Milton and Cheng (2010) describe a toolkit for helping Chinese learners of English become more independent writers. The toolkit gives the learners access to online resources including web searches, online concordance tools, and dictionaries. Users are provided with snapshots of the word or structure in context. In Milton (2006), 500 revisions to 323 journal entries were made using an earlier version of this tool. Around 70 of these revisions had misinterpreted the evidence presented or were careless mistakes; the remaining revisions resulted in more natural sounding sentences.

3 Wikipedia Revisions

Our goal is to build a tool that can provide explicit feedback about errors to writers. We take advantage of the recently released Wikipedia preposition error corpus (Cahill et al., 2013) and design our tool based on this large corpus containing sentences annotated for preposition errors and their corrections. The corpus was produced automatically by mining a total of 288 million revisions for 8.8 million articles present in a Wikipedia XML snapshot from 2011. The Wikipedia error corpus, as we refer to in the rest of the paper, contains 2 million sentences annotated with preposition errors and their respective corrections.

There are two possible approaches to building an explicit feedback tool for preposition errors based on this corpus:

1. **Classifier-based**. We could train a classifier on the Wikipedia error corpus to predict the correct preposition in a given context, as Cahill et al. (2013) did. Although this would allow us to suggest corrections for contexts that are unseen in the Wikipedia data, the suggestions would likely be quite noisy given the inherent difficulty of a classification problem with a large number of classes.[1] In addition, this approach would not facilitate pro-

[1]Cahill et al. (2013) used a list of 36 prepositions as classes.

viding evidence for each correction to the user.

2. **Corpus-based**. We could use the Wikipedia error corpus *directly* for feedback. Although this means that suggestions can only be generated for contexts occurring in the Wikipedia data, it also means that all suggestion would be grounded in actual revisions made by other humans on Wikipedia.

We believe that anchoring suggestions to human-authored corrections affords greater utility to a language learner, in line with the current practice in lexicography that emphasizes authentic usage examples (Collins COBUILD learner's dictionary, Sketch Engine (Kilgarriff et al., 2004)). Therefore, in this paper, we choose the second approach to build our tool.

4 Methodology

In order to use the Wikipedia error corpus directly for feedback, we first index the sentences in the corpus using the following fields:

- The incorrect preposition.
- The correct preposition.
- The words, bigrams, and trigrams before (and after) the preposition error (indexed separately).
- The part-of-speech tags, tag bigrams, and tag trigrams before (and after) the error (indexed separately).
- The title and URL of the Wikipedia article in which the sentence occurred.
- The ID of the article revision containing the preposition error.
- The ID of the article revision in which the correction was made.

Once the index is constructed, eliciting explicit feedback is straightforward. The input to the system is a tokenized sentence with a marked up preposition error (e.g. from an automated preposition error detection system). For each input sentence, the Wikipedia index is then searched with the identified preposition error and the words (or n-grams) present in its context. The index returns a list of the possible corrections occurring in the given context. The tool then counts how often each possible preposition is returned as a possible correction and orders its suggestions from most frequent to least frequent. In addition, the tool also displays five randomly chosen sentences from the index as evidence for each correction in order to help the learner make a better choice. The tool can use either the lexical n-grams (n=1,2,3) or the part-of-speech n-grams (n=1,2,3) around the error for the contextualized search of the Wikipedia index.

Figure 1 shows a screenshot of the tool in operation. The input sentence is entered into the text box at the top, with the preposition error enclosed in asterisks. In this case, the tool is using parts-of-speech on either side of the error for context. By default, the tool shows the top five possible corrections as a bar chart, sorted according to how many times the erroneous preposition was changed to the correction in the Wikipedia revision index. In this example, the preposition *of* with the left context of `<DT, NNS>` and the right context of `<DT, NN>` was changed to the preposition *in* 242 times in the Wikipedia revisions. When the user clicks on a bar, the box on the top shows the sentence with the change and the gray box on the right shows 5 (randomly chosen) actual sentences from Wikipedia where the change represented by the bar was made.

If parts-of-speech are chosen as context, the tool uses WebSockets to send the sentence to the Stanford Tagger (Toutanova et al., 2003) in the background and compute its part-of-speech tags before searching the index.

5 Evaluation

In order to determine how well the tool performs at suggesting corrections, we used sentences containing preposition errors from the **CLC FCE dataset**. The CLC FCE Dataset is a collection of 1,244 exam scripts written by learners of English as part of the Cambridge ESOL First Certificate in English (Yannakoudakis et al., 2011). Our evaluation set consists of 3,134 sentences, each containing a single preposition error.

We evaluate the tool on two criteria:

- **Coverage**. We define coverage as the proportion of errors for which the tool is able to suggest any corrections.
- **Accuracy**. The obvious definition of accu-

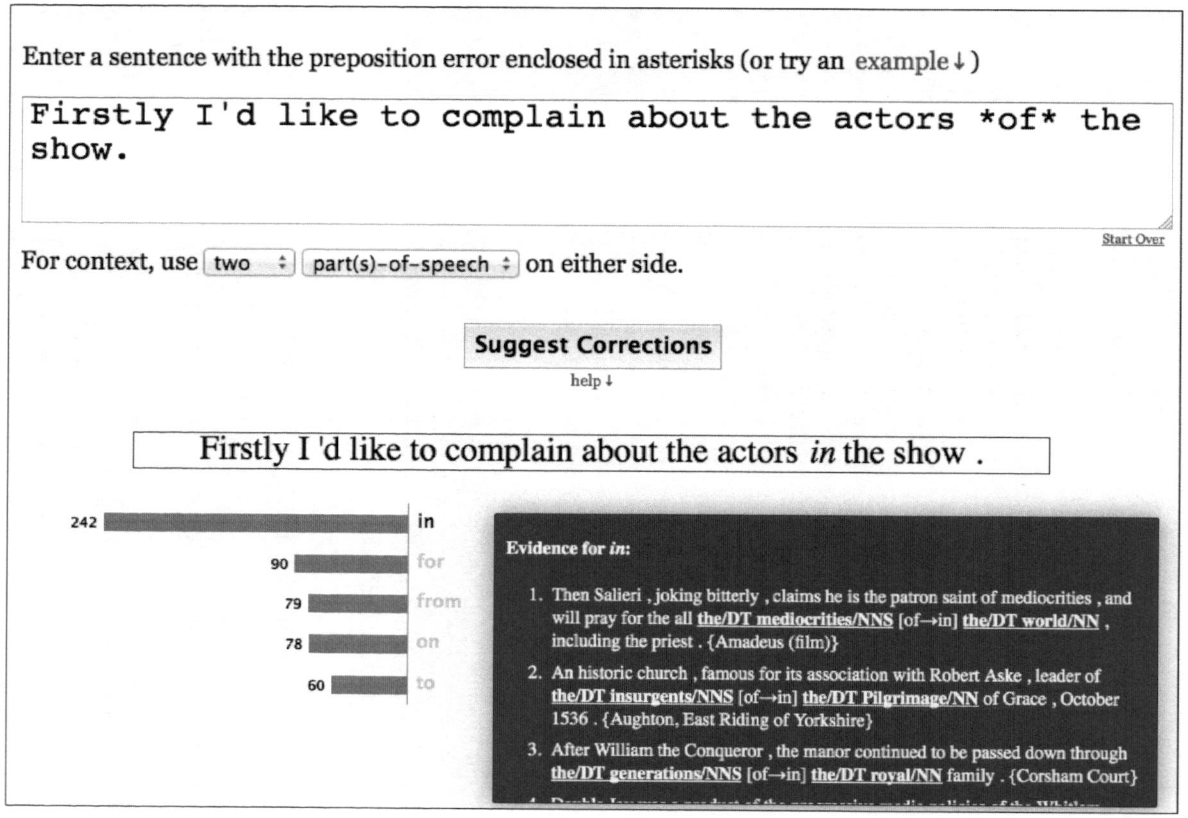

Figure 1: A screenshot of the tool suggesting the top 5 corrections for a sentence using two parts-of-speech on either side of the marked error as context. The corrections are displayed in ranked fashion as a histogram and clicking on one displays the "corrected" sentence above and the corresponding evidence from Wikipedia revisions on the left.

Context	Found	Missed	Blank	MRR
`words1`	889 (28.4%)	356 (11.4%)	1889 (60.3%)	.522
`words2`	55 (1.8%)	22 (0.7%)	3057 (97.5%)	.619
`words3`	16 (0.5%)	5 (0.2%)	3113 (99.3%)	.762
`tags1`	2821 (90.0%)	241 (7.7%)	72 (2.3%)	.419
`tags2`	1896 (60.5%)	718 (22.9%)	520 (16.6%)	.390
`tags3`	661 (21.1%)	633 (20.2%)	1840 (58.7%)	.325

Table 1: A detailed breakdown of the **Found**, **Missing** and **Blank** classes along with the Mean Reciprocal Rank (MRR) values, for different types (`words`, `tags`) and sizes (`1`, `2`, or `3` around the error) of contextual information used in the search.

racy would be the proportion of errors for which the tool's best suggestion is the correct one. However, since the tool returns a ranked list of suggestions, it is important to award partial credit for errors where the tool made a correct suggestion but it was not ranked at the top. Therefore, we use the Mean Reciprocal Rank (MRR), a standard metric used for evaluating ranked retrieval systems (Voorhees, 1999). MRR is computed as follows:

$$\text{MRR} = \frac{1}{|S|} \sum_{i=1}^{|S|} \frac{1}{R_i}$$

where S denotes the set of sentences for which ranked lists of suggestions are generated and R_i denotes the rank of the true correction in the list of suggestions the tool returns for sentence i. A higher MRR is better since that means that the tool ranked the true correction closer to the top of the list.

To conduct the evaluation on the FCE dataset, we run each of the sentences through the tool and extract the top 5 suggestions for each error annotated in the sentence.[2] At this point, each error instance input to the tool can be classified as one of three classes:

1. **Found**. The true correction for the error was found in the ranked list of suggestions made by the tool.

2. **Missing**. The true correction for the error was *not* found in the ranked list of suggestions.

3. **Blank**. The tool did not return any suggestions for the error.

[2]In this paper, we separate the tasks of error detection and correction and use the gold standard as an oracle to detect errors and then use our system to propose and rank corrections.

First, we examine the distribution of the three classes across the types and sizes of the contextual information used to conduct the search. Table 1 shows, for each context type and size, a detailed breakdown of the distribution of the three classes along with the mean reciprocal rank (MRR) values.[3] We observe that, with words as contexts, using larger contexts certainly produces more accurate results (as indicated by the larger MRR values). However, we also observe that employing larger contexts reduces coverage (as indicated by the decreasing percentage of **Found** sentences and by the the increasing percentage of the **Blank** sentences).

With part-of-speech tags, we observe that although using larger tag contexts can find corrections for a significantly larger number of sentences as compared to similar-sized word contexts (as indicated by the larger percentages of **Found** sentences), doing so yields overall worse MRR values. This is primarily due to the fact that with larger part-of-speech contexts the system produces more suggestions that never contain the true correction, i.e., an increasing percentage of **Missed** sentences. The most likely reason is that significantly reducing the vocabulary size by using part-of-speech tags introduces a lot of noise.

Figure 2 shows the distribution of the rank R of the true correction in the list of suggestions.[4] The figure uses a rank of 10+ to denote all ranks greater than 10 to conserve space. We observe similar trends in the figure as in Table 1 — using larger word contexts yield higher accuracies but significantly lower coverage and using larger

[3]We do not include **Blank** sentences when computing the MRR values.

[4]Note that in this figure, the bar for $R = 0$ includes both sentences where no ranked list was produced (**Blank**) and those where the true correction was not produced as a suggestion at all (**Missing**).

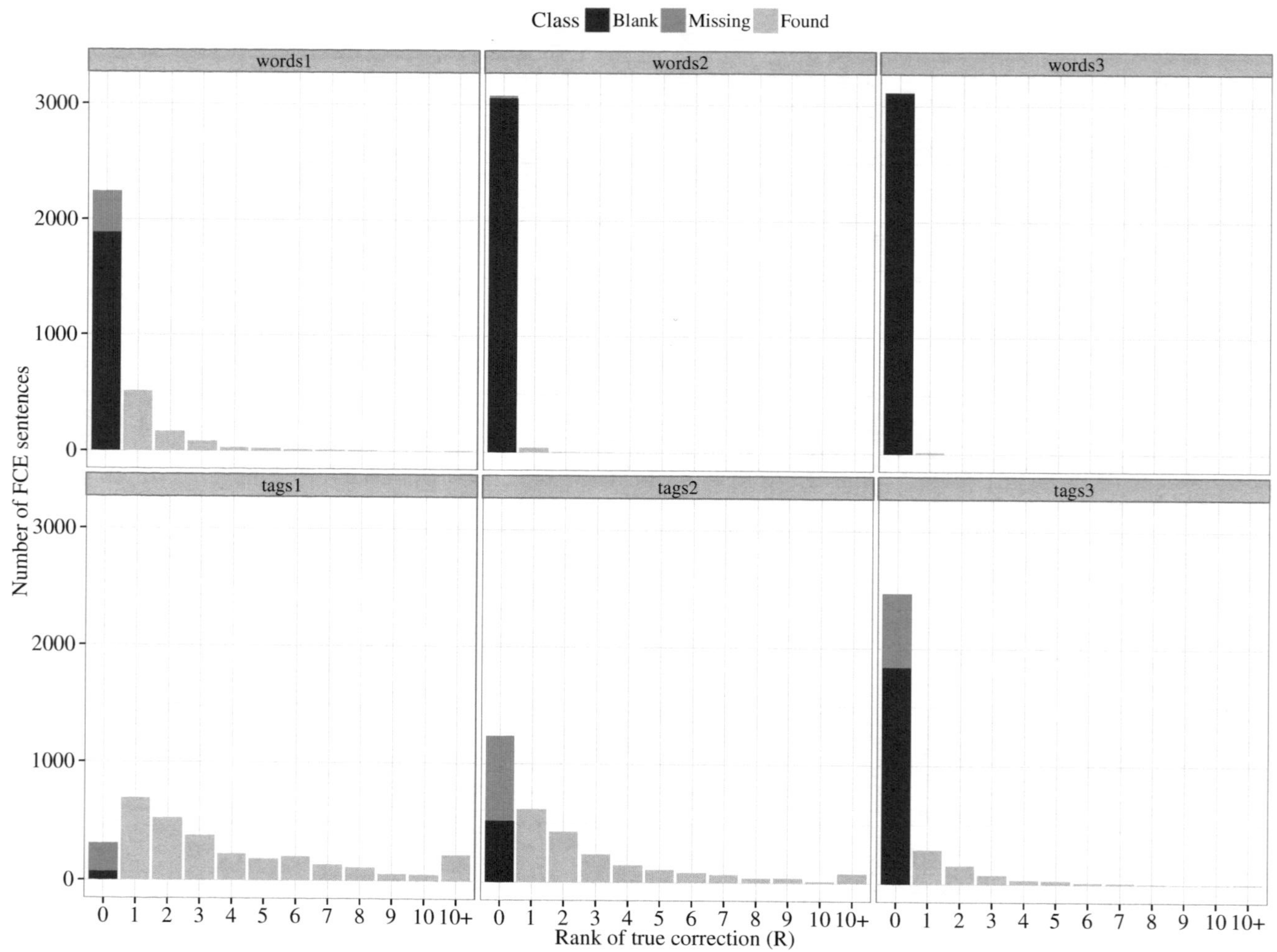

Figure 2: The distribution of the rank that the true correction has in the list of suggestions for the FCE sentences, across each context type and size used.

tag contexts yield lower accuracies and lower coverage, even though the coverage is significantly larger than that of the correspondingly sized word context.

6 Query Expansion

The results in the previous section indicate that although we could use part-of-speech tags as contexts to improve the coverage of the tool (as indicated by the number of **Found** sentences), doing so leads to a significant reduction in accuracy, as indicated by the lower MRR values.

In the field of information retrieval, a common practice is to expand the query with words similar to words in the query in order to increase the likelihood of finding documents relevant to the query (Spärck-Jones and Tait, 1984). In this section, we examine whether we can use a similar technique to improve the coverage of the tool.

We employ a simple query expansion technique for the cases where no results would otherwise be returned by the tool. For these cases, we first obtain a list of K words similar to the two words around the error from a distributional thesaurus (Lin, 1998), ranked by similarity. We then generate a list of additional queries by combining these two ranked lists of similar words. We then run each query in the list against the Wikipedia index until one of them yields results. Note that since we are using a word-based thesaurus, this expansion technique can only increase coverage when applied to the `words1` condition, i.e., single word contexts. We investigate K = 1, 2, 5, or 10 expansions for each of the context words.

Table 2 shows the a detailed breakdown of the distribution of the three classes and the MRR values with query expansion integrated into the tool for sentences where it would generally produce no output. Each row corresponds to a different value of K – the number of expansions used per context word – is varied. Note that $K = 0$ corresponds to the condition where query expansion is not used. From the table, we observe that using query expansion indeed seems to increase the coverage of the tool as indicated by the increasing percentage of **Found** sentences and decreasing percentage of **Blank** sentences. However, we also find that using query expansion yields worse MRR values, again because of the increasing percentage of **Missed** sentences. This represents a traditional trade-off scenario where accuracy can be traded off for an increase in coverage, depending on the desired operating characteristics.

7 Discussion and Future Work

There are several issues that merit further discussion and possibly provide future extensions to the work described in this paper.

- **Need for an extrinsic evaluation**. Although our intrinsic evaluation clearly shows that the tool has reasonably good coverage as well as accuracy on publicly available data containing preposition errors, it does not provide any evidence that the explicit feedback provided by the tool is useful to English language learners in a classroom setting. In the future, we plan to conduct a controlled study in a classroom setting that measures, for example, whether the students that see the improved feedback from the tool learn more or better than those who either see no feedback at all or those who see only implicit feedback. Biber et al. (2011) review several previously published studies on the effects of feedback on writing development in classrooms. Although the number of studies that were included in the analysis is small, some patterns did emerge. In general, students improve their writing when they receive feedback, however greater gains are made when they are presented with comments rather than direct location and correction of errors. It is unclear how students would react to a ranked list of suggestions for a particular error at a given location. An interesting finding was that L2-English students showed greater improvements in writing when they received either feedback from peers or computer-generated feedback than when they received feedback from teachers.

- **Assuming a single true correction**. Our evaluation setup assumes that the single correction provided as part of the FCE data set is the only correct preposition for a given sentence. However, it is well known in the grammatical error detection community that this is not always the case. Most usage errors such as preposition selection errors are a matter of degree rather than simple rule violations such as number agreement. As a consequence, it is common for two native English speakers

Context	K	Found	Missed	Blank	MRR
`words1`	0	889 (28.4%)	356 (11.4%)	1889 (60.3%)	.522
`words1`	1	932 (29.7%)	417 (13.3%)	1785 (57.0%)	.513
`words1`	2	1033 (33.0%)	550 (17.6%)	1551 (49.5%)	.493
`words1`	5	1118 (35.7%)	691 (22.1%)	1325 (42.3%)	.476
`words1`	10	1160 (37.0%)	780 (24.9%)	1194 (38.1%)	.465

Table 2: A detailed breakdown of the **Found**, **Missing** and **Blank** classes along with the Mean Reciprocal Rank (MRR) values, for different number of query expansions (K).

to have different judgments of usage. In fact, this is exactly why the tool is designed to return a ranked list of suggestions rather than a single suggestion. Therefore, it is possible that our intrinsic evaluation is underestimating the performance of the tool.

- **Practical considerations for deployment**. In this study, we used the gold standard error annotations for detecting preposition errors before querying the tool for suggestions. Such a setup allowed us to separate the problems of error detection and the generation of feedback and likely gives an upper bound on performance. Using a fully automatic error detection system will likely introduce additional noise into the pipeline, however, we believe that tuning the detection system for higher precision could mitigate that effect. Another useful idea would be to use the classifier-based approach (see §3) as a backup for the corpus-based approach for providing suggestions, i.e., using the classifier to predict the suggested corrections when no corrections can be found in the Wikipedia revisions.

- **Using other types of expansions**. In this paper, we used a very simple method of generating query expansions – a distributional thesaurus. However, in the future, it may be worth exploring other distributional similarity methods such as Brown clusters (Brown et al., 1992; Miller et al., 2004; Liang, 2005) or *word2vec* (Mikolov et al., 2013).

8 Conclusions

In this paper, we presented our work on building a proof-of-concept tool that can provide automated explicit feedback for preposition errors. We used an existing, error-annotated preposition corpus produced by mining Wikipedia revisions (Cahill et al., 2013) to not only provide a ranked list of suggestions for any given preposition error but also to produce human-authored evidence for each suggested correction. The tool can use either words or part-of-speech tags around the error as context. We evaluated the tool in terms of both accuracy and coverage and found that: (1) using larger context window sizes for words increases accuracy but reduces coverage due to sparsity (2) using part-of-speech tags leads to increased coverage compared to using words as contexts but decreases accuracy. We also experimented with query expansion for single words around the error and found that it led to an increase in coverage with only a slight decrease in accuracy; using a larger set of expansions added more noise. In general, we find that the approach of using a large error-annotated corpus to provide explicit feedback to writers performs reasonably well in terms of providing ranked lists of alternatives. It remains to be seen how useful this tool is in a practical situation.

Acknowledgments

We would like to thank Beata Beigman Klebanov, Michael Heilman, Jill Burstein, and the anonymous reviewers for their helpful comments about the paper. We also thank Ani Nenkova, Chris Callison-Burch, Lyle Ungar and their students at the University of Pennsylvania for their feedback on this work.

References

Yigal Attali. 2004. Exploring the Feedback and Revision Features of *Criterion*. Paper presented at the National Council on Measurement in Education (NCME), Educational Testing Service, Princeton, NJ.

Douglas Biber, Tatiana Nekrasova, and Brad Horn. 2011. The Effectiveness of Feedback for L1-English and L2-Writing Development: A Meta-Analysis.

Research Report RR-11-05, Educational Testing Service, Princeton, NJ.

Peter F. Brown, Vincent J. Della Pietra, Peter V. de Souza, Jennifer C. Lai, and Robert L. Mercer. 1992. Class-Based n-gram Models of Natural Language. *Computational Linguistics*, 18(4):467–479.

Jill Burstein, Martin Chodorow, and Claudia Leacock. 2003. Criterion online essay evaluation: An application for automated evaluation of student essays. In *Proceedings of IAAI*, pages 3–10, Acapulco, Mexico.

Aoife Cahill, Nitin Madnani, Joel Tetreault, and Diane Napolitano. 2013. Robust Systems for Preposition Error Correction Using Wikipedia Revisions. In *Proceedings of NAACL*, pages 507–517, Atlanta, GA, USA.

Martin Chodorow, Michael Gamon, and Joel Tetreault. 2010. The Utility of Article and Preposition Error Correction Systems for English Language Learners: Feedback and Assessment. *Language Testing*, 27(3):419–436.

Daniel Dahlmeier and Hwee Tou Ng. 2011. Grammatical Error Correction with Alternating Structure Optimization. In *Proceedings of ACL-HLT*, pages 915–923, Portland, Oregon, USA.

Rachele De Felice and Stephen G. Pulman. 2009. Automatic detection of preposition errors in learner writing. *CALICO Journal*, 26(3):512–528.

Michael Gamon, Claudia Leacock, Chris Brockett, William B Dolan, Jianfeng Gao, Dmitriy Belenko, and Alexandre Klementiev. 2009. Using Statistical Techniques and Web Search to Correct ESL Errors. *CALICO Journal*, 26(3):491–511.

Adam Kilgarriff, Pavel Rychly, Pavel Smrz, and David Tugwell. 2004. The Sketch Engine. In *Proceedings of EURALEX*, pages 105–116.

Percy Liang. 2005. Semi-supervised Learning for Natural Language. Master's thesis, Massachusetts Institute of Technology.

Dekang Lin. 1998. Automatic Retrieval and Clustering of Similar Words. In *Proceedings of ACL-COLING*, pages 768–774, Montreal, Quebec, Canada.

Anastasiya A. Lipnevich and Jeffrey K. Smith. 2008. Response to Assessment Feedback: The Effects of Grades, Praise, and Source of Information. Research Report RR-08-30, Educational Testing Service, Princeton, NJ.

Tomas Mikolov, Ilya Sutskever, Kai Chen, Gregory S. Corrado, and Jeffrey Dean. 2013. Distributed Representations of Words and Phrases and their Compositionality. In *Proceedings of NIPS*, pages 3111–3119.

Scott Miller, Jethran Guinness, and Alex Zamanian. 2004. Name Tagging with Word Clusters and Discriminative Training. In *Proceedings of HLT-NAACL*, pages 337–342, Boston, MA, USA.

John Milton and Vivying SY Cheng. 2010. A Toolkit to Assist L2 Learners Become Independent Writers. In *Proceedings of the NAACL Workshop on Computational Linguistics and Writing: Writing Processes and Authoring Aids*, pages 33–41, Los Angeles, CA, USA.

John Milton. 2006. Resource-rich Web-based Feedback: Helping learners become Independent Writers. *Feedback in second language writing: Contexts and issues*, pages 123–139.

JoAnn Leah Rock. 2007. The Impact of Short-Term Use of Criterion on Writing Skills in Ninth Grade. Research Report RR-07-07, Educational Testing Service, Princeton, NJ.

Alla Rozovskaya and Dan Roth. 2010. Training Paradigms for Correcting Errors in Grammar and Usage. In *Proceedings of NAACL-HLT*, pages 154–162, Los Angeles, California.

Hongsuck Seo, Jonghoon Lee, Seokhwan Kim, Kyusong Lee, Sechun Kang, and Gary Geunbae Lee. 2012. A Meta Learning Approach to Grammatical Error Correction. In *Proceedings of ACL (short papers)*, pages 328–332, Jeju Island, Korea.

Mark D. Shermis, Jill C. Burstein, and Leonard Bliss. 2004. The Impact of Automated Essay Scoring on High Stakes Writing Assessments. In *Annual Meeting of the National Council on Measurement in Education*.

Karen Spärck-Jones and J. I. Tait. 1984. Automatic Search Term Variant Generation. *Journal of Documentation*, 40(1):50–66.

Joel R. Tetreault and Martin Chodorow. 2008. The Ups and Downs of Preposition Error Detection in ESL Writing. In *Proceedings of COLING*, pages 865–872, Manchester, UK.

Joel Tetreault, Jennifer Foster, and Martin Chodorow. 2010. Using Parse Features for Preposition Selection and Error Detection. In *Proceedings of ACL (short papers)*, pages 353–358, Uppsala, Sweden.

Kristina Toutanova, Dan Klein, Christopher D. Manning, and Yoram Singer. 2003. Feature-rich part-of-speech tagging with a cyclic dependency network. In *Proceedings of NAACL*, pages 173–180, Edmonton, Canada.

John Truscott. 2007. The Effect of Error Correction on Learners' Ability to Write Accurately. *Journal of Second Language Writing*, 16(4):255–272.

Ellen M. Voorhees. 1999. The TREC-8 Question Answering Track Report. In *Proceedings of the Text REtrieval Conference (TREC)*, volume 99, pages 77–82.

Helen Yannakoudakis, Ted Briscoe, and Ben Medlock. 2011. A New Dataset and Method for Automatically Grading ESOL Texts. In *Proceedings of the ACL: HLT*, pages 180–189, Portland, OR, USA.

Syllable and language model based features for detecting non-scorable tests in spoken language proficiency assessment applications

Angeliki Metallinou, Jian Cheng
Knowledge Technologies, Pearson
4040 Campbell Ave., Menlo Park, California 94025, USA
angeliki.metallinou@pearson.com jian.cheng@pearson.com

Abstract

This work introduces new methods for detecting non-scorable tests, i.e., tests that cannot be accurately scored automatically, in educational applications of spoken language proficiency assessment. Those include cases of unreliable automatic speech recognition (ASR), often because of noisy, off-topic, foreign or unintelligible speech. We examine features that estimate signal-derived syllable information and compare it with ASR results in order to detect responses with problematic recognition. Further, we explore the usefulness of language model based features, both for language models that are highly constrained to the spoken task, and for task independent phoneme language models. We validate our methods on a challenging dataset of young English language learners (ELLs) interacting with an automatic spoken assessment system. Our proposed methods achieve comparable performance compared to existing non-scorable detection approaches, and lead to a 21% relative performance increase when combined with existing approaches.

1 Introduction

Automatic language assessment systems are becoming a valuable tool in education, and provide efficient and consistent student assessment that can complement teacher assessment. Recently, there has been a great increase of English Language Learners (ELLs) in US education (Pearson, 2006). ELLs are students coming from non-English speaking backgrounds, and often require additional teacher attention. Thus, assessing ELL student language proficiency is a key issue.

Pearson has developed an automatic spoken assessment system for K-12 students and collected a large dataset of ELL students interacting with the system. This is a challenging dataset, containing accented speech and speech from young students. Thus, for a small percentage of tests, it is technically challenging to compute an accurate automatic score, often because of background/line noise, off-topic or non-English responses or unintelligible speech. Such tests as referred to as non-scorable. Here, our goal is to propose new methods for better classifying non-scorable tests and describe a system for non-scorable detection.

We propose two new sets of features: syllable based and language model (LM) based. The intuition is to contrast information from different sources when processing a test, in order to detect inconsistencies in automatic speech recognition (ASR), that often appear in non-scorable tests. Syllable features measure similarity between different estimates of syllable locations, one extracted from ASR and the second from the raw signal. LM features measure similarity between two ASR results, one using a standard item specific word LM, and the second using a item independent phoneme LM. Finally, an additional set of ASR confidence scores and log-likelihoods is computed using the proposed phoneme LM.

Compared to existing work, our new methods achieve comparable performance, although they approach the problem from a different perspective. Furthermore, our proposed features carry complementary information to existing ones, and lead to a 21% relative performance increase when combined with existing work.

2 Related Work

A review of spoken language technologies for education can be found in Eskanazi (2009). There is a considerable amount of previous work on automatic speech assessment. Pearson's automated speech scoring technologies that measure the candidates' speaking skill (pronunciation, flu-

Proceedings of the Ninth Workshop on Innovative Use of NLP for Building Educational Applications , pages 89–98,
Baltimore, Maryland USA, June 26, 2014.

ency, content) have been used in the Versant series tests: English, Aviation English, Junior English, Spanish, Arabic, French, Dutch, Chinese (Bernstein et al., 2000; Bernstein and Cheng, 2007; Cheng et al., 2009; Bernstein et al., 2010; Xu et al., 2012), and Pearson Test of English Academic (Pearson, 2011). A non-scorable detection component (Cheng and Shen, 2011) is usually required for such systems. Educational Testing Service described a three-stage system on spoken language proficiency scoring, that rates open-ended speech and includes a non-scorable detection component (Higgins et al., 2011).

The system described here evaluates spoken English skills of ELL students in manner and content. Past work on children's automatic assessment of oral reading fluency includes systems that score performance at the passage-level (Cheng and Shen, 2010; Downey et al., 2011) or word-level (Tepperman et al., 2007).

Regarding detecting problematic responses in speech assessment applications, related work includes off-topic and non-scorable detection. Non-scorable detection is a more general problem which includes not only off-topic responses, but also noisy, poor quality, foreign or unintelligible responses, etc. Higgins et al. (2011) describe a system that uses linear regression and four informative features (number of distinct words, average ASR confidence, average and standard deviation of speech energy) for filtering out non-scorable responses. Yoon et al. (2011) use a set of 42 signal-derived and ASR features along with a decision tree classifier for non-scorable response detection. Many of their features are also extracted here for comparison purposes (see Section 7).

Chen and Mostow (2011) focus on off-topic detection for a reading tutor application. They use signal features (energy, spectrum, cepstrum and voice quality features) and ASR features (percentage of off-topic words) with a Support Vector Machine (SVM) classifier. In our previous work (Cheng and Shen, 2011), we described an off-topic detection system, where we computed three variations for ASR confidence scores, along with features derived from acoustic likelihood, language model likelihood, and garbage modeling. Linear regression was used for classification.

Here, we focus on non-scorable test detection, using aggregate information from multiple test responses. We propose new similarity features that are derived from syllable location estimation and the use of a item independent phoneme LM.

3 The ELL student dataset

3.1 The asessment system

Pearson has developed an English proficiency assessment test, which has been administered in a large number of K-12 ELL students in a U.S. state. The speaking component of the test is delivered via speakerphone, and the student performance is automatically scored. Each tests consists of a series of spoken tasks which are developed by professional educators to elicit various displays of speaking ability. There are repeat tasks, where students repeat a short sentence, and open ended tasks, where students are required to answer questions about an image or a topic, give instructions, ask a question about an image, etc. Each test contains multiple test prompts (also referred to as items), some of which may belong to the same task. For example, for the 'question about image' task, there may be items refering to different images. Each test contains student responses to the items. Responses which are typically two or three sentences long.

Figure 1 summarizes the components of Pearson's automatic proficiency assessment system. Assessment is done through combination of ASR, speech and text processing, and machine learning to capture the linguistic content, pronunciation and fluency of the student's responses. In this work, we focus on the lower block of Figure 1 that illustrates the non-scorable detection component, whose purpose is to detect the tests that cannot be reliably scored. It exploits signal related and ASR information to extract features that are later used by a binary classifier to decide whether a test is scorable or not. Our goal is to filter out non-scorable tests, to be graded by humans. The proficiency assessment system (upper part of Figure 1) is described elsewhere (Cheng and Shen, 2010; Downey et al., 2011). The word error rate (WER) over the test set using the final acoustic models is around 35%.

3.2 The non-scorable tests

This research focuses on data obtained from four stages; elementary, primary, middle school and high school. Those consist of 6000 spoken tests (1500 per stage), of which 4800 were used for training (1200 per stage) and the remaining 1200

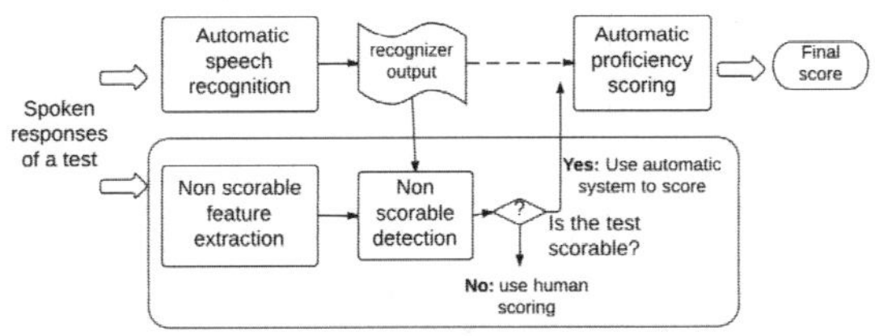

Figure 1: Outline of the assessment system. The lower block is the non-scorable test detection module, that is the focus of this work.

were used for testing. Professional human graders were recruited to provide a grade for each test response, following pre-defined rubrics per item. The grades per test are then summed up to compute an overall human grade in the range 0-14. Each test was double graded and the final human grade was computed by averaging. Our automatic scoring system was also used to estimate an overall machine grade in the range 0-14 for each test, after considering all student responses.

We define a test as non-scorable when the overall machine and human grades differ by more than 3 points. For our dataset of 6000 tests, only 308 (or approx. 5.1%) are non-scorable, according to this definition. Inspecting a subset of those tests, revealed various reasons that may cause a test to be non-scorable. Those include poor audio quality (recording or background noise, volume too loud or too soft), excessive mouth noises and vocalizations, foreign language, off-topic responses and unintelligible speech (extremely disfluent and mispronounced). As expected, the above issues are more common among younger test takers. Although the cases above can be very different, a commonality is that their ASR results are unreliable, therefore making subsequent automatic scoring inaccurate. In the following sections, we propose new methods for detecting problematic ASR outputs and filtering out non-scorable tests.

4 Syllable based features

The intuition behind the syllable based features is to compare information coming from the ASR component with information that is derived directly from the speech signal. If these two sources are inconsistent, this may indicate problems in the recognition output, which often results in non-scorable tests. Here, we focus on syllable locations as the type of information to compare. Syllable locations can be approximated as the vowel locations of the speech recognition output. Alternatively, they can be approximated using the speech pitch and intensity signals. By examining intensity, we may find intensity peaks that are preceded by intensity dips, and by examining pitch, we may select voiced intensity peaks as estimates of syllable locations. This method for identifying syllables was described by Jong and Wempe (2009), and the number of syllables has been used as a feature for non-scorable detection in Yoon et al. (2011). In this work, we propose to use the syllable information in order to compute features that measure similarities between signal-derived and ASR-derived syllable locations.

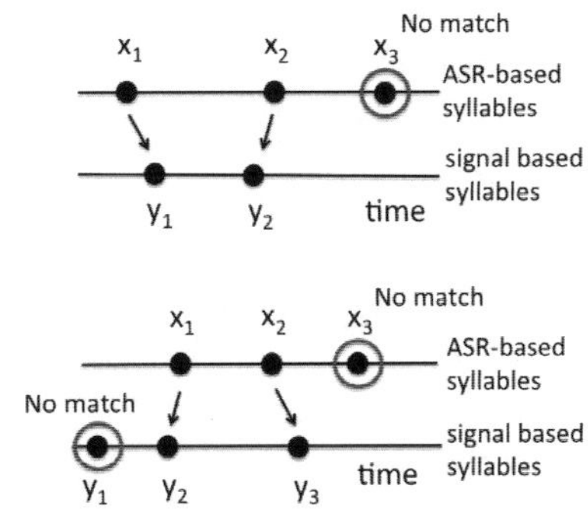

Figure 2: Two examples of mapping between ASR-derived and signal-derived syllable locations.

Assume that we have a sequence of n ASR-derived syllable locations: $X = \{x_1, x_2, \ldots, x_n\}$ and a sequence of m signal-derived locations: $Y = \{y_1, y_2, \ldots, y_m\}$. The first step in computing similarity features is finding a mapping between the two sequences. Specifically, we want to find an appropriate mapping that pairs points $(x_i, y_j), x_i \in X, y_j \in Y$ such that the smallest possible distances $d(x_i, y_j)$ are preferred. Potentially inconsistent points can be discarded. Two examples are presented in Figure 2. In the upper example $n > m$, therefore some syllable locations of the longer sequence will be discarded (here location x_3). In the lower example, although $n = m$, the mapping that produces location pairs with the smallest distances is (x_1, y_2) and (x_2, y_3), while locations y_1, x_3 will be discarded. A mapping (x_3, y_1) would be invalid as it violates time constraints, given the existing mappings. We use a greedy algorithm for finding the mapping, which iteratively searches all available valid paired locations and finds the pair (x_i, y_j) with the smallest distance. A mapping (x_i, y_j) is valid if no time constraints are violated, e.g., there is no previously selected mapping (x_k, y_l), where $k < i, l > j$ or $k > i, l < j$.

The algorithm is described in Algorithm 1. Our implementation is recursive: after finding the locations that define the best available mapping at each step, the algorithm is recursively called to search for mappings between points that are both either at the right subsequences, or at the left subsequences, with respect to the recent mapping. The right subsequences contain points on the right of the selected mapping (similarly for left subsequences). That way we avoid searching for mappings that would violate the time constraints.

Data: Syllable locations $X = \{x_1, x_2, \ldots, x_n\}$ and $Y = \{y_1, y_2, \ldots, y_m\}$
Result: Mapping between X and Y. Some locations in X or Y may be discarded
Compute pairwise distances: $d(x_i, y_j), x_i \in X, y_j \in Y$;
Set of pairs: $E =$ **mapping**$(1, n, 1, m)$;

function mapping(i, j, k, l) returns set of pairs ;
if $i > j$ *or* $k > l$ **then**
  return empty set
end
Find $\min(d(x_u, y_v)), u \in [i, j], v \in [k, l]$;
$E_{now} = (u, v)$;
//check left subsequences
$E_{left} =$ **mapping**$(i, u-1, k, v-1)$;
//check right subsequences
$E_{right} =$ **mapping**$(u+1, j, v+1, l)$;
return $union(E_{left}, E_{now}, E_{right})$;

Algorithm 1: Compute mapping between ASR-based and signal-based syllable locations

Based on the mapping of Algorithm 1, we estimate a set similarity features including number of pairs found, number of syllables that were not paired, the absolute length difference between the two sequences, as well as normalized versions of these features (we normalize the features by dividing with the maximum sequence length). For example, in the lower part of Figure 2, there are two pairs and the longest sequence has length three, so the normalized number of pairs found is $2/3$. Other features include average, min, max and standard deviation of the distances of the pairs found, as well as the lengths of the two sequences. These features are a set of descriptions of the quality of the mapping or, in other words, of the similarity between the two syllable sequences.

Algorithm 1 follows a greedy approach, however, one could derive a similar mapping using dynamic programming (DP) to minimize the average distance over all selected pairs. In practice, we do

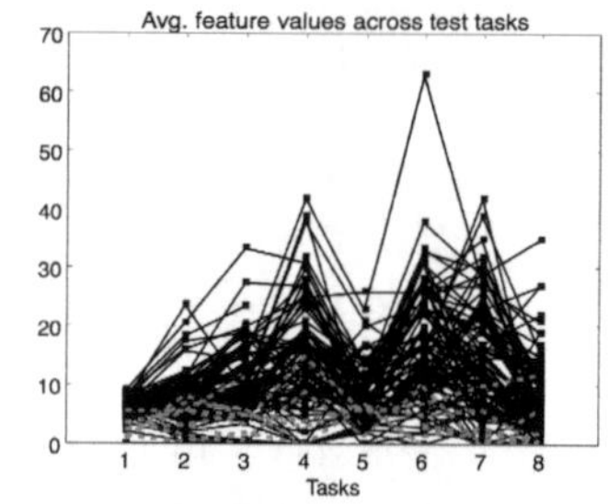

(a) Number of syllable pairs found.

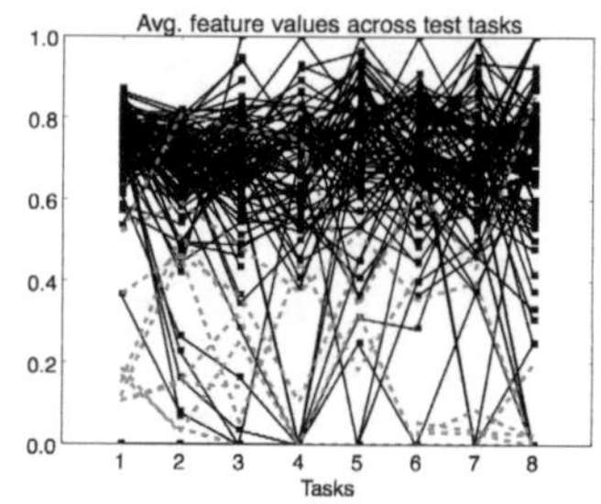

(b) Number of pairs over length of largest sequence.

Figure 3: Visualization of feature values across tasks during a test, for sampled tests. Scorable tests are in black, non-scorable in dashed red lines. For tasks that contain multiple responses, we average the feature values of the responses of a task.

not expect the choice of greedy or DP approach to greatly affect the final computed similarity features, and we chose the greedy approach for simplicity (although DP implementations could be explored in the future).

To visualize the feature information, we plot the feature values across tasks of a test, for randomly sampled tests. For tasks that contain multiple responses (multiple items), we average the feature values of the responses of a task. Figure 3(a) visualizes the number of pairs found. Each test is represented by a set of feature values (one per task) connected by lines between tasks. Values of some tasks may be missing if they are undefined, e.g., the student did not reply. Scorable tests are represented in black, and non-scorable tests in dashed red lines. We notice that the number of pairs found for non-scorable tests is consistently low throughout the tasks of the test. This agrees with our intuition that for non-scorable tests there will be less similarity between the ASR-based and signal-based syllable locations, thus there will be fewer pairs between these two location sequences, compared to scorable tests. Similarly, Figure 3(b) visualizes the normalized pairs found, and again this percentage is lower for non-scorable tests, indicating that fewer pairs were found for those tests.

In our implementation, we computed the ASR-based syllable sequences by performing phoneme-level forced alignment of the ASR, and approximating the syllable location as the center of each vowel segment of the force aligned result. We computed the signal-based syllable sequence by augmenting the open source Praat script developed by Jong and Wempe (2009) to output syllable locations. The syllable locations are approximate: computing the syllable detection accuracy would require human annotation of syllables in our corpus, which is out of the scope of this work. Our focus is to estimate syllables well enough, so as to compute useful features. Based on Figures 3(a) and (b) and the results of Section 9, our syllable detection works sufficiently well for our purpose.

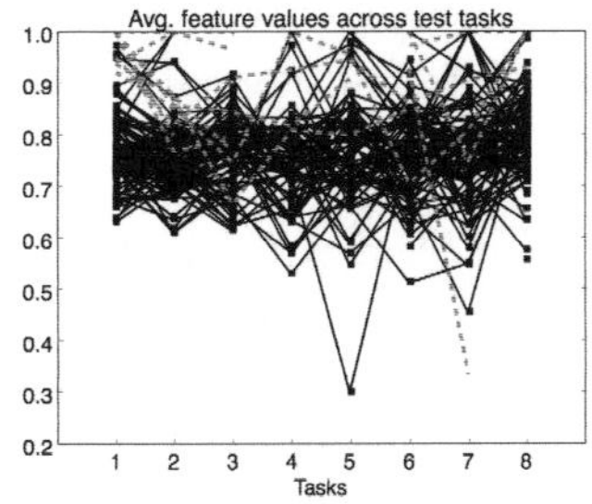

(a) Edit distance over longest sequence length.

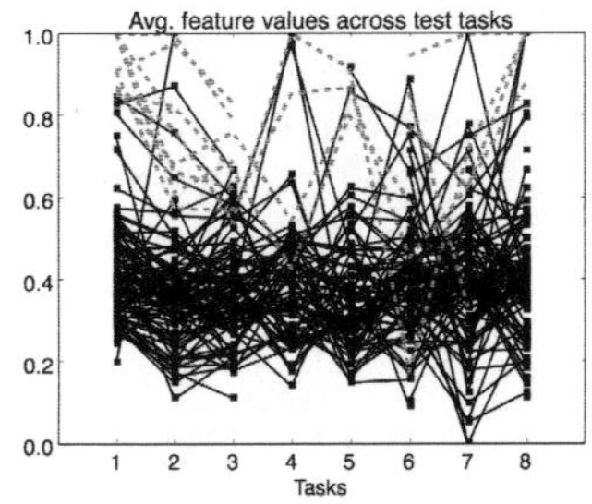

(b) Length difference over longest sequence length.

Figure 4: Visualization of feature values across tasks during a test, for sampled tests. Scorable tests are in black, non-scorable in dashed red lines.

5 Language model based features

Language models (LMs) are used to model word transition probabilities in ASR systems, and are learnt using large text corpora. For cases where the input speech belongs to a specific topic, it is common to use constrained LMs, e.g., learn the word transitions from corpora related to the topic in question. Here we explore the idea of using different LMs for our ASR system, either highly constrained or unconstrained ones, and comparing the corresponding recognition results. If the ASR results of the two LMs are very different, then it is likely that the ASR result is problematic, which may be indicative of a non-scorable test. To detect those cases, we introduce a set of features that measure the similarity between ASR results obtained using different language models.

In our system, each item requires the user to talk about a specific known topic. The default LM used by our ASR component is item dependent and is constrained on the topic of the item. In general, this is beneficial to our system as it allows the ASR to focus on words that have a high enough likelihood of appearing given the item topic. However, for some non-scorable tests, we noticed that this approach may result in misrecognizing phrases that are off-topic or non-English as valid on-topic phrases. Therefore, we introduce an unconstrained LM to detect cases where the constrained LM causes our system to misrecognize topic specific words that were not actually spoken. We create the unconstrained LM independent of the vocabulary used, by training a phoneme bigram LM that models phoneme transition probabilities. Hence, our LM can handle out of vocabulary or non-English words that often appear in non-scorable tests.

We use item specific training data to build a standard bigram word LM for each item. For the unconstrained LM, we perform phoneme-level forced alignment of all training data, and build a item independent bigram phoneme LM. We perform recognition using both LMs and compare the resulting phoneme-level recognition results. Comparison is performed by computing the edit distance between the two phoneme sequences, obtained from the two LMs. Edit distance is a common metric for measuring similarity between sequences and estimates the minimum number of insertions, deletions or substitutions required to change one sequence to the other. We compute a number of similarity features including edit distance, length difference between the sequences, number of insertions, deletions and substitutions, as well as normalized versions of those features (by dividing with the maximum sequence length). We also include the two phoneme sequence lengths as features.

Similarly to Section 4, we visualize feature information by plotting feature values across tasks, for randomly sampled tests. The resulting plots for edit distance and length difference between sequences, both normalized, are presented in Figures 4 (a) and (b) respectively. Scorable tests are in black and non-scorable in red dashed lines. Intuitively, the more dissimilar the sequences from the two LMs are, the larger the features values will be for these two features. Looking at the plots, we notice that, as expected, non-scorable tests tend to have larger feature values compared to scorable ones. This indicates that the proposed phoneme LM can help detect cases of non-scorable tests.

6 Confidence features

The ASR component of the Pearson assessment system assigns confidence scores to the recognized words. Three variants of confidence scores are computed: mconf (based on normalized acoustic scores), aconf (based on force alignment and phoneme recognition) and lconf (lattice-based). They are described in our previous work (Cheng and Shen, 2011), where they were used for off-topic detection. Here, we use them for non-scorable detection, and compute them separately using the ASR result obtained from either the item specific word LM or the item independent phoneme LM. For each confidence score, our feature set includes the average score value over words of a response, and the maximum, minimum and standard deviation. We also compute the word-level recognition log-likelihood using each of the two LMs, and include as features the average, minimum, maximum and standard deviation of these log-likelihoods over words of a response.

Although the confidence scores are described in Cheng and Shen (2011), here we compute them using the proposed phoneme LM (in addition to the standard word LM), thus they are significantly different from prior work. Indeed, scores computed by the proposed phoneme LM prove to be highly informative (see Section 9, Table 3).

7 Signal derived and ASR features

A variety of signal-derived and ASR-based features have been used in the literature for non-scorable detection (Cheng and Shen, 2011; Yoon et al., 2011; Chen and Mostow, 2011), as well as related work on pronunciation and fluency assessment (Bernstein et al., 2010; Higgins et al., 2011). In this study, we extract and include a set of common features.

Signal-derived features typically describe properties of the pitch and energy of the speech signal. Our feature set includes maximum and minimum energy, number of nonzero pitch frames and average pitch. We also extract features that estimate noise level, specifically Signal to Noise Ratio (SNR). For SNR estimation we used the NIST Speech Quality Assurance package (NIST, 2009)

Furthermore, we use features extracted from the ASR result, including utterance duration, number of words spoken, number of interword pauses, average interword pause duration, average pause duration before the first spoken word (response latency), and number of hesitations. Pauses, hesitations and response latency have been found informative of speaking fluency (Bernstein et al., 2010), and could be indicative of problematic, non-scorable tests. We also compute two variations of speech rate: words over total response duration and words over duration of speech (excluding pauses). Other ASR features we use include recognition log-likelihood, average LM likelihood, number of phonemes pruned during recognition, and average word lattice confidence. We include some additional confidence-related features, like percentage of low confidence words or phonemes in the response (low confidence is defined based on an experimental threshold).

We compute ASR features that are specific to the task: either repeat or non-repeat. For the repeat tasks, where the student is asked to repeat a prompt sentence, we compute the number of insertions, deletions and substitutions of the recognized response compared to the prompt, as well as the number and percentage of the recognized prompt words. For the open question (non-repeat) tasks, where the student gives an open ended response on a topic, we estimate the number of key words recognized in the response, from a set of predefined, topic key words.

Finally, we also include some features that are not used in previous work, and were devised to enhance earlier versions of our non-scorable detection system. Specifically, we compute the number of clipped energy frames, where clipping happens when energy exceeds a max value (often because the student is speaking too close to the microphone). Also, we include an indicator feature that indicates when the number of non zero pitch frames exceeds a certain threshold but the ASR recognizes only silence. This is a rough way to detect inconsistencies between the ASR and the pitch signal, where pitch indicates the presence of voiced speech, but the ASR recognizes silence. Although these features are new, for simplicity, we merge them in our baseline feature set.

Overall, we have extracted a diverse and powerful set of representative features, which will be referred as 'base' feature set, and is summarized in Table 1.

Table 1: Summary of features included in the 'Base' feature set

	description
signal	max and min energy, nonzero pitch frames, avg. pitch, number of clipped frames, SNR
ASR	number of words spoken, pauses and hesitations, utterance duration, speech rate (2 variations), avg. interword pause duration, leading pause duration.
	ASR log-likelihood, average LM likelihood, number of phonemes pruned, average word lattice confidence, percentage of low confidence words and phonemes
	Repeat types: number of insertions, deletions, substitutions, number of recognized prompt words, percentage of recognized prompt words. Non repeat types: number of recognized key words
indicator	indicator when number of zero pitch frames exceeds a threshold while ASR recognizes silence

8 Random forest classification

We use a binary random forest classifier to decide if a test is scorable or not. A random forest is an ensemble of decision trees where each tree decides using a subset of the features and the final decision is computed by combining the tree decisions (Breiman, 2001). Random forests can take advantage of feature combinations to construct a complex, non-linear decision region in the feature space. In addition, they can be trained fast, have good generalization properties and do not require much parameter tuning, which makes them popular classifiers in the machine learning literature. In our work, a variety of diverse reasons may cause a test to be non-scorable, including background or line/static noise, off-topic responses, non-English or unintelligible speech. Random forests combine a number of decision trees that could correspond to the different sub-cases of our problem, therefore they seem well suited for non-scorable test detection. According to our experiments, random forests outperform decision trees and maximum entropy classifiers. Therefore, all results of Section 9 are based on random forest classification.

Up to now, we have described feature extraction for each test response. The non-scorable detection system needs to aggregate multiple response information to make an overall decision at the test level. We can combine response-level features in a straightforward manner by taking their average over a test. However, responses may belong to different types of tasks, either repeat or non repeat ones, and some of the features are task specific. Also, repeat task responses often resemble recited speech, while non-repeat ones tend to be more spontaneous. To preserve this information, we separately average features that belong to repeat responses and non-repeat responses of a test (two averaged features are extracted per test and per feature). There are cases where a feature cannot be extracted for a response, because it is undefined, i.e., for a response that is recognized as silence the average interword pause duration is undefined. Therefore, we also include the percentage of repeat or non-repeat responses used to compute the average, i.e., two percentage features (for repeat and non-repeat cases) are extracted per test and per response. More statistics could be extracted when combining response features, e.g., variance, max and min values, and others. However, our preliminary experiments indicated that including just averages and corresponding percentages is sufficient, and adding more statistics greatly increases the feature vector size without significant performance gains. Therefore, our final feature set includes only averages and percentages.

9 Experiments and results

9.1 Experimental setup

Our experiments are organized in 5-fold cross validation: we randomly split the 6000 tests into five sets, and each time we use three sets for training the random forest classifier, one set as a development for optimizing the number of trees, and one set for testing non-scorable classification performance. Performance is computed after merging all test set results. Because the percentage of non-scorable tests in our dataset is small (approx. 5%) and random forests are trained with a degree of randomness, different runs of an experiment can cause small variations in performance. To minimize this effect, we repeat each 5-fold cross validation experiment 10 times, and report the average and standard deviation over the 10 runs.

Performance is estimated using the ROC curve of false acceptance rate (FAR) versus false rejection rate (FRR) for the binary (scorable vs non-scorable) classification task. Our goal is to minimize the area under the curve (AUC), e.g., achieve low values for both FAR and FRR. Our experiments were performed using the Python Scikit-Learn toolbox (Scikit-Learn, 2014).

9.2 Results

Table 2 presents the average AUC performance of non-scorable test detection over 10 experiment runs, using different feature sets and random forests. 'Base' denotes the set of standard ASR-based and signal-based features described in Section 7. Syllable based and LM based denote the similarity features introduced in Sections 4 and 5 respectively. Finally, 'confidence' denotes the confidence and log-likelihood features derived from the standard and the proposed phoneme LM, as described in Section 6. According to our results, 'base' features are the best performing. However, it is encouraging that our proposed comparison-based syllable and LM approaches, that approach the problem from a different perspective and only use similarity features, still achieve comparable performance.

Table 2: Average and standard deviation of AUC over 10 experiment runs for the different feature sets, and combinations of feature sets.

features	AUC (Avg ± Std.dev)
Base	0.102 ± 0.007
Syllable based	0.122 ± 0.011
LM based	0.123 ± 0.008
Confidence	0.106 ± 0.011
Feature Combination	
Base+Syllable	0.091 ± 0.007
Base+LM	0.091 ± 0.011
Base+Confidence	0.094 ± 0.011
All	0.097 ± 0.011
Feature Combination (select top 300 features)	
Base+Syllable	0.092 ± 0.008
Base+LM	0.088 ± 0.012
Base+Confidence	0.097 ± 0.010
All	0.092 ± 0.008
Classifier Decision Combination	
Base+Syllable	0.087 ± 0.008
Base+LM	0.085 ± 0.007
Base+Confidence	0.084 ± 0.007
All	**0.081 ± 0.006**

Table 2 also presents the AUC performance after concatenating the feature vectors of different feature sets, under 'Feature Combination'. We notice that adding separately each of our proposed syllable based, LM based and confidence features to the base features improves performance by decreasing AUC. This further indicates that the proposed features carry useful information, which is complementary to the 'base' feature set. Combining all features together leads to a relatively small performance increase, possibly because the large number of features may cause overfitting.

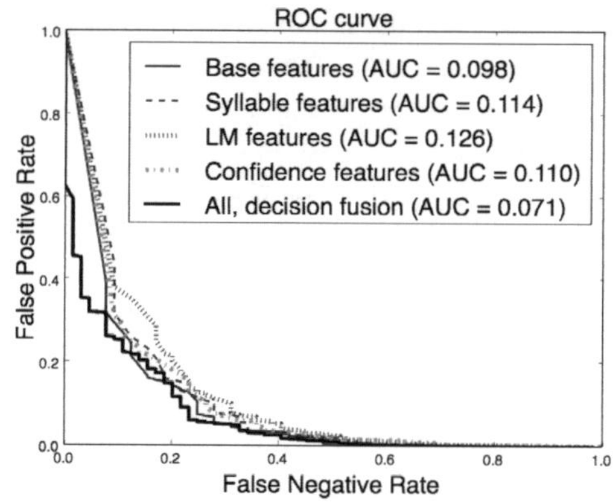

Figure 5: Test set ROC curves for different feature sets, and their combination using decision fusion (averaging), for one run of the experiment.

We also perform feature selection by selecting the top 300 features from each feature set. Features are ranked based on their positions in the trees of the random forest: features closer to the root of a tree contribute to the decision of a larger number of input samples, thus, the expected fraction of the samples that each feature contributes to, can be used as an estimate of feature importance. We use Scikit-Learn to compute the feature importance for each feature, and rank features based on their average importance over the 10 experiment runs. The results, presented in Table 2, show that feature selection helps for cases of large feature sets, i.e., when combining all features together. However, for cases when fewer features are used, the performance does not change much compared to no feature selection.

Finally, instead of concatenating features, we perform decision combination by averaging the decisions of classifiers trained on different feature sets. For simplicity, we perform simple averaging (in future when a larger train set will be available, we can explore learning appropriate classifier weights, and performing weighted average). From the results of Table 2, we notice that this approach is advantageous and leads to a significant performance increase, especially when we combine all four classifiers: one using existing 'base' features, and the rest using our new features. Overall, we

Table 3: Top-10 ranked features from each feature set. 'Av' and 'prc' denote that the feature is an average or percentage respectively, while 'r' and 'nr' denote that the feature is computed over repeat or non-repeat responses, respectively. For the confidence features, 'wLM' denotes the feature is computed using regular bigram word LM and 'pLM' denotes proposed bigram phoneme LM.

feature set	description	
signal and ASR	n_hesitations (av, r)	indicator_pitch_asr (av,r)
	min_energy (av,r)	n_pitch_frames (av, nr)
	n_pitch_frames (av,r)	asr_loglik (av, nr)
	asr_loglik (av,r)	min_energy (av, nr)
	avg_pitch(av,nr)	snr (av, nr)
syllable based	diff_lengths_norm (av,r)	diff_lengths_norm (av,nr)
	min_pair_distances(av,nr)	diff_lengths (av,r)
	n_pairs_norm (av,nr)	diff_lengths(av,nr)
	avg_pair_distances (av,r)	min_pair_distances (av,r)
	n_pairs_norm (av,r)	max_pair_distances (av,nr)
LM based	edit_dist_norm (av,r)	diff_lengths_norm (av,r)
	n_insert_norm (av,r)	edit_dist_norm (av,nr)
	diff_lengths_norm (av, nr)	n_insert_norm (av,nr)
	n_substitute_norm (av,nr)	min_length (av,nr)
	min_length (av,r)	n_substitute (av, nr)
Confidence	avg_aconf_pLM (av,nr)	min_loglik_pLM (av,r)
	min_loglik_pLM (av,nr)	max_lconf_pLM (av,r)
	min_aconf_pLM (av,nr)	stddev_loglik_pLM (av,nr)
	min_loglik_wLM (av,r)	min_aconf_pLM (av,r)
	std_loglik_pLM (av,r)	avg_loglik_pLM (av,r)

achieved a decrease in AUC from 0.102 to 0.081, a 21% relative performance improvement.

Figure 5 presents the ROC curves for one run of the experiment, for the four feature sets, and their combination using averaging of the classifier decisions. Combining all feature sets leads to a lower AUC (thick black line). We notice improvement especially in reducing false positives, e.g., misclassifying scorable test as non-scorable.

In Table 3, we present the top 10 selected features from each feature set, based on their averaged feature importance. Overall, we notice that both repeat and non-repeat features are among the top ranked, indicating that both types are informative. Only average features are among the top ranked, which suggests that averages carry more information than percentage features. For the syllable and LM features, we can see many intuitive similarity features being at the top, such as difference of sequence lengths, edit distance and number of insertions (LM based feature set), and average, min and max of the distances of paired syllables (syllable based feature set). For confidence, we note that many log-likelihood features are at the top (here log-likelihood statistics are computed over words of a response). Also, note that the great majority of top-ranked confidence features are computed using our proposed item independent phoneme LM, instead of the regular item dependent word LM, indicating the usefulness of this approach.

10 Conclusion and future work

In this work, we have proposed new methods for detecting non-scorable tests in spoken language proficiency assessment applications. Our methods compare information extracted from different sources when processing a test, and compute similarity features. Inconsistencies suggest problematic ASR, which is often indicative of non-scorable tests. We extract two sets of features: syllable based, which compare syllable location information, and LM based, which compare ASR obtained using item specific and item independent LMs. Our proposed item independent LM is a bigram phoneme LM, which can handle out-of-vocabulary or non-English words, that often appear in non-scorable tests. By visualizing the proposed similarity features, we verify that they can highlight inconsistencies that are common in non-scorable tests. We experimentally validate our methods in a large, challenging dataset of young ELLs interacting with the Pearson spoken assessment system. Our features carry complementary information to existing features, and when combined with existing work, they achieve a 21% relative performance improvement. Our final, non-scorable detection system combines the decisions of four random forest classifiers: one using baseline features, and the rest using proposed features.

We are currently collecting human annotations for non-scorable tests in our dataset, which contain additional annotation of the different non-scorable subcases in these tests, e.g., noise, off-topic, non-English, unintelligible speech etc. In the future, we plan to use these annotations to further validate our methods, as well as perform detailed evaluation of the usefulness of our proposed feature sets for each of the non-scorable test subcases.

References

J. Bernstein and J. Cheng. 2007. Logic and validation of a fully automatic spoken English test. In V. M. Holland and F. P. Fisher, editors, *The Path of Speech Technologies in Computer Assisted Language Learning*, pages 174–194. Routledge, New York.

J. Bernstein, J. De Jong, D. Pisoni, and B. Townshend. 2000. Two experiments on automatic scoring of spoken language proficiency. In *Proc. of STIL (Integrating Speech Technology in Learning)*.

J. Bernstein, A. Van Moere, and J. Cheng. 2010. Validating automated speaking tests. *Language Testing*, 27.

L. Breiman. 2001. Random forests. *Machine Learning*, 45.

W. Chen and J. Mostow. 2011. A tale of two tasks: Detecting children's off-task speech in a reading tutor. In *Proc. of Interspeech*.

J. Cheng and J. Shen. 2010. Towards accurate recognition for children's oral reading fluency. In *Proc. of IEEE-SLT*, pages 91–96.

J. Cheng and J. Shen. 2011. Off-topic detection in automated speech assessment applications. In *Proc. of Interspeech*.

J. Cheng, J. Bernstein, U. Pado, and M. Suzuki. 2009. Automated assessment of spoken modern standard arabic. In *Proc. of the Fourth Workshop on Innovative Use of NLP for Building Educational Applications*.

R. Downey, D. Rubin, J. Cheng, and J. Bernstein. 2011. Performance of automated scoring for children's oral reading. In *Proc. of the 6th Workshop on Innovative Use of NLP for Building Educational Applications*.

M. Eskanazi. 2009. An overview of spoken language technology for education. *Speech Communication*, 51.

D. Higgins, X. Xi, K. Zechner, and D. Williamson. 2011. A three-stage approach to the automated scoring of spontaneous spoken responses. *Computer Speech and Language*, 25.

N. H. De Jong and T. Wempe. 2009. Praat script to detect syllable nuclei and measure speech rate automatically. *Behavior research methods*, 41:385–390.

NIST. 2009. The NIST SPeech Quality Assurance (SPQA) Package. `http://www.nist.gov/speech/tools/index.htm`.

G. Pearson. 2006. Ask NCELA No.1: How many school-aged English-language learners (ELLs) are there in the U.S.? Washington, D.C: National Clearing House for English-Language Acquisition and Language Instruction Educational Programs 2006, Retrieved Online February 2007 at `http://www.ncela.gwu.edu/expert/faq/01leps.htm`.

Pearson. 2011. Skills and scoring in PTE Academic. `http://www.pearsonpte.com/SiteCollectionDocuments/US_Skills_Scoring_PTEA_V3.pdf`.

Scikit-Learn. 2014. The Scikit-Learn Machine Learning Python Toolbox. `http://scikit-learn.org/`.

J. Tepperman, M. Black, P. Price, S. Lee, A. Kazemzadeh, M. Gerosa, M. Heritage, A. Alwan, and S. Narayanan. 2007. A Bayesian network classifier for word-level reading assessment. In *Proc. of Interspeech*.

X. Xu, M. Suzuki, and J. Cheng. 2012. An automated assessment of spoken Chinese: Technical definition of hanyu standards for content and scoring development. In *Proc. of the Seventh International Conference & Workshops on Technology & Chinese Language Teaching*.

S.-Y. Yoon, K. Evanini, and K. Zechner. 2011. Non-scorable response detection for automated speaking proficiency assessment. In *Proc. of the Sixth Workshop on Innovative Use of NLP for Building Educational Applications*.

Improving Peer Feedback Prediction: The Sentence Level is Right

Huy V. Nguyen
Department of Computer Science
University of Pittsburgh
Pittsburgh, PA 15260
hvn3@pitt.edu

Diane J. Litman
Department of Computer Science & LRDC
University of Pittsburgh
Pittsburgh, PA 15260
litman@cs.pitt.edu

Abstract

Recent research aims to automatically predict whether peer feedback is of high quality, e.g. suggests solutions to identified problems. While prior studies have focused on peer review of papers, similar issues arise when reviewing diagrams and other artifacts. In addition, previous studies have not carefully examined how the level of prediction granularity impacts both accuracy and educational utility. In this paper we develop models for predicting the quality of peer feedback regarding argument diagrams. We propose to perform prediction at the sentence level, even though the educational task is to label feedback at a multi-sentential comment level. We first introduce a corpus annotated at a sentence level granularity, then build comment prediction models using this corpus. Our results show that aggregating sentence prediction outputs to label comments not only outperforms approaches that directly train on comment annotations, but also provides useful information for enhancing peer review systems with new functionality.

1 Introduction

Peer review systems are increasingly being used to facilitate the teaching and assessment of student writing. Peer feedback can complement and even be as useful as teacher feedback; students can also benefit by producing peer feedback. Past research has shown that feedback implementation is significantly correlated to the presence of desirable feedback features such as the description of solutions to problems (Nelson and Schunn, 2009). Since it would be very time-consuming for instructors to identify feedback of low quality post-hoc, recent research has used natural language processing (NLP) to automatically predict whether peer feedback contains useful content for guiding student revision (Cho, 2008; Ramachandran and Gehringer, 2011; Xiong et al., 2012). Such real-time predictions have in turn been used to enhance existing online peer-review systems, e.g. by triggering tutoring that is designed to improve feedback quality (Nguyen et al., June 2014).

While most prior research of peer review quality has focused on feedback regarding papers, similar issues arise when reviewing other types of artifacts such as program code, graphical diagrams, etc. (Nguyen and Litman, July 2013). In addition, previous studies have not carefully examined how the level of prediction granularity (e.g. multi-sentential review comments versus sentences) impacts both the accuracy and the educational utility of the predictive models. For example, while the tutoring intervention of (Nguyen et al., June 2014) highlighted low versus high quality feedback comments, such a prediction granularity could not support the highlighting of specific text spans that also might have been instructionally useful.

In this paper, we first address the problem of predicting **feedback type** (i.e. *problem, solution, non-criticism*) in peer reviews of student argument diagrams. In *problem* feedback, the reviewer describes what is wrong or needs to be improved in the diagram. In *solution* feedback, the reviewer provides a way to fix a problem or to improve the diagram quality. Feedback is *non-criticism* when it is neither a *problem* nor a *solution* (e.g. when it provides only positive feedback or summarizes). Examples are shown in Figure 1.[1]

The second goal of our research is to design our prediction framework so that it can support real-time tutoring about feedback quality. We hypoth-

[1] Our peer review corpus comes from a system that uses an end-comment feedback approach as shown in Figure 1. While it is possible to instead directly annotate a reviewed artifact, this has been shown to encourage feedback on low-level issues, and is not good for more global feedback.

Proceedings of the Ninth Workshop on Innovative Use of NLP for Building Educational Applications , pages 99–108,
Baltimore, Maryland USA, June 26, 2014.

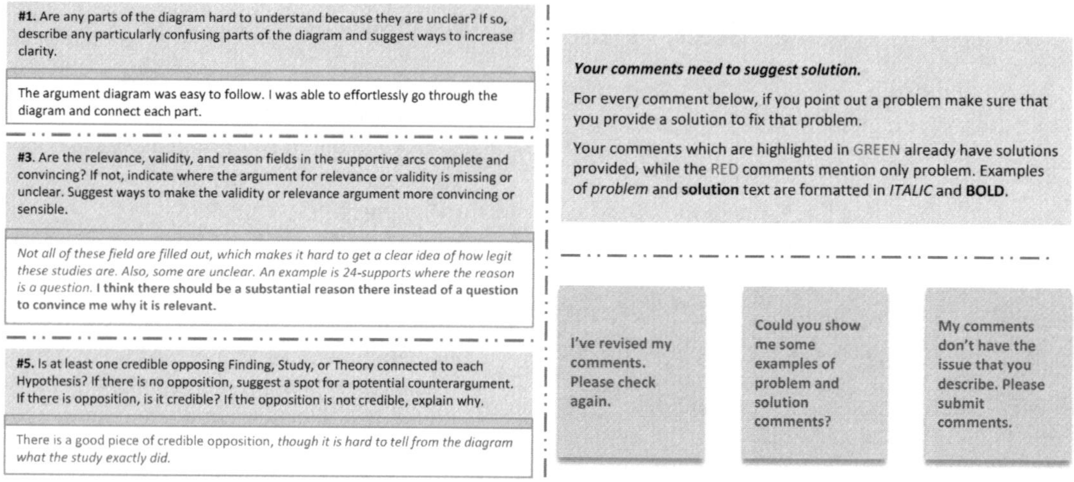

Figure 1: A mock-up interface of a peer review system where the prediction of feedback type triggers a system tutoring intervention. Left: three sample feedback comments including a *non-criticism* (top), a *solution* (middle), and a *problem* (bottom). Right-top: a system tutoring intervention to teach the student reviewer to provide a solution whenever a problem is mentioned. Right-bottom: possible student responses to the system's tutoring.

esize that using a student's own high-quality reviews during tutoring, and identifying the explicit text that makes the review high quality, will help students learn how to improve their lower quality reviews. To facilitate this goal, we develop prediction models that work at the sentence level of granularity.

Figure 1 presents a mock-up of our envisioned peer review interface. To tutor the student about solutions (figure right), the system uses live examples taken from the student's current review (figure left). Color is used to display the feedback type predictions: here a *non-criticism* is displayed in black, while the criticisms that are positive and negative examples of *solution* are displayed in green and red, respectively. In addition, to help the student focus on the important aspect of the (green) positive example, the sentence that actually specifies the solution is highlighted in bold.

This paper presents our first results towards realizing this vision. The contributions of our work are two-fold. First, we develop a sentence-level model for predicting feedback type in a diagram review corpus. While our peer review system works at the level of *feedback comments* (text of each box in Figure 1), we find it is more accurate to annotate and predict at finer-grained granularity levels, then use these predictions to infer the comment's feedback type. By introducing a small overhead to annotate peer feedback, we created a phrase level-annotated corpus of argument diagram reviews. Our experimental results show that our learned prediction models using labeled sentences outperform models trained and tested at comment level. In addition, our models outperform models previously developed for paper rather than diagram feedback, and also show potential generality by avoiding the use of domain-specific features. Second, we demonstrate that our sentence-level prediction can be used to support visualizations useful for tutoring. Particular sentences that are predicted to express the comment's feedback type are highlighted for instructional purposes (e.g. the bold highlighting in Figure 1).

2 Related work

In instructional science, research has been conducted to understand what makes peer feedback helpful. At the secondary school level, Gielen *et al.* (2010) found that the presence of justification in feedback significantly improved students' writing performance. At the university level, Nelson and Schunn (2009) found that feedback on papers was more likely to be implemented when the feedback contained solutions or pinpointed problem locations. Lippman *et al.* (2012) found that similar feedback properties led to greater implementation of feedback on diagrams as well.

Building on such findings, researchers have begun to develop automated methods to identify helpful feedback. Cho (2008) was the first to take a machine learning approach. Peer feedback, i.e. comments, were manually segmented into idea units[2] and human-coded for various features including problem detection, solution suggestion, praise, criticism, and summary. Feedback was then labeled as helpful or not-helpful based on the presence of such features. The study showed that feedback could be classified regarding helpfulness with up to 67% accuracy using simple NLP techniques including ngrams and part-of-speech. Our work is different from (Cho, 2008) in that we focus on predicting particular feedback types (i.e. solution and problem) rather than helpfulness in general. Also, as the raw feedback to peer-review systems is typically at the comment-level, and being aware that idea-units are difficult to automatically segment, we instead predict at the sentence-level to make model deployment more practical.

Our work is more similar to (Xiong and Litman, 2010; Xiong et al., June 2010; Xiong et al., 2012), in which NLP and machine learning were used to automatically predict whether peer reviews of student papers contained specific desirable feedback features. Xiong and Litman used NLP-based features including paper ngrams, predefined keyword lists, and dependency parses to predict feedback type. For feedback of type criticism, they also developed models to further predict problem localization and solution. Following (Cho, 2008), Xiong and Litman evaluated their models on peer review data that had been manually segmented into idea units. As noted above, the difficulty of automatically segmenting raw comments into idea units makes deployment of such models less practical than our sentence-level approach. Also like Cho (2008), while their models predicted a label for each idea unit, the relevant text that led to the prediction was not identified. We will address this limitation by introducing a more fine-grained annotated corpus.

Regarding peer reviews of student argument diagrams rather than papers, Nguyen and Litman (July 2013) developed a rule-based algorithm for predicting feedback that contained localization text (e.g. "Hypothesis 4"). Their approach was to first identify common words between a peer comment and its diagram, then classify phrases containing these words into different localization patterns. Although we similarly focus on diagram rather than paper feedback, our work addresses a different prediction task (namely, predicting feedback type rather than localization). We also use statistical machine learning rather than a rule-based approach, in conjunction with more general linguistic features, to allow us to ultimately use our models for papers as well as diagrams with minimal modification or training.

Outside of peer review, research has been performed recently to mine wishes and suggestions in product reviews and political discussion. Goldberg *et al.* (2009) analyzed the WISH[3] corpus and built wish detectors based on simple word cues and templates. Focusing on product reviews only, Ramanand *et al.* (2010) created two corpora of suggestion wishes (wishes for a change in an existing product or service) and purchasing wishes (explicit expressions of a desire to purchase a product), and developed rules for identifying wish sentences from non-wish ones. Both (Goldberg et al., 2009; Ramanand et al., 2010) created rules manually by examining the data. Although we hypothesize that wishes are related to solutions in peer review, our educational data makes direct application of product-motivated rules difficult. We thus currently use statistical machine learning for our initial research, but plan to explore incorporating expression rules to enhance our model.

Sub-sentence annotation has gained much interest in sentiment analysis and opinion mining. One notable work is (Wilson et al., 2005) in which the author addressed the problem that the contextual polarity (i.e. *positive*, *negative*, or *neutral*) of the phrase in which a word appears may be different from the word's prior polarity. We will also use a phrase-level annotation, as described below.

3 Argument diagram review corpus

Diagramming software tools such as LASAD (Scheuer et al., 2010) are increasingly being used to teach student argumentation skills through graphical representations. Graphical argument environments typically allow students to create diagrams in which boxes represent statements and links represent argumentative or rhetorical relations. This helps students focus on abstract argu-

[2]Cf. (Cho, 2008) "a self-contained message on a single piece of strength or weakness found in peer writing."

[3]http://www.timessquarenyc.org/nye/nye_interactive.html

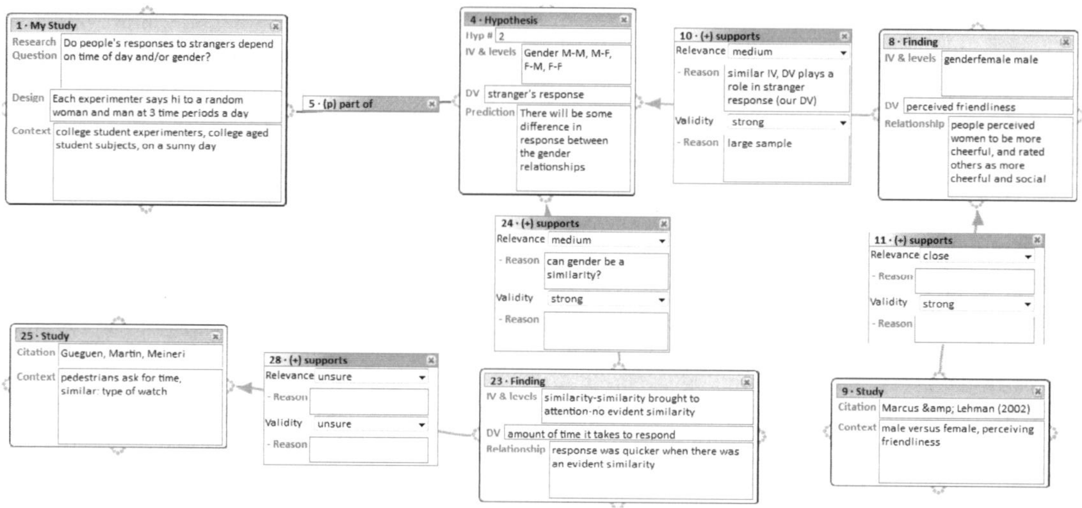

Figure 2: Part of a student argument diagram.

ment schemes before learning how to write argumentative essays. To further help students create good argument diagrams, it has recently been suggested that receiving and providing feedback on argument diagrams might yield useful pedagogical benefits (Falakmassir et al., July 2013), analogously to improving writing via peer review of papers.

Our corpus consists of a subset of comments from diagram reviews collected from nine separate sections of an undergraduate psychology course. Student argument diagrams were created using an instructor-defined diagram ontology. The diagram ontology defines five different types of nodes: *Current study, Hypothesis, Theory, Finding*, and *Study (for reference)*. The ontology also defines four different types of arcs that connect nodes: *Supports, Opposes, Part-of*, and *Undecided*. Figure 2 shows part of a student argument diagram that includes two studies, each of which supports a finding which in turn supports or opposes a hypothesis. In the course that generated our corpus, students first created graphical argument diagrams using LASAD to justify given hypotheses. Student argument diagrams were then distributed, using the SWoRD (Cho and Schunn, 2007) web-based peer-review system, to other students in the class for reviewing. Student authors potentially revised their argument diagrams based on peer feedback, then used the diagrams to write the introduction of associated papers. Diagram reviews consist of multiple written feedback comments in response

<IU> <Pr>*Not all of these field are filled out, which makes it hard to get a clear idea of how legit these studies are.*</Pr> **</IU>** **<IU>** <Pr>*Also, some are unclear. An example is 24-supports where the reason is a question.*</Pr> <Sl>**I think there should be a substantial reason there instead of a question to convince me why it is relevant.**</Sl> **</IU>**

Table 1: Example of an annotated comment. Markers <IU>: idea unit, <Sl>: solution, <Pr>: problem. Problem text is italic and solution text is bold for illustration purpose.

to rubric prompts, i.e. review dimensions. Student reviewers were required to provide at least one but no more than three comments for each of five review dimensions. Figure 1 shows three sample peer comments for three review dimensions (i.e. dimensions 1, 3 and 5).

Following prior work on peer review analysis (Lippman et al., 2012; Nguyen and Litman, July 2013), the first author composed a coding manual for peer reviews of argument diagrams. An annotator first segments each comment into idea units (defined as contiguous feedback referring to a single topic). Note that idea-unit segmentation is necessary to make coding reliable. We however do not exploit idea unit information for our current prediction tasks. Then the annotator codes each idea unit for different features among which *solution* and *problem* are

Label	Number of comments
`Solution`	178
`Problem`	194
`Combined`	135
`Non-criticism`	524
Total	1031

Table 2: Comment label distribution.

the two labels used in this study. These labels are then used to assign a **feedback type** (i.e. `solution`, `problem`, `combined`, and `non-criticism`) to the comment as a whole. The comment is labeled `Solution` if at least one of its idea units presents a solution but no problem unit is explicitly present. If no solution idea is found, the comment is labeled `Problem` if at least one of its idea units presents a problem. The comment is labeled `Combined` if it has both solution and problem idea units, or `Non-criticism` if it does not have solution or problem. `Non-criticism` units can be praise, summary or text that does not express any idea, e.g. *"Yes, it is."* Table 1 shows an example annotated feedback comment that consists of two idea units. The first idea unit is about *empty fields*, and the second is about *reason is a question*. Based on the annotations shown, the comment as a whole has the label `Combined`.

We had one undergraduate psychology major annotate the 1031 comments in our corpus, yielding the label distribution shown in Table 2. The first author also annotated 244 randomly selected comments, solely to evaluate inter-coder agreement. The obtained agreement of comment labels was high, with accuracy 0.81 and kappa 0.74.

In addition to comment labeling, the annotator also highlighted[4] text spans that explain the labels. The marked text span must either express solution or problem information but cannot express both. Therefore we require the annotator to highlight at the phrase (i.e. sub-sentence) level, and that each marked text must be completely within an idea unit. Generally speaking this requirement does not increase cognitive workload because annotators already have to read the comment and notice any solution or problem mentioned before labeling.

[4]Highlighting was made possible using macros in Microsoft Word. Annotators select the text of interest, then click a button corresponding to the relevant label, e.g. problem.

Label	Sentence
Problem	Not all of these field are filled out, which makes it hard to get a clear idea of how legit these studies are.
Problem	Also, some are unclear.
Problem	An example is 24-supports where the reason is a question.
Solution	I think there should be a substantial reason there instead of a question to convince me why it is relevant.

Table 3: Examples of labeled sentences extracted from the annotated comment.

Category	Number of sentences
Solution	389
Problem	458
Non-criticism	1061
Total	1908

Table 4: Sentence label distribution.

Although we asked the annotator to mark text spans which convey problem or solution information, we did not ask the annotator to break each text span into sentences. The first reason is that the problem or solution text might only be part of a sentence and highlighting only the informative part will give us more valuable data. Second, sentence segmentation can be performed automatically with high accuracy. After the corpus was annotated, we ran a sentence segmentation procedure using NLTK[5] to create a labeled corpus at the sentence level as follows. Each comment is broken into three possible parts: *solution* including all solution text marked in the comment, *problem* including all problem text, and *other* for non-criticism text. Each part is then segmented into sentences and each sentence is assigned the label of the part to which it belongs. It may happen that the segmented text is a phrase rather than a complete sentence. We consider such phrases as reduced sentential-like text, and we use the term *sentence(s)* to cover such sub-sentence forms, as well. Labeled sentences of the comment in Table 1 are shown in Table 3. After discarding empty sentences and those of length 1 (all of those are in the *non-criticism* category), there are 1908 sentences remaining, distributed as shown in Table 4.

[5]www.nltk.org

4 Experimental setup

Sections 6 and 7 report the results of two different experiments involving the prediction of feedback types at the comment level. While each experiment differs in the exact classes to be predicted, both compare the predictive utility of the same two different model-building approaches:

- *Trained using comments* (CTRAIN): our baseline[6] approach learns comment prediction models using labeled feedback comments for training.
- *Trained using sentences* (STRAIN): our proposed approach learns sentence prediction models using labeled sentences, then aggregates sentence prediction outputs to create comment labels. For example, the aggregation used for the experiment in Section 6 is as follows: if at least one sentence is predicted as *Solution/Problem* then the comment is assigned *Solution/Problem*.

We hypothesize that the proposed approach will yield better predictive performance than the baseline because the former takes advantage of cleaner and more discriminative training data.

To make the features of the two approaches comparable, we use the same set of generic linguistic features:

- Ngrams to capture word cues: word unigrams, POS/word bigrams, POS/word trigrams, word and POS pairs, punctuation, word count.
- Dependency parse to capture structure cues.

We skip domain and course-specific features (e.g. review dimensions, diagram keywords like *hypothesis*) in order to make the learned model more applicable to different diagram review data. Instead, we search for diagram keywords in comments and replace them with the string "KEYWORD". The keyword list can be extracted automatically from LASAD's diagram ontology. Adding metadata features such as comment and sentence ordering did not seem to improve performance so we do not include such features in the experiments below.

Following (Xiong et al., 2012), we learn prediction models using logistic regression. However, in our work both feature extraction and model learning are performed using the LightSide[7] toolkit. As our data is collected from nine separate sections of the same course, to better evaluate the models, we perform cross-section evaluation in which for each fold we train the model using data from 8 sections and test on the remaining section. Reported results are averaged over 9-fold cross validations. Four metrics are used to evaluate prediction performance. Accuracy (Acc.) and Kappa (κ) are used as standard performance measurements. Since our annotated corpus has imbalanced data which makes the learned models bias to the majority classes, we also report the Precision (Prec.) and Recall (Recl.) of predicting the minor classes.

5 Sentence prediction performance

We first evaluate models for predicting binary versions of the sentence labels from Table 4 (e.g. solution or not), as this output will be aggregated in our proposed STRAIN approach. The results of using sentence training (STr) and sentence testing (STe) are shown in the STR/STE row of Table 5. For comparison, the first row of the table shows the performance of a majority baseline approach (MAJOR), which assigns all sentences the label of the relevant major class in each prediction task. To confirm that a sentence-level annotated corpus is necessary to train sentence prediction models, a third approach that uses labeled comment data for training (CTr) but sentences for testing (STe) is included in the CTR/STE row. As we can see, STR/STE models outperform those of CTR/STE and MAJOR for all 4 metrics[8]. The comment versus sentence training yields significant differences for predicting *Problem* and *Criticism* sentences.

6 Three feedback type prediction tasks

In this experiment we evaluate our hypothesis that STRAIN outperforms CTRAIN by comparing performance on three feedback type prediction tasks at the comment level (derived from Table 2):

- *Problem v. Non-problem*. The *Problem* class includes problem and combined comments.

[6]The use of comment-level annotations for training and testing is similar to (Nguyen and Litman, July 2013).

[7]http://ankara.lti.cs.cmu.edu/side/download.html

[8]Note that κ in general, and precision and recall of minor classes, are not applicable when evaluating MAJOR.

	Solution				*Problem*				*Criticism*			
Model	Acc.	κ	Prec.	Recl.	Acc.	κ	Prec.	Recl.	Acc.	κ	Prec.	Recl.
MAJOR	0.80	-	-	-	0.76	-	-	-	0.56	-	-	-
CTR/STE	0.87	0.57	0.70	0.62	0.75	0.22	0.48	0.29	0.75	0.48	0.76	0.63
STR/STE	0.88	0.61	0.76	0.63	**0.81**	**0.44**	**0.62**	**0.51**	*0.80*	*0.59*	*0.79*	*0.74*

Table 5: Prediction performance of three tasks at the sentence level. Comparing STR/STE to CTR/STE: *Italic* means higher with $p < 0.05$, **Bold** means higher with $p < 0.01$.

- *Solution v. Non-solution.* The *Solution* class includes solution and combined comments.
- *Criticism v. Non-criticism.* The *Criticism* class includes problem, solution and combined comments.

The two approaches are also compared to majority baselines (MAJOR) and a hybrid approach (HYBRD) that trains models using labeled sentence data but tests on labeled comments.

As shown in Table 6, both MAJOR and HYBRD perform much worse than CTRAIN and STRAIN. We note that while HYBRD gives comparably high precision, its kappa and recall do not match those of CTRAIN and STRAIN. Comparing CTRAIN and STRAIN, the results confirm our hypothesis that STRAIN outperforms CTRAIN. The major advantage of STRAIN is that it only needs one correctly predicted sentence to yield the correct comment label. This is particularly beneficial for predicting problem comments, where the improvement is significant for 3 of 4 metrics.

As our evaluation is cross-section, folds do not have identical label distributions. Therefore we look at prediction performance for each of the nine individual sections. We find that the sentence level approach yields higher performance on all four metrics in six sections when predicting both *Solution* and *Problem* task, but only two sections for *Criticism*. For the *Criticism* task – where it is not necessary to exclusively differentiate between *Solution* and *Problem*, training prediction models using labeled sentences does not yield higher performance than the traditional approach.

Roughly comparing predicting at the sentence level (Table 5) versus the comment level (Table 6), we note that the sentence level tasks are more difficult (e.g. lower absolute kappas) despite an intuition that the labeled sentence corpus is cleaner and more discriminative compared to the labeled comment corpus. The observed performance disparity shows the necessity of developing better sentence prediction models, which we leave to future work.

7 A case study experiment

To the best of our knowledge, (Xiong et al., June 2010; Xiong et al., 2012) contain the only published models developed for predicting feedback types. A comment-level solution prediction model has since been deployed in their peer review software to evaluate student reviewer comments in classroom settings, using the following 3-way classification algorithm[9]. Each student comment is classified as either a criticism (i.e. presents problem/solution information) or a non-criticism. The non-criticism comment is labeled *NULL*. The criticism comment is labeled *SOLUTION* if it contains solution information, and labeled *PROBLEM* otherwise.

To evaluate our proposed STRAIN approach in their practically-motivated setting, we follow the description above to relabel peer feedback comments in our corpus to new labels: *NULL, PROBLEM*, and *SOLUTION*. We also asked the authors of (Xiong et al., 2012) for access to their current model and we were able to run their model on our feedback comment data. While it is not appropriate to directly compare model performance as Xiong *et al.* were working with paper (not diagram) review data, we report their model output, named PAPER, to provide a reference baseline. We expect the PAPER model to work on our diagram review data to some extent, particularly due to its predefined seed words for solution and problem cues. Our CTRAIN baseline, in contrast, trains models regarding the new label set using relabeled diagram comment data, with the same features and learning algorithm from the prior sections. The majority baseline, MAJOR, assigns all comments the major class label (which is now *NULL*).

Regarding our STRAIN sentence level ap-

[9] Personal communication.

Model	*Solution*				*Problem*				*Criticism*			
	Acc.	κ	Prec.	Recl.	Acc.	κ	Prec.	Recl.	Acc.	κ	Prec.	Recl.
MAJOR	0.70	-	-	-	0.68	-	-	-	0.51	-	-	-
HYBRD	0.82	0.52	0.87	0.48	0.75	0.36	0.68	0.41	0.78	0.56	0.84	0.68
CTRAIN	0.87	0.67	0.84	0.71	0.76	0.43	0.65	0.55	0.83	0.66	0.85	0.80
STRAIN	0.88	*0.71*	0.86	*0.74*	**0.81**	**0.55**	*0.71*	**0.66**	0.85	0.70	0.84	*0.85*

Table 6: Prediction performance of three tasks at comment level. Comparing STRAIN to CTRAIN: *Italic* means higher with $p < 0.1$, **Bold** means higher with $p < 0.05$.

1. For each sentence, label it *SOLUTION* if it is predicted as *Solution* by the *Solution* model.
2. For a predicted *Non-solution* sentence, label it *NULL* if it is predicted as *Non-criticism* by the *Criticism* model.
3. For a predicted *Criticism* sentence, label it *PROBLEM* if it is predicted as *Problem* by the *Problem* model.
4. For a predicted *Non-problem* sentence, label it *SOLUTION*

Table 7: Relabel procedure.

Model	Acc.	κ
MAJOR	0.51	-
PAPER	0.71	0.49
CTRAIN	0.76	0.60
RELABELFIRST	0.79	0.66
INFERFIRST	0.79	0.66

Table 8: Prediction performance of different approaches in a case study.

proach, we propose two aggregation procedures to infer comment labels given sentence prediction output. In the first procedure, RELABELFIRST, we infer new sentence labels regarding *NULL, PROBLEM*, and *SOLUTION* using a series of conditional statements. The order of statements is chosen heuristically given the performance of individual models (see Table 5) and is described in Table 7. Given the sentences' inferred labels, the comment is labeled *SOLUTION* if it has at least one *SOLUTION* sentence. Else, it is labeled *PROBLEM* if at least one of its sentences is *PROBLEM*, and labeled *NULL* otherwise. Our second aggregation procedure, called INFERFIRST, follows an opposite direction in which we infer comment labels regarding *Solution, Problem*, and *Criticism* before re-labeling the comment regarding *SOLUTION, PROBLEM*, and *NULL* following the order of conditional statements in the relabel procedure.

As shown in Table 8, the MAJOR and PAPER models perform much worse than the other three models. While the PAPER model has accuracy close to that of the other models, its kappa is far lower. Regarding the three models trained on diagram review data, the two sentence level models outperform the CTRAIN model. Particularly, kappas of the two sentence level models are either significantly higher (for INFERFIRST) or marginally higher (for RELABELFIRST) compared to kappa of CTRAIN. To further investigate performance disparity between models, we report in Table 9 precision and recall of different models for each class. The PAPER model achieves high precision but low recall for *SOLUTION* and *PROBLEM* classes. We reason that the model's seed words help its precision, but its ngram features, which were trained using paper review data, cannot adequately cover positive instances in our corpus. The two sentence level models perform better for the *PROBLEM* class than the other two models, which is consistent with what is reported in Table 6. Comparing the two sentence level models, INFERFIRST better balances precision and recall than RELABELFIRST.

8 The sentence level is right

The experimental results in the previous two sections have demonstrated that sentence prediction output helps improve prediction performance at the comment level. This supports our hypothesis that sentence prediction is the right level for enhancing peer review systems to detect and respond to multi-sentence review comments of low quality. In our labeled sentence corpus, each instance either expresses a solution, a problem, or is a non-criticism, so the data is cleaner and more discrim-

	SOLUTION		*PROBLEM*		*NULL*	
Model	Prec.	Recl.	Prec.	Recl.	Prec.	Recl.
MAJOR	-	-	-	-	0.51	1.00
PAPER	0.81	0.62	0.58	0.29	0.70	0.92
CTRAIN	0.84	0.75	0.55	0.41	0.78	0.90
RELABELFIRST	0.72	0.90	0.66	0.48	0.88	0.84
INFERFIRST	0.75	0.86	0.61	0.55	0.88	0.84

Table 9: Precision and recall of different models in a case study.

inative than the labeled comment corpus. This is a nice property that helps reduce feature collocation across exclusive classes, *Problem vs. Solution* for example, which is a danger of training on feedback comments due to *Combined* instances. Moreover, our annotated comment corpus has solution and problem text marked at the sub-sentence level, which is a valuable resource for learning solution and problem patterns and linguistic cues.

Improving peer feedback prediction accuracy is not the only reason we advocate for the sentence level. We envision that the sentence level is the necessary lower bound that a peer review system needs to handle new advanced functionalities such as envisioned in Figure 1. Being able to highlight featured text in a peer comment is a useful visualization function that should help peer reviewers learn from live examples, and may also help student authors quickly notice the important point of the comment.

Sentence and phrase level annotation is made easy with the availability of many text annotation toolkits; BRAT[10] (Stenetorp et al., 2012) is an example. From our work, marking text spans by selecting and clicking requires a minimal additional effort from annotators and does not cause more cognitive workload. Moreover, we hypothesize that through highlighting the text, an annotator has to reason about why she would choose a label, which in turn makes the annotation process more reliable. We plan to test whether annotation performance does indeed improve in future work.

9 Conclusions and future work

In this paper we present a sentence-level annotated corpus of argument diagram peer review data, which we use to develop comment-level predictions of peer feedback types. Our work is the first of its kind in building an automated feedback type assessment component for reviews of argument diagrams rather than papers. We have demonstrated that using sentence prediction outputs to label the corresponding comments outperforms the traditional approach that learns models using labeled comments. The improvement of using sentence prediction outputs is more significant for more difficult tasks, i.e. *Problem vs. Non-problem*, in which textual expression varies greatly from explicit to implicit. In a case study mimicking a real application setting to experiment with the proposed models, we achieved a similar verification of the utility of sentence models. Given our imbalanced training data labels and our avoidance of using domain-specific features, these first results of our two experiments are promising.

In these first studies, our models were trained using generic prediction procedures, e.g., using basic linguistic features without feature selection or tuning. Thus our next step is to analyze prediction features for their predictiveness. We also plan to incorporate human-engineered rules for solution and problem text. We aim to improve performance while keeping feature generality. An interesting experiment we may conduct is to test our learned models on paper review data to evaluate performance and generality in an extreme setting.

Acknowledgments

This work is supported by NFS Grant No. 1122504. We are grateful to our colleagues for sharing the data. We thank Kevin Ashley, Wencan Luo, Fan Zhang, other members of the Argument-Peer and ITSPOKE groups as well as the anonymous reviewers for their valuable feedback.

References

Kwangsu Cho and Christian D. Schunn. 2007. Scaffolded writing and rewriting in the discipline: A web-based reciprocal peer review system. *Computers and Education*, 48(3):409–426.

[10]http://brat.nlplab.org/

Kwangsu Cho. 2008. Machine classification of peer comments in physics. In *Proceedings 1st international conference on Educational Data Mining (EDM)*, pages 192–196.

Mohammad Falakmassir, Kevin Ashley, and Christian Schunn. July 2013. Using argument diagramming to improve peer grading of writing assignments. In *Proceedings of the 1st Workshop on Massive Open Online Courses at 16th International Conference on Artificial Intelligence in Education (AIED), Memphis, TN*, pages 41–48.

Sarah Gielen, Elien Peeters, Filip Dochy, Patrick Onghena, and Katrien Struyven. 2010. Improving the effectiveness of peer feedback for learning. *Learning and Instruction*, 20(4):304–315.

Andrew B. Goldberg, Nathanael Fillmore, David Andrzejewski, Zhiting Xu, Bryan Gibson, and Xiaojin Zhu. 2009. May all your wishes come true: A study of wishes and how to recognize them. In *Proceedings Human Language Technologies: The 2009 Annual Conference of the North American Chapter of the Association for Computational Linguistics, NAACL-HTL*, pages 263–271.

Jordan Lippman, Mike Elfenbein, Matthew Diabes, Cori Luchau, Collin Lynch, Kevin Ashley, and Chris Schunn. 2012. To revise or not to revise: What influences undergrad authors to implement peer critiques of their argument diagrams? In *International Society for the Psychology of Science and Technology 2012 Conference*. Poster.

Melissa M. Nelson and Christian D. Schunn. 2009. The nature of feedback: how different types of peer feedback affect writing performance. *Instructional Science*, 37(4):375–401.

Huy V. Nguyen and Diane J. Litman. July 2013. Identifying localization in peer reviews of argument diagrams. In *Proceedings 16th International Conference on Artificial Intelligence in Education (AIED), Memphis, TN*, pages 91–100.

Huy Nguyen, Wenting Xiong, and Diane Litman. June 2014. Classroom evaluation of a scaffolding intervention for improving peer review localization. In *Proceedings 12th International Conference on Intelligent Tutoring Systems (ITS), Honolulu, HI*, pages 272–282.

Lakshmi Ramachandran and Edward F. Gehringer. 2011. Automated assessment of review quality using latent semantic analysis. In *Proceedings 11th IEEE International Conference on Advanced Learning Technologies (ICALT)*, pages 136–138.

J. Ramanand, Krishna Bhavsar, and Niranjan Pedanekar. 2010. Wishful thinking: finding suggestions and 'buy' wishes from product reviews. In *Proceedings the NAACL-HLT 2010 Workshop on Computational Approaches to Analysis and Generation of Emotion in Text*, pages 54–61.

Oliver Scheuer, Frank Loll, Niels Pinkwart, and Bruce M. McLaren. 2010. Computer-supported argumentation: A review of the state of the art. *International Journal of Computer-Supported Collaborative Learning*, 5(1):43–102.

Pontus Stenetorp, Sampo Pyysalo, Goran Topic, Tomoko Ohta, Sophia Ananiadou, and Jun'ichi Tsujii. 2012. Brat: a web-based tool for nlp-assisted text annotation. In *Proceedings the Demonstrations at the 13th Conference of the European Chapter of the Association for Computational Linguistics*, pages 102–107.

Theresa Wilson, Janyce Wiebe, and Paul Hoffmann. 2005. Recognizing contextual polarity in phrase-level sentiment analysis. In *Joint Human Language Technology Conference and the Conference on Empirical Methods in Natural Language Processing (HLT-EMNLP)*, pages 347–354.

Wenting Xiong and Diane Litman. 2010. Identifying problem localization in peer-review feedback. In *Proceedings 10th International Conference on Intelligent Tutoring System (ITS), Pittsburgh, PA*. Poster.

Wenting Xiong, Diane Litman, and Christian Schunn. 2012. Natural language processing techniques for researching and improving peer feedback. *Journal of Writing Research*, 4(2):155–176.

Wenting Xiong, Diane Litman, and Christian Schunn. June 2010. Assessing reviewer's performance based on mining problem localization in peer-review data. In *Proceedings 3rd International Conference on Educational Data Mining (EDM), Pittsburgh, PA*, pages 211–220.

ArCADE: An Arabic Corpus of Auditory Dictation Errors

C. Anton Rytting
Paul Rodrigues
Tim Buckwalter
Valerie Novak
Aric Bills
University of Maryland
7005 52nd Avenue
College Park, MD 20742
{crytting,prr,tbuckwal,
vnovak,abills}@umd.edu

Noah H. Silbert
Communication
Sciences & Disorders
University of Cincinnati
2600 Clifton Avenue
Cincinnati, Ohio
silbernh
@ucmail.uc.edu

Mohini Madgavkar
Independent Researcher
6120 Dhaka Pl. 20189-6120
Dhaka, Bangladesh
mohini.madgavkar
@gmail.com

Abstract

We present a new corpus of word-level listening errors collected from 62 native English speakers learning Arabic designed to inform models of spell checking for this learner population. While we use the corpus to assist in automated detection and correction of auditory errors in electronic dictionary lookup, the corpus can also be used as a phonological error layer, to be combined with a composition error layer in a more complex spell-checking system for non-native speakers. The corpus may be useful to instructors of Arabic as a second language, and researchers who study second language phonology and listening perception.

1 Introduction

Learner corpora have received attention as an important resource both for guiding teachers in curriculum development (Nesselhauf, 2004) and for providing training and evaluation material the development of tools for computer-assisted language learning (CALL). One of the most commonly used technologies in CALL is spell correction. Spell correction is used for providing automated feedback to language learners (cf. Warschauer and Ware, 2006), automatic assessment (Bestgen and Granger, 2011), and in providing cleaner input to downstream natural language processing (NLP) tools, thereby improving their performance (e.g. Nagata et al., 2011). However, off-the-shelf spell correctors developed for native speakers of the target language are of only limited use for repairing language learners' spelling errors, since their error patterns are different (e.g. Hovermale, 2011; Mitton and Okada, 2007; Okada, 2005).

Most learner corpora (and spell correctors) are understandably focused on learner-written texts. Thus, they allow a greater understanding (and improvement) of learners' writing skills. However, another important aspect of language learning is listening comprehension (cf. Field, 2008; Prince, 2012). A better understanding of listening errors can guide teachers and curriculum development just as written production errors do. Listening error data may also be helpful for improving technologies for listening training tools, by helping prioritize the most critical pairs of phonemes for discrimination, and pointing out the most troublesome contexts for phoneme discrimination.

Finally, spell correction specifically designed to correct listening errors may aid listening comprehension and vocabulary acquisition. If learners are unable to hear, recall and record accurately what they heard, they will be less able to search dictionaries or the Web for more information on new vocabulary items they otherwise could have learned from listening exercises. While data-driven spelling correction on popular search engines may catch some non-native errors, native errors are likely to 'drown out' any non-native errors they conflict with due to larger numbers of native users of these search engines. On the other hand, if the most common listening and transcription errors are automatically corrected within a search tool, learners will have greater success in finding the new vocabulary items they may have misheard in speech.

Learner corpora focused on written production may not have enough samples of phonologically-based errors to aid in developing such tools, and

Proceedings of the Ninth Workshop on Innovative Use of NLP for Building Educational Applications, pages 109–115,
Baltimore, Maryland USA, June 26, 2014.

even in a large corpus, word avoidance strategies and other biases would make the source unreliable for estimating relative magnitudes of listening problems accurately. It may be more effective to target listening errors directly, through other tasks such as listening dictation.

2 Related Work

Tools for language learning and maintenance, and learner corpora from which to build them, typically focus on language pairs for which there is a large market. Learner corpora for native English learners of low resource languages such as Arabic have been until recently comparatively rare, and often too small to be of practical use for the development of educational technology. In the past few years, however, a number of learner corpora for Arabic have become available, including a corpus of 19 non-native (mostly Malaysian) students at Al Al-Bayt University (Abu al-Rub, 2007); the *Arabic Interlanguage Database* (ARIDA; Abuhakema et al., 2008, 2009); the *Arabic Learners Written Corpus* from the University of Arizona Center for Educational Resources in Culture, Language, and Literacy (CERCLL; Farwaneh and Tamimi, 2012);[1] and the *Arabic Learner Corpus v1* (Alfaifi and Atwell, 2013).[2]

These corpora are all derived from learner writing samples, such as essays, and as such they contain many different types of errors, including errors in morphology, syntax, and word choice. Spelling errors are also observed, but relatively rarely, and the relevance of these spelling errors to listening competence is unclear. Hence, while they are likely to be useful for many applications in teaching Arabic writing, their usefulness for other purposes, such as examining listening skills and the effects of learner phonology on spelling, is limited.

Corpora or datasets focused on speaking and listening skills in Arabic are rarer. One such corpus, the West Point Arabic Speech Corpus, available from the LDC, contains one hour of non-native (learner) speech (LaRocca and Chouairi, 2002) Sethy et al. (2005) describe a corpus of elicited Arabic speech, but because none of the participants had prior exposure to Arabic, its use for understanding learner Arabic is limited. While there have been a few studies of Arabic listening skills (e.g. Huthaily, 2008; Faircloth, 2013), their coverage was not sufficiently broad to make reuse of their data likely to inform such purposes as the development of phoneme discrimination training or other CALL technology.

3 Motivation

We present here the *Arabic Corpus of Auditory Dictation Errors* (ArCADE) version 1, a corpus of Arabic words as transcribed by 62 native English speakers learning Arabic. This corpus fills the current gap in non-native spelling error corpora, and particularly for spelling errors due to listening difficulties. Unlike error corpora collected from non-native Arabic writing samples, it is designed to elicit spelling errors arising from perceptual errors; it provides more naturalistic data than is typical in phoneme identification or confusion studies.

A principal purpose for creating the corpus was to aid in the development and evaluation of tools for detecting and correcting listening errors to aid in dictionary lookup of words learners encountered in spoken language (cf. Rytting et al., 2010). As such, it serves as a complementary dataset for the dictionary search engine's query logs, since in this case the intended target of each transcription is known (rather than having to be inferred, in the case of query logs). We list three other potential uses for this corpus in Section 5.

4 Corpus Design and Creation

The ArCADE corpus was created through an elicitation experiment, similar in structure to an American-style spelling test. The principal difference (other than the language) is that in this case, the participants are expected to be unfamiliar with the words, and thus forced to rely on what they hear in the moment, rather than their lexical knowledge. We selected words from a commonly-used dictionary of Modern Standard Arabic such that the set of words would contain a complete set of non-glide consonants in various phonetic contexts.

4.1 Selection of Stimulus Words

Since the corpus was originally collected for a study focused on the perception of consonants within the context of real Arabic words, the stimulus set was designed with three purposes in

[1] Available from `http://l2arabiccorpus.cercll.arizona.edu/?q=homepage`.

[2] As of February 2014, a second version, with about 130K words from non-native speakers, is available from `http://www.arabiclearnercorpus.com/`. It also has a small (three hour) speech component.

mind: coverage of target sounds, exclusion of basic words, and brevity (so that participants could complete the task in one sitting).

In order to differentiate consonants that are relatively unpredictable (and thus test listening ability) from consonants whose value could be predicted from non-acoustic cues (such as prior knowledge of morphological structure), the corpus is annotated for *target* consonants vs. non-target consonants. A target consonant is defined as a consonant that should not be predictable (assuming the word is unknown to the listener) except by the acoustic cues alone. Glides */w/* and */j/* were not targeted in the study because orthographic ambiguities between glides and vowels would complicate the error analysis.

Each Arabic consonant other than the glides occurs as a target consonant in the stimulus set in six consonant/vowel/word-boundary contexts: C_V, V_C, V_V, #_V, V_#, and C_#.[3] (The contexts #_C and C_C are phonotactically illegal in Modern Standard Arabic.)

Consonants that were judged morphologically predictable within a word were considered non-target consonants. These included: (1) non-root consonants, when Semitic roots were known to the researchers; (2) consonants participating in a reduplicative pattern such as */tamtam/* and */zalzala/*; and (3) Consonants found in doubled (R2=R3) roots if the two consonants surfaced separately (e.g., in broken plurals such as */ʔasnan/*).

We excluded words from our stimulus set if we anticipated that an intermediate Arabic student would already be familiar with them or would easily be able to guess their spellings. Items found in vocabulary lists associated with two commonly-used introductory textbooks (*Al-Kitaab* and *Alif-Baa*) were excluded (Brustad et al., 2004a,b). Loanwords from Western languages were also excluded, as were well-known place names (e.g., */ʔiskotlanda/* = "Scotland"). Words found only in colloquial dialects and terms that might be offensive or otherwise distracting (as judged by native speaker of Arabic) were removed, as well.

In order to keep the stimulus set as short as possible while maintaining coverage of the full set of target stimuli consonants in each targeted context, we chose words with multiple target consonants whenever possible. The final set of 261 words contained 649 instances of target consonants: one instance of each geminate consonant and between 17 and 50 instances of each singleton consonant (at least two instances for each of the six contexts), with a few exceptions.[4] Although glides and vowels were not specifically targeted, 6 instances of */w/*, 10 instances of */j/*, and at least 12 instances of each of the monophthong vowels (*/a/, /i/, /u/, /a:/, /i:/, /u:/*) occur in the stimulus set.

4.2 Recording of the Stimuli

The audio data used in the dictation was recorded in a sound-proof booth with a unidirectional microphone (Earthworks SR30/HC) equipped with a pop filter, and saved as WAV files (stereo, 44.1kHz, 32-bit) with Adobe Audition. The stimuli were spoken at a medium-fast rate. The audio files were segmented and normalized with respect to peak amplitude with Matlab.

The native Arabic speaker in the audio recording is of Egyptian and Levantine background, but was instructed to speak with a neutral ("BBC Arabic") accent.

4.3 Participants and Methodology

Seventy-five participants were recruited from six universities. To be eligible, participants had to be 18 years of age or older, native speakers of English, and have no known history of speech language pathology or hearing loss. Participants were required to have completed at least two semesters of university level Arabic courses in order to ensure that they were able to correctly write the Arabic characters and to transcribe Arabic speech. Heritage speakers of Arabic and non-English dominant bilinguals were excluded from the study. The corpus contains responses from 62 participants. The mean duration of Arabic study completed was 5.6 semesters (median 4).

Before beginning the experiment, participants were asked to fill out a biographical questionnaire. This included questions about language exposure during childhood and languages studied in a classroom setting. There were additional questions about time spent outside of the United States to ascertain possible exposure to languages not addressed in previous questions.

[3] C = consonant, V = vowel, # = word boundary, and '_' (underscore) = location of target consonant.

[4] These exceptions include only one instance of a phone rather than two for the following contexts: (1) */h/* in the context C_#, (2) */f/* in the context V_#, and (3) */z/* in the context #_V. One geminate consonant, */x:/*, was inadvertently omitted from the stimulus set.

Participants wrote their responses to the 261 stimulus words on a response sheet that contained numbered boxes. They were asked to use Arabic orthography with full diacritics and short vowels (*fatha, damma, kasra, shadda* and *sukun*). The *shadda* (gemination) mark was required in order to analyze the participants' perception of geminate consonants; the other diacritics were included so as to not single out *shadda* for special attention (since participants were naïve to the purpose of the study) and also to increase the value of the resulting error corpus for later analysis of short vowels.

4.4 Presentation of the Stumuli

The proctors who ran the experiment supplied an iPod Touch tablet to each participant, pre-loaded with a custom stimuli presentation application.

In this custom iPod application, 261 Arabic words were randomized into 9 stimulus sets. Each stimulus set was preceded by four practice items which were not scored; thus each participant saw 265 items. Each touch screen tablet was initialized by the testers to deliver a specific stimulus set. A button on the touch screen allowed the participants to begin the experiment. After a few seconds' delay, the first word was played. A stimulus number identifying the word appeared in a large font to aid the participants in recording the word on paper. Participants were given 15 seconds to write their response, before the tablet automatically advanced to the next word. Participants were not able to replay a word.

The participants used noise-canceling headphones (Audio-Technica ATH-ANC7 or ATH-ANC7B) for listening to the audio stimuli. The experiment was performed in a quiet classroom.

4.5 Data Coding

The participants' handwritten responses were typed in as they were written, using Arabic Unicode characters. Any diacritics (short vowels or gemination) written by the participants were preserved. An automatic post-process was used to ensure that the gemination mark was ordered properly with respect to an adjacent short vowel mark.

The corpus consists of two main sections: orthographic and phonemic. The orthographic section is very simple: each stimulus word is given in its target orthography (with diacritics) and in each participant's corresponding orthographic transcription (including diacritics if the participant provided them as instructed). The phonemic section is more elaborate, containing additional fields designed for a phone level analysis of target consonants. Its construction is described in further detail below.

Both the orthographic response and the canonical (reference) spelling were automatically converted to a phonemic representation. This conversion normalizes certain orthographic distinctions, such as various spellings for word-final vowels. This phonemic representation of the response for each stimulus item was then compared with the phonemic representation of the item's canonical pronunciation, and each phoneme of the response was aligned automatically with the most probable phoneme (or set of equally plausible phonemes) in the canonical phonemic representation of the auditory stimulus. This alignment was done via dynamic programming with a weighted Levenshtein edit distance metric. Specifically, weights were used to favor the alignment of vowels and glides with each other rather than with non-glide consonants (since the scope of our original study was non-glide consonants). Thus substitutions between short vowels, long vowels, and glides are given preference over other confusions. This is intended to reduce the ambiguity of the alignments and to ensure that non-glide consonants are aligned with non-glide consonants when possible, without introducing any bias in the non-glide consonants alignments. When one unique alignment had the lowest cost, it was used as the alignment for that item. In some cases, multiple alignments were tied for minimal cost. In this case, all alignments were used and assigned equal probability.

Once the least-cost alignment(s) were found between a response string and the reference string for an item, the target consonants within the reference string were then each paired with the corresponding phonemes in the response, and an error category (<substitution>, <deletion>, or <match> for no error) was assigned. In the case of geminate phonemes, two subtypes of <substitution> were introduced: <gemination> and <degemination>.

Where an entire word had no response, 'NA' was used to indicate that no edit operation can be assigned. (A total of 112 items were missing).

Note that insertions were not marked, because only the 649 instances of target consonants were analyzed for the phonemic portion of the corpus, and no other material in each stimulus word (including any possible insertion points for additional material) were annotated for errors. Insertions can be recovered from the orthographic portion of the corpus.

The coding method described above yielded a set of 41,121 target consonant records of participants' responses to target consonants (not counting the 112 non-response items), including 29,634 matches (72.1%) and 11,487 errors (27.9%). At the word level, there are 16,217 words, of which 8321 (48.2%) contain at least one error in a targeted consonant, and 5969 (37.1%) are spelled perfectly (excluding diacritics).

5 Potential Uses of the Corpus

In addition to the uses described in Section 3, we believe the data could be used for several other uses, such as examining linguistic correlates of proficiency, developing phonemic training, and investigating non-native Arabic handwriting.

One potential use of the corpus is to analyze the errors by individual learners to determine which sounds are confused only by relatively beginning learners (after two semesters) and which are confused by beginning and experienced learners alike. While hard measures of proficiency are not available for the participants, the language questionnaire includes time of study and self-report measures of proficiency. To the extent to which these proxies are reliable, the corpus may lead to the development of hypotheses which can be tested in more targeted studies.

Since the corpus allows quantitative evidence for the relative difficulty of particular sound pairs in particular contexts, it may guide the prioritization of foci for phonemic discrimination training and other listening exercises. At the most basic level, a teacher can take our original audio stimuli and use them as dictation exercises for beginning students (who may not be ready for sentence or paragraph level dictation). It may also form the basis for automated phonemic discrimination training, such as Michael et al. (2013). Cf. Bradlow (2008) for a review.

Since the participants handwrote their responses, the corpus contains, as a byproduct, a set of 16,329 words in non-native handwriting and their digital transcriptions. As Alfaifi and Atwell (2013) note, this could be used as a corpus of non-native handwriting for training or evaluating OCR on L2 Arabic script. If corresponding native transcriptions of the same (or similar) strings were obtained, the corpus could also be used to differentiate native from non-native handwriting (cf. Farooq et al., 2006; Ramaiah et al., 2013).

6 Limitations and future work

The corpus as it currently stands has some limitations worth noting. First, there is no control set of native Arabic listeners to provide a comparison point for distinguishing non-native perceptual errors from acoustic errors that even native speakers are subject to. Second, the survey does not contain proficiency ratings (except self-report) for the participants, making direct correlation of particular confusion patterns with proficiency level more difficult.

Statistical analysis of the participants' accuracy at distinguishing Arabic consonants is currently underway (Silbert et al., in preparation). An investigation of the utility of the corpus for training and evaluating spelling correction for L1 English late learners of Arabic, including the effects of training corpus size on accuracy, is also in progress.

7 Conclusion

The Arabic Corpus of Auditory Dictation Errors (ArCADE) version 1 provides a corpus of word-level transcriptions of Arabic speech by native English speakers learning Arabic, ideal for the analysis of within-word listening errors, as well as the development and evaluation of NLP tools that seek to aid either in developing listening skill or in compensating for typical non-native deficits in listening. Since most learner corpora only include written composition or spoken production from students, this corpus fills a gap in the resources available for the study of Arabic as a second language.

The corpus, along with the original audio stimuli and participants' handwriting samples, is available at `http://www.casl.umd.edu/datasets/cade/arcade/index.html`.

Acknowledgments

This material is based on work supported, in whole or in part, with funding from the United States Government. Any opinions, findings, and conclusions or recommendations expressed in this material are those of the authors and do not necessarily reflect the views of the University of Maryland, College Park and/or any agency or entity of the United States Government.

References

Muhammad Abu al-Rub. 2007. تحليل الأخطاء الكتابية على مستوى الإملاء لدى متعلمي اللغة العربية الناطقين بغيرها. Taḥlīl al-akhṭā' al-kitābīyah 'ala mustawá al-imlā' ladá muta'allimī al-lughah al-'arabīyah al-nāṭiqīna bi-ghayrihā [Analysis of written spelling errors among non-native speaking learners of Arabic]. دراسات، العلوم الإنسانية والاجتماعية. *Dirāsāt, al-'Ulūm al-Insānīyah wa-al-Ijtimā'īyah [Humanities and Social Sciences]*, 34(2). http://journals.ju.edu.jo/DirasatHum/article/view/1911/1898.

Ghazi Abuhakema, Anna Feldman, and Eileen Fitzpatrick. 2008. Annotating an Arabic learner corpus for error. In *Proceedings of the International Conference on Language Resources and Evaluation (LREC 2008)*. Marrakech, Morocco.

Ghazi Abuhakema, Anna Feldman, and Eileen Fitzpatrick. 2009. ARIDA: An Arabic interlanguage database and its applications: A pilot study. *Journal of the National Council of Less Commonly Taught Languages (NCOLCTL)*, 7:161–184.

Abdullah Alfaifi and Eric Atwell. 2013. Potential uses of the Arabic Learner Corpus. In *Leeds Language, Linguistics, and Translation PGR Conference 2013*. University of Leeds, Leeds, UK.

Yves Bestgen and Sylvaine Granger. 2011. Categorising spelling errors to assess L2 writing. *International Journal of Continuing Engineering Education and Life-Long Learning*, 21(2/3):235–252.

Ann Bradlow. 2008. Training non-native language sound patterns. In *Phonology and Second Language Acquisition*, Benjamins, Amsterdam and Philadelphia, pages 287–308.

Kristin Brustad, Mahmoud Al-Batal, and Abbas Al-Tonsi. 2004a. *Al-Kitaab fii Ta'allum al-'Arabiyya*, volume 1. Georgetown University Press, Washington, DC, 1st edition.

Kristin Brustad, Mahmoud Al-Batal, and Abbas Al-Tonsi. 2004b. *Alif Baa: Introduction to Arabic Letters and Sounds*. Georgetown University Press, Washington, DC, 2nd edition.

Laura Rose Faircloth. 2013. *The L2 Perception of Phonemic Distinctions in Arabic by English Speakers*. BA Thesis, The College of William and Mary. https://digitalarchive.wm.edu/bitstream/handle/10288/18160/FairclothLauraRose2013Thesis.pdf?sequence=1.

Faisal Farooq, Liana Lorigo, and Venu Govindaraju. 2006. On the accent in handwriting of individuals. In *Tenth International Workshop on Frontiers in Handwriting Recognition*. La Baule, France. http://hal.inria.fr/docs/00/11/26/30/PDF/cr103741695994.pdf.

Samira Farwaneh and Mohammed Tamimi. 2012. Arabic learners written corpus: A resource for research and learning. Available from the University of Arizona Center for Educational Resources in Culture, Language, and Literacy web site. http://l2arabiccorpus.cercll.arizona.edu/?q=homepage.

John Field. 2008. *Listening in the Language Classroom*. Cambridge University Press, Cambridge, UK.

DJ Hovermale. 2011. *Erron: A Phrase-Based Machine Traslation Approach to Customized Spelling Correction*. Ph.D. thesis, The Ohio State University.

Khaled Yahya Huthaily. 2008. *Second Language Instruction with Phonological Knowledge: Teaching Arabic to Speakers of English*. Ph.D. thesis, The University of Montana.

Col. Stephen A. LaRocca and Rajaa Chouairi. 2002. West Point Arabic speech corpus. Technical report, LDC, Philadelphia.

Erica B. Michael, Greg Colflesh, Valerie Karuzis, Michael Key, Svetlana Cook, Noah H. Silbert, Christopher Green, Evelyn Browne, C. Anton Rytting, Eric Pelzl, and Michael Bunting. 2013. Perceptual training for second language speech perception: Validation study to assess the efficacy of a new training regimen (TTO 2013). Technical report, University of Maryland Center for Advanced Study of Language, College Park, MD.

Roger Mitton and Takeshi Okada. 2007. The adaptation of an English spellchecker for Japanese writers. Birbeck ePrints, London. http://eprints.bbk.ac.uk/archive/00000592.

Ryo Nagata, Edward Whittaker, and Vera Sheinman. 2011. Creating a manually error-tagged and shallow-parsed learner corpus. In *Proceedings of the 49th Annual Meeting of the Asso-*

ciation for Computational Linguistics. Association for Computational Linguistics, Portland, OR, pages 1210–1219.

Nadja Nesselhauf. 2004. Learner corpora and their potential in language teaching. In *How to Use Corpora in Language Teaching*, Benjamins, Amsterdam and Philadelphia, pages 125–152.

Takeshi Okada. 2005. Spelling errors made by Japanese EFL writers: with reference to errors occurring at the word-initial and word-final positions. In Vivian Cook and Benedetta Bassetti, editors, *Second language writing systems*, Multilingual Matters, Clevedon, UK, pages 164–183.

Peter Prince. 2012. Writing it down: Issues relating to the use of restitution tasks in listening comprehension. *TESOL Journal*, 3(1):65–86.

Chetan Ramaiah, Arti Shivram, and Venu Govindaraju. 2013. A Baysian framework for modeling accents in handwriting. In *12th International Conference on Document Analysis and Recognition (ICDAR)*. `http://ieeexplore.ieee.org/xpls/abs_all.jsp?arnumber=6628752`.

C. Anton Rytting, Paul Rodrigues, Tim Buckwalter, David M. Zajic, Bridget Hirsch, Jeff Carnes, Nathanael Lynn, Sarah Wayland, Chris Taylor, Jason White, Charles Blake, Evelyn Browne, Corey Miller, and Tristan Purvis. 2010. Error correction for Arabic dictionary lookup. In *Seventh International Conference on Language Resources and Evaluation (LREC 2010)*. Valletta, Malta.

Abhinav Sethy, Shrikanth Narayanan, Nicolaus Mote, and W. Lewis Johnson. 2005. Modeling and automating detection of errors in Arabic language learner speech. In *INTERSPEECH-2005*. pages 177–180.

Noah H. Silbert, C. Anton Rytting, Paul Rodrigues, Tim Buckwalter, Valerie Novak, Mohini Madgavkar, Katharine Burk, and Aric Bills. in preparation. Similarity and bias in non-native Arabic consonant perception.

Mark Warschauer and Paige Ware. 2006. Automated writing evaluation: Defining the classroom research agenda. *Language Teaching Research*, 10(2):157–180.

Similarity-Based Non-Scorable Response Detection for Automated Speech Scoring

Su-Youn Yoon
Educational Testing Service
Princeton, NJ, USA
syoon@ets.org

Shasha Xie
Microsoft
Sunnyvale, CA, USA
shxie@microsoft.com

Abstract

This study provides a method that identifies problematic responses which make automated speech scoring difficult. When automated scoring is used in the context of a high stakes language proficiency assessment, for which the scores are used to make consequential decisions, some test takers may have an incentive to try to game the system in order to artificially inflate their scores. Since many automated proficiency scoring systems use fluency features such as speaking rate as one of the important features, students may engage in strategies designed to manipulate their speaking rate as measured by the system.

In order to address this issue, we developed a method which filters out non-scorable responses based on text similarity measures. Given a test response, the method generated a set of features which calculated the topic similarity with the prompt question or the sample responses including relevant content. Next, an automated filter which identified these problematic responses was implemented using the similarity features. This filter improved the performance of the baseline filter in identifying responses with topic problems.

1 Introduction

In spoken language proficiency assessment, some responses may include sub-optimal characteristics which make it difficult for the automated scoring system to provide a valid score. For instance, some test takers may try to game the system by speaking in their native languages or by citing memorized responses for unrelated topics. Others may repeat questions or part of questions with modifications instead of generating his/her own response. Hereafter, we call these problematic responses non-scorable (NS) responses. By using these strategies, test takers can generate fluent speech, and the automated proficiency scoring system, which utilizes fluency as one of the important factors, may assign a high score. In order to address this issue, the automated proficiency scoring system in this study used a two-step approach: these problematic responses were filtered out by a "filtering model," and only the remaining responses were scored using the automated scoring model. By filtering out these responses, the robustness of the automated scoring system can be improved.

The proportion of NS responses, in the assessment of which the responses are scored by human raters, are likely to be low. For instance, the proportion of NS responses in the international English language assessment used in this study was 2%. Despite this low proportion, it is a serious problem which has a strong impact on the validity of the test. In addition, the likelihood of students engaging in gaming strategies may increase with the use of automated scoring. Therefore, an automated filtering model with a high accuracy is a necessary step to use the automated scoring system as a sole rater.

Both off-topic and copy responses have topic-related problems, although they are at the two extremes in the degree of similarity. Focusing on the intermediate levels of similarity, Metzler et al. (2005) presented a hierarchy of five similarity levels: unrelated, on the general topic, on the specific topic, same facts, and copied. In the automated scoring of spontaneous speech, responses that fell into *unrelated* can be considered as off-topic, while the ones that fell into *copied* can be considered as repetition or plagiarism. Following this approach, we developed a non-scorable response identification method utilizing similar-

Proceedings of the Ninth Workshop on Innovative Use of NLP for Building Educational Applications , pages 116–123,
Baltimore, Maryland USA, June 26, 2014.

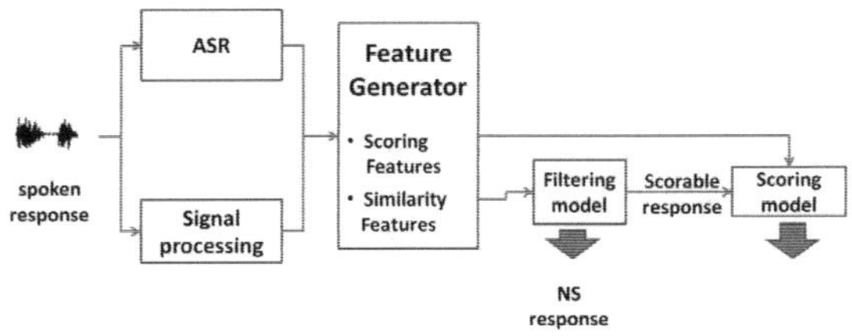

Figure 1: A diagram of the overall architecture of our method.

ity measures. We will show that this similarity based method is highly efficient in identifying off-topic or repetition responses. Furthermore, we will show that the method can effectively detect NS responses that are not directly related to the topicality issue (e.g, non-English responses).

Figure 1 shows the overall architecture of our method including the automated speech proficiency scoring system. For a given spoken response, the system performs speech processing including speech recognition and generates a word hypotheses and time stamps. In addition, the system computes pitch and power; the system calculates descriptive statistics such as the mean and standard deviation of pitch and power at both the word level and response level. Given the word hypotheses and descriptive features of pitch/power, it derives features for automated proficiency scoring. In addition, the similarity features are generated based on the word hypotheses and topic models. Finally, given both sets of features, the filtering model filters out non-scorable responses, and the remainder of the responses are scored using a scoring model. A detailed description of the system is available from Zechner et al. (2009). In this study, we will only focus on the filtering model.

This paper will proceed as follows: we first review previous studies in section 2, then describe the data in section 3, and present the method and experiment set-up in sections 4 and 5. The results and discussion are presented in section 6, and the conclusions are presented in section 7.

2 Related Work

Filtering of NS responses for automated speech scoring has been rarely recognized. Only a few pieces of research have focused on this task, and most studies have targeted highly restricted speech. van Doremalen et al. (2009) and Lo et al. (2010) used normalized confidence scores of a speech recognizer in recasting speech. They identified non-scorable responses with promising performances (equal error rates ranged from 10 to 20%). Cheng and Shen (2011) extended these studies and combined an acoustic model score, a language model score, and a garbage model score with confidence scores. They applied this new filter to less constrained items (e.g., picture description) and identified off-topic responses with an accuracy rate of 90% with a false positive rate of 5%.

Although normalized confidence scores achieved promising performances in restricted speech, they may not be appropriate for the items that elicit unconstrained spontaneous speech. Low confidence scores signal the use of words or phrases not covered by the language model (LM) and this is strongly associated with off-topic responses in restricted speech in which the target sentence is given. However, in spontaneous speech, this is not trivial; it may be associated with not only off-topic speech but also mismatch between the LM and speech input due to the low coverage of the LM. Due to the latter case, the decision based on the confidence score may not be effective in measuring topic similarity.

The topic similarity between two documents has been frequently modeled by relative-frequency measures (Hoad and Zobel, 2003; Shivakumar and Garcia-Molina, 1995), document fingerprinting (Brin et al., 1995; Shivakumar and Garcia-Molina, 1995; Shivakumar and Garcia-Molina, 1996)), and query based information retrieval methods using vector space models or language model (Sanderson, 1997; Hoad and Zobel, 2003).

Document similarity measures have been applied in automated scoring. Foltz et al. (1999) evaluated the content of written essays using latent semantic analysis (LSA) by comparing the test essays with essays of known quality in regard to their degree of conceptual relevance and the amount of relevant content. In another approach, the lexical content of an essay was evaluated by comparing the words contained in each essay to the words found in a sample of essays from each score category (Attali and Burstein, 2006). More recently, Xie et al. (2012) used a similar approach in automated speech scoring; they measured the similarity using three similarity measures, including a lexical matching method (Vector Space Model) and two semantic similarity measures (Latent Semantic Analysis and Pointwise Mutual Information). They showed moderately high correlations between the similarity features and human proficiency scores on even the output of an automatic speech recognition system. Similarity measures have also been used in off-topic detection for non-native speakers' essays. Higgins et al. (2006) calculated overlaps between the question and content words from the essay and obtained an error rate of 10%.

Given the promising performance in both automated scoring and off-topic essay detection, we will expand these similarity measures in NS response detection for speech scoring.

3 Data

In this study, we used a collection of responses from an international English language assessment. The assessment was composed of items in which speakers were prompted to provide spontaneous speech.

Approximately 48,000 responses from 8,000 non-native speakers were collected and used for training the automated speech recognizer (ASR set). Among 24 items in the ASR set, four items were randomly selected. For these items, a total of 11,560 responses were collected and used for the training and evaluation of filtering model (FM set). Due to the extremely skewed distribution of NS responses (2% in the ASR set), it was not easy to train and evaluate the filtering model. In order to address this issue, we modified the distribution of NS responses in the FM set. Initially, we collected 90,000 responses including 1,560 NS responses. While maintaining all NS responses, we downsampled the scorable responses in the FM set to include 10,000 responses. Finally, the proportion of NS responses was 6 times higher in FM set (13%) than ASR set. This artificial increase of the NS responses reduces the current problem of the skewed NS distribution and may make the task easier. However, the likelihood of students engaging in gaming strategies may increase with the use of automated scoring, and this increased NS distribution may be close to this situation.

Each response was rated by trained human raters using a 4-point scoring scale, where 1 indicated a low speaking proficiency and 4 indicated a high speaking proficiency. The raters also labeled responses as NS, when appropriate. NS responses are defined as responses that cannot be given a score according to the rubrics of the four-point scale. NS responses were responses with technical difficulties (TDs) that obscured the content of the responses or responses that would receive a score of 0 due to participants' inappropriate behaviors. The speakers, item information, and distribution of proficiency scores are presented in Table 1. There was no overlap in the sets of speakers in the ASR and FM sets.

In addition, 1,560 NS responses from the FM set were further classified into six types by two raters with backgrounds in linguistics using the rubrics presented in Table 2. This annotation was used for the purpose of analysis: to identify the frequent types of NS responses and prioritize the research effort.

Type	Proportion in total NSs	Description
NR	73%	No response. Test taker doesn't speak.
OR	16%	Off-topic responses. The response is not related to the prompt.
TR	5%	Generic responses. The response only include filler words or generic responses such as, "I don't know, it is too difficult to answer, well", etc.
RE	4%	Question copy. Full or partial repetition of question.
NE	1%	Non-English. Responses is in a language other than English.
OT	1%	Others

Table 2: Types of zero responses and proportions

Some responses belonged to more than one type, and this increased complexity of the annotation task. For instance, one response was comprised of a question copy and generic sentences, while another response was comprised of a question copy and off-topic sentences. An example of this type was presented in Table 3. This was a response for the question "Talk about an interesting book that you read recently. Explain why it was interesting[1]."

For these responses, annotators first segmented them into sentences and assigned the type that was most dominant.

Each rater annotated approximately 1,000 responses, and 586 responses were rated by both

[1]In order to not reveal the real test question administered in the operational test, we invented this question. Based on the question, we also modified a sample response; the question copy part was changed to avoid disclosure of the test question, but the other part remained the same as the original response.

Data set	Num. responses	Num. speakers	Num. items	Average score	Score distribution				
					NS	1	2	3	4
ASR	48,000	8,000	24	2.63	773 2%	1953 4%	16834 35%	23106 48%	5334 11%
FM	11,560	11,390	4	2.15	1560 13%	734 6%	4328 37%	4263 37%	675 6%

Table 1: Data size and score distribution

Sentence	Type
Well in my opinion are the interesting books that I read recently is.	RE
Talking about a interesting book.	RE
One interesting book oh God interesting book that had read recently.	RE
Oh my God.	TR
I really don't know how to answer this question.	TR
Well I don't know.	TR
Sorry.	TR

Table 3: Manual transcription of complex-type response

raters. The Cohen's kappa between two raters was 0.76. Among five different NS responses, non-response was the most frequent type (73%), followed by off-topic (16%). The combination of the two types was approximately 90% of the entire NS responses.

4 Method

In this study, we generated two different types of features. First, we developed similarity features (both chunk-based and response-based) to identify the responses with problems in topicality. Secondly, we generated acoustic, fluency, and ASR-confidence features using a state-of-art automated speech scoring system. Finally, using both feature sets, classifiers were trained to make a binary distinction of NS response vs. scorable response.

4.1 Chunk-based similarity features

Some responses in this study included more than two different types of the topicality problems. For instance, the first three sentences in Table 3 belonged to the "copied" category, while the other sentences fell into "unrelated". If the similarity features were calculated based on the entire response, the feature values may fall into neither the "copied" nor "unrelated" range because of the trade-off between the two types at two extremes. In order to address this issue, we calculated chunk-based similarity features similar to Metzler et al. (2005)'s sentence-based features.

First, the response was split into the chunks which were surrounded by long silences with durations longer than 0.6 sec. For each chunk, the proportion of word overlap with the question (WOL) was calculated based on the formula (1). Next, chunks with a WOL higher than 0.5 were considered as ***question copies***.

$$WOL = \frac{|S \cap Q|}{|S|}$$

where S is a response and Q is a question,
$|S \cap Q|$ is the number of word types that appear both in S and Q,
$|S|$ is the number of word types in S

(1)

Finally, the following three features were derived for each response based on the chunk-based WOL.

- numwds: the number of word tokens after removing question copies, fillers, and typical generic sentences[2];
- copyR: the proportion of question copies in the response in terms of number of word tokens;
- meanWOL: the mean of WOLs for all chunks in the response.

4.2 Response-based similarity features

We implemented three features based on a vector space model (VSM) using cosine similarity and term frequency-inverse document frequency (tf-idf) weighting to estimate the topic relevance at the response-level.

[2]Five sentences "it is too difficult", "thank you", "I don't know", "I am sorry", and "oh my God" were stored as typical sentences and removed from responses

Since the topics of each question were different from each other, we trained a VSM for each question separately. For the four items in the FM set, we selected a total of 485 responses (125 responses per item) from the ASR set for topic model training. Assuming that the responses with the highest proficiency scores contain the most diverse and appropriate words related to the topic, we only selected responses with a score of 4. We obtained the manual transcriptions of the responses, and all responses about the same question were converted into a single vector. In this study, the term was a unigram word, and the document was the response. *idf* was trained from the entire set of 48,000 responses in the ASR training partition, while tf was trained from the question-specific topic model training set.

In addition to the response-based VSM, we trained a question-based VSM. Each question was composed of two sentences. Each question was converted into a single vector, and a total of four VSMs were trained. *idf* was trained in the same way as the response-based VSMs, while tf was trained only using the question sentences.

Using these two different types of VSMs, the following three features were generated for each response.

- $sampleCosine$: a similarity score based on the response-based VSM. Assuming that two documents with the same topic shared common words, it measured the similarity in the words used in a test response and the sample responses. The feature was implemented to identify off-topic responses (OR);

- $qCosine$: a similarity score based on the question-based VSM. It measured the similarity between a test response and its question. The feature was implemented to identify both off-topic responses (OR) and question copy responses (RE); a low score is highly likely to be an off-topic response, while a high score signals a full or partial copy;

- $meanIDF$: mean of *idf*s for all word tokens in the response. Generic responses (TR) tend to include many high frequency words such as articles and pronouns, and the mean *idf* value of these responses may be low.

4.3 Features from the automated speech scoring system

A total of 61 features (hereafter, A/S features) were generated using a state-of-the-art automated speech scoring system. A detailed description of the system is available from (Jeon and Yoon, 2012). Among these features, many features were conceptually similar but based on different normalization methods, and they showed a strong inter-correlation. For this study, 30 features were selected and classified into three groups according to their characteristics: acoustic features, fluency features, and ASR-confidence features.

The acoustic features were related to power, pitch, and MFCC. First, power, pitch and MFCC were extracted at each frame using Praat (Boersma, 2002). Next, we generated response-level features from these frame-level features by calculating mean and variation. These features captured the overall distribution of energy and voiced regions in a speaker's response. These features are relevant since NS responses may have an abnormal distribution in energy. For instance, non-responses contain very low energy. In order to detect these abnormalities in the speech signal, pitch and power related features were calculated.

The fluency features measure the length of a response in terms of duration and number of words. In addition, this group contains features related to speaking rate and silences, such as mean duration and number of silences. In particular, these features are effective in identifying non-responses which contain zero or only a few words.

The ASR-confidence group contains features predicting the performance of the speech recognizer. Low confidence scores signal low speech recognition accuracy.

4.4 Model training

Three filtering models were trained to investigate the impact of each feature group: a filtering model using similarity features (hereafter, the Similarity-filter), a filtering model using A/S features (hereafter, the A/S-filter), and a filtering model using a combination of the two groups of features (hereafter, the Combined-filter).

5 Experiments

An HMM-based speech recognizer was trained using the ASR set. A gender independent triphone acoustic model and a combination of bigram, trigram, and four-gram language models were used. A word error rate (WER) of 27% on the held-out test dataset was observed.

For each response in the FM set, the word hypotheses was generated using this recognizer. From this ASR-based transcription, the six similarity features were generated. In addition, the 30 A/S features described in 4.3 were generated.

Using these two sets of features, filtering models were trained using the Support Vector Machine algorithm (SVM) with the RBF kernel of the WEKA machine-learning toolkit (Hall et al., 2009). A 10 fold cross-validation was conducted using the FM dataset.

6 Results and discussion

First, we will report the performance for the subset only topic-related NS responses. The similarity features were designed to detect NS responses with topicality issues, but the majority in the FM set were non-response (73%). The topic-related NS responses (off-topic responses, generic responses, and question copy responses) were only 25%. In the entire set, the advantage of the similarity features over the A/S features might not be salient due to the high proportion of non-response. In order to investigate the performance of the similarity features in the topic related NS responses, we excluded all responses other than 'OR', 'TR', and 'RE' from the FM set and conducted a 10 fold cross-validation.

Table 4 presents the average of the 10 fold cross-validation results in this subset. In this set, the total number of NS responses is 314, and the accuracy of the majority voting (to classify all responses as scorable responses) is 0.962.

	acc.	prec.	recall	fscore
Similarity-filter	0.975	0.731	0.548	0.626
A/S-filter	0.971	0.767	0.341	0.472
Combined-filter	0.977	0.780	0.566	0.656

Table 4: Performance of filters in topic-related NS detection

Not surprisingly, the Similarity-filter outperformed the A/S-filter: the F-score was approximately 0.63 which was 0.15 higher than that of the A/S-filter in absolute value. The lack of features specialized for detection of topic abnormality resulted in the low recall of the A/S-filter. The combination of the two features achieved a slight improvement: the F-score was 0.66 and it was 0.03 higher than the Similarity-filter.

In Metzler et al. (2005)'s study, the system using both sentence-based features and document-based features did not achieve further improvement over the system based on the document-based features alone. In order to explore the impact of chunk-based features, similarity features were classified into two groups (chunk-based features vs. document-based features), and two filters were trained using each group separately. Table 5 compares the performance of the two filters (Similarity-chunk and Similarity-doc) with the filter using all similarity features (Similarity).

	acc.	prec.	recall	fscore
Similarity-chunk	0.972	0.700	0.442	0.542
Similarity-doc	0.971	0.730	0.396	0.514
Similarity	0.975	0.731	0.548	0.626

Table 5: Comparison of chunk-based and document-based similarity features

In this study, the chunk-based features were comparable to the document-based features. Furthermore, combination of the two features improved F-score. The performance improvement mostly resulted from higher recall.

Finally, Table 6 presents the results using the entire FM set, including the OR, TR, and RE responses that were not included in the previous experiment. The accuracy of the majority class baseline (classifying all responses as scorable responses) is 0.865.

	acc.	prec.	recall	fscore
Similarity-filter	0.976	0.926	0.895	0.910
A/S-filter	0.974	0.953	0.849	0.898
Combined-filter	0.977	0.941	0.884	0.911

Table 6: Performance of filters in all types of NS detection

Both the Similarity-filter and the A/S-filter achieved high performance. Both accuracies and F-scores were similar and the difference between the two filters was approximately 0.01. The Similarity-filter achieved better performance than the A/S-filter in recall: it was 0.89, which was substantially higher than the A/S-filter (0.85).

It is an encouraging result that the Similarity-filter could achieve a performance comparable to the A/S-filter, which was based on multiple resources such as signal processing, forced-alignment, and ASR. But, the combination of the two feature groups did not achieve further improvement: the increase in both accuracy and F-measure was less than 0.01.

7 Conclusions

In this study, filtering models were implemented as a supplementary module for an automated speech proficiency scoring system. In addition to A/S features, which have shown promising performance in previous studies, a set of similarity features were implemented and a filtering model was developed. The Similarity-filter was more accurate than the A/S-filter in identifying the responses with topical problems. This result is encouraging since the proportion of these responses is likely to increase when the automated speech scoring system becomes a sole rater of the assessment.

Although the Similarity-filter achieved better performance than the A/S-filter, it should be further improved. The recall of the system was low, and approximately 45% of NS responses could not be identified. In addition, the model requires substantial amount of sample responses for each item, and it will cause serious difficulty when it is used the real test situation. In future, we will explore the similarity features trained only using the prompt question or the additional prompt materials such as visual and audio materials.

References

Yigal Attali and Jill Burstein. 2006. Automated essay scoring with e–rater R v.2. *The Journal of Technology, Learning, and Assessment*, 4(3).

Paul Boersma. 2002. Praat, a system for doing phonetics by computer. *Glot International*, 5(9/10):341–345.

Sergey Brin, James Davis, and Hector Garcia-Molina. 1995. Copy detection mechanisms for digital documents. In *ACM SIGMOD Record*, volume 24, pages 398–409. ACM.

Jian Cheng and Jianqiang Shen. 2011. Off-topic detection in automated speech assessment applications. In *Proceedings of InterSpeech*, pages 1597–1600. IEEE.

Peter W. Foltz, Darrell Laham, and Thomas K. Landauer. 1999. The Intelligent Essay Assessor: Applications to educational technology. *Interactive multimedia Electronic Journal of Computer-Enhanced Learning*, 1(2).

Mark Hall, Eibe Frank, Geoffrey Holmes, Bernhard Pfahringer, Peter Reutemann, and Ian H Witten. 2009. The weka data mining software: an update. *ACM SIGKDD Explorations Newsletter*, 11(1):10–18.

Derrick Higgins, Jill Burstein, and Yigal Attali. 2006. Identifying off-topic student essays without topic-specific training data. *Natural Language Engineering*, 12(02):145–159.

Timothy C Hoad and Justin Zobel. 2003. Methods for identifying versioned and plagiarized documents. *Journal of the American society for information science and technology*, 54(3):203–215.

Je Hun Jeon and Su-Youn Yoon. 2012. Acoustic feature-based non-scorable response detection for an automated speaking proficiency assessment. In *Proceedings of the InterSpeech*, pages 1275–1278.

Wai-Kit Lo, Alissa M Harrison, and Helen Meng. 2010. Statistical phone duration modeling to filter for intact utterances in a computer-assisted pronunciation training system. In *Proceedings of Acoustics Speech and Signal Processing (ICASSP), 2010 IEEE International Conference on*, pages 5238–5241. IEEE.

Donald Metzler, Yaniv Bernstein, W Bruce Croft, Alistair Moffat, and Justin Zobel. 2005. Similarity measures for tracking information flow. In *Proceedings of the 14th ACM international conference on Information and knowledge management*, pages 517–524. ACM.

Mark Sanderson. 1997. Duplicate detection in the reuters collection. *" Technical Report (TR-1997-5) of the Department of Computing Science at the University of Glasgow G12 8QQ, UK"*.

Narayanan Shivakumar and Hector Garcia-Molina. 1995. Scam: A copy detection mechanism for digital documents.

Narayanan Shivakumar and Hector Garcia-Molina. 1996. Building a scalable and accurate copy detection mechanism. In *Proceedings of the first ACM international conference on Digital libraries*, pages 160–168. ACM.

Joost van Doremalen, Helmet Strik, and Cartia Cucchiarini. 2009. Utterance verification in language learning applications. In *Proceedings of the SLaTE*.

Shasha Xie, Keelan Evanini, and Klaus Zechner. 2012. Exploring content features for automated speech scoring. In *Proceedings of the 2012 Conference of the North American Chapter of the Association for Computational Linguistics: Human Language Technologies*, pages 103–111. Association for Computational Linguistics.

Klaus Zechner, Derrick Higgins, Xiaoming Xi, and David M. Williamson. 2009. Automatic scoring of non-native spontaneous speech in tests of spoken English. *Speech Communication*, 51(10):883–895.

Natural Language Generation with Vocabulary Constraints

Ben Swanson
Brown University
Providence, RI
chonger@cs.brown.edu

Elif Yamangil
Google Inc.
Mountain View, CA
leafer@google.com

Eugene Charniak
Brown University
Providence, RI
ec@cs.brown.edu

Abstract

We investigate data driven natural language generation under the constraints that all words must come from a fixed vocabulary and a specified word must appear in the generated sentence, motivated by the possibility for automatic generation of language education exercises. We present fast and accurate approximations to the ideal rejection samplers for these constraints and compare various sentence level generative language models. Our best systems produce output that is with high frequency both novel and error free, which we validate with human and automatic evaluations.

1 Introduction

Freeform data driven Natural Language Generation (NLG) is a topic explored by academics and artists alike, but motivating its empirical study is a difficult task. While many language models used in statistical NLP are generative and can easily produce sample sentences by running their "generative mode", if all that is required is a plausible sentence one might as well pick a sentence at random from any existing corpus.

NLG becomes useful when constraints exist such that only certain sentences are valid. The majority of NLG applies a semantic constraint of "what to say", producing sentences with communicative goals. Other work such as ours investigates constraints in structure; producing sentences of a certain form without concern for their specific meaning.

We study two constraints concerning the words that are allowed in a sentence. The first sets a fixed vocabulary such that only sentences where all words are in-vocab are allowed. The second demands not only that all words are in-vocab, but also requires the inclusion of a specific word somewhere in the sentence.

These constraints are natural in the construction of language education exercises, where students have small known vocabularies and exercises that reinforce the knowledge of arbitrary words are required. To provide an example, consider a Chinese teacher composing a quiz that asks students to translate sentences from English to Chinese. The teacher cannot ask students to translate words that have not been taught in class, and would like ensure that each vocabulary word from the current book chapter is included in at least one sentence. Using a system such as ours, she could easily generate a number of usable sentences that contain a given vocab word and select her favorite, repeating this process for each vocab word until the quiz is complete.

The construction of such a system presents two primary technical challenges. First, while highly parameterized models trained on large corpora are a good fit for data driven NLG, sparsity is still an issue when constraints are introduced. Traditional smoothing techniques used for prediction based tasks are inappropriate, however, as they liberally assign probability to implausible text. We investigate smoothing techniques better suited for NLG that smooth more precisely, sharing probability only between words that have strong semantic connections.

The second challenge arises from the fact that both vocabulary and word inclusion constraints are easily handled with a rejection sampler that repeatedly generates sentences until one that obeys the constraints is produced. Unfortunately, for

Proceedings of the Ninth Workshop on Innovative Use of NLP for Building Educational Applications , pages 124–133,
Baltimore, Maryland USA, June 26, 2014.

models with a sufficiently wide range of outputs the computation wasted by rejection quickly becomes prohibitive, especially when the word inclusion constraint is applied. We define models that sample directly from the possible outputs for each constraint without rejection or backtracking, and closely approximate the distribution of the true rejection samplers.

We contrast several generative systems through both human and automatic evaluation. Our best system effectively captures the compositional nature of our training data, producing error-free text with nearly 80 percent accuracy without wasting computation on backtracking or rejection. When the word inclusion constraint is introduced, we show clear empirical advantages over the simple solution of searching a large corpus for an appropriate sentence.

2 Related Work

The majority of NLG focuses on the satisfaction of a communicative goal, with examples such as Belz (2008) which produces weather reports from structured data or Mitchell et al. (2013) which generates descriptions of objects from images. Our work is more similar to NLG work that concentrates on structural constraints such as generative poetry (Greene et al., 2010) (Colton et al., 2012) (Jiang and Zhou, 2008) or song lyrics (Wu et al., 2013) (Ramakrishnan A et al., 2009), where specified meter or rhyme schemes are enforced. In these papers soft semantic goals are sometimes also introduced that seek responses to previous lines of poetry or lyric.

Computational creativity is another subfield of NLG that often does not fix an a priori meaning in its output. Examples such as Özbal et al. (2013) and Valitutti et al. (2013) use template filling techniques guided by quantified notions of humor or how catchy a phrase is.

Our motivation for generation of material for language education exists in work such as Sumita et al. (2005) and Mostow and Jang (2012), which deal with automatic generation of classic fill in the blank questions. Our work is naturally complementary to these efforts, as their methods require a corpus of in-vocab text to serve as seed sentences.

3 Freeform Generation

For clarity in our discussion, we phrase the sentence generation process in the following general terms based around two classes of atomic units : *contexts* and *outcomes*. In order to specify a generation system, we must define

1. the set $\mathcal{C}$ of contexts c
2. the set $\mathcal{O}$ of outcomes o
3. the "Imply" function $I(c, o) \rightarrow List[c \in \mathcal{C}]$
4. $\mathcal{M}$: derivation tree $\rightleftarrows$ sentence

where $I(c, o)$ defines the further contexts implied by the choice of outcome o for the context c. Beginning with a unique root context, a derivation tree is created by repeatedly choosing an outcome o for a leaf context c and expanding c to the new leaf contexts specified by $I(c, o)$. $\mathcal{M}$ converts between derivation tree and sentence text form.

This is simply a convenient rephrasing of the Context Free Grammar formalism, and as such the systems we describe all have some equivalent CFG interpretation. Indeed, to describe a traditional CFG, let $\mathcal{C}$ be the set of symbols, $\mathcal{O}$ be the rules of the CFG, and $I(c, o)$ return a list of the symbols on the right hand side of the rule o. To define an n-gram model, a context is a list of words, an outcome a single word, and $I(c, o)$ can be procedurally defined to drop the first element of c and append o.

To perform the sampling required for derivation tree construction we must define $P(o|c)$. Using $\mathcal{M}$, we begin by converting a large corpus of sentence segmented text into a training set of derivation trees. Maximum likelihood estimation of $P(o|c)$ is then as simple as normalizing the counts of the observed outcomes for each observed context. However, in order to obtain contexts for which the conditional independence assumption of $P(o|c)$ is appropriate, it is necessary to condition on a large amount of information. This leads to sparse estimates even on large amounts of training data, a problem that can be addressed by smoothing. We identify two complementary types of smoothing, and illustrate them with the following sentences.

The furry dog bit me.
The cute cat licked me.

An unsmoothed bigram model trained on this data can only generate the two sentences verbatim. If, however, we know that the tokens "dog" and "cat" are semantically similar, we can smooth by assuming the words that follow "cat" are also likely to follow "dog". This is easily handled with traditional smoothing techniques that interpolate between distributions estimated for both coarse, $P(w|w_{-1}$=[*animal*]), and fine, $P(w|w_{-1}$="dog"), contexts. We refer to this as *context smoothing*.

However, we would also like to capture the intuition that words which can be followed by "dog" can also be followed by "cat", which we will call *outcome smoothing*. We extend our terminology to describe a system that performs both types of smoothing with the following

- the set $\bar{\mathcal{C}}$ of smooth contexts $\bar{c}$
- the set $\bar{\mathcal{O}}$ of smooth outcomes $\bar{o}$
- a smoothing function $S_C : \mathcal{C} \to \bar{\mathcal{C}}$
- a smoothing function $S_O : \mathcal{O} \to \bar{\mathcal{O}}$

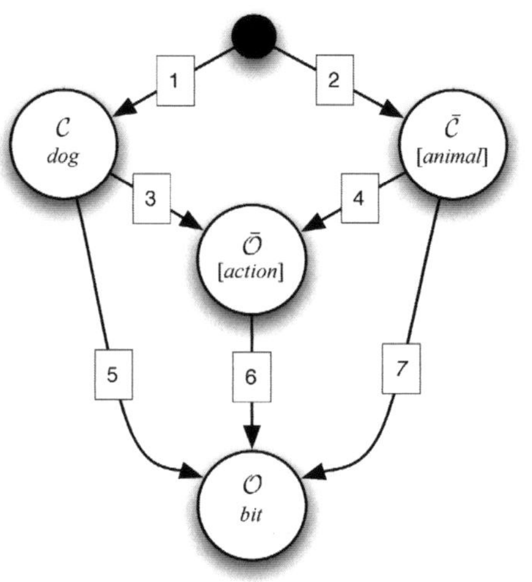

Figure 1: A flow chart depicting the decisions made when choosing an outcome for a context. The large circles show the set of items associated with each decision, and contain examples items for a bigram model where S_C and S_O map words (e.g. *dog*) to semantic classes (e.g. [*animal*]).

We describe the smoothed generative process with the flowchart shown in Figure 1. In order to choose an outcome for a given context, two decisions must be made. First, we must decide which context we will employ, the true context or the smooth context, marked by edges 1 or 2 respectively. Next, we choose to generate a true outcome or a smooth outcome, and if we select the latter we use edge 6 to choose a true outcome given the smooth outcome. The decision between edges 1 and 2 can be sampled from a Bernoulli random variable with parameter λ_c, with one variable estimated for each context c. The decision between edges 5 and 3 and the one between 4 and 7 can also be made with Bernoulli random variables, with parameter sets γ_c and $\gamma_{\bar{c}}$ respectively.

This yields the full form of the unconstrained probabilistic generative model as follows

$$
\begin{aligned}
P(o|c) &= \lambda_c P_1(o|c) + (1-\lambda_c)P_2(o|S_C(c)) \\
P_1(o|c) &= \gamma_c P_5(o|c) + \\
&\quad (1-\gamma_c)P_7(o|\bar{o})P_3(\bar{o}|c) \qquad (1) \\
P_2(o|\bar{c}) &= \gamma_{\bar{c}} P_6(o|c) + \\
&\quad (1-\gamma_{\bar{c}})P_7(o|\bar{o})P_4(\bar{o}|\bar{c})
\end{aligned}
$$

requiring estimation of the λ and γ variables as well as the five multinomial distributions P_{3-7}. This can be done with a straightforward application of EM.

4 Limiting Vocabulary

A primary concern in the generation of language education exercises is the working vocabulary of the students. If efficiency were not a concern, the natural solution to the vocabulary constraint would be rejection sampling: simply generate sentences until one happens to obey the constraint. In this section we show how to generate a sentence directly from this constrained set with a distribution closely approximating that of the rejection sampler.

4.1 Pruning

The first step is to prune the space of possible sentences to those that obey the vocabulary constraint. For the models we investigate there is a natural predicate $V(o)$ that is true if and only if an outcome introduces a word that is out of vocab, and so the vocabulary constraint is equivalent to the requirement that $V(o)$ is false for all possible outcomes o. Considering transitions along edges in Figure 1, the removal of all transitions along edges 5,6, and 7 that lead to outcomes where $V(o)$ is true satisfies this property.

Our remaining concern is that the generation process does not reach a failure case. Again considering transitions in Figure 1, failure occurs when we require $P(o|c)$ for some c and there is no transition to c on edge 1 or $S_C(c)$ along edge 2. We refer to such a context as *invalid*. Our goal, which we refer to as *consistency*, is that for all valid contexts c, all outcomes o that can be reached in Figure 1 satisfy the property that all members of $I(c, o)$ are valid contexts.

To see how we might end up in failure, consider a trigram model on POS/word pairs for which S_C is the identity function and S_O backs off to the POS tag. Given a context $c = (\binom{t_{-2}}{w_{-2}}, \binom{t_{-1}}{w_{-1}})$ if we generate along a path using edge 6 we will choose a smooth outcome t_0 that we have seen following c in the data and then independenently choose a w_0 that has been observed with tag t_0. This implies a following context $(\binom{t_{-1}}{w_{-1}}, \binom{t_0}{w_0})$. If we have estimated our model with observations from data, there is no guarantee that this context ever appeared, and if so there will be no available transition along edges 1 or 2.

Let the list $\bar{I}(c, o)$ be the result of the mapped application of S_C to each element of $I(c, o)$. In order to define an efficient algorithm, we require the following property **D** referring to the amount of information needed to determine $\bar{I}(c, o)$. Simply put, **D** states if the smoothed context and outcome are fixed, then the implied smooth contexts are determined.

$$\mathbf{D} \quad \{S_C(c), S_O(o)\} \rightarrow \bar{I}(c, o)$$

To highlight the statement **D** makes, consider the trigram POS/word model described above, but let S_C also map the POS/word pairs in the context to their POS tags alone. **D** holds here because given $S_C(c) = (t_{-2}, t_{-1})$ and $S_O(o) = t_0$ from the outcome, we are able to determine the implied smooth context (t_{-1}, t_0). If context smoothing instead produced $S_C(c) = (t_{-2})$, **D** would not hold.

If **D** holds then we can show consistency based on the transitions in Figure 1 alone as any complete path through Figure 1 defines both $\bar{c}$ and $\bar{o}$. By **D** we can determine $\bar{I}(c, o)$ for any path and verify that all its members have possible transitions along edge 2. If the verification passes for all paths then the model is consistent.

Algorithm 1 produces a consistent model by verifying each complete path in the manner just described. One important feature is that it preserves the invariant that if a context c can be reached on edge 1, then $S_C(c)$ can be reached on edge 2. This means that if the verification fails then the complete path produces an invalid context, even though we have only checked the members of $\bar{I}(c, o)$ against path 2.

If a complete path produces an invalid context, some transition along that path must be removed. It is never optimal to remove transitions from edges 1 or 2 as this unnecessarily removes all downstream complete paths as well, and so for invalid complete paths along 1-5 and 2-7 Algorithm 1 removes the transitions along edges 5 and 7. The choice is not so simple for the complete paths 1-3-6 and 2-4-6, as there are two remaining choices. Fortunately, **D** implies that breaking the connection on edge 3 or 4 is optimal as regardless of which outcome is chosen on edge 6, $\bar{I}(c, o)$ will still produce the same invalid $\bar{c}$.

Algorithm 1 Pruning Algorithm

```
Initialize with all observed transitions
for all out of vocab o do
    remove ? → o from edges 5,6, and 7
end for
repeat
    for all paths in flow chart do
        if ∃c̄ ∈ Ī(c, o) s.t. c̄ is invalid then
            remove transition from edge 5,7,3 or 4
        end if
    end for
    Run FIXUP
until edge 2 transitions did not change
```

After removing transitions in this manner, some transitions on edges 1-4 may no longer have any outgoing transitions. The subroutine FIXUP removes such transitions, checking edges 3 and 4 before 1 and 2. If FIXUP does not modify edge 2 then the model is consistent and Algorithm 1 terminates.

4.2 Estimation

In order to replicate the behavior of the rejection sampler, which uses the original probability model $P(o|c)$ from Equation 1, we must set the probabilities $P_V(o|c)$ of the pruned model appropriately. We note that for moderately sized vocabularies it is feasible to recursively enumerate $\mathcal{C}_V$, the set of all reachable contexts in the pruned model. In further discussion we simplify the representation of the model to a standard PCFG with $\mathcal{C}_V$ as its symbol set and its PCFG rules indexed by outcomes. This also allows us to construct the *reachability graph* for $\mathcal{C}_V$, with an edge from c_i to c_j for each $c_j \in I(c_i, o)$. Such an edge is given weight $P(o|c)$, the probability under the unconstrained model, and zero weight edges are not included.

Our goal is to retain the form of the standard incremental recursive sampling algorithm for PCFGs. The correctness of this algorithm comes from the fact that the probability of a rule R expanding a symbol X is precisely the probability of all trees rooted at X whose first rule is R. This implies that the correct sampling distribution is simply the distribution over rules itself. When constraints that disallow certain trees are introduced, the probability of all trees whose first rule is R only includes the mass from valid trees, and the correct sampling distribution is the renormalization of these values.

Let the *goodness* of a context $G(c)$ be the probability that a full subtree generated from c using the unconstrained model obeys the vocabulary constraint. Knowledge of $G(c)$ for all $c \in \mathcal{C}_V$ allows the calculation of probabilities for the pruned model with

$$P_V(o|c) \propto P(o|c) \prod_{c' \in I(c,o)} G(c') \tag{2}$$

While $G(c)$ can be defined recursively as

$$G(c) = \sum_{o \in \mathcal{O}} P(o|c) \prod_{c' \in I(c,o)} G(c') \tag{3}$$

its calculation requires that the reachability graph be acyclic. We approximate an acyclic graph by listing all edges in order of decreasing weight and introducing edges as long as they do not create cycles. This can be done efficiently with a binary search over the edges by weight. Note that this approximate graph is used only in recursive estimation of $G(c)$, and the true graph can still be used in Equation 2.

5 Generating Up

In this section we show how to efficiently generate sentences that contain an arbitrary word w^* in addition to the vocabulary constraint. We assume the ability to easily find $\mathcal{C}_{w^*}$, a subset of $\mathcal{C}_V$ whose use guarantees that the resulting sentence contains w^*. Our goal is once again to efficiently emulate the rejection sampler, which generates a derivation tree T and accepts if and only if it contains at least one member of $\mathcal{C}_{w^*}$.

Let $\mathcal{T}_{w^*}$ be the set of derivation trees that would be accepted by the rejection sampler. We present a three stage generative model and its associated probability distribution $P_{w^*}(\tau)$ over items τ for which there is a functional mapping into $\mathcal{T}_{w^*}$.

In addition to the probabilities $P_V(o|c)$ from the previous section, we require an estimate of $\mathbb{E}(c)$, the expected number of times each context c appears in a single tree. This can be computed efficiently using the mean matrix, described in Miller and Osullivan (1992). This $|\mathcal{C}_V| \times |\mathcal{C}_V|$ matri x M has its entries defined as

$$M(i,j) = \sum_{o \in \mathcal{O}} P(o|c_i)\#(c_j, c_i, o) \tag{4}$$

where the operator $\#$ returns the number of times context c_j appears $I(c_i, o)$. Defining a $1 \times |\mathcal{C}_V|$ start state vector z_0 that is zero everywhere and 1 in the entry corresponding to the root context gives

$$\mathbb{E}(z) = \sum_{i=0}^{\infty} z_0 M^i$$

which can be iteratively computed with sparse matrix multiplication. Note that the ith term in the sum corresponds to expected counts at depth i in the derivation tree. With definitions of context and outcome for which very deep derivations are improbable, it is reasonable to approximate this sum by truncation.

Our generation model operates in three phases.

1. Chose a start context $c_0 \in \mathcal{C}_{w^*}$
2. Generate a spine S of contexts and outcomes connecting c_0 to the root context
3. Fill in the full derivation tree T below all remaining unexpanded contexts

In the first phase, c_0 is sampled from the multinomial

$$P_1(c_0) = \frac{\mathbb{E}(c_0)}{\sum_{c \in \mathcal{C}_{w^*}} \mathbb{E}(c)} \tag{5}$$

The second step produces a spine S, which is formally an ordered list of triples. Each element of S records a context c_i, an outcome o_i, and the index k in $I(c_i, o_i)$ of the child along which the spine progresses. The members of S are sampled independantly given the previously sampled context, starting from c_0 and terminating when the root context is reached. Intuitively this is equivalent to generating the path from the root to c_0 in a bottom up fashion.

We define the probability P_σ of a triple (c_i, o_i, k) given a previously sampled context c_j

as

$$P_\sigma(\{c_i, o_i, k\}|c_j) \propto \begin{cases} \mathbb{E}(c_i)P_V(o_i|c_i) & I(c_i, o_i)[k] = c_j \\ 0 & \text{otherwise} \end{cases} \quad (6)$$

Let $S = (c_1, o_1, k_1) \ldots (c_n, o_n, k_n)$ be the results of this recursive sampling algorithm, where c_n is the root context, and c_1 is the parent context of c_0. The total probability of a spine S is then

$$P_2(S|c_0) = \prod_{i=1}^{|S|} \frac{\mathbb{E}(c_i)P_V(o_i|c_i)}{Z_{i-1}} \quad (7)$$

$$Z_{i-1} = \sum_{(c,o)\in\mathbb{I}_{c_{i-1}}} \mathbb{E}(c)P_V(o|c)\#(c_{i-1}, c, o) \quad (8)$$

where $\mathbb{I}_{c-1}$ is the set of all (c, o) for which $P_\sigma(c, o, k|c_{i-1})$ is non-zero for some k. A key observation is that $Z_{i-1} = \mathbb{E}(c_{i-1})$, which cancels nearly all of the expected counts from the full product. Along with the fact that the expected count of the root context is one, the formula simplifies to

$$P_2(S|c_0) = \frac{\prod_{i=1}^{|S|} P_V(o_i|c_i)}{\mathbb{E}(c_0)} \quad (9)$$

The third step generates a final tree T by filling in subtrees below unexpanded contexts on the spine S using the original generation algorithm, yielding results with probability

$$P_3(T|S) = \prod_{(c,o)\in T/S} P_V(o|c) \quad (10)$$

where the set T/S includes all contexts that are not ancestors of c_0, as their outcomes are already specified in S.

We validate this algorithm by considering its distrubution over complete derivation trees $T \in \mathcal{T}_{w^*}$. The algorithm generates $\tau = (T, S, c_0)$ and has a simple functional mapping into $\mathcal{T}_{w^*}$ by extracting the first member of τ.

Combining the probabilities of our three steps gives

$$P_{w^*}(\tau) = \frac{\mathbb{E}(c_0)}{\sum_{c\in\mathcal{C}_{w^*}} \mathbb{E}(c)} \frac{\prod_{i=1}^{|S|} P_V(o_i|c_i)}{\mathbb{E}(c_0)} \prod_{(c,o)\in T/S} P_V(o|c)$$

$$P_{w^*}(\tau) = \frac{P_V(T)}{\sum_{c\in\mathcal{C}_{w^*}} \mathbb{E}(c)} = \frac{1}{\rho} P_V(T) \quad (11)$$

where ρ is a constant and

$$P_V(T) = \prod_{(c,o)\in T} P_V(o|c)$$

is the probability of T under the original model. Note that several τ may map to the same T by using different spines, and so

$$P_{w^*}(T) = \frac{\eta(T)}{\rho} P_V(T) \quad (12)$$

where $\eta(T)$ is the number of possible spines, or equivalently the number of contexts $c \in \mathcal{C}_{w^*}$ in T.

Recall that our goal is to efficiently emulate the output of a rejection sampler. An ideal system P_{w^*} would produce the complete set of derivation trees accepted by the rejection sampler using P_V, with probabilities of each derivation tree T satisfying

$$P_{w^*}(T) \propto P_V(T) \quad (13)$$

Consider the implications of the following assumption

A each $T \in \mathcal{T}_{w^*}$ contains exactly one $c \in \mathcal{C}_{w^*}$

A ensures that $\eta(T) = 1$ for all T, unifying Equations 12 and 13. **A** does not generally hold in practice, but its clear exposition allows us to design models for which it holds most of the time, leading to a tight approximation.

The most important consideration of this type is to limit redundancy in $\mathcal{C}_{w^*}$. For illustration consider a dependency grammar model with parent annotation where a context is the current word and its parent word. When specifying $\mathcal{C}_{w^*}$ for a particular w^*, we might choose all contexts in which w^* appears as either the current or parent word, but a better choice that more closely satisfies **A** is to choose contexts where w^* appears as the current word only.

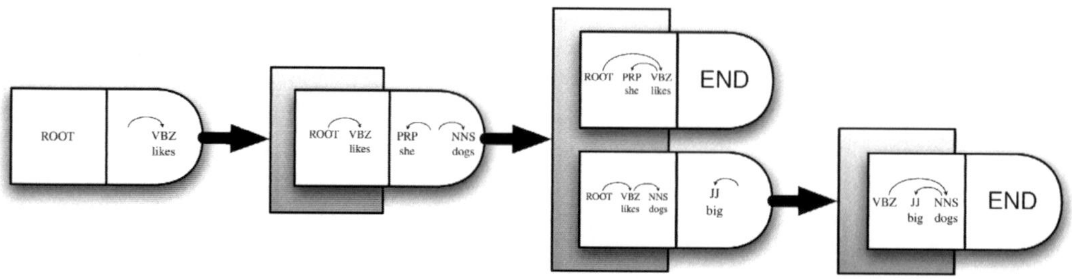

Figure 2: The generation system SPINEDEP draws on dependency tree syntax where we use the term *node* to refer to a POS/word pair. Contexts consist of a node, its parent node, and grandparent POS tag, as shown in squares. Outcomes, shown in squares with rounded right sides, are full lists of dependents or the END symbol. The shaded rectangles contain the results of $I(c, o)$ from the indicated (c, o) pair.

6 Experiments

We train our models on sentences drawn from the Simple English Wikipedia[1]. We obtained these sentences from a data dump which we liberally filtered to remove items such as lists and sentences longer than 15 words or shorter then 3 words. We parsed this data with the recently updated Stanford Parser (Socher et al., 2013) to Penn Treebank constituent form, and removed any sentence that did not parse to a top level S containing at least one NP and one VP child. Even with such strong filters, we retained over 140K sentences for use as training data, and provide this exact set of parse trees for use in future work.[2]

Inspired by the application in language education, for our vocabulary list we use the English Vocabulary Profile (Capel, 2012), which predicts student vocabulary at different stages of learning English as a second language. We take the most basic American English vocabulary (the A1 list), and retrieve all inflections for each word using SimpleNLG (Gatt and Reiter, 2009), yielding a vocabulary of 1226 simple words and punctuation.

To mitigate noise in the data, we discard any pair of context and outcome that appears only once in the training data, and estimate the parameters of the unconstrained model using EM.

6.1 Model Comparison

We experimented with many generation models before converging on SPINEDEP, described in Figure 2, which we use in these experiments.

	Corr(%)	% uniq
SPINEDEP unsmoothed	87.6	5.0
SPINEDEP WordNet	78.3	32.5
SPINEDEP word2vec 5000	72.6	52.9
SPINEDEP word2vec 500	65.3	60.2
KneserNey-5	64.0	25.8
DMV	33.7	71.2

Figure 3: System comparison based on human judged correctness and the percentage of unique sentences in a sample of 100K.

SPINEDEP uses dependency grammar elements, with parent and grandparent information in the contexts to capture such distinctions as that between main and clausal verbs. Its outcomes are full configurations of dependents, capturing coordinations such as subject-object pairings. This specificity greatly increases the size of the model and in turn reduces the speed of the true rejection sampler, which fails over 90% of the time to produce an in-vocab sentence.

We found that large amounts of smoothing quickly diminishes the amount of error free output, and so we smooth very cautiously, mapping words in the contexts and outcomes to fine semantic classes. We compare the use of human annotated hypernyms from Wordnet (Miller, 1995) with automatic word clusters from word2vec (Mikolov et al., 2013), based on vector space word embeddings, evaluating both 500 and 5000 clusters for the latter.

We compare these models against several baseline alternatives, shown in Figure 3. To determine

[1] http://simple.wikipedia.org
[2] data url anon for review

correctness, used Amazon Mechanical Turk, asking the question: "Is this sentence plausible?". We further clarified this question in the instructions with alternative definitions of plausibility as well as both positive and negative examples. Every sentence was rated by five reviewers and its correctness was determined by majority vote, with a .496 Fleiss kappa agreement. To avoid spammers, we limited our hits to Turkers with an over 95% approval rating.

Traditional language modeling techniques such as such as the Dependency Model with Valence (Klein and Manning, 2004) and 5-gram Kneser Ney (Chen and Goodman, 1996) perform poorly, which is unsurprising as they are designed for tasks in recognition rather than generation. For n-gram models, accuracy can be greatly increased by decreasing the amount of smoothing, but it becomes difficult to find long n-grams that are completely in-vocab and results become redundant, parroting the few completely in-vocab sentences from the training data. The DMV is more flexible, but makes assumptions of conditional independence that are far too strong. As a result it is unable to avoid red flags such as sentences not ending in punctuation or strange subject-object coordinations. Without smoothing, SPINEDEP suffers from a similar problem as unsmoothed n-gram models; high accuracy but quickly vanishing productivity.

All of the smoothed SPINEDEP systems show clear advantages over their competitors. The tradeoff between correctness and generative capacity is also clear, and our results suggest that the number of clusters created from the word2vec embeddings can be used to trace this curve. As for the ideal position in this tradeoff, we leave such decisions which are particular to specific application to future work, arbitrarily using SPINEDEP WordNet for our following experiments.

6.2 Fixed Vocabulary

To show the tightness of the approximation presented in Section 4.2, we evaluate three settings for the probabilities of the pruned model. The first is a weak baseline that sets all distributions to uniform. For the second, we simply renormalize the true model's probabilities, which is equivalent to setting $G(c) = 1$ for all c in Equation 2. Finally, we use our proposed method to estimate $G(c)$.

We show in Figure 4 that our estimation method more closely approximates the distribution of the rejection sampler by drawing 500K samples from each model and comparing them with 500K samples from the rejection sampler itself. We quantify this comparison with the likelihood ratio statistic, evaluating the null hypothesis that the two samples were drawn from the same distribution. Not only does our method more closely emulate that of the rejection sampler, be we see welcome evidence that closeness to the true distribution is correlated with correctness.

	Corr(%)	-LLR
True RS	79.3	–
Uniform	47.3	96.2
$G(c) = 1$	77.0	25.0
$G(c)$ estimated	**78.3**	**1.0**

Figure 4: A comparison of our system against both a weak and a strong baseline based on correctness and the negative log of the likelihood ratio measuring closeness to the true rejection sampler.

6.3 Word Inclusion

To explore the word inclusion constraint, for each word in our vocabulary list we sample 1000 sentences that are constrained to include that word using both unsmoothed and WordNet smoothed SPINEDEP. We compare these results to the "Corpus" model that simply searches the training data and uniformly samples from the existing sentences that satisfy the constraints. This corpus search approach is quite a strong baseline, as it is trivial to implement and we assume perfect correctness for its results.

This experiment is especially relevant to our motivation of language education. The natural question when proposing any NLG approach is whether or not the ability to automatically produce sentences outweighs the requirement of a post-process to ensure goal-appropriate output. This is a challenging task in the context of language education, as most applications such as exam or homework creation require only a handful of sentences. In order for an NLG solution to be appropriate, the constraints must be so strong that a corpus search based method will frequently produce too few options to be useful. The word inclusion constraint highlights the strengths of our method as it is not only highly plausible in a language ed-

	# < 10	# > 100	Corr(%)
Corpus	987	26	100
Unsmooth	957	56	89.0
Smooth	544	586	79.0

Figure 5: Using systems that implement the word inclusion constraint, this table shows the number of words for which the amount of unique sentences out of 1000 samples was less than 10 or greater than 100, along with the correctness of each system.

ucation setting but difficult to satisfy by chance in large corpora.

Figure 5 shows that the corpus search approach fails to find more than ten sentences that obey the word inclusion constraints for most target words. Moreover, it is arguably the case that unsmoothed SPINEDEP is even worse due to its inferior correctness. With the addition of smoothing, however, we see a drastic shift in the number of words for which a large number of sentences can be produced. For the majority of the vocabulary words this model generates over 100 sentences that obey both constraints, of which approximately 80% are valid English sentences.

7 Conclusion

In this work we address two novel NLG constraints, fixed vocabulary and fixed vocabulary with word inclusion, that are motivated by language education scenarios. We showed that under these constraints a highly parameterized model based on dependency tree syntax can produce a wide range of accurate sentences, outperforming the strong baselines of popular generative language models. We developed a pruning and estimation algorithm for the fixed vocabulary constraint and showed that it not only closely approximates the true rejection sampler but also that the tightness of approximation is correlated with human judgments of correctness. We showed that under the word inclusion constraint, precise semantic smoothing produces a system whose abilities exceed the simple but powerful alternative of looking up sentences in large corpora.

SPINEDEP works surprisingly well given the widely held stigma that freeform NLG produces either memorized sentences or gibberish. Still, we expect that better models exist, especially in terms of definition of smoothing operators. We have presented our algorithms in the flexible terms of context and outcome, and clearly stated the properties that are required for the full use of our methodology. We have also implemented our code in these general terms[3], which performs EM based parameter estimation as well as efficient generation under the constraints discussed above. All systems used in this work with the exception of 5-gram interpolated Kneser-Ney were implemented in this way, are included with the code, and can be used as templates.

We recognize several avenues for continued work on this topic. The use of form-based constraints such as word inclusion has clear application in language education, but many other constraints are also desirable. The clearest is perhaps the ability to constrain results based on a "vocabulary" of syntactic patterns such as "Not only ... but also ...". Another extension would be to incorporate the rough communicative goal of response to a previous sentence as in Wu et al. (2013) and attempt to produce in-vocab dialogs such as are ubiquitous in language education textbooks.

Another possible direction is in the improvement of the context-outcome framework itself. While we have assumed a data set of one derivation tree per sentence, our current methods easily extend to sets of weighted derivations for each sentence. This suggests the use of techinques that have proved effective in grammar estimation that reason over large numbers of possible derivations such as Bayesian tree substitution grammars or unsupervised symbol refinement.

References

Anja Belz. 2008. Automatic generation of weather forecast texts using comprehensive probabilistic generation-space models. *Natural Language Engineering*, 14(4):431–455.

A. Capel. 2012. The english vocabulary profile. *http://vocabulary.englishprofile.org/.*

Stanley F. Chen and Joshua Goodman. 1996. An empirical study of smoothing techniques for language modeling. In *Proceedings of the 34th Annual Meeting on Association for Computational Linguistics*, ACL '96, pages 310–318, Stroudsburg, PA, USA. Association for Computational Linguistics.

Simon Colton, Jacob Goodwin, and Tony Veale. 2012. Full face poetry generation. In *Proceedings of the*

[3]url anon for review

Third International Conference on Computational Creativity, pages 95–102.

Albert Gatt and Ehud Reiter. 2009. Simplenlg: A realisation engine for practical applications. In *Proceedings of the 12th European Workshop on Natural Language Generation*, ENLG '09, pages 90–93, Stroudsburg, PA, USA. Association for Computational Linguistics.

Erica Greene, Tugba Bodrumlu, and Kevin Knight. 2010. Automatic analysis of rhythmic poetry with applications to generation and translation. In *Proceedings of the 2010 Conference on Empirical Methods in Natural Language Processing*, EMNLP '10, pages 524–533, Stroudsburg, PA, USA. Association for Computational Linguistics.

Long Jiang and Ming Zhou. 2008. Generating chinese couplets using a statistical mt approach. In *Proceedings of the 22nd International Conference on Computational Linguistics-Volume 1*, pages 377–384. Association for Computational Linguistics.

Dan Klein and Christopher D. Manning. 2004. Corpus-based induction of syntactic structure: Models of dependency and constituency. In *Proceedings of the 42Nd Annual Meeting on Association for Computational Linguistics*, ACL '04, Stroudsburg, PA, USA. Association for Computational Linguistics.

Tomas Mikolov, Kai Chen, Greg Corrado, and Jeffrey Dean. 2013. Efficient estimation of word representations in vector space. *CoRR*, abs/1301.3781.

Michael I. Miller and Joseph A. Osullivan. 1992. Entropies and combinatorics of random branching processes and context-free languages. *IEEE Transactions on Information Theory*, 38.

George A. Miller. 1995. Wordnet: A lexical database for english. *COMMUNICATIONS OF THE ACM*, 38:39–41.

Margaret Mitchell, Kees van Deemter, and Ehud Reiter. 2013. Generating expressions that refer to visible objects. In *HLT-NAACL*, pages 1174–1184.

Jack Mostow and Hyeju Jang. 2012. Generating diagnostic multiple choice comprehension cloze questions. In *Proceedings of the Seventh Workshop on Building Educational Applications Using NLP*, pages 136–146. Association for Computational Linguistics.

Gözde Özbal, Daniele Pighin, and Carlo Strapparava. 2013. Brainsup: Brainstorming support for creative sentence generation. In *Proceedings of the 51st Annual Meeting of the Association for Computational Linguistics (Volume 1: Long Papers)*, pages 1446–1455, Sofia, Bulgaria, August. Association for Computational Linguistics.

Ananth Ramakrishnan A, Sankar Kuppan, and Sobha Lalitha Devi. 2009. Automatic generation of tamil lyrics for melodies. In *Proceedings of the Workshop on Computational Approaches to Linguistic Creativity*, pages 40–46. Association for Computational Linguistics.

Richard Socher, John Bauer, Christopher D. Manning, and Andrew Y. Ng. 2013. Parsing With Compositional Vector Grammars. In *ACL*.

Eiichiro Sumita, Fumiaki Sugaya, and Seiichi Yamamoto. 2005. Measuring non-native speakers' proficiency of english by using a test with automatically-generated fill-in-the-blank questions. In *Proceedings of the second workshop on Building Educational Applications Using NLP*, pages 61–68. Association for Computational Linguistics.

Alessandro Valitutti, Hannu Toivonen, Antoine Doucet, and Jukka M. Toivanen. 2013. "let everything turn well in your wife": Generation of adult humor using lexical constraints. In *ACL (2)*, pages 243–248.

Dekai Wu, Karteek Addanki, Markus Saers, and Meriem Beloucif. 2013. Learning to freestyle: Hip hop challenge-response induction via transduction rule segmentation. In *EMNLP*, pages 102–112.

Automated Scoring of Speaking Items in an Assessment for Teachers of English as a Foreign Language

Klaus Zechner, Keelan Evanini, Su-Youn Yoon, Lawrence Davis,
Xinhao Wang, Lei Chen, Chong Min Lee, Chee Wee Leong
Educational Testing Service (ETS)
Princeton, NJ 08541, USA
{kzechner,kevanini,syoon,ldavis,xwang002,lchen,clee001,cleong}@ets.org

Abstract

This paper describes an end-to-end prototype system for automated scoring of spoken responses in a novel assessment for teachers of English as a Foreign Language who are not native speakers of English. The 21 speaking items contained in the assessment elicit both restricted and moderately restricted responses, and their aim is to assess the essential speaking skills that English teachers need in order to be effective communicators in their classrooms. Our system consists of a state-of-the-art automatic speech recognizer; multiple feature generation modules addressing diverse aspects of speaking proficiency, such as fluency, pronunciation, prosody, grammatical accuracy, and content accuracy; a filter that identifies and flags problematic responses; and linear regression models that predict response scores based on subsets of the features. The automated speech scoring system was trained and evaluated on a data set involving about 1,400 test takers, and achieved a speaker-level correlation (when scores for all 21 responses of a speaker are aggregated) with human expert scores of 0.73.

1 Introduction

As English has become increasingly important as a language of international business, trade, science, and communication, efforts to promote teaching English as a Foreign Language (EFL) have seen substantially more emphasis in many non-English-speaking countries worldwide in recent years. In addition, the prevailing trend in English pedagogy has been to promote the use of spoken English in the classroom, as opposed to the respective native languages of the EFL learners. However, due to the high demand for EFL teachers in many countries, the training of these teachers has not always caught up with these high expectations, so there is a need for both governmental and private institutions involved in the employment and training of EFL teachers to assess their competence in the English language, as well as in English pedagogy.

Against this background, we developed a language assessment for EFL teachers who are not native speakers of English that addresses the four basic English language skills of Reading, Listening, Writing and Speaking. This paper focuses only on the speaking portion of the English assessment, and, in particular, on the system that we developed to automatically compute scores for test takers' spoken responses.

Several significant challenges needed to be addressed during the course of building this automated speech scoring system, including, but not limited to:

- The 21 Speaking items belong to 8 different task types with different characteristics; therefore, we had to select features and build scoring models for each task type separately.
- The test takers speak a variety of native languages, and thus have very different non-native accents in their spoken English. Furthermore, the test takers also exhibit a wide range of speaking proficiency levels, which contributes to the diversity of their spoken responses. Our speech recognizer therefore had to be trained and adapted to a large database of non-native speech.
- Since content accuracy is very important for the types of tasks contained in the test, even small error rates by the automatic speech recognition (ASR) system can lead to a noticeable impact on feature performance. This fact motivated the development of a set of

Proceedings of the Ninth Workshop on Innovative Use of NLP for Building Educational Applications , pages 134–142,
Baltimore, Maryland USA, June 26, 2014.

features that are robust to speech recognition errors.

- A significant amount of responses (more than 7%) exhibit issues that make them hard or impossible to score automatically, e.g., high noise levels, background speech, etc. We therefore implemented a filter to identify these non-scorable responses automatically.

The paper is organized as follows: Section 2 discusses related work; in Section 3, we present the data used for system training and evaluation; Section 4 describes the system architecture of the automated speech scoring system. We detail the methods we used to build our system in Section 5, followed by an overview of the results in Section 6. Section 7 discusses our findings; finally, Section 8 concludes the paper.

2 Related Work

Automated speech processing and scoring technology has been applied to a variety of domains over the course of the past two decades, including evaluation and tutoring of children's literacy skills (Mostow et al., 1994), preparation for high stakes English proficiency tests for institutions of higher education (Zechner et al., 2009), evaluation of English skills of foreign-based call center agents (Chandel et al., 2007), and evaluation of aviation English (Pearson Education, Inc., 2011), to name a few (for a comprehensive overview, see (Eskenazi, 2009)).

Most of these applications elicit restricted speech from the participants, and the most common item type by far is the Read Aloud, in which the speaker reads a sentence or collection of sentences out loud. Due to the constrained nature of this task, it is possible to develop ASR systems that are relatively accurate, even with heavily accented non-native speech. Several types of features related to a non-native speaker's ability to produce English sounds and speech patterns effectively have been extracted from these types of responses. Some of the best performing of these types of features include pronunciation features, such as a phone's spectral match to native speaker acoustic models (Witt, 1999) and a phone's duration compared to native speaker models (Neumeyer et al., 2000); fluency features, such as the rate of speech, mean pause length, and number of disfluencies (Cucchiarini et al., 2000); and prosody features, such as F0 and intensity slope (Hoenig, 2002).

In addition to the large majority of applications that elicit restricted speech, a small number of applications have also investigated automated scoring of non-native spontaneous speech, in order to more fully evaluate a speaker's communicative competence (e.g., (Cucchiarini et al., 2002) and (Zechner et al., 2009)). In these systems, the same types of pronunciation, fluency, and prosody features can be extracted; furthermore, features related to additional aspects of a speaker's proficiency in the non-native language can be extracted, such as vocabulary usage (Yoon et al., 2012), syntactic complexity (Bernstein et al., 2010a; Chen and Zechner, 2011), and topical content (Xie et al., 2012).

As described in Section 1, the domain for the automated speaking assessment investigated in this study is teachers of EFL around the world. Based on the fact that many of the item types are designed to assess the test taker's ability to productively use English constructions and linguistic units that commonly recur in English teaching environments, several of the item types elicit semi-restricted speech (see Table 1 below for a description of the different item types). These types of responses fall somewhere between the heavily restricted speech elicited by a Read Aloud task and unconstrained spontaneous speech. In these semi-restricted responses, the test taker may be provided with a set of lexical items that should be used to form a sentence; in addition, the test taker is often asked to make the sentence conform to a given grammatical template. Thus, the responses provided for a given prompt of this type by multiple different speakers will often overlap with each other; however, it is not possible to specify a complete list of all possible responses. These types of items have only infrequently been examined in the context of automated speech scoring. Some related item types that have been explored previously include the Sentence Build and Short item types described in (Bernstein et al., 2010b); however, those item types typically elicited a much narrower range of responses than the semi-restricted ones in this study.

3 Data

The data used in this study was drawn from a pilot administration of a language assessment for teachers of English as a Foreign Language. This test is designed to assess the ability of a non-native teacher of English to use English in classroom settings. The language forms and functions included in this test are based on the materials included in a curriculum that the test takers studied prior to taking the assessment. The assessment includes items that cover the four language skills: Reading, Listening, Writing, and Speaking. There are a total of 8 different types of Speaking items included in the assessment. These can be divided into the following two categories, depending on how constrained the test taker's response is:

- *Restricted Speech*: In these item types, all of the linguistic content expected in the test taker's response is presented in the test prompt, and the test taker is asked to read or repeat it aloud.
- *Semi-restricted Speech*: In these item types, a portion of the linguistic content is presented in the prompt, and the test taker is required to provide the remaining content to formulate a complete response.

Sets of 7 Speaking items are presented to the test taker in thematic units, called "lessons", based on their instructional goals; in total, each test taker completed three lessons, and thus responded to 21 Speaking items. Table 1 presents descriptions of the 8 different item types included in the assessment.

The numbers of responses provided by the test takers to each type (along with their respective response durations) are as follows: four Multiple Choice (10 seconds each), six Read Aloud (four 40 second responses and two 60 second responses), two Repeat Aloud (15 seconds each), one Incomplete Sentence (20 seconds), one Key Words (15 seconds), five Chart (four 20 seconds and one 40 seconds), one Keyword Chart (15 seconds), and one Visuals (15 seconds). Thus, each test taker provided a total of approximately 9 minutes of audio.

The responses were all double-scored by trained human raters on a three-point scale (1 - 3). For the Restricted Speech items, the raters assessed the test taker's pronunciation, pacing, and intonation. For the Semi-restricted Speech items, the responses were also scored holistically on a 3-point scale, but raters were also asked to take into account the appropriateness of the language used

Restricted Speech	
Type	Description
Multiple Choice (MC)	The test taker selects the correct option and reads it aloud
Read Aloud (RA)	The test taker reads aloud a set of classroom instructions
Repeat Aloud (RP)	The test taker listens to a student utterance twice and then repeats it
Semi-restricted Speech	
Type	Description
Incomplete Sentence (IS)	The test taker is given a sentence fragment and completes the sentence according to the instructions
Key Words (KW)	The test taker uses the key words provided to speak a sentence as instructed
Chart (CH)	The test taker uses an example from a language chart and then formulates a similar sentence using a given grammatical pattern
Keyword Chart (KC)	The test taker constructs a sentence using keywords provided and information in a chart
Visuals (VI)	The test taker is given two visuals and is asked to give instructions to students based on the graphical information

Table 1: Types of speaking items included in the assessment

(e.g., grammatical accuracy and content correctness) in addition to aspects of fluency and pronunciation. For some responses, the raters were not able to provide a score on the 1 - 3 scale, e.g., because the audio response contained no speech input, the test taker responded in their native language, etc. These responses are labeled NS for Non-Scoreable.

After receiving scores, all of the responses were transcribed using standard English orthography (disfluencies, such as filled pauses and partial words are also included in the transcriptions). Then, the responses were partitioned (with no speaker overlap) into five sets for the training and evaluation of the ASR system and the linear regression scoring models. The amount of data and human score distributions in each of these partitions are displayed in Table 2.

4 System Architecture

The automated scoring system used for the teachers' spoken language assessment consists of the following four components, which are invoked one after the other in a pipeline fashion (ETS SpeechRater^{SM}, (Zechner et al., 2009; Higgins et al., 2011)):

- an automated speech recognizer, generating word hypotheses from input audio recordings of the test takers' responses
- a feature computation module that generates features based on the ASR output, e.g., measuring fluency, pronunciation, prosody, and content accuracy
- a filtering model that flags responses that should not be scored automatically due to issues with audio quality, empty responses, etc.
- linear regression scoring models that predict the score for each response based on a set of selected features

Furthermore, we use Praat (Boersma and Weenick, 2012) to extract power and pitch from the speech signal; this information is used for some of the feature computation modules, as well as for the filtering model.

The ASR is an HMM-based triphone system trained on approximately 800 hours of non-native speech from a different data set; a background Language Model (LM) was also trained on the same data set. Subsequently, 8 adapted LMs were trained (with an interpolation weight of 0.9 for the in-domain data) using the responses in the ASR Training partition for the 8 different item types listed in Table 1. The ASR system obtained an overall word error rate (WER) of 13.0% on the ASR Evaluation partition and 15.6% on the Model Evaluation partition. As would be expected, the ASR system performed best on the responses that were most restricted by the test item and performed worse on the responses that were less restricted. The WER ranged from 11.4% for the RA responses to 41.4% for the IS responses in the Model Evaluation partition.

5 Methodology

5.1 Speech features

The feature computation components of our speech scoring system compute more than 100 features based on a speaker's response. They belong to the following broad dimensions of speaking proficiency: fluency, pronunciation, prosody, vocabulary usage, grammatical complexity and accuracy, and content accuracy (Zechner et al., 2009; Chen and Yoon, 2012; Chen et al., 2009; Zechner et al., 2011; Yoon et al., 2012; Yoon and Bhat, 2012; Zechner and Wang, 2013).

After initial feature generation, we selected a set of about 10 features for each of the 8 item types, based on the following considerations[1] (Zechner et al., 2009; Xi et al., 2008):

- empirical performance, i.e., feature correlation with human scores
- construct[2] relevance, i.e., to what extent the feature measures aspects of speaking proficiency that are considered to be relevant and important by content experts
- overall construct coverage, i.e., the feature set should include features from all relevant construct dimensions
- feature independence, i.e., the intercorrelation between any two features of the set should be low

Furthermore, some features were transformed (e.g., by applying the inverse or log function), in order to increase the normality of their distributions (an assumption of linear regression classifiers). All feature values that exceeded a threshold of 4 standard deviations from the mean were replaced by the respective threshold (outlier truncation).

The composition of feature sets is slightly different for the two item type categories: for the 3 restricted item types, features related to fluency, pronunciation, prosody and read/repeat accuracy were chosen, whereas for the 5 semi-restricted item types, vocabulary and grammar features were also added to the set. Further, while accuracy

[1]While automated feature selection is conceivable in principle, in our experience it typically does not result in a feature set that meets all of these criteria well.

[2]A construct is the set of knowledge, skills, and abilities measured by a test.

Partition	Spk.	Resp.	Dur.	1	2	3	NS
ASR Training	773	16,049	116.7	1,587 (9.9)	4,086 (25.5)	8,796 (54.8)	1,580 (9.8)
ASR Development	25	525	3.8	53 (10.1)	133 (25.3)	327 (62.3)	12 (2.3)
ASR Evaluation	25	525	3.8	31 (5.9)	114 (21.7)	326 (62.1)	54 (10.3)
Model Training	300	6,300	45.8	675 (10.7)	1,715 (27.2)	3,577 (56.8)	333 (5.3)
Model Evaluation	300	6,300	45.7	647 (10.3)	1,637 (26.0)	3,487 (55.3)	529 (8.4)
Total	1,423	29,699	215.8	2,993 (9.38)	7,685 (25.14)	16,513 (58.26)	2,508 (7.22)

Table 2: Amount of data contained in each partition (speakers, responses, hours of speech) and distribution of human scores (percentages of scores per partition in brackets).

features for the restricted items were based only on string alignment measures, content accuracy features for the semi-restricted items were more diverse, e.g., based on regular expressions, keywords, and language model scores (Zechner and Wang, 2013). Table 3 lists the features that were used in the scoring models for restricted and semi-restricted item types, along with sub-constructs they measure and their description.

5.2 Filtering model

In order to automatically identify responses that have technical issues (e.g., loud background noise) or are otherwise not scorable (e.g., empty responses), a decision tree-based filtering model was developed using a combination of features derived from ASR output and from pitch and energy information (Yoon et al., 2011; Jeon and Yoon, 2012). The filtering model was tested on the scoring model evaluation data, and obtained an accuracy rate (the exact agreement between the filtering model and a human rater concerning the distinction between scorable and non-scorable responses) of 97%; it correctly identified 90% of the non-scorable responses in the data set with a false positive rate of 21% (recall=0.90, precision=0.79, F-score=0.84).

5.3 Scoring models

We used the Model Training set to train 8 linear regression models for the 8 different item types, using the previously determined feature sets. We used the features as independent variables in these models and the summed scores of two human raters as the dependent variable. These trained scoring models were then employed to score responses of the Model Evaluation data (excluding responses marked as non-scorable by human raters) and rounded to the nearest integer to predict the final scores for each response. These scores were then evaluated against the first human rater score (H1).

Item	N	S-H1	H1-H2	WER (%)
RA	1653	0.34	0.51	11.4
RP	543	0.41	0.73	21.8
MC	1036	0.67	0.83	17.1
CH	1372	0.44	0.67	26.3
KW	275	0.45	0.67	28.7
KC	274	0.57	0.74	28.8
IS	260	0.46	0.69	41.4
VI	272	0.43	0.80	30.4

Table 4: Correlations between system and first human rater (S-H1) and between two human raters (H1-H2), for all responses of each item type in the Model Evaluation partition (N). The last column provides the average ASR word error rate (WER) in percent.

Additionally, for responses flagged as non-scorable by the automatic filtering model, the second human rater score (H2) was used as final item score in order to mimic the operational scenario where human raters score responses that are flagged by the filtering model.

We also compute the agreement between system and human raters based on a set of all 21 responses of a speaker. Score imputation was used for responses that were labeled as non-scorable by both the system and H2; in this case, the response was given the mean score of the total scorable responses from the same speaker. Similarly, the same score imputation rule was applied to the H1 scores.

6 Results

Table 4 presents the Pearson correlation coefficients between human and automated scores for the responses from the 8 different item types along with the human-human correlation for each item type. Furthermore, we also provide the word error rates of the ASR system for the same 8 item types in the last column of the table.

Feature	Sub-construct	Description
Content_Ed1	Read/repeat accuracy / Fluency	Correctly read words per minute
Content_Ed2	Read/repeat accuracy	Read/repeat word error rate
Content_RegEx	Content accuracy	Matching of regular expressions
Content_WER	Content accuracy	Response discrepancy from high scoring responses
Content_NGram	Content accuracy	N-grams in response matching high scoring response n-grams
Fluency_Rate	Fluency	Speaking rate
Fluency_Chunk	Fluency	Average length of contiguous word chunks
Fluency_Sil1	Fluency	Frequency of long silences
Fluency_Sil2	Fluency / Grammar	Proportion of long within-clause-silences to all within-clause-silences
Fluency_Sil3	Fluency	Mean length of silences within a clause
Fluency_Disfl1	Fluency	Frequency of interruption points (repair, repetition, false start)
Fluency_Disfl2	Fluency	Number of disfluencies per second
Fluency_Disfl3	Fluency	Frequency of repetitions
Pron_Vowels	Pronunciation	Average vowel duration differences relative to a native-speaker model
Prosody1	Prosody	Percentage of stressed syllables
Prosody2	Prosody	Mean deviation of time intervals between stressed syllables
Prosody3	Prosody	Mean distance between stressed syllables
Vocab1	Vocabulary / Fluency	Number of word types divided by utterance duration
Grammar_POS	Grammar	Part-of-speech based distributional similarity score between a response and responses with different score levels
Grammar_LM	Grammar	Global language model score (normalized by response length)

Table 3: List of features used for item type scoring models, with the sub-constructs they represent and descriptions.

Comparison	Pearson r
S-H1	0.725
S-H2	0.742
H1-H2	0.934

Table 5: Speaker-level performance (Pearson r correlations) computed over the sum of all 21 scores from each speaker, N=272

Sub-construct	Restricted	Semi-restricted
Content	0.33–0.67	0.34–0.61
Fluency	0.19–0.33	0.20–0.33
Pronunciation	0.20–0.22	0.13–0.31
Prosody	0.18–0.24	0.12–0.27
Grammar	–	0.23–0.49
Vocabulary	–	0.21–0.32

Table 6: Range of Pearson r correlations for different features with human scores (H1) by sub-construct for restricted and semi-restricted item types.

Table 5 presents the Pearson correlation coefficients between the speaker-level scores produced by the automated scoring system (S) and the two sets of human scores (H1 and H2). These speaker-level scores were computed based on the sum of all 21 scores from each speaker in the Model Evaluation partition. Responses that received a non-scorable rating from the human raters were imputed, as described above. Furthermore, 28 speakers were excluded from this analysis because they had more than 7 non-scorable responses each.[3]

Finally, Table 6 provides an overview of Pearson correlation ranges with human rater scores (H1) for the different features used in the scoring models, summarized by the sub-constructs that the features represent.

7 Discussion

When looking at Table 4, we see that the inter-rater reliability for human raters ranges between 0.51 (for RA items) and 0.83 (for MC items). Inter-rater reliability varies less for the 5 semi-restricted item types (0.67–0.80), compared to the 3 restricted item types (0.51–0.83). As for automated score correlations with human raters, the Pearson r coefficients range from 0.34 (RA) to 0.67 (MC).

[3]In an operational setting, these test takers would not receive a test score; instead, they would have the opportunity to take the test again.

Again, the variability of Pearson r coefficients is larger for the 3 restricted item types (0.34–0.67) than for the 5 semi-restricted item types (0.43–0.57). The degradation in correlation between the inter-human results and the machine-human results varies from 0.16 (MC) to 0.37 (VI).

Speech recognition word error rate does not seem to have a strong influence on model performance (RA items have the lowest WER with S-H1 r=0.34, but r=0.46 for IS items that have the highest WER). However, we found other factors that affect model performance negatively; for example, multiple repeats of responses by test takers contribute to the large performance difference between S-H1 and H1-H2 for the RP items. In general, we conjecture that using features for a larger set of sub-construct areas—in the case of semi-restricted item types—may contribute to the lower variation of scoring model performance for this subset of the data.

As for speaker-level results (Table 5), the overall degradation between the inter-human correlation and the system-human correlations is of a similar magnitude (around 0.2) as observed for most of the individual item types. Still, the speaker-level correlation of 0.73 is 0.26 higher than the average item type correlation between the system and H1.

When we look into more detail at the Pearson r correlations between individual features used in the item type scoring models and human scores (Table 6), we can see that features related to content accuracy exhibit a substantially stronger performance (r=0.33–0.67) than features related to most other sub-constructs of speaking proficiency, namely fluency, pronunciation, prosody, and vocabulary ($r \sim 0.2$). One exception is features related to grammar, where correlations with human scores are as high as 0.49. Since related work on scoring speech using features indicative of fluency, pronunciation, etc. showed higher correlations (e.g., (Cucchiarini et al., 1997; Franco et al., 2000; Zechner et al., 2009)), we conjecture that the reason behind this difference is likely to be found in the fact that the responses in this assessment for teachers of English are quite short (6–14 words on average for all items except for Read Aloud items that are about 46 words on average). Since content features are less reliant on longer stretches of speech, they still work fairly well for most items in our corpus.

Finally, while the proportion of words contained in responses in restricted items is much larger than those contained in responses in semi-restricted items, these two item type categories are more evenly distributed over the whole test, i.e., each test taker responds to 9 semi-restricted and 12 restricted items, and the item scores are then aggregated for a final score with equal weight given to each item score.

8 Conclusion

This paper presented an overview of an automated speech scoring system that was developed for a language assessment for teachers of English as a Foreign Language (EFL) whose native language is not English. We described the main components of this prototype system and their performance: the ASR system, features generated from ASR output, a filtering model to flag non-scorable responses, and finally a set of linear regression models, one for each of 8 different types of test items.

We found that overall, the correlation between our speech scoring system's predicted scores and human rater scores range between 0.34 and 0.67, evaluated on responses from 8 item types. Furthermore, we found that correlations based on complete sets of 21 spoken responses per test taker improve to around $r = 0.73$.

Given the many significant challenges of this work, including 8 different item types in the assessment, responses from speakers from different native languages and speaking proficiency levels, sub-optimal audio conditions for a part of the data, and a relatively small data set for both ASR system adaptation and linear regression model training, we find that the overall performance achieved by our automated speech scoring system was a good starting point for an eventual deployment in a low-stakes assessment context.

Future work will aim at improving the performance of the prediction models by the addition of more features addressing different aspects of the construct as well as an improved filtering model for flagging the different types of problematic responses. Furthermore, agreement between human raters, in particular for read-aloud items, could be improved by refining rater rubrics and additional rater training and monitoring.

Acknowledgments

The authors would like to thank Anastassia Loukina and Jidong Tao for their comments on an earlier version of this paper, and are also indebted to the anonymous reviewers of BEA-9 and ASRU 2013 for their valuable comments and suggestions.

References

Jared Bernstein, Jian Cheng, and Masanori Suzuki. 2010a. Fluency and structural complexity as predictors of L2 oral proficiency. In *Proceedings of Interspeech*.

Jared Bernstein, Alistair Van Moere, and Jian Cheng. 2010b. Validating automated speaking tests. *Language Testing*, 27(3):355–377.

Paul Boersma and David Weenick. 2012. Praat: Doing phonetics by computer, version 5.3.32. `http://www.praat.org`.

Abhishek Chandel, Abhinav Parate, Maymon Madathingal, Himanshu Pant, Nitendra Rajput, Shajith Ikbal, Om Deshmuck, and Ashish Verma. 2007. Sensei: Spoken language assessment for call center agents. In *Proceedings of the IEEE Workshop on Automatic Speech Recognition and Understanding (ASRU)*.

Lei Chen and Su-Youn Yoon. 2012. Application of structural events detected on ASR outputs for automated speaking assessment. In *Proceedings of Interspeech*.

Miao Chen and Klaus Zechner. 2011. Computing and evaluating syntactic complexity features for automated scoring of spontaneous non-native speech. In *Proceedings of the 49th Annual Meeting of the Association for Computational Linguistics*, pages 722–731.

Lei Chen, Klaus Zechner, and Xiaoming Xi. 2009. Improved pronunciation features for construct-driven assessment of non-native spontaneous speech. In *Proceedings of NAACL-HLT*.

Catia Cucchiarini, Helmer Strik, and Lou Boves. 1997. Automatic evaluation of Dutch pronunciation by using speech recognition technology. In *Proceedings of the IEEE Workshop on Auotmatic Speech Recognition and Understanding (ASRU)*.

Catia Cucchiarini, Helmer Strik, and Lou Boves. 2000. Quantitative assessment of second language learners' fluency by means of automatic speech recognition technology. *Journal of the Acoustical Society of America*, 107(2):989–999.

Catia Cucchiarini, Helmer Strik, and Lou Boves. 2002. Quantitative assessment of second language learners' fluency: Comparisons between read and spontaneous speech. *Journal of the Acoustical Society of America*, 111(6):2862–2873.

Maxine Eskenazi. 2009. An overview of spoken language technology for education. *Speech Communication*, 51(10):832–844.

Horacio Franco, Leonardo Neumeyer, Vassilios Digalakis, and Orith Ronen. 2000. Combination of machine scores for automatic grading of pronunciation quality. *Speech Communication*, 30(1-2):121–130.

Derrick Higgins, Xiaoming Xi, Klaus Zechner, and David M. Williamson. 2011. A three-stage approach to the automated scoring of spontaneous spoken responses. *Computer Speech and Language*, 25(2):282–306.

Florian Hoenig. 2002. Automatic assessment of non-native prosody – Annotation, modelling, and evaluation. In *Proceedings of the International Symposium on Automatic Detection of Errors in Pronunciation Training (ISADEPT)*, pages 21–30, Stockholm, Sweden.

Je Hun Jeon and Su-Youn Yoon. 2012. Acoustic feature-based non-scorable response detection for an automated speaking proficiency assessment. In *Proceedings of Interspeech*.

Jack Mostow, Steven F. Roth, Alexander G. Hauptmann, and Matthew Kane. 1994. A prototype reading coach that listens. In *Proceedings of the Twelfth National Conference on Artificial Intelligence*.

Leonardo Neumeyer, Horacio Franco, Vassilios Digalakis, and Mitchel Weintraub. 2000. Automatic scoring of pronunciation quality. *Speech Communication*, 30:83–93.

Pearson Education, Inc. 2011. Versant™ Aviation English Test. `http://www.versanttest.com/technology/VersantAviationEnglishTestValidation.pdf`.

Silke Witt. 1999. *Use of speech recognition in computer-assisted language learning*. Ph.D. thesis, Cambridge University.

Xiaoming Xi, Derrick Higgins, Klaus Zechner, and David M. Williamson. 2008. Automated scoring of spontaneous speech using SpeechRater v1.0. *Educational Testing Service Research Report RR-08-62*.

Shasha Xie, Keelan Evanini, and Klaus Zechner. 2012. Exploring content features for automated speech scoring. In *Proceedings of the 2012 Conference of the North American Chapter of the Association for Computational Linguistics: Human Language Technologies*, pages 103–111, Montréal, Canada. Association for Computational Linguistics.

Su-Youn Yoon and Suma Bhat. 2012. Assessment of ESL learners' syntactic competence based on similarity measures. In *Proceedings of the 2012 Joint Conference on Empirical Methods in Natural Language Processing and Computational Natural Language Learning*, pages 600–608, Jeju Island, Korea. Association for Computational Linguistics.

Su-Youn Yoon, Keelan Evanini, and Klaus Zechner. 2011. Non-scorable response detection for automated speaking proficiency assessment. In *Proceedings of NAACL-HLT Workshop on Innovative Use of NLP for Building Educational Applications*.

Su-Youn Yoon, Suma Bhat, and Klaus Zechner. 2012. Vocabulary profile as a measure of vocabulary sophistication. In *Proceedings of the 7th Workshop on Innovative Use of NLP for Building Educational Applications, NAACL-HLT*, Montréal, Canada. Association for Computational Linguistics.

Klaus Zechner and Xinhao Wang. 2013. Automated content scoring of spoken responses in an assessment for teachers of english. In *Proceedings of the 8th Workshop on Innovative Use of NLP for Building Educational Applications, NAACL-HLT*, Atlanta. Association for Computational Linguistics.

Klaus Zechner, Derrick Higgins, Xiaoming Xi, and David M. Williamson. 2009. Automatic scoring of non-native spontaneous speech in tests of spoken English. *Speech Communication*, 51(10):883–895.

Klaus Zechner, Xiaoming Xi, and Lei Chen. 2011. Evaluating prosodic features for automated scoring of non-native read speech. In *Proceedings of the IEEE Workshop on Automatic Speech Recognition and Understanding (ASRU)*.

Automatic Generation of Challenging Distractors Using Context-Sensitive Inference Rules

Torsten Zesch
Language Technology Lab
University of Duisburg-Essen
torsten.zesch@uni-due.de

Oren Melamud
Computer Science Department
Bar-Ilan University
melamuo@cs.biu.ac.il

Abstract

Automatically generating challenging distractors for multiple-choice gap-fill items is still an unsolved problem. We propose to employ context-sensitive lexical inference rules in order to generate distractors that are semantically similar to the gap target word in some sense, but not in the particular sense induced by the gap-fill context. We hypothesize that such distractors should be particularly hard to distinguish from the correct answer. We focus on verbs as they are especially difficult to master for language learners and find that our approach is quite effective. In our test set of 20 items, our proposed method decreases the number of invalid distractors in 90% of the cases, and fully eliminates all of them in 65%. Further analysis on that dataset does not support our hypothesis regarding item difficulty as measured by average error rate of language learners. We conjecture that this may be due to limitations in our evaluation setting, which we plan to address in future work.

1 Introduction

Multiple-choice gap-fill items as illustrated in Figure 1 are frequently used for both testing language proficiency and as a learning device. Each item consists of a *carrier sentence* that provides the context to a *target word*. The target word is blanked and presented as one possible gap-fill answer together with a certain number (usually 3) of *distractors*. Given a desired target word, carrier sentences containing it can be automatically selected from a corpus. Some methods even select only sentences where the target word is used in a certain sense (Liu et al., 2005). Then, the main problem is to pick challenging distractors that are reasonably hard to distinguish from the correct answer (i.e. the target word) on one hand, yet cannot be considered as correct answers on the other.

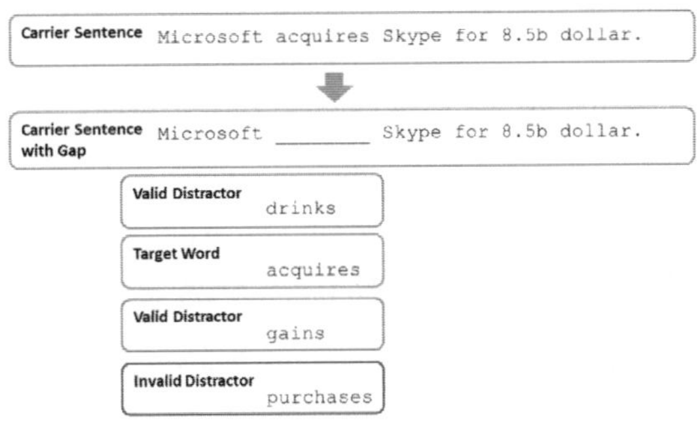

Figure 1: Multiple-choice gap-fill item.

In this paper we propose to generate distractors that are semantically similar to the gap target word in some sense, but not in the particular sense induced by the gap-fill context, thereby making them difficult to distinguish from the target word. For example, the distractor *gain* in Figure 1 is semantically similar to *acquire*, but is not appropriate in the particular context of purchasing companies, and therefore has high distractive potential. On the other hand, the distractor *purchase* is a correct answer in this context and is therefore an invalid distractor. To generate challenging distractors, we utilize context-sensitive lexical inference rules that can discriminate between appropriate substitutes of a target word given its context and other inappropriate substitutes.

In the next section, we give an overview of previous work in order to place our contribution into context.

2 Previous Work

The process of finding good distractors involves two steps: *Candidate Selection* controls the difficulty of the items, while *Reliability Checking* ensures that the items remain solvable, i.e. it ensures

Proceedings of the Ninth Workshop on Innovative Use of NLP for Building Educational Applications , pages 143–148,
Baltimore, Maryland USA, June 26, 2014.

that there is only one correct answer. We note that this work is focused on single-word distractors rather than phrases (Gates et al., 2011), and only on target isolated carrier sentences rather than longer texts as in (Mostow and Jang, 2012).

2.1 Candidates Selection

In some settings the set of possible distractors is known in advance, e.g. the set of English prepositions in preposition exercises (Lee and Seneff, 2007) or a confusion set with previously known errors like {two, too, to}. Sakaguchi et al. (2013) use data from the Lang-8 platform (a corpus of manually annotated errors[1]) in order to determine typical learner errors and use them as distractors. However, in the common setting only the target word is known and the set of distractors needs to be automatically generated.

Randomly selecting distractors is a valid strategy (Mostow and Jang, 2012), but it is only suitable for the most beginner learners. More advanced learners can easily rule out distractors that do not fit grammatically or are too unrelated semantically. Thus, more advanced approaches usually employ basic strategies, such as choosing distractors with the same part-of-speech tag as the target word, or distractors with a corpus frequency comparable to the target word (Hoshino and Nakagawa, 2007) (based on the assumption that corpus frequency roughly correlates with word difficulty). Pino and Eskenazi (2009) use distractors that are morphologically, orthographically, or phonetically similar (e.g. *bread – beard*).

Another approach used in previous works to make distractors more challenging is utilizing thesauri (Sumita et al., 2005; Smith and Avinesh, 2010) or taxonomies (Hoshino and Nakagawa, 2007; Mitkov et al., 2009) to select words that are semantically similar to the target word. In addition to the target word, some approaches also consider the semantic relatedness of distractors with the whole carrier sentence or paragraph (Pino et al., 2008; Agarwal and Mannem, 2011; Mostow and Jang, 2012), i.e. they pick distractors that are from the same domain as the target word.

Generally, selecting more challenging distractors usually means making them more similar to the target word. As this increases the probability that a distractor might actually be another correct answer, we need a more sophisticated approach for checking the reliability of the distractor set.

2.2 Reliability Checking

In order to make sure that there is only one correct answer to a gap-fill item, there needs to be a way to decide for each distractor whether it fits into the context of the carrier sentence or not. In those cases, where we have a limited list of potential target words and distractors, e.g. in preposition exercises (Lee and Seneff, 2007), a supervised classifier can be trained to do this job. Given enough training data, this approach yields very high precision, but it cannot be easily applied to open word classes like nouns or verbs, which are much larger and dynamic in nature.

When we do not have a closed list of potential distractors at hand, one way to perform reliability checking is by considering collocations involving the target word (Pino et al., 2008; Smith and Avinesh, 2010). For example, if the target word is *strong*, we can find the collocation *strong tea*. Then we can use *powerful* as a distractor because it is semantically similar to *strong*, yet **powerful tea* is not a valid collocation. This approach is effective, but requires strong collocations to discriminate between valid and invalid distractors. Therefore it cannot be used with carrier sentences that do not contain strong collocations, such as the sentence in Figure 1.

Sumita et al. (2005) apply a simple web search approach to judge the reliability of an item. They check whether the carrier sentence with the target word replaced by the distractor can be found on the web. If such a sentence is found, the distractor is discarded. We note that the applicability of this approach is limited, as finding exact matches for such artificial sentences can be unlikely due to sparseness of natural languages. Therefore not finding an exact match does not necessarily rule out the possibility of an invalid distractor.

3 Automatic Generation of Challenging Distractors

Our goal is to automatically generate distractors that are as 'close' to the target word as possible, yet do not fit the carrier sentence context. To accomplish this, our strategy is to first generate a set of distractor candidates, which are semantically similar to the target word. Then we use context-sensitive lexical inference rules to filter candidates that fit the context, and thus cannot be used as dis-

[1] http://cl.naist.jp/nldata/lang-8/

tractors. In the remainder of this section we describe this procedure in more detail.

3.1 Context-Sensitive Inference Rules

A lexical inference rule '*LHS* $\rightarrow$ *RHS*', such as '*acquire* $\rightarrow$ *purchase*', specifies a directional inference relation between two words (or terms). A rule can be *applied* when its LHS matches a word in a text T, and then that word is substituted for RHS, yielding the modified text H. For example, applying the rule above to "*Microsoft acquired Skype*", yields "*Microsoft purchased Skype*". If the rule is true then the meaning of H is inferred from the meaning of T. A popular way to learn lexical inference rules in an unsupervised setting is by using distributional similarity models (Lin and Pantel, 2001; Kotlerman et al., 2010). Under this approach, target words are represented as vectors of context features, and the score of a rule between two target words is based on vector arithmetics.

One of the main shortcomings of such rules is that they are *context-insensitive*, i.e. they have a single score, which is not assessed with respect to the concrete context T under which they are applied. However, the appropriateness of an inference rule may in fact depend on this context. For example, '*Microsoft acquire Skype* $\rightarrow$ *Microsoft purchase Skype*', is an appropriate application of the rule '*acquire* $\rightarrow$ *purchase*', while '*Children acquire skills* $\rightarrow$ *Children purchase skills*' is not. To address this issue, additional models were introduced that compute a different *context-sensitive* score per each context T, under which it is applied (Dinu and Lapata, 2010; Melamud et al., 2013).

In this work, we use the resource provided by Melamud et al. (2013), which includes both context-sensitive and context-insensitive rules for over 2,000 frequent verbs.[2] We use these rules to generate challenging distractors as we show next.

3.2 Distractor Selection & Reliability

We start with the following illustrative example to motivate our approach. While the words *purchase* and *acquire* are considered to be almost perfect synonyms in sentences like *Microsoft acquires Skype* and *Microsoft purchases Skype*, this is not true for all contexts. For example, in *Children acquire skills* vs. *Children purchase skills*, the meaning is clearly not equivalent. These context-dependent senses, which are particularly typical to verbs, make it difficult for learners to understand how to properly use these words.

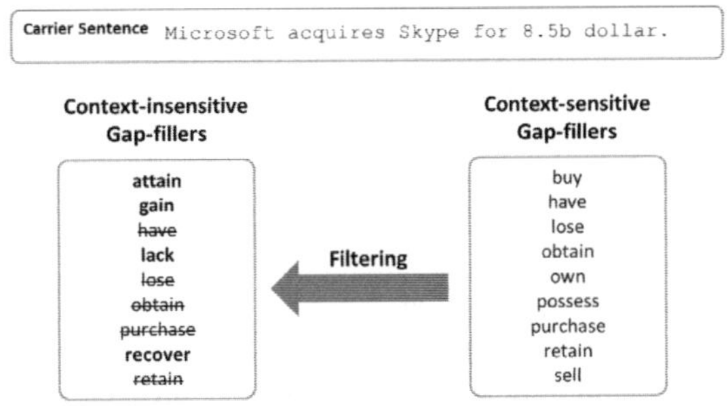

Figure 2: Filtering context-insensitive substitutions with context-sensitive ones in order to get challenging distractors.

Acquiring such fine-grained sense distinction skills is a prerequisite for really competent language usage. These skills can be trained and tested with distractors, such as *purchase* in the example above. Therefore, such items are good indicators in language proficiency testing, and should be specifically trained when learning a language.

To generate such challenging distractors, we first use the context-insensitive rules, whose LHS matches the carrier sentence target word, to create a *distractor candidate set* as illustrated on the left-hand side of Figure 2. We include in this set the top-n inferred words that correspond to the highest rule scores. These candidate words are inferred by the target word, but not necessarily in the particular context of the carrier sentence. Therefore, we expect this set to include both correct answers, which would render the item unreliable, as well as good distractors that are semantically similar to the target word in some sense, but not in the particular sense induced by the carrier sentence.

Next, we use context-sensitive rules to generate a *distractor black-list* including the top-m words that are inferred by the target word, but this time taking the context of the carrier sentence into consideration. In this case, we expect the words in the list to comprise only the gap-fillers that fit the given context as illustrated on the right-hand side of Figure 2. Such gap-fillers are correct answers and therefore cannot be used as distractors. Finally, we subtract the black-list distractors from the initial distractor candidate set and expect the remaining candidates to comprise only good distractors. We consider the candidates in this final set as our generated distractors.

[2]http://www.cs.biu.ac.il/nlp/downloads/wt-rules.html

3.3 Distractor Ranking

In case our approach returns a large number of good distractors, we should use ranking to select the most challenging ones. A simple strategy is to rely on the corpus frequency of the distractor, where less frequent means more challenging as it will not be known to the learner. However, this tends to put a focus on the more obscure words of the vocabulary while actually the more frequent words should be trained more often. Therefore, in this work we use the scores that were assigned to the distractors by the context-insensitive inference rules. Accordingly, the more similar a distractor is to the target word, the higher rank it will get (provided that it was not in the distractor black-list).

4 Experiments & Results

In our experiments we wanted to test two hypotheses: (i) whether context-sensitive inference rules are able to reliably distinguish between valid and invalid distractors, and (ii) whether the generated distractors are more challenging for language learners than randomly chosen ones.

We used the Brown corpus (Nelson Francis and Kuçera, 1964) as a source for carrier sentences and selected medium-sized (5-12 tokens long) sentences that contain a main verb. We then manually inspected this set, keeping only well-formed sentences that are understandable by a general audience without requiring too much context knowledge. In a production system, this manual process would be replaced by a sophisticated method for obtaining good carrier sentences, but this is beyond the scope of this paper. Finally, for this exploratory study, we only used the first 20 selected sentences from a much larger set of possible carrier sentences.

4.1 Reliability

Our first goal was to study the effectiveness of our approach in generating reliable items, i.e. items where the target word is the only correct answer. In order to minimize impact of pre-processing and lemmatization, we provided the context-sensitive inference rules with correctly lemmatized carrier sentences and marked the target verbs. We found that we get better results when using a distractor black-list that is larger than the distractor candidate set, as this more aggressively filters invalid distractors. We used the top-20 distractor black-list and top-10 distractor candidate set, which lead to generating on average 3.3 distractors per item.

Only valid distractors	13/20 (65%)
Mix of valid and invalid	5/20 (25%)
Only invalid distractors	2/20 (10%)

Table 1: Reliability of items after filtering

All our generated distractors were checked by two native English speakers. We count a distractor as "invalid" if it was ruled out by at least one annotator. Table 1 summarizes the results. We found that in 13 of the 20 items (65%) all distractors generated by our approach were valid, while only for 2 items all generated distractors were invalid. For the remaining 5 items, our approach returned a mix of valid and invalid distractors. We note that the unfiltered distractor candidate set always contained invalid distractors and in 90% of the items it contained a higher proportion of invalid distractors than the filtered one. This suggests that the context-sensitive inference rules are quite effective in differentiating between the different senses of the verbs.

A main source of error are sentences that do not provide enough context, e.g. because the subject is a pronoun. In *She [served] one four-year term on the national committee*, it would be acceptable to insert *sold* in the context of a report on political corruption, but a more precise subject like *Barack Obama* would render that reading much more unlikely. Therefore, more emphasis should be put on selecting better carrier sentences. Selecting longer sentences that provide a richer context would help to rule out more distractor candidates and may also lead to better results when using the context-sensitive inference rules. However, long sentences are also more difficult for language learners, so there will probably be some trade-off.

A qualitative analysis of the results shows that especially for verbs with clearly distinct senses, our approach yields good results. For example in *He [played] basketball there while working toward a law degree*, our method generates the distractors *compose* and *tune* which are both related to the "play a musical instrument" sense. Another example is *His petition [charged] mental cruelty*, where our method generates among others the distractors *pay* and *collect* that are both related to the "charge taxes" reading of the verb. *The ball [floated] downstream* is an example where our method did not work well. It generated the distractors *glide* and *travel* which also fit the context and

	Group 1	Group 2
Control Items	0.24 ± 0.12	0.20 ± 0.12
Test Items	0.18 ± 0.17	0.18 ± 0.15

Table 2: Average error rates on our dataset

should thus not be used as distractors. The verb *float* is different from the previous examples, as all its dominant senses involve some kind of "floating" even if only metaphorically used. This results in similar senses that are harder to differentiate.

4.2 Difficulty

Next, we wanted to examine whether our approach leads to more challenging distractors. For that purpose we removed the distractors that our annotators identified as invalid in the previous step. We then ranked the remaining distractors according to the scores assigned to them by the context-sensitive inference rules and selected the top-3 distractors. If our method generated less than 3 distractors, we randomly generated additional distractors from the same frequency range as the target word.

We compared our approach with randomly selected distractors that are in the same order of magnitude with respect to corpus frequency as the distractors generated by our method. This way we ensure that a possible change in distractor difficulty cannot simply be attributed to differences in the learners' familiarity with the distractor verbs due to their corpus frequency. We note that random selection repeatedly created invalid distractors that we needed to manually filter out. This shows that better methods for checking the reliability of items like in our approach are definitely required.

We randomly split 52 participants (all non-natives) into two groups, each assigned with a different test version. Table 2 summarizes the results. For both groups, the first 7 test items were identical and contained only randomly selected distractors. Average error rate for these items was 0.24 (SD 0.12) for the first group, and 0.20 (SD 0.12) for the second group, suggesting that the results of the two groups on the remaining items can be compared meaningfully. The first group was tested on the remaining 13 items with randomly selected distractors, while the second group got the same items but with distractors created by our method.

Contrary to our hypothesis, the average error rate for both groups was equal (0.18, SD_1=0.17, SD_2=0.15). One reason might be that the English language skills of the participants (mostly computer science students or faculty) were rather high, close to the native level, as shown by the low error rates. Furthermore, even if the participants were more challenged by our distractors, they might have been able to finally select the right answer with no measurable effect on error rate. Thus, in future work we want measure answer time instead of average error rate, in order to counter this effect. We also want to re-run the experiment with lower grade students, who might not have mastered the kind of sense distinctions that our approach is focused on.

5 Conclusions

In this paper we have tackled the task of generating challenging distractors for multiple-choice gap-fill items. We propose to employ context-sensitive lexical inference rules in order to generate distractors that are semantically similar to the gap target word in some sense, but not in the particular sense induced by the gap-fill context.

Our results suggest that our approach is quite effective, reducing the number of invalid distractors in 90% of the cases, and fully eliminating all of them in 65%. We did not find a difference in average error rate between distractors generated with our method and randomly chosen distractors from the same corpus frequency range. We conjecture that this may be due to limitations in the setup of our experiment.

Thus, in future work we want to re-run the experiment with less experienced participants. We also wish to measure answer time in addition to error rate, as the distractive powers of a gap-filler might be reflected in longer answer times more than in higher error rates.

Acknowledgements

We thank all participants of the gap-fill survey, and Emily Jamison and Tristan Miller for their help with the annotation study. This work was partially supported by the European Community's Seventh Framework Programme (FP7/2007-2013) under grant agreement no. 287923 (EXCITEMENT).

References

Manish Agarwal and Prashanth Mannem. 2011. Automatic Gap-fill Question Generation from Text Books. In *Proceedings of the Sixth Workshop on Innovative Use of NLP for Building Educational Applications*, pages 56–64.

Georgiana Dinu and Mirella Lapata. 2010. Measuring Distributional Similarity in Context. In *Proceedings of the 2010 Conference on Empirical Methods in Natural Language Processing (EMNLP)*, pages 1162–1172.

Donna Gates, Margaret Mckeown, Juliet Bey, Forbes Ave, and Ross Hall. 2011. How to Generate Cloze Questions from Definitions : A Syntactic Approach. In *Proceedings of the AAAI Fall Symposium on Question Generation*, pages 19–22.

Ayako Hoshino and Hiroshi Nakagawa. 2007. Assisting Cloze Test Making with a Web Application. In *Proceedings of the Society for Information Technology and Teacher Education International Conference*, pages 2807– 2814.

Lili Kotlerman, Ido Dagan, Idan Szpektor, and Maayan Zhitomirsky-Geffet. 2010. Directional Distributional Similarity for Lexical Inference. *Natural Language Engineering*, 16(4):359–389.

John Lee and Stephanie Seneff. 2007. Automatic Generation of Cloze Items for Prepositions. In *Proceedings of INTERSPEECH*, pages 2173–2176, Antwerp, Belgium.

Dekang Lin and Patrick Pantel. 2001. DIRT – Discovery of Inference Rules from Text. In *Proceedings of ACM SIGKDD Conference on Knowledge Discovery and Data Mining 2001.*

Chao-lin Liu, Chun-hung Wang, and Zhao-ming Gao. 2005. Using Lexical Constraints to Enhance the Quality of Computer-Generated Multiple-Choice Cloze Items. *Computational Linguistics and Chinese Language Processing*, 10(3):303–328.

Oren Melamud, Jonathan Berant, Ido Dagan, Jacob Goldberger, and Idan Szpektor. 2013. A Two Level Model for Context Sensitive Inference Rules. In *Proceedings of the 51st Annual Meeting of the Association for Computational Linguistics (Volume 1: Long Papers)*, pages 1331–1340, Sofia, Bulgaria.

Ruslan Mitkov, Le An Ha, Andrea Varga, and Luz Rello. 2009. Semantic Similarity of Distractors in Multiple-choice Tests: Extrinsic Evaluation. In *Proceedings of the Workshop on Geometrical Models of Natural Language Semantics*, pages 49–56.

Jack Mostow and Hyeju Jang. 2012. Generating Diagnostic Multiple Choice Comprehension Cloze Questions. In *Proceedings of the Seventh Workshop on Building Educational Applications Using NLP*, pages 136–146, Stroudsburg, PA, USA.

W. Nelson Francis and Henry Kuçera. 1964. Manual of Information to Accompany a Standard Corpus of Present-day Edited American English, for use with Digital Computers.

Juan Pino and Maxine Eskenazi. 2009. Semi-Automatic Generation of Cloze Question Distractors Effect of Students L1. In *SLaTE Workshop on Speech and Language Technology in Education.*

Juan Pino, Michael Heilman, and Maxine Eskenazi. 2008. A Selection Strategy to Improve Cloze Question Quality. In *Proceedings of the Workshop on Intelligent Tutoring Systems for Ill-Defined Domains at the 9th Internationnal Conference on Intelligent Tutoring Systems.*

Keisuke Sakaguchi, Yuki Arase, and Mamoru Komachi. 2013. Discriminative Approach to Fill-in-the-Blank Quiz Generation for Language Learners. In *Proceedings of the 51st Annual Meeting of the Association for Computational Linguistics (Volume 2: Short Papers)*, pages 238–242, Sofia, Bulgaria.

Simon Smith and P V S Avinesh. 2010. Gap-fill Tests for Language Learners: Corpus-Driven Item Generation. In *Proceedings of ICON-2010: 8th International Conference on Natural Language Processing.*

Eiichiro Sumita, Fumiaki Sugaya, and Seiichi Yamamoto. 2005. Measuring Non-native Speakers' Proficiency of English by Using a Test with Automatically-generated Fill-in-the-blank Questions. In *Proceedings of the second workshop on Building Educational Applications Using NLP*, EdAppsNLP 05, pages 61–68, Stroudsburg, PA, USA.

Sentence-level Rewriting Detection

Fan Zhang
University of Pittsburgh
Pittsburgh, PA, 15260
zhangfan@cs.pitt.edu

Diane Litman
University of Pittsburgh
Pittsburgh, PA, 15260
litman@cs.pitt.edu

Abstract

Writers usually need iterations of revisions and edits during their writings. To better understand the process of rewriting, we need to know what has changed between the revisions. Prior work mainly focuses on detecting corrections within sentences, which is at the level of words or phrases. This paper proposes to detect revision changes at the sentence level. Looking at revisions at a higher level allows us to have a different understanding of the revision process. This paper also proposes an approach to automatically detect sentence revision changes. The proposed approach shows high accuracy in an evaluation using first and final draft essays from an undergraduate writing class.

1 Introduction

Rewriting is considered to be an important process during writing. However, conducting successful rewriting is not an easy task, especially for novice writers. Instructors work hard on providing suggestions for rewriting (Wells et al., 2013), but usually such advice is quite general. We need to understand the changes between revisions better to provide more specific and helpful advice.

There has already been work on detecting corrections in sentence revisions (Xue and Hwa, 2014; Swanson and Yamangil, 2012; Heilman and Smith, 2010; Rozovskaya and Roth, 2010). However, these works mainly focus on detecting changes at the level of words or phrases. According to Faigley's definition of revision change (Faigley and Witte, 1981), these works could help the identification of *Surface Changes* (changes that do not add or remove information to the original text). However, *Text Changes* (changes that add or remove information) will be more difficult to identify if we only look at revisions within sentences. According to Hashemi and Schunn (2014), when instructors were presented a comparison of differences between papers derived from words, they felt the information regarding changes between revisions was overwhelming.

This paper proposes to look at the changes between revisions at the level of sentences. Comparing to detecting changes at the word level, detecting changes at the sentence level contains less information, but still keeps enough information to understand the authors' intention behind their modifications to the text. The sentence level edits could then be grouped and classified into different types of changes. The long-term goal of this project is to allow us to be able to identify both *Text Changes* and *Surface Changes* automatically. Students, teachers, and researchers could then perform analysis on the different types of changes and have a better understanding of the rewriting process. As a preliminary work, this paper explores steps toward this goal: First, automatically generate the description of changes based on four primitives: *Add*, *Delete*, *Modify*, *Keep*; Second, merge the primitives that come from the same purpose.

2 Related work

Hashemi and Schunn (2014) presented a tool to help professors summarize students' changes across papers before and after peer review. They first split the original documents into sentences and then built on the output of Compare Suite (CompareSuite, 2014) to count and highlight changes in different colors. Figure 1 shows a screenshot of their work. As we can see, the modifications to the text are misinterpreted. Line 66 in the final draft should correspond to line 55 and line 56 in the first draft, while line 67 and line 68 should be a split of line 57 in the first draft. However, line 67 is aligned to line 56 wrongly in their work. This wrong alignment caused many mis-

Proceedings of the Ninth Workshop on Innovative Use of NLP for Building Educational Applications , pages 149–154,
Baltimore, Maryland USA, June 26, 2014.

recognized modifications. According to Hashemi, the instructors who use the system think that the overwhelming information of changes make the system less useful. We hypothesize that since their work is based on analysis at the word level, although their approach might work for identifying differences within one sentence, it makes mistakes when sentence analysis is the primary concern.

Our work avoids the above problem by detecting differences at the sentence level. Sentence alignment is the first step of our method; further inferences about revision changes are then based on the alignments generated. We borrow ideas from the research on sentence alignment for monolingual corpora. Existing research usually focuses on the alignment from the text to its summarization or its simplification (Jing, 2002; Barzilay and Elhadad, 2003; Bott and Saggion, 2011). Barzilay and Elhadad (2003) treat sentence alignment as a classification task. The paragraphs are clustered into groups, and a binary classifier is trained to decide whether two sentences should be aligned or not. Nelken (2006) further improves the performance by using TF*IDF score instead of word overlap and also utilizing global optimization to take sentence order information into consideration. We argue that summarization could be considered as a special form of revision and adapted Nelken's approach to our approach.

Edit sequences are then inferred based on the results of sentence alignment. Fragments of edits that come from the same purpose will then be merged. Related work to our method is sentence clustering (Shen et al., 2011; Wang et al., 2009). While sentence clustering is trying to find and cluster sentences similar to each other, our work is to find a cluster of sentences in one document that is similar to one sentence in the other document after merging.

3 Sentence-level changes across revisions

3.1 Primitives for sentence-level changes

Previous work in educational revision analysis (Faigley and Witte, 1981; Connor and Asenavage, 1994) categorized revision changes to be either surface changes or text-based changes. With both categories, six kinds of changes were defined as shown in Table 1.

Code	Explanation
Addition	Adding a word or phrase
Deletion	Omitting a word or phrase
Substitutions	exchange words with synonyms
Permutation	rearrange of words or phrases
Distribution	one segment divided into two
Consolidation	combine two segments into one

Table 1: Code Definition by L.Faigley and S.Witte

Different from Faigley's definition, we define only 4 primitives for our first step of edit sequence generation: *Add*, *Delete*, *Modify* and *Keep*. This definition is similar to Bronner's work (Bronner and Monz, 2012). We choose this definition because these 4 primitives only correspond to one sentence at a time. *Add*, *Delete*, *Modify* indicates that the writer has added/deleted/modified a sentence. *Keep* means the original sentence is not modified. We believe *Permutation*, *Distribution* and *Consolidation* as defined by Faigley could be described with these four primitives, which could be recognized in the later merge step.

3.2 Data and annotation

The corpus we choose consists of paired first and final drafts of short papers written by undergraduates in a course "Social Implications of Computing Technology". Students are required to write papers on one topic and then revise their own papers. The revisions are guided by other students' feedback based on a grading rubric, using a web-based peer review system. Students first submitted their original paper into the system, and then were randomly assigned to review and comment others' work according to the writing rubric. The authors would receive the others' anonymous comments, and then could choose to revise their work based on others' comments as well as their own insights obtained by reviewing other papers.

The papers in the corpus contain two topics. In the first topic, the students discussed the role that Big Data played in Obama's presidential campaign. This topic contains 11 pairs of first and final drafts of short papers. We name this **C1**. The other topic, named **C2**, talks about intellectual property and contains 10 pairs of paper drafts. The students involved in these two topics are from the same class. Students make more modifications to their papers in **C2**. More details can be seen in Table 2.

Our revision change detection approach contains three steps: sentence alignment, edit sequence generation and merge of edit sequences. Thus we annotated for these three steps.

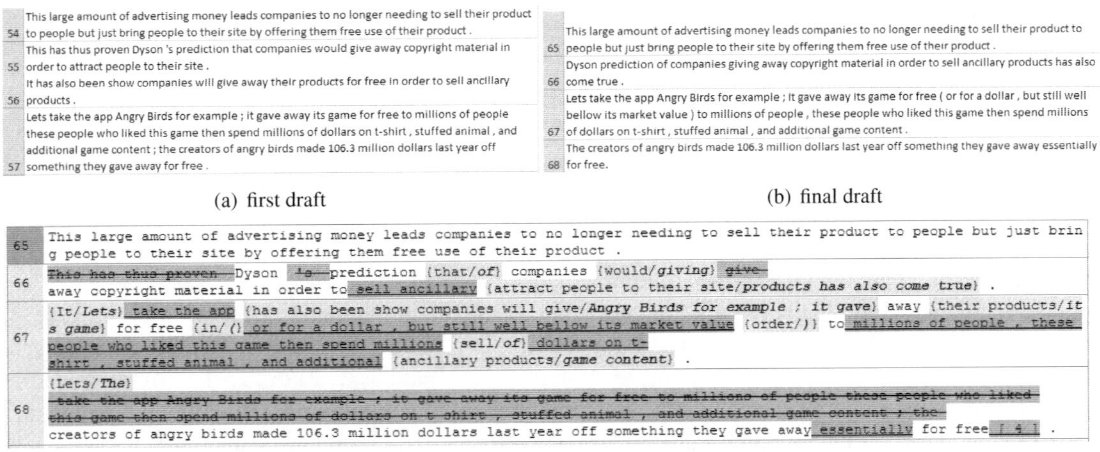

(a) first draft

(b) final draft

(c) Revision detection using Hashemi's approach

Figure 1: Fragments of a paper in corpus **C2** discussing intellectual property, (c) is Hashemi's work, green for recognized modifications, blue for insertions and red for deletion

For sentence alignment, each sentence in the final draft is assigned the index of its aligned sentence in the original draft. If a sentence is newly added, it will be annotated as ADD. Sentence alignment is not necessarily one-to-one. It can also be one-to-many (*Consolidation*) and many-to-one (*Distribution*). Table 3 shows a fragment of the annotation for the text shown in Figure 1.

For edit sequences, the annotators do the annotation based on the initial draft. For the same fragment in Table 3, the annotated sequence is: *Keep*, *Modify*, *Delete*, *Modify*, *Add*[1].

For edit sequence merging, we further annotate *Consolidation* and *Distribution* based on the edit sequences. In our example, 66 consolidates 55 and 56, while 57 distributes to 67 and 68.

	pairs	#D1	#D2	Avg1	Avg2
C1	11	761	791	22.5	22.7
C2	10	645	733	24.7	24.5

Table 2: Detailed information of corpora. #D1 and #D2 are the number of sentences in the first and final draft, Avg1 and Avg2 are the average number of words in one sentence in the first and final draft

As a preliminary work, we only have one annotator doing all the annotations. But for the annotation of sentence alignments, we have two annotators annotating on one pair of papers. The paper contains 76 sentences, and the annotators only disagree in one sentence. The kappa is 0.794 [2], which suggests that the annotation is reliable based on our annotation scheme.

4 Automatic detection of revision changes

The detection of revision changes contains three parts: sentence alignment, edit sequence generation and edit sequence merging. The first two parts generate edit sequences detected at the sentence level, while the third part groups edit sequences and classifies them into different types of changes. Currently the third step only covers the identification of *Consolidation* and *Distribution*.

Sentence Index (Final)	65	66	67	68
Sentence Index (First)	54	55,56	57	57

Table 3: An example of alignment annotation

Sentence alignment We adapted Nelken's approach to our problem.

Alignment based on sentence similarity

The alignment task goes through three stages.

1. Data preparation: for each sentence in the annotated final draft, if it is not a new sentence, create a sentence pair with its aligned sentence in the

[1] 66 consolidates 55, 56; while 57 distributes to 67, 68. Notice that *Consolidation* is illustrated as *Modify*, *Delete* and *Distribution* is illustrated as *Modify*, *Add*. As the annotators annotate based on the first draft, *Modify* always appears before *Add* or *Delete*

[2] We calculate the Kappa value following Macken's idea (Macken, 2010), where the aligned sentences are categorized as direct-link, while new added sentences are categorized as null-link (ADD).

first draft. The pair is considered to be an aligned pair. Also, randomly select another sentence from the first draft to make a negative sentence pair. Thus we ensure there are nearly equal numbers of positive and negative cases in the training data.

2. Training: according to the similarity metric defined, calculate the similarity of the sentence pairs. A logistic regression classifier predicting whether a sentence pair is aligned or not is trained with the similarity score as the feature. In addition to classification, the classifier is also used to provide a similarity score for global alignment.

3. Alignment: for each pair of paper drafts, construct sentence pairs using the Cartesian product of sentences in the first draft and sentences in the final. Logistic regression classifier is used to determine whether the sentence pair is aligned or not.

We added Levenshtein distance (LD) (Levenshtein, 1966) as another similarity metric in addition to Nelken's metrics. Together three similarity metrics were compared: Levenshtein Distance, Word Overlap(WO), and TF*IDF.

Global alignment

Sentences are likely to preserve the same order between rewritings. Thus, sentence ordering should be an important feature in sentence alignment. Nelken's work modifies the Needleman-Wunsch alignment (Needleman and Wunsch, 1970) to find the sentence alignments and goes in the following steps.

Step1: The logistic regression classifier previously trained assigns a probability value from 0 to 1 for each sentence pair $s(i,j)$. Use this value as the similarity score of sentence pair: $sim(i,j)$.

Step2: Starting from the first pair of sentences, find the best path to maximize the likelihood between sentences according to the formula $s(i,j) = max\{s(i-1,j-1) + sim(i,j), s(i-1,j) + \mathbf{sim(i,j)}, s(i,j-1) + \mathbf{sim(i,j)}\}$

Step3: Infer the sentence alignments by back tracing the matrix $s(i,j)$.

We found out that changing bolded parts in the formula to $s(i,j) = max\{s(i-1,j-1) + sim(i,j), s(i-1,j) + \mathit{insertcost}, s(i,j-1) + \mathit{deletecost}\}$ shows better performance in our problem. According to our experiment with **C1**, *insertcost* and *deletecost* are both set to 0.1 as they are found to be the most effective during practice.

Edit sequence generation This step is an intermediate step, which tries to generate the edit sequence based on the sentence alignment results from the previous step. The edit sequences generated would later be grouped together and classified into different types. In our current work, a rule-based method is proposed for this step.

Step1: The index of original document i and the index of the modified document j both start from 0. If sentence i in the original document is aligned to sentence j in the modified one, go to step 2, if not go to step 3.

Step2: If the two sentences are exactly the same, add *Keep* to the edit sequence, if not, add *Modify*. Increase i and j by 1, go to step 1.

Step3: Check the predicted alignment index of sentence j, if the predicted index is larger than sentence i in the original document, add *Delete* and increase i by 1, otherwise, mark as *Add* and increase j by 1, go to step 1.

Edit sequence merging *Distribution* means splitting one sentence into two or more sentences, while *Consolidation* means merging two or more sentences into one sentence. These two operations can be derived with primitives *Modify*, *Add* and *Delete*. They follow the following patterns:

Consolidation: *Modify-Delete-Delete-...*

Distribution: *Modify-Add-Add-...*

These sequences both start with *Modify* followed with a repetitive number of *Delete* or *Add*. A group of edit sequences can be merged if they can be merged to a sentence close to the sentence in the other draft. We applied a rule-based approach based on our observations.

We first scan through the sequence generated above. Sequences with *Modify-Add-...* or *Modify-Delete-...* are extracted. For each sequence extracted, if there are n consecutive *Add* or *Delete* following *Modify*, create n groups, $Group_i (i \leq n)$ contains sentences from the modified sentence to the next consecutive i sentences. For each group, merge all the sentences, and use the classifier trained above to get the similarity score Sim_{group_i} between the merged sentence and the original one. If there are multiple groups classified as aligned, choose group i that has the largest Sim_{group_i}, merge the basic edit operations into *Consolidation* or *Distribution*. If none of the groups are classified as aligned, do not merge.

5 Evaluation

Sentence alignment We use accuracy as the evaluation metric. For each pair of drafts, we count the number of sentences in the final draft

N_1. For each sentence in the final draft, we count the number of sentences that get the correct alignment as N_2. The accuracy of the sentence alignment is $\frac{N_2}{N_1}$. [3]

We use Hashemi's approach as the baseline. Compare Suite colors the differences out, as shown in Figure 1. We treat the green sentences as *Modify* and aligned to the original sentence.

For our method, we tried four groups of settings. Group 1 and group 2 perform leave-one-out cross validation on **C1** and **C2** (test on one pair of paper drafts and train on the others). Group 3 and group 4 train on one corpus and test on the other.

Group	LD	WO	TF*IDF	Baseline
1	0.9811	0.9863	**0.9931**	0.9427
2	0.9649	0.9593	**0.9667**	0.9011
3	**0.9727**	0.9700	**0.9727**	0.9045
4	0.9860	**0.9886**	0.9798	0.9589

Table 4: Accuracy of our approach vs. baseline

Table 4 shows that all our methods beat the baseline [4]. Among the three similarity metrics, TF*IDF is the most predictive.

Edit sequence generation We use WER (Word Error Rate) from speech recognition for evaluating the generated sequence by comparing the generated sequence to the gold standard.

WER is calculated based on edit distances between sequences. The ratio is calculated as: $WER = \frac{S+D+I}{N}$, where *S* means the number of modifications, *D* means the number of deletes, *I* means the number of inserts.

We apply our method on the gold standard of sentence alignment. The generated edit sequence is then compared with the gold standard edit sequence to calculate WER. Hashemi's approach is chosen as the baseline. The WER of our method is 0.035 on **C1** and 0.017 on **C2**, comparing to 0.091 on **C1** and 0.153 on **C2** for the baseline, which shows that our rule-based method has promise. Applying our method on the predicted alignment on the first step gets 0.067 on **C1** and 0.025 on **C2**, which although degraded still beats the baseline.

Edit sequence merging There are only a limited number of *Consolidation* and *Distribution* examples in our corpus. Together there are 9 *Consolidation* and 5 *Distribution* operations. In our current data, the number of sentences involved in these operations is always 2. Our rule-based method achieved 100% accuracy in the identification of these operations. It needs further work to see if this method would perform equally well in more complicated corpora.

6 Conclusion

This paper presents a preliminary work in the effort of describing changes across revisions at a higher level than words, motivated by a long term goal to build educational applications to support revision analysis for writing. Comparing to revision analysis based on words or phrases, our approach is able to capture higher level revision operations. We also propose algorithms to detect revision changes automatically. Experiments show that our method has a reliable performance.

Currently we are investigating applying sequence merging on the automatic generated edit sequences based on edit distances directly. Our next plan is to develop a tool for comparing drafts, and conduct user studies to have extrinsic evaluations on whether our method would provide more useful information to the user. We are also planning to do further analysis based on the revisions detected, and ultimately be able to distinguish between surface changes and text-based changes.

Acknowledgments

We would like to thank W. Wang, W. Luo, H. Xue, and the ITSPOKE group for their helpful feedback and all the anonymous reviewers for their suggestions.

This research is supported by the Institute of Education Sciences, U.S. Department of Education, through Grant R305A120370 to the University of Pittsburgh. The opinions expressed are those of the authors and do not necessarily represent the views of the Institute or the U.S. Department of Education.

[3] Notice that we have the case that one sentence is aligned to two sentences (i.e. *Consolidation*, as sentence 66 in Table 3). In our evaluation, an alignment is considered to be correct only if the alignment covers all the sentences that should be covered. For example, if Sentence 66 in Table 3 is aligned to Sentence 55 in the first draft, it is counted as an error.

[4] For Groups 1 and 2, we calculate the accuracy of Hashemi's approach under a leave-one-out setting, each time remove one pair of document and calculate the accuracy. A significance test is also conducted, the worst metric LD in Group 1 and WO in Group 2 both beat the baseline significantly ($p_1 = 0.025$,$p_2 = 0.017$) in two-tailed T-test.

References

Regina Barzilay and Noemie Elhadad. 2003. Sentence alignment for monolingual comparable corpora. In *Proceedings of the 2003 conference on Empirical methods in natural language processing*, pages 25–32. Association for Computational Linguistics.

Stefan Bott and Horacio Saggion. 2011. An unsupervised alignment algorithm for text simplification corpus construction. In *Proceedings of the Workshop on Monolingual Text-To-Text Generation*, pages 20–26. Association for Computational Linguistics.

Amit Bronner and Christof Monz. 2012. User edits classification using document revision histories. In *Proceedings of the 13th Conference of the European Chapter of the Association for Computational Linguistics*, pages 356–366. Association for Computational Linguistics.

CompareSuite. 2014. Compare suite, feature-rich file and folder compare tool. `http://www.comparesuite.com`.

Ulla Connor and Karen Asenavage. 1994. Peer response groups in esl writing classes: How much impact on revision? *Journal of Second Language Writing*, 3(3):257–276.

Lester Faigley and Stephen Witte. 1981. Analyzing revision. *College composition and communication*, pages 400–414.

Homa B. Hashemi and Christian D. Schunn. 2014. A tool for summarizing students' shanges across drafts. In *International Conference on Intelligent Tutoring Systems(ITS)*.

Michael Heilman and Noah A Smith. 2010. Tree edit models for recognizing textual entailments, paraphrases, and answers to questions. In *Human Language Technologies: The 2010 Annual Conference of the North American Chapter of the Association for Computational Linguistics*, pages 1011–1019. Association for Computational Linguistics.

Hongyan Jing. 2002. Using hidden markov modeling to decompose human-written summaries. *Computational linguistics*, 28(4):527–543.

Vladimir I Levenshtein. 1966. Binary codes capable of correcting deletions, insertions and reversals. In *Soviet physics doklady*, volume 10, page 707.

Lieve Macken. 2010. An annotation scheme and gold standard for dutch-english word alignment. In *7th conference on International Language Resources and Evaluation (LREC 2010)*, pages 3369–3374. European Language Resources Association (ELRA).

Saul B Needleman and Christian D Wunsch. 1970. A general method applicable to the search for similarities in the amino acid sequence of two proteins. *Journal of molecular biology*, 48(3):443–453.

Rani Nelken and Stuart M Shieber. 2006. Towards robust context-sensitive sentence alignment for monolingual corpora. In *EACL*.

Alla Rozovskaya and Dan Roth. 2010. Annotating esl errors: Challenges and rewards. In *Proceedings of the NAACL HLT 2010 fifth workshop on innovative use of NLP for building educational applications*, pages 28–36. Association for Computational Linguistics.

Chao Shen, Tao Li, and Chris HQ Ding. 2011. Integrating clustering and multi-document summarization by bi-mixture probabilistic latent semantic analysis (plsa) with sentence bases. In *AAAI*.

Ben Swanson and Elif Yamangil. 2012. Correction detection and error type selection as an esl educational aid. In *Proceedings of the 2012 Conference of the North American Chapter of the Association for Computational Linguistics: Human Language Technologies*, pages 357–361. Association for Computational Linguistics.

Dingding Wang, Shenghuo Zhu, Tao Li, and Yihong Gong. 2009. Multi-document summarization using sentence-based topic models. In *Proceedings of the ACL-IJCNLP 2009 Conference Short Papers*, pages 297–300. Association for Computational Linguistics.

Jaclyn M. Wells, Morgan Sousa, Mia Martini, and Allen Brizee. 2013. Steps for revising your paper. `http://owl.english.purdue.edu/owl/resource/561/05`.

Huichao Xue and Rebecca Hwa. 2014. Improved correction detection in revised esl sentences. In *Proceedings of The 52nd Annual Meeting of the Association for Computational Linguistics(ACL)*.

Exploiting Morphological, Grammatical, and Semantic Correlates for Improved Text Difficulty Assessment

Elizabeth Salesky, Wade Shen †
MIT Lincoln Laboratory Human Language Technology Group, 244 Wood Street, Lexington MA 02420, USA
{elizabeth.salesky, swade}@ll.mit.edu

Abstract

We present a low-resource, language-independent system for text difficulty assessment. We replicate and improve upon a baseline by Shen et al. (2013) on the Interagency Language Roundtable (ILR) scale. Our work demonstrates that the addition of morphological, information theoretic, and language modeling features to a traditional readability baseline greatly benefits our performance. We use the Margin-Infused Relaxed Algorithm and Support Vector Machines for experiments on Arabic, Dari, English, and Pashto, and provide a detailed analysis of our results.

1 Introduction

While there is a growing breadth of reading materials available in various languages, finding pertinent documents at suitable reading levels remains difficult. Information retrieval methods can find resources with desired vocabulary, but educators still need to filter these to find appropriate difficulty levels. This task is often more challenging than manually adapting the documents themselves. Reading level assessment systems can be used to automatically find documents at specific Interagency Language Roundtable (ILR) levels, aiding both instructors and learners by providing proficiency-tailored materials.

While interest in readability assessment has been gaining momentum in many languages, the majority of previous work is language-specific. Shen et al. (2013) introduced a baseline for language-independent text difficulty assessment, based on the ILR proficiency scale. In this work, we replicate and extend their results.

† This work is sponsored by the Defense Language Institute under Air Force Contract FA8721-05-C-0002. Opinions, interpretations, conclusions and recommendations are those of the authors and are not necessarily endorsed by the United States Government.

The ILR scale is the standard language proficiency measure for the U.S. federal government. It ranges from no proficiency to native proficiency on a scale of 0-5, with half-level denotations where proficiency meets some but not all of the criteria for the next level (Interagency Language Roundtable, 2013). For second language learners, it is sufficient to use up to ILR level 4. Since proficiency is a continuous spectrum, text difficulty assessment is often treated as a regression problem, as we do here. Though the ILR levels may appear to be discrete categories, documents can fall between levels. The degree to which they do is important for us to measure.

Level	Description
1	***Elementary***: can fulfill basic needs, limited to fundamental vocabulary
2	***Limited working***: routine social demands, gist of non-technical works, elementary grasp of grammar
3	***General professional***: general vocabulary, good control of grammar, errors do not interfere with understanding
4	***Advanced professional***: fluent language use on all levels, only rare & minute errors

Table 1: Description of proficiency at ILR levels

The ILR scale addresses semantic and grammatical capabilities, and to model it appropriately, a system needs to reflect both. The baseline system developed by Shen et al. (2013) uses both term frequency log-weighted (TFLOG) word-usage features and z-normalized word, sentence, and document length features. However, their results are not equally significant across its set of test languages, which this paper addresses with additional features.

The utilization of types for TFLOG weighted vectors is not as representative for morphologically rich languages, where multiple types can represent different word-forms within a single

Proceedings of the Ninth Workshop on Innovative Use of NLP for Building Educational Applications , pages 155–162,
Baltimore, Maryland USA, June 26, 2014.

paradigm. By incorporating morphology, we can improve our TFLOG vectors' representation of semantic complexity for these languages. We employ the Morfessor Categories-MAP algorithm for segmentation (Creutz & Lagus, 2007). Relative entropy and statistical language models (LMs) can also measure semantic complexity, and class-based language models (cLMs) can give us a measure of the grammatical complexity of the text. All of these methods are low-resource and unsupervised; they can be easily applied to new languages. We have compared their performance to language-specific methods where possible.

The remainder of this paper is structured as follows; Section 2 summarizes previous research on readability assessment. Section 3 introduces our corpus and approach, while Section 4 details our results and their analyses. Section 5 provides a summary and description of future work.

2 Background & Related Work

Early work on readability assessment approximated grammatical and lexical complexity using shallow features like sentence length and the number of syllables in a word, like the prominent Flesch-Kincaid measure, in large part due to their low computational cost (Kincaid et al., 1975). Such features over-generalize what makes a text difficult; it is not always the case that longer words and sentences are more grammatically complex than their shorter counterparts. Subsequent work such as the Dale-Chall model (Dale & Chall, 1995) added representation on static word lists: in this case, one of 3,000 words familiar to 4th graders. Such lists, however, are not readily available for many difficulty scales and languages.

Ensuing approaches have employed more sophisticated methods, such as word frequency estimates to measure lexical complexity (Stenner, 1996) and statistical language models to measure semantic and syntactic complexity, and have seen significant performance gains over previous work (Collins-Thompson & Callan, 2004; Schwarm & Ostendorf, 2005; Petersen & Ostendorf, 2009). In the case of Heilman et al. (2007), the combination of lexical and grammatical features specifically addressed the order in which vocabulary and grammar are acquired by second language learners, where grasp of grammar often trails other markers of proficiency.

The extension of readability research to languages beyond English necessitated the introduction of new features such as morphology, which have long been proven useful in other areas. Dell'Orletta et al. (2011) developed a two-class readability model for Italian based on its verbal morphology. François and Fairon (2012) built a six-class readability model, but for adult learners of French, utilizing verb tense and mood-based features. Most recently, Hancke et al. (2012) built a two-class German reading level assessment system heavily utilizing morphology. In addition to traditional syntactic, lexical, and language modeling features used in English readability research, Hancke et al. (2012) tested a broad range of features based on German inflectional and derivational morphology. While all of these systems were very effective, they required many language-specific resources, including part-of-speech tags.

Recent experiments have several noteworthy characteristics in common. While some systems discriminate between multiple grade-level categories, most are two- or three-class classification tasks between 'easy' and 'difficult' which do not require such fine-grained feature discrimination. Outside of English, there are few multi-level graded datasets; for those that do exist, they are very small, averaging less than a hundred labeled documents per level. Further, though recent work has been increasingly motivated by second language learners, most systems have only been implemented for a single language (Schwarm & Ostendorf, 2005; Petersen & Ostendorf, 2009); Vajjala & Meurers, 2012). The language-specific morphological and syntactic features used by many systems outside of English would make it difficult to apply them to other languages. Shen et al. (2013) address this problem by using language-independent features and testing their work on four languages. In this work, we extend their system in order to improve upon their results.

3 Approach

3.1 Corpus

We conducted our experiments on the corpus used by Shen et al. (2013). The dataset was collected by the Defense Language Institute Foreign Language Center (DLIFLC) for instructional use. It comprises approximately 1390 documents for each of Arabic, Dari, English, and Pashto. The documents are evenly distributed across seven test ILR levels: {1, 1+, 2, 2+, 3, 3+, 4}. This equates to close to

200 documents per level per language. We use an 80/20 train test split.

Lang.	Tokens	Types	Stems	Morphs / Word
Arabic	593,113	84,160	14,591	2.60
Dari	761,412	43,942	13,312	2.61
English	796,406	44,738	35,594	1.80
Pashto	840,673	59,031	20,015	2.34

Table 2: Corpus statistics

The documents were chosen by language instructors as representative of a particular level and range from news articles to excerpts from philosophy to craigslist postings. Three graders hand-leveled each document. The corpus is annotate only with the aggregate scores; we use only this score for comparison. The creation of the corpus took 70 hours per language on average. We assume the ILR scale is linear and measure performance by mean squared error (MSE), typical for regression. MSE reflects the variance and bias of our predictions, and is therefore a good measure of performance uniformity within levels.

3.2 Experimental Design

We compare our results to the best performing Support Vector Machine (SVM) and Margin-Infused Relaxed Algorithm (MIRA) baselines from Shen et al. (2013). Both of these baselines have the same features: TFLOG weighted word vectors, average sentence length by document, average word length by document, and document word count. We used an implementation of the MIRA algorithm for regression (Crammer & Singer, 2003). We embedded Morfessor for unsupervised morphological segmentation and preprocessed our data as required by this algorithm (Creutz & Lagus, 2007). To verify our results across classifiers, we compare with SVM (Chang & Lin, 2001). We also compare Morfessor to ParaMor (Monson 2009), an unsupervised system with a different level of segmentation aggression, as well as to language-specific analyzers.

Our experiments apply word-usage features, shallow length features, and language models. For the first, we compare TFLOG vectors based on word types, all morphemes, and stems only. For the second, we tested the three baseline shallow length features (average word length in characters per document, average sentence length per document, and document word count) as well as measures of relative entropy, average stem fertility, average morphemes per word, and the ratio of types to tokens. Of these, only relative entropy positively impacted performance, and only its results are reported in this paper. All length features were z-normalized. We compare both word- and class-based language models. We trained LMs for each ILR level and used the document perplexity measured against each as features.

Optimal settings were determined by sweeping algorithm parameters, and Morfessor's perplexity threshold for each language. We conducted a feature analysis for all combinations of word, length, and LM features across all four languages.

4 Results & Analysis

We first replicate the baseline results of Shen et al. (2013) using both the MIRA and SVM algorithms. We find there is very overall little performance difference between the two algorithms, and the difference is language-dependent. It is inconclusive which algorithm performs best.

Algorithm	AR	DA	EN	PA
MIRA	0.216	0.296	0.154	0.348
SVM	0.198	0.301	0.147	0.391

Table 3: Baseline results in MSE, SVM vs. MIRA

Table 3 shows the average MSE across the seven ILR levels for each language. Figure 1 depicts MSE performance on each individual ILR level.

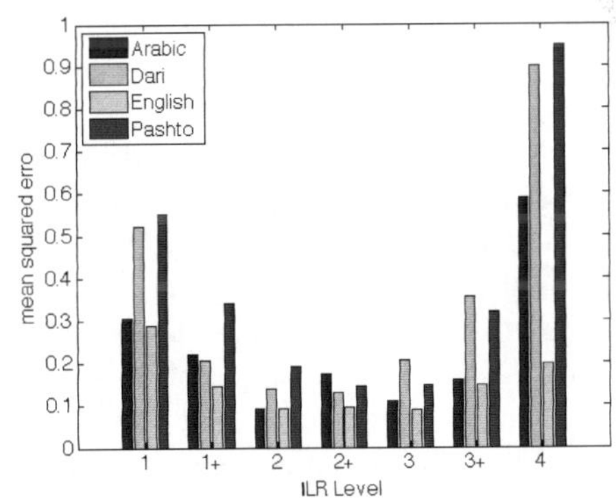

Figure 1: MSE by ILR level, baseline

4.1 Morphological Analysis

Reading level assessment in English does not necessitate the use of morphological features, and so they have not been researched for this task until recently. Morphology has long been shown to be useful in other areas; it is unsurprising that segmentation should help with this task for morphologically rich languages. What we demonstrate is that unsupervised methods perform similarly to language-specific methods, at a lower cost.

Language	TYPES	MORPHS	STEMS
Arabic	0.216	0.198	0.208
Dari	0.296	0.304	0.294
English	0.154	0.151	0.151
Pashto	0.348	0.303	0.293

Table 4: Average MSE results comparing the use of types, all morphs, and stems for TFLOG vectors. Morfessor algorithm used for segmentation.

Table 4 compares the performance of the baseline, which utilizes types for its TFLOG weighted word vectors, to our configurations that alternatively use all morphemes or stems only. We see that morphological information improves performance for all cases but one, all morphs for Dari, and that using stems only shows the greatest improvement.

Our greatest improvement was seen in Pashto, which has the most unique stems in our dataset both outright and compared to types (see Table 4). Without stemming, TFLOG word vectors were heavily biased by the frequency of alternate word forms within a paradigm. With stemming, which reduced overall MSE compared to the baseline by 16%, the number of word vectors in the optimized configuration increased by 18%, and were much more diverse, reflecting the actual semantic complexity of the documents. We posit that the reason Dari, which has a similar ratio of morphemes per word to Pashto, does not improve in this way is due to its much smaller and more uniform vocabulary in our data. Our Pashto documents have 1.5 times as many unique words as our Dari, and in fact, with stemming, the number of word vectors utilized in our optimized configuration was reduced by 20%, as fewer units were necessary to reflect the same content.

We compare our results using Morfessor to another unsupervised segmentation system, ParaMor (Monson 2009). ParaMor is built on a different mathematical framework than Morfessor, and so has a very different splitting pattern. Morfessor has a tunable perplexity threshold that dictates how aggressively the algorithm segments. Even set at its highest, ParaMor still segments much more aggressively, sometimes isolating single characters, which can be useful for downstream applications (Kurimo et al. 2009). This is not the case here, as shown in Table 5. All further results use Morfessor for stemming.

Algorithm	AR	DA	EN	PA
Morfessor	0.208	0.294	0.151	0.293
ParaMor	0.227	0.321	0.158	0.301

Table 5: Comparison of unsupervised segmenters

To our knowledge, no Pashto-specific morphological analyzer yet exists for comparison. However, in lacking both a standardized writing system and spelling conventions, one word in Pashto may be written in many different ways (Kathol, 2005). To account for this, we normalized the data using the Levenshtein distance between types. We swept possible cutoff thresholds up to 0.25, evaluated by the overall MSE of the subsequent results. Using normalized data did not improve results; in many cases the edit distance between alternate misspellings is just as high or higher as the distance between word types.

We believe that the limited change in Dari performance is primarily related to corpus characteristics; relatively uniform data provides low perplexity, making it more difficult for Morfessor to discover all morphological segmentations. Using the Perstem stemmer in place of Morfessor, the number of word vectors in the optimized system rose 143% and our results improved 8%. This increase affirms that Morfessor is under-splitting. Perstem is tailored to Farsi, and while the two dialects are mutually intelligible, they have grammatical, phonological, and loan word differences (Shah et al. 2007).

We highlight that the overall MSE of all configurations in Table 4 vary only 2% for English, with identical results using all morphs and only stems. This is expected, as English is not morphologically complex. Given the readily available rule-based systems for English, we compared results with Morfessor to the traditional Porter and Paice stemmers, as well as the multi-lingual FreeLing stemmer, as seen in Table 6.

Performance variance between all analyzers of only 3% points us to the similar and limited grammatical rules found in the different algorithms, as well as the relatively limited number of unique

Baseline	Morf.	Porter	Paice	FreeLing
0.154	0.151	0.149	0.148	0.153

Table 6: Comparison of English segmenters

stems and affixes to be found in English. Topical similarities in our data are also possible.

Like Pashto, Arabic has a rich morphological structure, but in addition to affixes it contains templatic morphology. It is difficult for unsupervised analyzers not specifically tailored to templatic morphology to capture non-contiguous morphemes. Here, Morfessor consistently segments vowelized types into sequences of two character stems. When compared with MADA, a rule-based Arabic analyzer (Habash, 2010), we found that Morfessor outperformed MADA by 10%. This is likely because the representations present in the dataset are what is significant; if a form is 'morphologically correct' but perpetuates a sparsity problem, linguistically-accurate stemming will not help. Neither stemmer contributes much to Arabic results, however, as MIRA does not weight word-usage features very heavily for either Arabic analyzer.

4.2 Relative Entropy and Word LMs

As mentioned in Section 2, traditional features like document word count and average sentence length overstate the importance of length to difficulty. To capture the significance of the length of the document, rather than merely the length itself, we utilized relative entropy. Relative entropy, also known as the Kullback-Leibler divergence (KL), is a measure of the information lost by using one probability distribution as compared to another. Expressed as an equation, we have:

$$D(p,q) = \sum_{x \in \varepsilon} p(x) \log \frac{\mathrm{p}(x)}{\mathrm{q}(x)}. \qquad (1)$$

In this work, we are comparing a unigram probability distribution of a document $q(x)$ to a uniform distribution over the same length $p(x)$. This provides both a measure of the semantic and structural complexity of a document, allowing us to differentiate between documents of similar length. Figure 2 shows the normalized distribution of the relative entropy feature for Pashto.

The separability of ILR levels suggests we will be able to discriminate between them. As demonstrated by the improved performance in Figure 3, where the inclusion of relative entropy is superimposed over the baseline, this feature greatly contributes to the separability of outlier levels of our corpus. Common z-scores between levels 2 and 3 explain the system's poorer performance on the ILR levels 2.0 and 2.5 (Figure 3). Adding the relative entropy feature to the baseline produced an average MSE reduction of 15%.

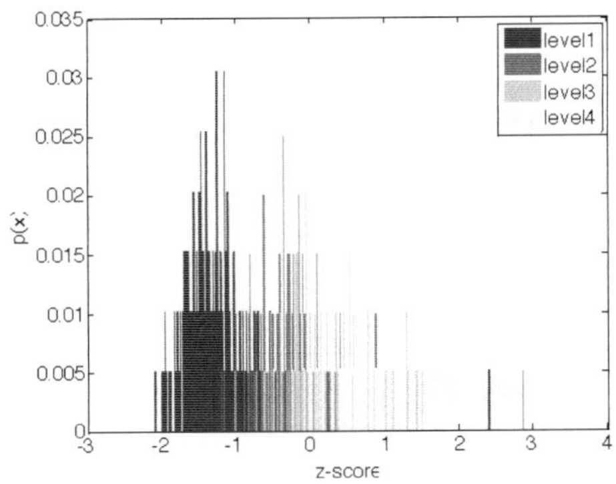

Figure 2: Pashto, normalized KL distribution

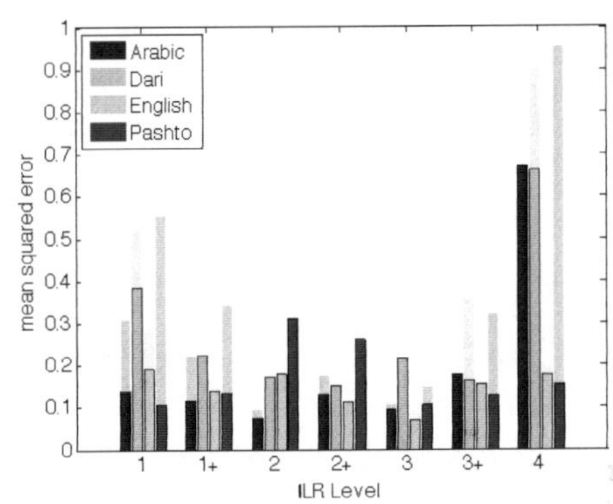

Figure 3: MSE by ILR level, baseline +stems +KL

The combination of stemming for TFLOG vectors and relative entropy together is more effective than either alone. Further removing document word count improved performance by an average 1%. As seen in Figure 3, the combination of all these changes produces significant gains over the baseline, particularly in Dari and Pashto. The combination configuration reduced overall MSE by 52% for Pashto documents and by 18% for Dari. From Figure 3 above, we see that the +stems+KL configuration exhibits very poor performance in Arabic level 4, and on outlying levels for Dari. While these MSE values are clear outliers in this figure, they values are less than 0.1 greater than their MIRA baseline counterparts. This may be due to data similarity between level 3+ and 4 documents, or MIRA may have been overfit during training. In contrast, the variance for English and Pashto is much smaller; overall, the variance has been greatly reduced.

Statistical language models (LMs) are a probability distribution over text. An n-gram language predicts a word w_n given the preceding context $w_1 ... w_{n-1}$. We used the SRI Language Modeling Toolkit to train LMs on our training data for each ILR level (Stolcke, 2002). To account for unseen n-grams, we used Kneser-Ney smoothing. To score documents against these LMs, we calculate their perplexity (PP), a measure of how well a probability distribution represents data. Perplexity represents the average number of bits necessary to encode each word. For each document in our dataset, we use the perplexities against each ILR level LM as features in MIRA. We compared n-gram orders 2-5, and while we found an average decrease of 3% MSE between orders 2 and 3 across languages, there was a difference of less than 1% between 3-gram and 5-gram LMs.

Features	AR	DA	EN	PA
baseline	0.216	0.296	0.154	0.348
+stems +KL	0.208	0.269	0.147	0.173
+LM	0.208	0.176	0.117	0.171
+LM -WVs	0.567	0.314	0.338	0.355
+stems +KL +LM	0.168	0.167	0.096	0.137

Table 7: Average MSE results comparing features from Sections 4.1 and 4.2. LMs are order 5.

As we can see from Table 7, the addition of language models alone can provide a huge measure of improvement from the baseline. For Arabic and Pashto, it is the same improvement seen by stemming TFLOG vectors and adding relative entropy. For Dari and English, however, the performance improvement is unmatched by any other features presented thus far. We compare these results to the same configuration without TFLOG vectors, in order to measure the overlap between these features; see Table 7. Based on the relative results, it seems that word vector and LM features are orthogonal. The addition of all three new features (stemmed word vectors, relative entropy, and language models) provides considerable further improvement upon any previous configuration. It appears that the interactions between these features have a further positive influence on our discriminative ability.

4.3 Class-Based LMs

It is possible to group words based on similar meaning and syntactic function. It is reasonable to think that the probability distributions of words in such groups would be similar (though not the same). By assigning classes to words, we can calculate the probability of a word based not on the sequence of preceding *words*, but rather, *word classes*. Doing so decreases the size of resulting models and also allows for better predictions of unseen word sequences. Sparsity is a concern with language models, where we rely on the frequency of sequences, not just words. Using word classes assuages some of this concern. These word classes are generated in an unsupervised manner. We train our class-based language models (cLMs) using c-discounting to account for data sparsity.

Features	AR	DA	EN	PA
baseline	0.216	0.296	0.154	0.348
+LM	0.208	0.176	0.117	0.171
+cLM	0.130	0.286	0.144	0.211
+LM +cLM	0.094	0.155	0.051	0.084
+stems +KL +LM +cLM	0.092	0.152	0.049	0.079

Table 8: Average MSE results comparing all features. LMs and cLMs are order 5.

Class-based and word-based LMs each help different languages in our test set. The two types of LMs model different information, with word-based LMs providing a measure of semantic complexity and class-based modeling grammatical complexity. As seen in Table 8, the combination of this complementary information is highly beneficial and strongly correlated to ILR level. We see average MSE reductions of 56%, 48%, 67%, and 77% in Arabic, Dari, English, and Pashto, respectively, using both types of language model.

Algorithm	AR	DA	EN	PA
MIRA	0.091	0.156	0.049	0.079
SVM	0.089	0.159	0.069	0.070

Table 9: Final system results, comparing avg. MSE with the MIRA and SVM algorithms

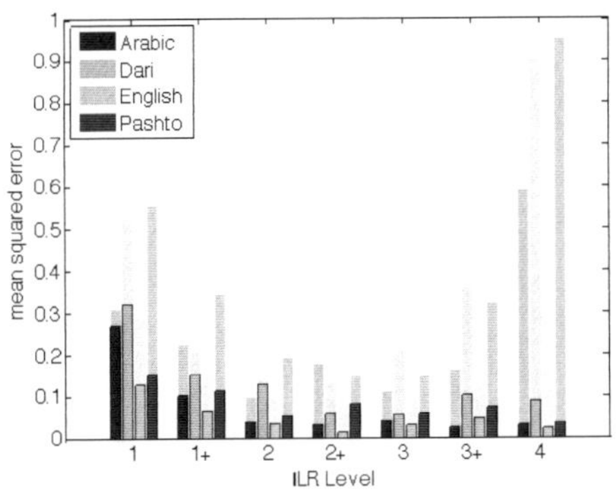

Figure 4: Comparison of final configuration with all features to baseline by MSE, MIRA algorithm

The further inclusion of TFLOG stemming and relative entropy reduces average MSE an additional 1%. Figure 4 reflects this configuration's performance across the seven ILR levels.

Figure 4 superimposes our final error results over those of the baseline. It is clear that error has become much less language-specific; performance on all seven ILR levels has become considerably more consistent across the four languages, as has the accuracy at each individual ILR level. It seems likely that our error measures would be similar to inner-annotator disagreement, a measure that we would like to quantify in the future.

We find that our results are significant across classifiers. Table 9 shows the performance of our final feature set with both MIRA and SVM. The MSE exhibits the same trends across ILR levels and languages with both algorithms. The average difference in error between the algorithms remains the same as it was with the baseline features.

5 Conclusions and Future Work

Our experiments demonstrate that language-independent methods can improve text difficulty assessment performance on the ILR scale for four languages. Morphological segmentation for TFLOG word vectors improves our measure of semantic complexity and allows us to do topic analysis better. Unsupervised methods perform similarly to language-specific and linguistically-accurate analyzers on this task; we are not sacrificing performance for a language-independent system. Relative entropy gives structural context to more traditional shallow length features, and with word-based LM features provide another way to measure semantic complexity. Class-based LM features measure grammatical complexity and to some degree account for data sparsity issues. All of these features are low-cost and require no language-specific resources to be applied to new languages. The combination of all these features significantly improves our performance as measured by mean square error across a diverse set of languages.

We would like to expand our work to more diverse languages and datasets in future work. There is room to improve upon features described in this paper, such as new frequency-based measures for word vectors and unsupervised morphological segmentation methods. In the future, we would like to directly compare inner-annotator error and well-known formulas with our results. It would also be interesting to look at performance on subsets of the corpus to test dependence on dataset size. We would also like to investigate the ILR scale; while we assume that it is linear, this is not likely to be the case.

Acknowledgments

This paper benefited from valuable discussion with Jennifer Williams.

References

J. Chall, E. Dale. 1995. Readability revisited: The new Dale-Chall readability formula. *Brookline Books*, Cambridge, MA.

C-C. Chang, C-J. Lin. 2001. LIBSVM: a library for support vector machines. *Software available at http://www.csie.ntu.edu.tw/ cjlin/libsvm.*

K. Collins-Thompson, J. Callan. 2005. Predicting reading difficulty with statistical language models. *Journal of the American Society for Information Science and Technology* 56(13), 1448-1462.

K. Crammer, Y. Singer. 2003. Ultraconservative Online Algorithms for Multiclass Problems. *Journal of Machine Learning Research*, 3(2003):951-991.

M. Creutz, K. Lagus. 2007. Unsupervised models for morpheme segmentation and morphology learning. *Association for Computing Machinery Transactions on Speech and Language Processing (ACM TSLP)*, 4(1):1-34.

F. Dell'Orletta, S. Montemagni, G. Venturi. 2011. Read-it: Assessing readability of italian texts with a view to text simplification. *Proceedings of the 2nd Workshop on Speech and Language Processing for Assistive Technologies (SLPAT)* 73-83.

T. François, C. Fairon. 2012. An AI readability formula for French as a foreign language. *Proceedings of the 2012 Joint Conference on Empirical Methods in Natural Language Processing (EMNLP) and Computational Natural Language Learning (CoNLL)*. 466-477.

N. Habash, O. Rambow, R. Roth. 2010. Mada+Tokan: A toolkit for arabic tokenization, diacritization, morphological disambiguation, pos tagging, stemming and lemmatization. *Proceedings of the 2nd International Conference on Arabic Language Resources and Tools (MEDAR)*.

J. Hancke, S. Vajjala, D. Meurers 2012. Readability Classification for German using lexical, syntactic, and morphological features. *Proceedings of CoLING 2012: Technical Papers*, 1063-1080.

K.S. Hasan, M.A. ur Rahman, V. Ng. 2009. Learning-Based Named Entity Recognition for Morphologically-Rich, Resource-Scarce Languages. *Proceedings of the 12th Conference of the European Chapter of the Association for Computational Linguistics (EACL)*, 354-362.

M. Heilman, K. Collins-Thompson, J. Callan, M. Eskenazi. 2007. Combining Lexical and Grammatical Features to Improve Readability Measures for First and Second Language Texts. *Proceedings of NAACL HLT*, 460-467.

Interagency Language Roundtable. ILR Skill Scale. `http://www.govtilr.org/Skills/ILRscale4.htm`. 2013.

A. Jadidinejad, F. Mahmoudi, J. Dehdari. 2010. Evaluation of perstem: a simple and efficient stemming algorithm for Persian. *Multilingual Information Access Evaluation Text Retrieval Experiments*.

A. Kathol, K. Precoda, D. Vergyri, W. Wang, S. Riehemann. 2005. Speech translation for low-resource languages: The case of pashto. *Proceedings of INTERSPEECH*, 2273-2276.

J.P. Kincaid, R.P Fishburne Jr., R.L. Rodgers, and B.S. Chisson 1975. Derivation of new readability formulas for Navy enlisted personnel. *Research Branch Report, U.S. Naval Air Station, Memphis*, 8-75.

M. Kurimo, V. Turunen, M. Varjokallio. 2009. Overview of Morpho Challenge 2008. *Evaluating Systems for Multilingual and Multimodal Information Access*, Springer Berlin Heidelberg, 951-966.

C. Monson. 2009. ParaMor: From Paradigm Structure to Natural Language Morphology Induction. *PhD thesis. Carnegie Mellon University*.

R. Munro, C.D. Manning. 2010. Subword Variation in Text Message Classification. *The 2010 Annual Conference of the North American Chapter of the Association for Computational Linguistics*, 510-518.

M. Padr. 2004. FreeLing: An Open-Source Suite of Language Analyzers. *Proceedings of the 4th International Conference on Language Resources and Evaluation (LREC'04)*.

C.D. Paice. 1990. Another Stemmer. *SIGIR Forum*, 24:56-61.

S. E. Petersen and M. Ostendorf. 2009. A machine learning approach to reading level assessment. *Computer Speech and Language*, 23(2009):89-106.

M.F. Porter. 1980. An algorithm for suffix stripping. *Program*, 14(3): 130-137.

A. Ratnaparkhi. 1997. A simple introduction to maximum entropy models for natural language processing. *IRCS Technical Reports Series*, 81.

S. E. Schwarm and M. Ostendorf. 2005. Reading Level Assessment Using Support Vector Machines and Statistical Language Models. In *Proceedings of the 43rd Annual Meeting of the Association for Computational Linguistics (ACL)*.

M.I. Shah, J. Sadri, C.Y. Suen, N. Nobile. 2007. A New Multipurpose Comprehensive Database for Handwritten Dari Recognition. *11th International Conference on Frontiers in Handwriting Recognition*, Montreal, 635-40.

W. Shen, J. Williams, T. Marius, E. Salesky. 2013. A language-independent approach to automatic text difficulty assessment for second-language learners. *Proceedings of the 2nd Workshop on Predicting and Improving Text Readability for Target Reader Populations (PITR) 2013*.

A. Stolcke. 2002. SRILM - an extensible language modeling toolkit. *Proceedings of the ICSLP*, vol. 2, 901-4.

S. Vajjala, D. Meurers. 2012. On improving the accuracy of readability classification using insights from second language acquisition. *Proceedings of the Seventh Workshop on Building Educational Applications Using NLP. Association for Computational Linguistics, 2012*. 163-173.

Assessing the Readability of Sentences: Which Corpora and Features?

Felice Dell'Orletta[◇], **Martijn Wieling**[•∘], **Andrea Cimino**[◇], **Giulia Venturi**[◇] **and Simonetta Montemagni**[◇]
[◇]Istituto di Linguistica Computazionale "Antonio Zampolli" (ILC–CNR)
ItaliaNLP Lab - *www.italianlp.it*
{name.surname}@ilc.cnr.it
[•]Department of Humanities Computing, University of Groningen, The Netherlands
[∘]Department of Quantitative Linguistics, University of Tübingen, Germany
wieling@gmail.com

Abstract

The paper investigates the problem of sentence readability assessment, which is modelled as a classification task, with a specific view to text simplification. In particular, it addresses two open issues connected with it, i.e. the corpora to be used for training, and the identification of the most effective features to determine sentence readability. An existing readability assessment tool developed for Italian was specialized at the level of training corpus and learning algorithm. A maximum entropy–based feature selection and ranking algorithm (grafting) was used to identify to the most relevant features: it turned out that assessing the readability of sentences is a complex task, requiring a high number of features, mainly syntactic ones.

1 Introduction

Over the last ten years, work on automatic readability assessment employed sophisticated NLP techniques (such as syntactic parsing and statistical language modeling) to capture highly complex linguistic features, and used statistical machine learning to build readability assessment tools. A variety of different NLP–based approaches has been proposed so far in the literature, differing at the level of the number of identified readability classes, the typology of features taken into account, the intended audience of the texts under evaluation, or the application within which readability assessment is carried out, etc.

Research focused so far on readability assessment at the document level. However, as pointed out by Skory and Eskenazi (2010), methods developed perform well when the task is characterizing the readability level of an entire document, while they are unreliable for short texts, including single sentences. Yet, for specific applications, assessing the readability level of individual sentences would be desirable. This is the case, for instance, for text simplification: in current approaches, text readability is typically assessed with respect to the entire document, while text simplification is carried out at the sentence level, as e.g. done in Aluísio et al. (2010), Bott and Saggion (2011) and Inui et al. (2003). By decoupling the readability assessment and simplification processes, the impact of simplification operations on the overall readability level of a given text may not always be clear. With sentence–based readability assessment, this is expected to be no longer a problem. Sentence readability assessment thus represents an open issue in the literature which is worth being further explored. To our knowledge, the only attempts in this direction are represented by Dell'Orletta et al. (2011) and Sjöholm (2012) for the Italian and Swedish languages respectively, followed more recently by Vajjala and Meurers (2014) dealing with English.

In this paper, we tackle the challenge of assessing the readability of individual sentences as a first step towards text simplification. The task is modelled as a classification task, with the final aim of shedding light on two open issues connected with it, namely the reference corpora to be used for training (i.e. collections of sentences classified according to their readability level), and the identification of the most effective features to determine sentence readability. For what concerns the former, sentence readability assessment poses the remarkable issue of classifying sentences according to their difficulty: if all sentences occurring in simplified texts can be assumed to be easy–to–read sentences, the reverse does not necessarily hold since not all sentences occurring in complex texts are to be assumed difficult–to–read. This fact has important implications at the level of the composition of the corpora to be used for training. The sec-

Proceedings of the Ninth Workshop on Innovative Use of NLP for Building Educational Applications , pages 163–173,
Baltimore, Maryland USA, June 26, 2014. ©2014 Association for Computational Linguistics

ond issue is concerned with whether and to what extent the features playing a significant role in the assessment of readability at the sentence level coincide with those exploited at the level of document. In particular, the following research questions are addressed:

1. in assessing sentence readability, is it better to use a small gold standard training corpus of manually classified sentences or a much bigger training corpus automatically constructed from readability–tagged documents possibly containing misclassified sentences?

2. which are the features maximizing sentence readability assessment?

3. to what extent do important features for sentence readability classification match those playing a role in the document readability classification?

We will try to answer these questions by working on Italian, which is a less–resourced language as far as readability is concerned. To this end, READ–IT (Dell'Orletta et al., 2011; Dell'Orletta et al., 2014), which represents the first NLP–based readability assessment tool for Italian, was specialized in different respects, namely at the level of the training corpus and of the learning algorithm; to investigate questions 2. and 3. above, a maximum entropy–based feature selection and ranking algorithm (i.e. grafting) was selected. The specific target audience of readers addressed in this study is represented by people characterised by low literacy skills and/or by mild cognitive impairment. The paper is organized as follows: Section 2 describes the background literature, Section 3 introduces our approach to the task, in terms of used corpora, features and learning algorithm. Finally, Sections 4 and 5 describe the experimental setting and discuss achieved results.

2 Background

In spite of the acknowledged need of performing readability assessment at the sentence level, so far very few attempts have been made to systematically investigate the issues and challenges concerned with the readability assessment of sentences (as opposed to documents). The first two studies in this direction focused on languages other than English, namely Italian (Dell'Orletta et al., 2011) and Swedish (Sjöholm, 2012). In both cases, the authors start from the assumption that while all sentences occurring in simplified texts can be assumed to be easy–to–read sentences, the reverse is not true, since not all sentences occurring in complex texts are difficult–to–read. This has important consequences at the level of the evaluation of sentence classification results: i.e. erroneous readability assessments within the class of difficult–to–read texts may either correspond to those easy–to–read sentences occurring within complex texts or represent real classification errors. To overcome this problem in the readability assessment of individual sentences, a notion of distance with respect to easy-to-read sentences was introduced by Dell'Orletta et al. (2011). Focusing on English, a similar issue is addressed more recently by Vajjala and Meurers (2014) who developed a binary sentence classifier trained on Wikipedia and Simple English Wikipedia: they showed that the low accuracy obtained by their classifier stems from the incorrect assumption that all Wikipedia sentences are more complex than the Simple Wikipedia ones.

Besides readability, sentence–based analyses are reported in the literature for related tasks: for instance, in a text simplification scenario by Drndarević et al. (2013), Aluísio et al. (2008), Štajner and Saggion (2013) and Barlacchi and Tonelli (2013); or to predict writing quality level by Louis and Nenkova (2013). Sheikha and Inkpen (2012) report the results of both document– and sentence–based classification in the different but related task of assessing formal vs. informal style of a document/sentence. For students learning English, Andersen et al. (2013) made a self–assessment and tutoring system available which was able to assign a quality score for each individual sentence they write: this provides automated feedback on learners' writing.

A further important issue, largely investigated in previous readability assessment studies, is the identification of linguistic factors playing a role in assessing the readability of documents. If traditional readability metrics (see e.g., Kincaid et al. (1975)) typically rely on raw text characteristics, such as word and sentence length, the new NLP–based readability indices exploit wider sets of features ranging across different linguistic levels. Starting from Schwarm and Ostendorf (2005) and Heilman et al. (2007), the role of syntactic features in this task was considered, and more recently, the role of discourse features (e.g., discourse topic, discourse cohesion and coherence) has also been taken into account (see e.g., Barzilay and Lapata (2008), Pitler and Nenkova (2008), Kate et al. (2010), Feng et al. (2010) and Tonelli et al. (2012)). Many of these studies also explored the usefulness of features belonging to individual levels of linguistic description in predicting text readability. For example, Feng et al. (2010) systematically evaluated a wide range of features and compared the results of different statistical classifiers trained on different classes of features. Similarly, the correlation between level–specific features has been calculated by Pitler and Nenkova (2008) with respect to human readability judgments, and by François and Fairon (2012) with respect to readability levels. In both cases, the classes of features which turned out to be highly correlated with readability judgments were used in a readability assessment tool to test their efficacy. Note, however, that in all cases the predictive power of the selected features was evaluated at the document level only.

3 Our Approach

In this section, we introduce the main ingredients of our approach to sentence readability assessment, corpora used for training and testing, selected features and the learning and feature selection algorithm.

3.1 Corpora

We relied on two different corpora: a newspaper corpus, *La Repubblica* (henceforth, *Rep*), and an easy–to–read newspaper, *Due Parole* (henceforth, *2Par*). *2Par* includes articles specifically written by Italian linguists experts in text simplification for an audience of adults with a rudimentary literacy level or with mild intellectual disabilities (Piemontese, 1996), which represents the target audience of this study. The two corpora – selected as representative of complex vs. simplified texts within the journalistic genre – differ significantly with respect to the distribution of features typically correlated with text complexity (Dell'Orletta et al., 2011) and thus represent reliable training datasets. However, whereas such a distinction is valid as far as documents are concerned, it appears to be a simplistic generalization when the focus is on sentences. In other words, whereas we can consider all sentences of *2Par* as easy–to–read, not all *Rep* sentences are expected to be difficult–to–read. From this it follows that whereas the internal composition of *2Par* is homogeneous at the sentence level, this is not the case for *Rep*.

To overcome this asymmetry and in particular to assess the impact of the noise in the *Rep* training corpus, we constructed different training sets differing in size and internal composition, going from a noisy set which assumes all *Rep* sentences to be difficult–to–read to a clean but smaller set in which the easy–to–read sentences occurring in *Rep* were manually filtered out. These training sets were used in different experiments whose results are reported in Section 4.2.

The corpus containing only difficult–to–read sentences was manually built by annotating *Rep* sentences according to their readability (i.e. easy vs. difficult). The annotation process was carried out by two annotators with a background in computational linguistics. In order to assess the reliability of their judgements, we started with a small annotation experiment: the two annotators were provided with the same 5 articles from the *Rep* corpus (for a total of 107 sentences) and were asked to extract the difficult–to–read sentences (as opposed to both easy–to–read and not–easy–to–classify sentences). The first annotator carried out the task in 5 minutes and 46 seconds, while the second annotator took 9 minutes and 8 seconds. The two annotators agreed on the classification of 81 difficult–to–read sentences out of 107 considered ones (in particular, the first annotator identified 90 difficult–to–read–sentences and the second one 93 sentences). The agreement between the two annotators was calculated in terms of precision, by taking one of the annotation sets as the gold standard and the other as response: on average, we obtained a precision of 0.88 in the retrieval of sentences definitely classified as difficult–to–read. Given the high level of agreement, the two annotators were asked to select difficult sentences from two sets of distinct *Rep* articles. This resulted in a set of 1,745 difficult–to–read sentences which were used together with a random selection of easy–to–read sentences from *2Par* for training and testing.[1]

[1]The collection can be downloaded from www.italianlp.it/?page_id=22.

Feature	Ranking position		Feature	Ranking position	
	Sent. class.	Doc. class.		Sent. class.	Doc. class.
Raw text features:					
[1] Sentence length	**1**	**1**	[2] Word length	**2**	**2**
Lexical features:					
[3] Word types in the *Basic Italian Vocabulary*	**14**	42	[6] "High availability words"	**21**	22
[4] "Fundamental words"	**10**	**9**	[7] TTR (form)		**7**
[5] "High usage words"	**22**	38	[8] TTR (lemma)		53
Morpho–syntactic features:					
[9] Adjective		46	[26] Aux. verb – inf. mood	64	
[10] Adverb	**29**	59	[27] Aux. verb – part. mood	51	
[11] Article	49	25	[28] Aux. verb – subj. mood	55	
[12] Conjunction		40	[29] Main verb – cond. mood	40	43
[13] Determiner	43	54	[30] Main verb – ger. mood	48	48
[14] Interjection			[31] Main verb – imp. mood	37	57
[15] Noun	**12**	19	[32] Main verb – indic. mood	**16**	**11**
[16] Number	65	44	[33] Main verb – inf. mood	**13**	**13**
[17] Predeterminer			[34] Main verb – part. mood	**26**	28
[18] Preposition	61		[35] Main verb – subj. mood	46	32
[19] Pronoun	**27**	30	[36] Modal verb - inf. mood	54	56
[20] Punctuation		35	[37] Modal verb – cond. mood	41	36
[21] Residual			[38] Modal verb – imp. mood		
[22] Verb	63	34	[39] Modal verb – indic. mood	**18**	23
[23] Lexical density	34	33	[40] Modal verb – part. mood		
[24] Aux. verb – cond. mood	59	60	[41] Modal verb – subj. mood	60	58
[25] Aux. verb – indic. mood	**17**	17			
Syntactic features:					
[42] Argument	62		[65] Sentence root	35	62
[43] Auxiliary		70	[66] Subject	39	52
[44] Clitic		63	[67] Subordinate clause		64
[45] Complement	**28**	29	[68] Temporal complement	45	55
[46] Concatenation		66	[69] Temporal modifier		
[47] Conjunct in a disjunctive compound	58	67	[70] Temporal predicate		
[48] Conjunct linked by a copulative conjunction	38	37	[71] Parse tree depth	**5**	**4**
[49] Copulative conjunction	31	39	[72] Embedded complement 'chains'	**8**	24
[50] Determiner	50	26	[73] Verbal Root	**6**	**3**
[51] Direct object	44	27	[74] Arity of verbal predicates	**3**	15
[52] Disjunctive conjunction	57	68	[75] Pre–verbal subject	**4**	**12**
[53] Indirect complement/object	66		[76] Post–verbal subject	**25**	16
[54] Locative complement	52	51	[77] Pre–verbal object	36	41
[55] Locative modifier			[78] Post–verbal object	**9**	21
[56] Locative predicate			[79] Main clauses	**23**	**14**
[57] Modal verb		61	[80] Subordinate clauses	42	45
[58] Modifier	**20**	47	[81] Subordinate clauses in pre–verbal position	32	**10**
[59] Negative	56	69	[82] Subordinate clauses in post–verbal position	**19**	20
[60] Passive subject			[83] 'Chains' of embedded subordinate clauses	**11**	**5**
[61] Predicative complement		49	[84] Finite complement clauses	**30**	18
[62] Preposition			[85] Infinitive clauses	53	50
[63] Punctuation	**24**	31	[86] Length of dependency links	**15**	**8**
[64] Relative modifier	47	65	[87] Maximum length of dependency links	**7**	**6**

Table 1: Typology of features and ranking position in sentence and document readability assessment experiments. Only about 14 features are needed for an adequate model of document readability, whereas this number increases to 30 for sentence readability (marked in boldface). Features which were not selected during ranking have no rank.

3.2 Linguistic Features

The set of features used in the experiments reported in this paper is wide, spanning across different levels of linguistic analysis. They can be broadly classified into four main classes, as reported in Table 1: raw text features, lexical features, morpho–syntactic features and syntactic features, shortly described below.[2]

Raw text features (Features [1–2] in Table 1) refer to those features typically used within traditional readability metrics and include *sentence length*, calculated as the average number of words per sentence, and *word length*, calculated as the average number of characters per words.

The cover category of lexical features (Features [3–8] in Table 1) includes features referring to

[2]For an exhaustive discussion including the motivations underlying this selection of features, the interested reader is referred to Dell'Orletta et al. (2011, 2014) where these features were successfully used for assessing the readability of Italian texts.

both the internal composition of the vocabulary and the lexical richness of the text. For what concerns the former, the *Basic Italian Vocabulary* by De Mauro (2000) was taken as a reference resource, including a list of 7000 words highly familiar to native speakers of Italian. In particular, we consider: a) the percentage of all unique words (types) on this reference list occurring in the text, and b) the internal distribution of the occurring basic Italian vocabulary words into the usage classification classes of 'fundamental words' (very frequent words), 'high usage words' (frequent words) and 'high availability words' (relatively lower frequency words referring to everyday life). Lexical richness of texts is monitored by computing the Type/Token Ratio (TTR), which refers to the ratio between the number of lexical types and the number of tokens within a text. Due to its sensitivity to sample size, this feature is computed for text samples of equivalent length.

The set of morpho–syntactic features (Features [9–41] in Table 1) is aimed at capturing different aspects of the linguistic structure affecting in one way or another the readability of a text. They range from the probability distribution of part–of–speech (POS) types, to the lexical density of the text, calculated as the ratio of content words (verbs, nouns, adjectives and adverbs) to the total number of lexical tokens in a text. This class also includes features referring to the distribution of verbs by mood and/or tense, which can be seen as a language–specific feature exploiting the predictive power of the Italian rich morphology.

The set of syntactic features (Features [42–87] in Table 1) captures different aspects of the syntactic structure which are taken as reliable indicators for automatic readability assessment, namely:

- the unconditional probability of syntactic dependency types, e.g. subject, direct object, modifier, etc. (Features 42–70);
- parse tree depth features (71–72), going from the *depth of the whole parse tree*, calculated in terms of the longest path from the root of the dependency tree to some leaf, to a more specific feature referring to the *average depth of embedded complement 'chains'* governed by a nominal head and including either prepositional complements or nominal and adjectival modifiers;
- verbal predicate features (73–78) aimed at capturing different aspects of the behaviour of verbal predicates: they range from the *number of verbal roots* with respect to number of all sentence roots occurring in a text, to more specific features such as the *arity of verbs*, meant as the number of instantiated dependency links sharing the same verbal head (covering both arguments and modifiers) and the *relative ordering of subject and object with respect to the verbal head*;
- as subordination is widely acknowledged to be an index of structural complexity in language, subordination features (79–85) include: the *distribution of subordinate vs. main clauses*; for subordinates, the *distribution of infinitives vs finite complement clauses*, their *relative ordering with respect to the main clause* and the *average depth of 'chains' of embedded subordinate clauses*;
- the length of dependency links is another characteristic connected with the syntactic complexity of sentences. Features 86–87 measure dependency length in terms of the words occurring between the syntactic head and the dependent: they focus on all dependency links vs. maximum dependency links only.

3.3 Model Training and Feature Ranking

Given the twofold goal of this study, i.e. reliably assessing sentence readability and finding the most predictive features undelying it, we used GRAFTING (Perkins et al., 2003), as this approach allows to train a maximum entropy model while simultaneously including incremental feature selection. The method uses a gradient–based heuristic to select the most promising feature (to add to the set of selected features S), and then performs a full weight optimization over all features in S. This process is repeated until a certain stopping criterion is reached. As the grafting approach we use integrates the l_1 regularization (preventing overfitting), features are only included (i.e. have a nonzero weight) when the reduction of the objective function is greater than a certain treshold. In our case, the l_1 prior we use was selected on the basis of evaluating maximum entropy models with varying l_1 values (range: 1e-11, 1e-10, ..., 0.1, 1) via 10–fold cross validation. We used TinyEst[3], a

[3]http://github.com/danieldk/tinyest

grafting-capable maximum entropy parameter estimator for ranking tasks (de Kok, 2011; de Kok, 2013), to select the features and estimate their weights. Whereas our task is not a ranking task, but rather a binary classification problem, we were able to model it as a ranking task by assigning a high score (1) to difficult–to–read sentences and a low score (0) to easy–to–read sentences. Consequently, a sentence having a score < 0.5 was interpreted as an easy–to–read sentence, whereas a sentence which was assigned a score ≥ 0.5 was interpreted to be a difficult–to–read sentence.

4 Experiments and Results

4.1 Experimental Setup

In all experiments, the corpora were automatically tagged by the part–of–speech tagger described in Dell'Orletta (2009) and dependency–parsed by the DeSR parser (Attardi, 2006) using Support Vector Machines as learning algorithm. We devised two different experiments, aimed at exploring the research questions investigated in this paper. To this end, READ–IT was adapted by integrating a specialized training corpus and a maximum entropy–based feature selection and ranking algorithm (i.e. grafting).

Experiment 1

This experiment, investigating the first research question, is aimed at identifying what is the most effective training data for sentence readability assessment. In particular, the goal is to compare the results on the basis of using a small set of gold standard data with respect to a (potentially larger, but) noisy data set (i.e. without manual revision) where every *Rep* sentence was assumed to be difficult–to–read. In particular, the comparison involved four datasets:

- a collection of gold standard data consisting of 1,310 easy–to–read sentences randomly extracted from the *2Par* corpus and 1,310 manually selected difficult–to–read sentences from the *Rep* corpus;
- a large and unbalanced collection of uncorrected data consisting of the whole *2Par* corpus (3,910 easy–to–read sentences) and the whole *Rep* corpus (8,452 sentences, classified *a priori* as difficult–to–read);
- a balanced collection of uncorrected sentences, consisting of 3,910 sentences from *2Par* and 3,910 sentences from *Rep*;
- a balanced collection of uncorrected sentences having the same size as the gold standard dataset, namely 1,310 sentences from *2Par* and 1,310 sentences from *Rep*.

To assess similarities and differences at the level of the different corpora used for training in this experiment, in Table 2 we report a selection of linguistic features (see Section 3.2) characterizing the four datasets with respect to the whole *2Par* corpus.We can observe that *2Par* differs from all four *Rep* corpora for all reported features, and that the four *Rep* corpora show similar trends. Interestingly, however, the *Rep* Gold corpus is almost always the most distant one from *2Par* (i.e. at the level of sentence length, word length, distribution of adjectives and subjects, average length of dependency links and parse tree depth).

On the basis of the four *Rep* datasets, four models were built which we evaluated using a held–out test set consisting of 435 sentences from *2Par* and 435 manually classified difficult–to–read sentences from *Rep*. Using the grafting method, we calculated the classification score for each sentence in our test set on the basis of an increasing number of features (ranging from 1 to all non-zero weighted features for the specific dataset): sentences with a score below 0.5 were classified as easy–to–read, whereas sentences having a score greater or equal to 0.5 were classified as difficult–to–read. This procedure was repeated for each of the four models.

Experiment 2

The second experiment is aimed at answering our second and third research questions, focusing on the features relevant for sentence readability, and the relationship of those features with document readability classification. For this purpose, we compared sentence– and document–based readability classification results. In particular, we compared the features used by the sentence–based readability model trained on the gold standard data and the features used by the document–based model trained on *Rep* and *2Par*. With respect to the document classification, we used a corpus of 638 documents (319 extracted from *2Par* representating easy–to–read texts, and 319 extracted from *Rep* representing difficult–to–read texts) with 20% of the documents constituting the held–out test set.

Features	*Rep* Unbalan. large	*Rep* Balan. small	*Rep* Balan. large	*Rep* Gold	*2Par*
Sentence length	24.98	26.03	25.26	28.14	18.66
Word length	5.14	5.24	5.14	5.28	5
"Fundamental words"	75.05%	75.08%	74.83%	74.99%	76.38
Adjective	6.19%	6.25%	6.36%	6.42%	6.03%
Noun	25.65%	27.09%	25.74%	26.10%	29.13%
Subject	4.62%	4.75%	4.64%	4.42%	6%
Max. length of dependency links	9.73	10.13	9.85	10.98	7.67
Parse tree depth	6.18	6.57	6.30	6.83	5.2

Table 2: Distribution of some linguistic features in *Rep* and *2Par* training data

	Accuracy					Precision (all ft)	
Training data	**2 ft**	**10 ft**	**30 ft**	**50 ft**	**all ft**	**Easy**	**Difficult**
Unbalanced large	50	63.7	74.9	78.4	78.9 (85 ft)	69.2	***88.5***
Balanced small	64	67.9	79.2	80.8	82.5 (82 ft)	82.5	82.5
Balanced large	63.9	**70.6**	79.7	81.0	82.3 (85 ft)	83.0	81.6
Gold data	**65.6**	69.8	**79.9**	**81.3**	**83.7 (66 ft)**	***84.8***	82.5

Table 3: Sentence classification results using four training datasets and a varying number of features

4.2 Which Training Corpus for Sentence Classification?

Table 3 reports the results for the sentence classification task using the four training datasets described above. Results are reported in terms of both overall accuracy (calculated as the proportion of correct answers against all answers) and precision within each readability class (when using all features), defined as the number of easy or difficult sentences correctly identified as such (in their respective columns).

Accuracy was computed for all training models tested using an increasing number of features (2, 10, 30, 50 and all features) as resulting from the GRAFTING–based ranking and detailed in Table 1. Note that the first two features correspond in all cases to the traditional readability features of sentence length and word length. The classification model trained on the small gold standard dataset turned out to almost always outperform all other models: it achieved the best accuracy (83.7%) using a relatively small number of features (66), and also for a fixed number of features (i.e. 2, 30 and 50). Only when using the top–10 features, the uncorrected balanced large dataset slightly outperformed the gold standard dataset. The accuracy when using the unbalanced dataset for training was always significantly ($p < 0.05$) worse (using McNemar's test) than the accuracy based on the other training data. The only other significant difference existed between the balanced small and large dataset for 10 features. All other differences are non–significant.

It is also interesting to note that in the results reported in column *2 ft* of Table 3 a significant difference is observed when comparing the accuracy achieved using the unbalanced large data set with that achieved with the gold standard data: i.e. about 15.5 percentage points of difference for the *2 ft* model against $3 - 6\%$ using higher numbers of features. This result originates from the fact that the unbalanced corpus contains to a larger extent sentences which are short and complex at the same time whose correct readability assessment requires linguistically–grounded features (see below).

The last two columns of Table 3 report precision results for easy– vs. difficult–to–read sentences for each of the four training datasets (all features). It is clear that for the class of difficult–to–read sentences the highest precision (88.5%) is obtained when using the whole *2Par* and *Rep* corpora for training (i.e. unbalanced large), whereas for the class of easy–to–read sentences the best precision results (84.8%) are obtained with the system trained on the gold standard dataset. Interestingly, the worst precision results (69.2%) are reported for the class of easy–to–read sentences with the unbalanced large training data set.

These results suggest that the advantages of using the gold standard data over the uncorrected training data sets are limited. From this it follows that treating the whole *Rep* corpus as a collection of difficult–to–read sentences is not completely unjustified: this is in line with the satisfactory results reported by Dell'Orletta et al. (2011) where *Rep* was used for training a sentence readability classifier without any manual filtering of sentences. Nevertheless, the results of this experiment demonstrate that readability assessment accuracy and in particular the precision in identifying easy–to–read sentences can be improved by using a manually selected training dataset. Balancing the size of larger but potentially noisy (i.e. without manual revision) data sets appears to create a positive trade–off between accuracy and precision for both classes, thus representing a viable alternative to the construction of a gold standard dataset.

4.3 Sentence vs. Document Classification: which and how many features?

To identify the typology of features needed for sentence readability assessment and compare them to those needed for assessing document readability, we compared the results obtained by the grafting–based feature selection in the sentence classification task (using the gold standard dataset for training, see Table 3) to those obtained in the document classification task whose accuracy on the test set is reported in Table 4 for increasing numbers of features selected via GRAFTING.

Train. data	2 ft	10 ft	30 ft	50 ft	70 ft (all)
Rep - 2Par	80	93.3	**96.6**	96.6	95

Table 4: Accuracy of document classification for a varying number of features

By comparing the document classification results with respect to those obtained for sentences, it can be noticed that the best accuracy is achieved using a set of 30 features: in contrast to sentence classification where adding features keeps increasing the performance, more features do not appear to help for document classification. Sentence readability classification thus seems to be a more complex task, requiring a higher amount of features. This trend emerges more clearly in Figures 1(a) and 1(b), where the classification results on the training set (using 10–fold cross–validation) and the held–out test set are visualized for increasing amounts of features selected via GRAFTING. As Figure 1(a) shows, the document classification task requires about 14 features after which the performance appears to stabilize (97.4% accuracy for the ten–fold cross-validation and 96.7% for the held–out test set). In contrast, Figure 1(b) shows that sentence classification requires at least 30 features (83.4% accuracy for the ten–fold cross-validation and 79.9% for the test set).

Noticeable differences can also be observed in the typology of features playing a prominent role in the two tasks. For each feature taken into account, Table 1 reports its ranking as resulting from sentence– and document–based classification experiments (columns "Sent. class." and "Doc. class." respectively). Note that in interpreting the rank associated with each feature it should be considered that in sentence– and document–classification the number of required features is significantly different, i.e. 30 and 14 respectively: this is to say that approximately the same rank associated to the same feature does not entail a comparable role across the two classification tasks.

As already pointed out, for both sentences and documents raw text features (i.e. *Sentence length* and *Word length*) turned out to be the top features, leading however to significantly different results: i.e. 80% accuracy for documents vs. 65% for sentences. Among the remaining features, grafting results show that syntactic features do play a central role in both sentence– and document–based readability assessment: many of these are highly ranked, with some differences. Syntactic features playing a similar role in both readability classification tasks include: *Verbal root* [73], *Parse tree depth* [71], *'Chains' of embedded subordinate clauses* [83] and *Max. length of dependency links* [87], covering important aspects of syntactic complexity such as depth of the syntactic dependency (sub–)tree and length of dependency links. Features that are mainly useful for sentence readability turned out to be *Arity of verbal predicates* [74], *Pre–verbal subject* [75], *Post–verbal object* [78] and *Embedded complement 'chains'* [72], which can all be seen as representing local features referring to sentence parts. The feature *Subordinate clauses in pre–verbal position* [81], focusing on the global distribution of pre–verbal subordinate clauses within the document, is relevant for document classification only. It is interesting to note that features capturing different facets of the same phenomenon can play quite a different role for assessing the readability of sentences vs. documents: this is the case of dependency length, measured in terms of the words occurring between the syntactic head and the dependent, where feature [86] refers to the average length of all dependency links and [87] to the average length of

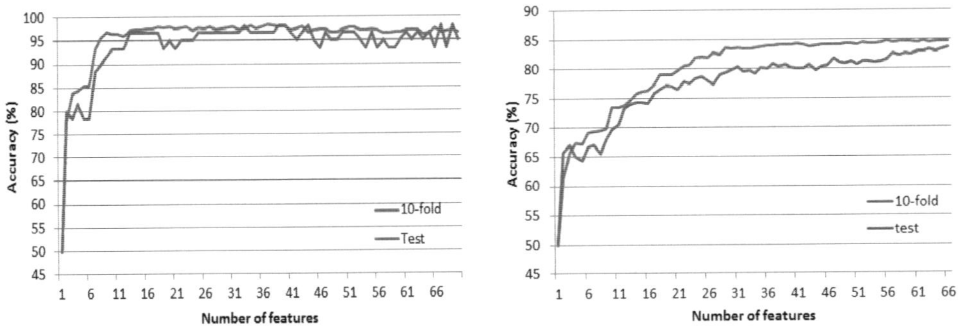

(a) Document classification

(b) Sentence classification

Figure 1: Document vs Sentence classification results

maximum dependency links from each sentence. Whereas [86] plays a similar role for sentences and documents (in both cases it is a middle rank feature), [87] is a global feature playing a more prominent role in document classification.

At the morpho–syntactic level, the feature ranking is more comparable. However, it is interesting to note that very few morpho–syntactic features were selected by the feature selection process: this is particularly true for document classification. This can follow from the fact that these features can be considered as proxies of the syntactic structure which in these experiments was represented through specific features: in this situation, the grafting process preferred syntactic features over morpho–syntactic ones, in spite of the lower accuracy of the dependency parser with respect to the part–of–speech tagger. Interestingly, this result is in contrast with what reported by Falkenjack and Jönsson (2014) for what concerns document readability assessment, who claim that an optimal subset of text features for readability based document classification does not need features induced via parsing. Among the morpho–syntactic features, it appears that verbal features play an important role: this can follow both by the language dealt with which is a a morphologically rich language, and by the fact that these features do not have a counterpart at the syntactic level.

Lexical features show a much more mixed result. Type–Token Ratio (TTR) is only important for document classification, whereas most of the other features are important for sentence readability, but not for document readability (with the exception of the presence of 'fundamental words' of the *Basic Italian Vocabulary*).

5 Discussion

In this study we have focused on three research questions. First, we asked which type of training corpus is best to assess sentence readability. Whereas we found that using a set of manually selected complex sentences was better than using a simple corpus–based distinction, the extra effort needed to construct the training corpus might not be worthwhile as observed improvements were quite modest. However, we did not consider a more sensitive measure of the difficulty of a sentence (such as a number ranging between 0 and 1), and this might be able to offer a more substantial improvement (at the cost of needing more time to create the training material). Of course, when the goal is to identify the best features for assessing sentence readability, it does make sense to have high–quality training data to prevent selecting inadequate features. The second research question involved identifying which features were most useful for assessing sentence readability. Besides raw text features, syntactic but also morpho–syntactic features turned out to play a central role to achieve adequate performance. The third research question investigated the overlap between the features needed for document and sentence readability classification. Whereas there certainly was overlap between the top features (with different levels of performance), most of the features had a different rank across the two tasks, with local features being more predictive for sentence classification and global ones for documents. This suggests that the sentence readability task is more complex than assessing document readability, given that there is much less information available for a sentence than for a document.

Acknowledgments

The research reported in this paper was carried out in the framework of the Short Term Mobility program of international exchanges funded by CNR (Italy). We thank Daniël de Kok for his help in applying TINYEST to our data and Giulia Benotto for her help in manual revision of training data.

References

Sandra M. Aluísio, Lucia Specia, Thiago A.S. Pardo, Erick G. Maziero, and Renata P.M. Fortes. 2008. Towards brazilian portuguese automatic text simplification systems. In *Proceedings of the Eighth ACM Symposium on Document Engineering*, pages 240–248.

Sandra Aluísio, Lucia Specia, Caroline Gasperin, and Carolina Scarton. 2010. Readability assessment for text simplification. In *Proceedings of the NAACL HLT 2010 Fifth Workshop on Innovative Use of NLP for Building Educational Applications*, pages 1–9.

Øistein E. Andersen, Helen Yannakoudakis, Fiona Barker, and Tim Parish. 2013. Developing and testing a self-assessment and tutoring system. In *Proceedings of the Eighth Workshop on Innovative Use of NLP for Building Educational Applications*, pages 32–41.

Giuseppe Attardi. 2006. Experiments with a multilanguage non-projective dependency parser. In *Proceedings of the Tenth Conference on Computational Natural Language Learning (CoNLL-X '06), New York City, New York*, pages 166–170.

Gianni Barlacchi and Sara Tonelli. 2013. Ernesta: A sentence simplification tool for children's stories in italian. In *Proceedings of the 14th Conferences on Computational Linguistics and Natural Language Processing (CICLing 2013)*, pages 476–487.

Regina Barzilay and Mirella Lapata. 2008. Modeling local coherence: An entity-based approach. volume 34.

Stefan Bott and Horacio Saggion. 2011. An unsupervised alignment algorithm for text simplification corpus construction. In *Proceedings of the Workshop on Monolingual Text-To-Text Generation*, pages 20–26.

Daniël de Kok. 2011. Discriminative features in reversible stochastic attribute-value grammars. In *Proceedings of the EMNLP Workshop on Language Generation and Evaluation*, pages 54–63. Association for Computational Linguistics.

Daniël de Kok. 2013. *Reversible Stochastic Attribute-Value Grammars*. Ph.D. thesis, Rijksuniversiteit Groningen.

Tullio De Mauro. 2000. *Il dizionario della lingua italiana*. Paravia, Torino.

Felice Dell'Orletta, Simonetta Montemagni, and Giulia Venturi. 2011. Read-it: Assessing readability of italian texts with a view to text simplification. In *Proceedings of the Workshop on Speech and Language Processing for Assistive Technologies (SLPAT 2011)*, pages 73–83.

Felice Dell'Orletta, Simonetta Montemagni, and Giulia Venturi. 2014. Assessing document and sentence readability in less resourced languages and across textual genres. In *International Journal of Applied Linguistics (ITL). Special Issue on Readability and Text Simplification*. To appear.

Felice Dell'Orletta. 2009. Ensemble system for part-of-speech tagging. In *Proceedings of Evalita'09, Evaluation of NLP and Speech Tools for Italian, Reggio Emilia, December*.

Biljana Drndarević, Sanja Štajner, Stefan Bott, Susana Bautista, and Horacio Saggion. 2013. Automatic text simplification in spanish: A comparative evaluation of complementing modules. In *Computational Linguistics and Intelligent Text Processing*, pages 488–500. Springer Berlin Heidelberg.

Johan Falkenjack and Arne Jönsson. 2014. Classifying easy-to-read texts without parsing. In *Proceedings of the Proceedings of the 3rd Workshop on Predicting and Improving Text Readability for Target Reader Populations (PITR)*, Gothenburg, Sweden. Association for Computational Linguistics.

Lijun Feng, Martin Jansche, Matt Huenerfauth, and Noémie Elhadad. 2010. A comparison of features for automatic readability assessment. In *Proceedings of the 23rd International Conference on Computational Linguistics (COLING 2010)*, pages 276–284.

Thomas François and Cédrick Fairon. 2012. An "AI readability" formula for french as a foreign language. In *Proceedings of the 2012 Joint Conference on Empirical Methods in Natural Language Processing and Computational Natural Language Learning, Jeju Island, Korea*, pages 466–477.

Michael J. Heilman, Kevyn Collins, and Jamie Callan. 2007. Combining lexical and grammatical features to improve readability measures for first and second language texts. In *Proceedings of the Human Language Technology Conference*, pages 460–467.

Kentaro Inui, Atsushi Fujita, Tetsuro Takahashi, Ryu Iida, and Tomoya Iwakura. 2003. Text simplification for reading assistance: A project note. In *Proceedings of the Second International Workshop on Paraphrasing*, pages 9–16.

Rohit J. Kate, Xiaoqiang Luo, Siddharth Patwardhan, Martin Franz, Radu Florian, Raymond J. Mooney, Salim Roukos, and Chris Welty. 2010. Learning to predict readability using diverse linguistic features. In *oceedings of the 23rd International Conference on Computational Linguistics*, pages 546–554.

J. Peter Kincaid, Lieutenant Robert P. Fishburne, Richard L. Rogers, and Brad S. Chissom. 1975. Derivation of new readability formulas for navy enlisted personnel. In *Research Branch Report, Millington, TN: Chief of Naval Training*, pages 8–75.

Annie Louis and Ani Nenkova. 2013. A corpus of science journalism for analysing writing quality. volume 4.

Simon Perkins, Kevin Lacker, and James Theiler. 2003. Grafting: Fast, incremental feature selection by gradient descent in function space. *The Journal of Machine Learning Research*, 3:1333–1356.

Maria Emanuela Piemontese. 1996. *Capire e farsi capire. Teorie e tecniche della scrittura controllata.* Tecnodid, Napoli.

Emily Pitler and Ani Nenkova. 2008. Revisiting readability: A unified framework for predicting text quality. In *Proceedings of the 2008 Conference on Empirical Methods in Natural Language Processing*, pages 186–195.

Sarah E. Schwarm and Mari Ostendorf. 2005. Reading level assessment using support vector machines and statistical language models. In *Proceedings of the 43rd Annual Meeting on Association for Computational Linguistics (ACL 05)*, pages 523–530.

Fadi Abu Sheikha and Diana Inkpen. 2012. Learning to classify documents according to formal and informal style. volume 8.

Johan Sjöholm. 2012. *Probability as readability: A new machine learning approach to readability assessment for written Swedish.* LiU Electronic Press, Master thesis.

Adam Skory and Maxine Eskenazi. 2010. Predicting cloze task quality for vocabulary training. In *Proceedings of the NAACL HLT 2010 Fifth Workshop on Innovative Use of NLP for Building Educational Applications*, pages 49–56.

Sara Tonelli, Ke Tran Manh, and Emanuele Pianta. 2012. Making readability indices readable. In *Proceedings of the First Workshop on Predicting and Improving Text Readability for Target Reader Populations*, pages 40–48.

Sowmya Vajjala and Detmar Meurers. 2014. On assessing the reading level of individual sentences for text simplification. In *Proceedings of the 14th Conference of the European Chapter of the Association for Computational Linguistics (EACL-14)*, Gothenburg, Sweden. Association for Computational Linguistics.

Sanja Štajner and Horacio Saggion. 2013. Readability indices for automatic evaluation of text simplification systems: A feasibility study for spanish. In *Proceedings of the International Joint Conference on Natural Language Processing*.

Rule-based and machine learning approaches for second language sentence-level readability

Ildikó Pilán, Elena Volodina and Richard Johansson
Språkbanken, University of Gothenburg
Box 200, Gothenburg, Sweden
{ildiko.pilan, elena.volodina, richard.johansson}@svenska.gu.se

Abstract

We present approaches for the identification of sentences understandable by second language learners of Swedish, which can be used in automatically generated exercises based on corpora. In this work we merged methods and knowledge from machine learning-based readability research, from rule-based studies of Good Dictionary Examples and from second language learning syllabuses. The proposed selection methods have also been implemented as a module in a free web-based language learning platform. Users can use different parameters and linguistic filters to personalize their sentence search with or without a machine learning component assessing readability. The sentences selected have already found practical use as multiple-choice exercise items within the same platform. Out of a number of deep linguistic indicators explored, we found mainly lexical-morphological and semantic features informative for second language sentence-level readability. We obtained a readability classification accuracy result of 71%, which approaches the performance of other models used in similar tasks. Furthermore, during an empirical evaluation with teachers and students, about seven out of ten sentences selected were considered understandable, the rule-based approach slightly outperforming the method incorporating the machine learning model.

1 Introduction and motivation

Despite the fact that there is a vast selection of existing materials, many language teachers opt for completing course syllabuses with either invented examples or authentic resources, customized to the need of specific learners (Howard and Major, 2004). Collections with millions of tokens of digital text are available for several languages today, part of which would offer adequate practice material for learners of a second or foreign language (L2) to develop their skills further. However, a necessary first step representing a major challenge when reusing copora for automatic exercise generation is how to assess the suitability of the available material. In this study, we explored how we could exploit existing Natural Language Processing (NLP) tools and resources for this purpose.

To overcome copyright issues often limiting full-text access to certain corpora, we decided to work with sentences as linguistic unit when assessing the characteristics of suitability and when generating exercise items. Although a large number of studies exist investigating readability, i.e. understandability, at the text level, the sentence level remains little explored. Similarly, the focus of previous investigations has mainly been readability from native language (L1) readers' perspective, but aspects of L2 readability have been less widely studied. To our knowledge no previous research have explored this latter dimension for Swedish before, hence we aim at filling this gap, which can be useful, besides the purposes mentioned above, also in future sentence and text simplification and adaptation tasks.

We propose a rule-based as well as a combination of rule-based and machine learning methods for the identification of sentences understandable by L2 learners and suitable as exercise items. During the selection of linguistic indicators, we have taken into consideration previously studied features of readability (François and Fairon, 2012; Heimann Mühlenbock, 2013; Vajjala and Meurers, 2012), L2 Swedish curricula (Levy Scherrer and Lindemalm, 2009; Folkuniversitet, 2013) and aspects of Good Dictionary Examples (GDEX)

Proceedings of the Ninth Workshop on Innovative Use of NLP for Building Educational Applications , pages 174–184,
Baltimore, Maryland USA, June 26, 2014.

(Husák, 2010; Kilgarriff et al., 2008), being that we believe they have some properties in common with exercise items. The current version of the machine learning model distinguishes sentences readable by students at an intermediate level of proficiency from sentences of a higher readability level. The approaches have been implemented and integrated into an online Intelligent Computer-Assisted Language Learning (ICALL) platform, Lärka (Volodina et al., 2013). Besides a module where users can experiment with the filtering of corpus hits, a module with inflectional and vocabulary exercises (making use of the selected sentences with our method) is also available. An initial evaluation with students, teachers and linguists indicated that more than 70% of the sentences selected were understandable, and about 60% of them would be suitable as exercise items according to the two latter respondent groups.

2 Background

2.1 Text-level readability

Readability of texts in different languages has been the subject of several studies and they range from simpler formulas, taking into account superficial text properties, to more sophisticated NLP methods. Traditional readability measures for L1 Swedish at the text level include *LIX* (Läsbarthetsindex, "Readability index") (Björnsson, 1968) and the *Nominal Ratio* (Hultman and Westman, 1977). In recent years a number of studies, mostly focusing on the L1 context, appeared which take into consideration linguistic features based on a deeper text processing. Morphosyntactic aspects informative for L1 readability include, among others, parse tree depth, subordination features and dependency link depth (length) (Dell'Orletta et al., 2011). Language models have also been commonly used for readability predictions (Collins-Thompson and Callan, 2004; Schwarm and Ostendorf, 2005). A recently proposed measure, the *Coh-Metrix* (Graesser et al., 2011), aims at a multilevel analysis of texts, inspired by psycholinguistic principles. It measures not only linguistic difficulty, but also cohesion in texts.

Research on L1 readability for Swedish, using machine learning, is described in Heimann Mühlenbock (2013) and Falkenjack et al. (2013). Heimann Mühlenbock (2013) examined readability along five dimensions: surface features, word usage, sentence structure, idea density and human interest. Mean dependency distance, subordinate clauses and modifiers proved good predictors for L1 Swedish.

Although a number of readability formulas exist for native language users, these might not be suitable predictors of L2 difficulty being that the acquisition processes of L1 and L2 present a number of differences (Beinborn et al., 2012). Studies focusing on L2 readability are considerably fewer in the literature. The linguistic features in this context include, among others, relative clauses, passive voice (Heilman et al., 2007) and the number of coordinate phrases per clause (Vajjala and Meurers, 2012). Crossley et al. (2008) applied some Coh-Metrix indicators to English L2 readability. The authors found that lexical coreferentiality, syntactic similarity and word frequency measures outperformed traditional L1 readability formulas. A language-independent approach to L2 readability assessment, using an online machine learning algorithm, is presented by Shen et al. (2013) which, however, employed only the surface features of average sentence and word length, and word frequencies as lexical feature. The authors found that none of the features in isolation was able to clearly distinguish between the levels.

In the second language teaching scenario, a widely used scale is the Common European Framework of Reference for Languages (CEFR) (Council of Europe, 2001), which, however, has been less frequently adopted so far in readability studies. The CEFR guidelines for L2 teaching and assessment define six different proficiency levels: A1 (beginner), A2 (elementary), B1 (intermediate), B2 (upper intermediate), C1 (advanced) and C2 (proficiency). François and Fairon (2012) proposed a CEFR-based readability formula for L2 French. Some of the predictive features proved to be structural properties, including shallow length features as well as different morpho-syntactic categories (e.g. present participles) and the presence of words in a list of easy words.

2.2 Sentence-level readability

Many of the text readability measures mentioned above have shortcomings when used on very short passages containing 100 words or less (Kilgarriff et al., 2008). The concept of readability at the sentence level can be related to the selection of appropriate vocabulary example sentences. GDEX

(Husák, 2010; Kilgarriff et al., 2008) is a sentence evaluation algorithm, which, on the basis of lexical and syntactical criteria, automatically ranks example candidates from corpora. Some of the influential linguistic aspects of appropriate example sentences are: their length and structure, the presence of short and common vocabulary items which do not need disambiguation and the absence of anaphoric pronouns. Segler (2007) focuses on the L2 rather than on the lexicographic context. He explores the characteristics of helpful vocabulary examples to be used via an ICALL system for L2 German and underlines the importance of syntactic complexity. Research about ranking Swedish corpus examples is presented in Volodina et al. (2012b). Their first algorithm includes four heuristic rules concerning sentence length, infrequent lexical items, keyword position and the presence of finite verbs, complemented by a sentence similarity measure in the second algorithm. Readability experiments focusing at the sentence level have started to appear recently both for language learning purposes (Pilán et al., 2013) and for detecting differences between simplified and unsimplified sentence pairs (Vajjala and Meurers, 2014).

3 Resources

Our sentence selection module utilizes a number of tools, resources and web services available for Swedish. *Korp*[1], an infrastructure for accessing and maintaining corpora (Borin et al., 2012), contains a large number of Swedish texts which are equipped with automatic annotations (with some exceptions) for part-of-speech (POS), syntactic (dependency) relations, lemma forms and sense ids. Korp offers, among others, a web service for concordances, which makes a search in corpora based on a query (e.g. a keyword and its POS) and returns hits with a sentence-long context. Moreover, with the corpus pipeline of Korp, tools for automatically annotating corpora are also available. A variety of different modern Swedish corpora from Korp have been used throughout this study including novel, newspaper and blog texts.

Another source for sentences was the *CEFR corpus* (Volodina and Johansson Kokkinakis, 2013), a collection of CEFR-related L2 Swedish course book texts. The corpus contains: (a) manual annotations indicating the structure of each lesson in the book (exercises, instructions, texts etc.); (b) automatic linguistic annotations obtained with the annotation tools available through Korp. The CEFR corpus at the time of writing included B1 texts from three course books and B2 texts from one course book. The annotation of additional material covering other CEFR levels was ongoing.

Not only corpora, but also information from frequency word lists has been used for determining the appropriateness of a sentence. The *Kelly list* (Volodina and Kokkinakis, 2012) is a frequency-based vocabulary list mostly built on a corpus of web texts from 2010. Besides frequency information, an associated CEFR level is available for each item. Another frequency-based word list employed for the machine learning experiments is the *Wikipedia list* (Volodina et al., 2012b). It contains the POS and the number of occurrences for each word form in a corpus of Swedish Wikipedia texts.

A central resource of the present study is *Lärka*[2] (Volodina et al., 2013), a freely available online ICALL platform. Currently its exercise generator module offers tasks both for students of linguistics and learners of L2 Swedish (Figure 1). Additional parts include a corpus editor used for the annotation of the CEFR corpus and the sentence selection module presented in this paper, *Hit-Ex*[3] (*Hitta Exempel*, "Find Examples" or Hit Examples). The version under development contains also dictation and spelling exercises (Volodina et al., 2013).

4 Machine learning experiments for readability

4.1 Dataset

We distinguished two different classes in the dataset for the machine learning experiments: (a) sentences understandable at (*within*) B1 level and (b) sentences *above* B1 level. For the former group, sentences were collected from B1-level texts from the CEFR corpus. Sentences above B1 level consisted partly of B2-level sentences from the CEFR corpus, and partly of native language sentences from Korp retrieved on the basis of keywords between B2 and C2 levels according to the Kelly list. Only sentences between the length of 5 and 30 tokens were collected from all resources to decrease the influence of sentence length on the decisions made by the classifiers and to increase the importance of other linguistic features. The

[1] http://spraakbanken.gu.se/korp/

[2] http://spraakbanken.gu.se/larka/

[3] http://spraakbanken.gu.se/larka/larka_hitex_index.html

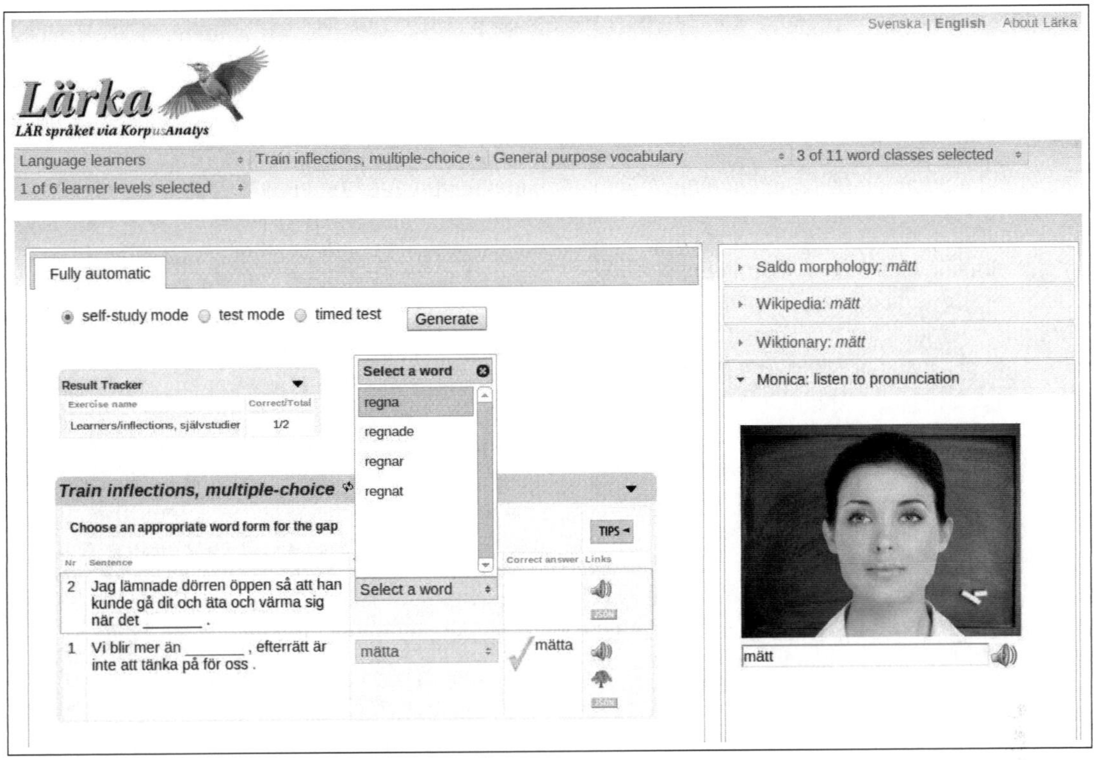

Figure 1: Inflectional exercise.

size of the dataset and the number of sentences per level are illustrated in Table 1.

Level	Source	Nr. sentences
Within B1	B1 (CEFR) texts	2358
Above B1	B2 (CEFR) texts	795
	Korp corpora	1528
Total size of dataset		**4681**

Table 1: The source and the number of sentences in the dataset.

4.2 Method

We performed supervised classification using as training and test data the set of sentences described in section 4.1. Thus, we aimed at a two-way classification distinguishing sentences within B1 level from those above. This level, besides being approximately a middle point of the CEFR scale, is typically divided into sub-levels in language courses (Folkuniversitet, 2013) which indicates a more substantial linguistic content. Consequently, additional practice for learners can be beneficial at this stage. Self-study activities may also be more common in this phase since students have sufficient L2 autonomy. We experimented with different classification algorithms[4] available through the Scikit-learn Python package (Pedregosa et al., 2011), out of which we present the results only of the best performing one here, a linear Support Vector Machine (SVM) classifier. The SVM classifier aims at separating instances into classes with a hyperplane (Tanwani et al., 2009), equivalent to a line in a two-dimensional space. This hyperplane is defined based on the feature values of instances and weights associated with them. Once extracted, the values for each feature were scaled and centered.

Evaluation was carried out with stratified 10-fold cross-validation, i.e. the proportion of labels in each fold was kept the same as that in the whole training set during the ten iterations of training and testing. The evaluation measures taken into consideration were accuracy, precision, recall and the F1 score, a combination of precision and recall, the two of them being equally important (Pedregosa et al., 2011).

[4]The other classification methods used were a Naïve Bayes classifier, a decision tree and two linear algorithms: perceptron and logistic regression.

4.3 Features

After a thorough overview of the machine learning approaches for readability in the literature, a number of features were chosen to be tested in our experiments. The features selected aimed at a deep analysis of the sentences at different linguistic levels. Besides traditional readability indicators, a number of syntactic, morphological, lexical and semantic aspects have been taken into consideration. Our initial set contained altogether 28 features, as presented in Table 2 on the next page.

A number of popular traditional (shallow) features were included in the feature set (features 1-4). These required less sophisticated text processing and had previously been used in several studies with success (Beinborn et al., 2012; Dell'Orletta et al., 2011; François and Fairon, 2012; Heimann Mühlenbock, 2013; Vajjala and Meurers, 2012). We computed sentence length as the number of tokens including punctuation, and token length as the number of characters per token.

Part of the syntactic features was based on the depth (length) and direction of dependency arcs (features 5-8). Another group of these features relied on the type of dependency relations. In feature 9 (Mod) nominal pre-modifiers (e.g. adjectives) and post-modifiers (e.g. relative clauses, prepositional phrases) were counted, similarly to Heimann Mühlenbock (2013). Variation features (ModVar, AdvVar) measured the ratio of a morphosyntactic category to the number of lexical (content) words in the sentence, as in Vajjala and Meurers (2012). These lexical categories comprised nouns, verbs, adverbs and adjectives. Subordinates (11) were detected on the basis of the "UA" (subordinate clause minus subordinating conjunction) dependency relation tag (Heimann Mühlenbock, 2013). Features DepDepth, Mod, Sub and RightDep, PrepComp have previously been empoyed for Swedish L1 readability at the text level in Heimann Mühlenbock (2013) and Falkenjack et al. (2013) respectively.

The lexical-morphological features (features 13-25) constituted the largest group. Difficulty at the lexical level was determined based on both the TTR feature mentioned above, expressing vocabulary diversity, and on the basis of the rarity of words (features 13-17) according to the Kelly list and the Wikipedia word list. An analogous approach was adopted also by François and Fairon (2012), Vajjala and Meurers (2012) and Heimann Mühlenbock (2013) with positive results. The LexD feature considers the ratio of lexical words (nouns, verbs, adjectives and adverbs) to the sum of tokens in the sentence (Vajjala and Meurers, 2012). The NN/VB ratio feature, which has a higher value in written text, can also indicate a more complex sentence (Biber et al., 2004; Heimann Mühlenbock, 2013). Features 21-25 are based on evidence from the content of L2 Swedish course syllabuses (Folkuniversitet, 2013) and course books (Levy Scherrer and Lindemalm, 2009), part of them being language-dependent, namely S-VB/VB and S-VB%. These two features cover different types of Swedish verbs ending in *-s* which can indicate either a reciprocal verb, a passive construction or a deponent verb, active in meaning but passive in form (Fasth and Kannermark, 1989).

Our feature set included three semantic features (26-28). The intuition behind 28 is that words with multiple senses (polysemous words), increase reading complexity as, in order to understand the sentence, word senses need to be disambiguated (Graesser et al., 2011). This feature was computed by counting the number of sense IDs per token according to a lexical-semantic resource for Swedish, SALDO (Borin et al., 2013), and dividing this value by the number of tokens in the sentence. As pronouns indicate a potentially more difficult text (Graesser et al., 2011), we included PN/NN in our set. Both NomR and PN/NN capture idea density, i.e. how complex the relation between the ideas expressed are (Heimann Mühlenbock, 2013).

4.4 Classification results

The results obtained using the complete set of 28 features is shown in Table 3. The results of the SVM are presented in comparison to a baseline classifier assigning the most frequent output label in the dataset to each instance.

Classifier	Acc	F1	B1 Prec	B1 Recall
Baseline	0.50	0.66	0.50	1.00
SVM	0.71	0.70	0.73	0.68

Table 3: Classification results with the complete feature set.

The baseline classifier tagged sentences with 50% accuracy being that the split between the two

Nr.	Feature Name	Feature ID	Nr.	Feature Name	Feature ID
Traditional			*Lexical-morphological*		
1	Sentence length	SentLen	13	Average word frequency (Wikipedia list)	WikiFr
2	Average token length	TokLen	14	Average word frequency (Kelly list)	KellyFr
3	Percentage of words longer than 6 characters	LongW%	15	Percentage of words above B1 level	DiffW%
4	Type-token ratio	TTR	16	Number of words above B1 level	DiffWs
Syntactic			17	Percentage of words at B1 level	B1W%
5	Average dependency depth	DepDepth	18	Lexical density	LexD
6	Dependency arcs deeper than 4	DeepDep	19	Nouns/verbs	NN/VB
7	Deepest dependency / sentence length	DDep / SentLen	20	Adverb variation	AdvVar
8	Ratio of right dependency arcs	RightDep	21	Modal verbs / verbs	MVB/VB
9	Modifiers	Mod	22	Participles / verbs	PCVB/VB
10	Modifier variation	ModVar	23	S-verbs / verbs	S-VB/VB
11	Subordinates	Sub	24	Percentage of S-verbs	S-VB%
12	Prepositional complements	PrepComp	25	Relative pronouns	RelPN
			Semantic		
			26	Nominal ratio	NomR
			27	Pronoun/noun	PN/NN
			28	Average number of senses per word	Sense/W

Table 2: The complete feature set.

classes was about 50-50%. The SVM classified 7 out of 10 sentences accurately. The precision and recall values for the identification of B1 sentences was 73% and 68%. Previous classification results for a similar task obtained an average of 77.25% of precision for the classification of easy-to-read texts within an L1 Swedish text-level readability study (Heimann Mühlenbock, 2013). Another classification at the sentence level, but for Italian and from an L1 perspective achieved an accuracy of 78.2%, thus 7% higher compared to our results (Dell'Orletta et al., 2011). The 73% precision of our SVM model for classifying B1 sentences was close to the precision of 75.1% obtained for the easy-to-read sentences from Dell'Orletta et al. (2011). François and Fairon (2012) in a classification study from the L2 perspective, aiming at distinguishing all 6 CEFR levels for French at the text level, concluded that intermediate levels are harder to distinguish than the levels at the edges of the CEFR scale. The authors reported an adjacent accuracy of 67% for B1 level, i.e. the level of almost 7 out of 10 texts was predicted either correctly or with only one level of difference compared to the original level. Precise comparison with previous results is, however, difficult since, to our knowledge, there are no results reported for L2 readability at the sentence level. Thus, the values mentioned above serve more as a side-by-side illustration.

Besides experimenting with the complete feature set, groups of features were also separately tested. The results are presented in Table 4.

Feature group (Nr of features)	Acc	F1
Traditional (4)	0.59	0.55
Syntactic (8)	0.59	0.54
Lexical (13)	**0.70**	**0.70**
Semantic (3)	0.61	0.55

Table 4: SVM results per feature group.

The group of traditional and syntactic features performed similarly, with an accuracy of 59%. In-

Rank	Feature ID	Weight
1	DiffW%	0.576
2	Sense/W	0.438
3	DiffWs	0.422
4	SentLen	0.258
5	Mod	0.223
6	KellyFr	0.215
7	NomR	0.132
8	AdvVar	0.114
9	Ddep/SentLen	0.08
10	DeepDep	0.08

Table 5: The 10 most informative features according to the SVM weights.

terestingly, although semantic features represented the smallest group, they performed 2% better than traditional or syntactic features. The largest group of features including lexical-morphological indicators performed around 10% more accurately than other feature groups.

Among the 10 features that influenced most the decisions of our SVM classifier, we can find attributes from different feature groups. The ID of these features together with the SVM weights are reported in Table 5. An informative traditional measure was sentence length, similarly to the results of previous studies (Beinborn et al., 2012; Dell'Orletta et al., 2011; François and Fairon, 2012; Heimann Mühlenbock, 2013; Vajjala and Meurers, 2012). Lexical-morphological features based on information about the frequency and the CEFR level of items in the Kelly list (DiffW%, DiffWs and KellyFr) also proved to be influential for the classification, as well as AdvVar. Two out of our three semantic features, namely NomR and, in particular, Sense/W, were also highly predictive. Syntactic features Ddep/SentLen and DeepDep, based on information about dependency arcs, were also among the ten features with highest weights, but they were somewhat less useful, as the weights in Table 5 show.

Contrary to our results, François and Fairon (2012) found syntactic features more informative than semantic ones for L2 French. This may depend either on the difference between the features used or the target languages. Moreover, in the case of Swedish L1 text readability the noun/pronoun ratio and modifiers proved to be indicative of text-level difficulty (Heimann Mühlenbock, 2013), but at the sentence level from the L2 perspective only the latter seemed influential in our experiments.

The data used for the experiments was labeled for CEFR levels at the text level, not at the sentence level. This introduced some noise in the data and made the classification task somewhat harder. In the future, the availability of data labeled at the sentence level could contribute to more accurate results. Excluding potentially lower level sentences from those appearing in higher level texts based on the distance between feature vectors could also be explored, in a similar fashion to Dell'Orletta et al. (2011).

5 Heuristics: GDEX parameters for sentence filtering and ranking

Besides SVM classification, our sentence selection module, Hit-Ex, offers also a number of heuristic parameter options[5], usable either in combination or as an alternative to the machine learning model (for further details see section 6). Part of these search parameters are generic preferences including the keyword to search for, its POS, the corpora from Korp to be used during selection and the desired CEFR level of the sentences. Furthermore, it is possible to avoid sentences containing: abbreviations, proper names, keyword repetition, negative formulations (*inte* "not" or *utom* "except" in the sentence), modal verbs, participles, s-verbs and sentences lacking finite verbs. Users can also allow these categories and choose a penalty point between 0 and -50 for them. The penalty score for each filtering criteria is summed for obtaining a final score per sentence, based on which a final ranking is produced for all sentences retrieved from Korp, the ranking reflecting the extent to which they satisfy the search criteria. Some additional parameters, partly overlapping with the machine learning model's features, are also available for users to experiment with, being that the machine learning model does not cover all CEFR levels. Based on statistical evidence from corpora, we suggested default values for all parameters for retrieving sentences of B1, B2, C1 level with rule-based parameters only. However, additional data and further testing is required to verify the appropriateness of the proposed values.

[5]See Pilán (2013) or the Hit-Ex webpage, http://spraakbanken.gu.se/larka/larka_hitex_index.html, for a complete list of parameters.

6 Combined approach

As mentioned in the previous subsection, the heuristic parameters and the machine learning approach have been implemented and tested also in combination. Parameters are kept to perform a GDEX-like filtering, whilst the SVM model is employed to ensure that hits were of a suitable level for learners. During this combined filtering, first a ranking for each unfiltered sentence coming from the web service of Korp is computed with heuristics. During these calculations, the parameters partly or fully overlapping with certain features of the machine learning model are deactivated, i.e. receive penalty points set to 0, thus, they do not influence the ranking. Instead, those aspects are taken care of by the machine learning model, in a subsequent step. Only the 100 sentences ranked highest are given for classification to the machine learning model for efficiency reasons. Finally, once the classification has been performed, sentences classified as understandable at B1 level are returned in the order of their heuristic ranking. Figure 2 shows part of the interface of Hit-Ex, as well as the highest ranked three sentences[6] of an example search for the noun *hund* "dog" at B1 level. Besides the Hit-Ex page, both the heuristics-only and the combined approaches are available also as web services.

7 Evaluation

The purpose of the evaluation was to explore how many sentences, collected from native language corpora in Korp with our algorithms, were understandable at B1 level (at B1 or below) and thus, appropriate to be presented to learners of L2 Swedish of that CEFR level. Participants included three L2 Swedish teachers, twenty-six L2 Swedish students at B1 level, according to their current or most recent language course, and five linguists familiar with the CEFR scale. Besides the criteria of understandability (readability), the aspect of being an appropriate exercise item was also explored. We selected altogether 196 sentences using both our approaches, with two different parameter settings for the rule-based method (See Pilán et al. (2013) and Pilán (2013) for further details about the evaluation). Evaluators were asked to indicate whether they found the sentences understandable at B1 level or not. Teachers and linguists (TL) rated the sentences also as potential exercise items. The results of the evaluation are presented in Table 6.

Understandability		Exercise item
TL	Students	TL
76%	69%	**59%**
73%		

Table 6: Evaluation results.

Respondents found overall 73% percent of the sentences selected by both our methods understandable at B1 level, whilst somewhat less, about six out of ten items, proved to be suitable for being included in exercises for L2 Swedish learning.

According to our evaluators, the two settings of the rule-based approach (Alg1-s1 and Alg1-s2) satisfied the two criteria observed between 1-5% more of the cases. On average, teachers, linguists and students considered 75% of the sentences selected with Alg1-s1 understandable, but only 70% of those identified with the combined approach (Alg2). The detailed results per algorithm, criteria and user group are shown in Figure 3.

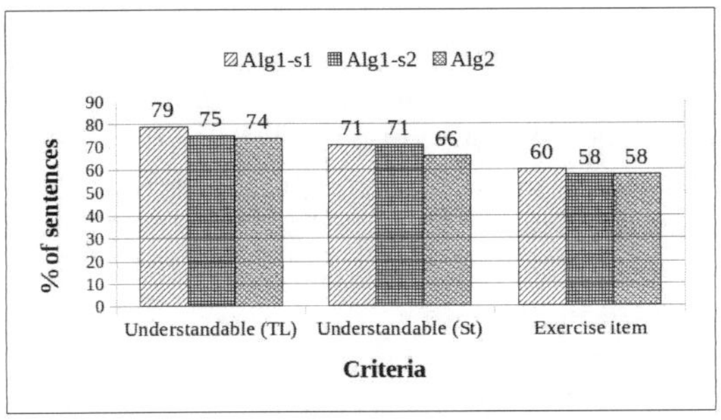

Figure 3: Comparison of algorithms.

According to our evaluators' comments, some of the selected sentences contained difficult aspects at the syntactic level, among others, difficult word order, subordinates and relative clauses. Moreover, at the lexical level, a stricter lexical filtering, and checking for a sufficient amount of lexical words in the sentence would be required. Respondents' comments revealed also the potential future improvement of filtering for context dependency which would make sentences more suitable as exercise items.

[6]English translations of the selected sentences: (1)"It would be enough for a normal dog."; (2)"They left the body in the form of a dog."; (3)"There was a person with a dog."

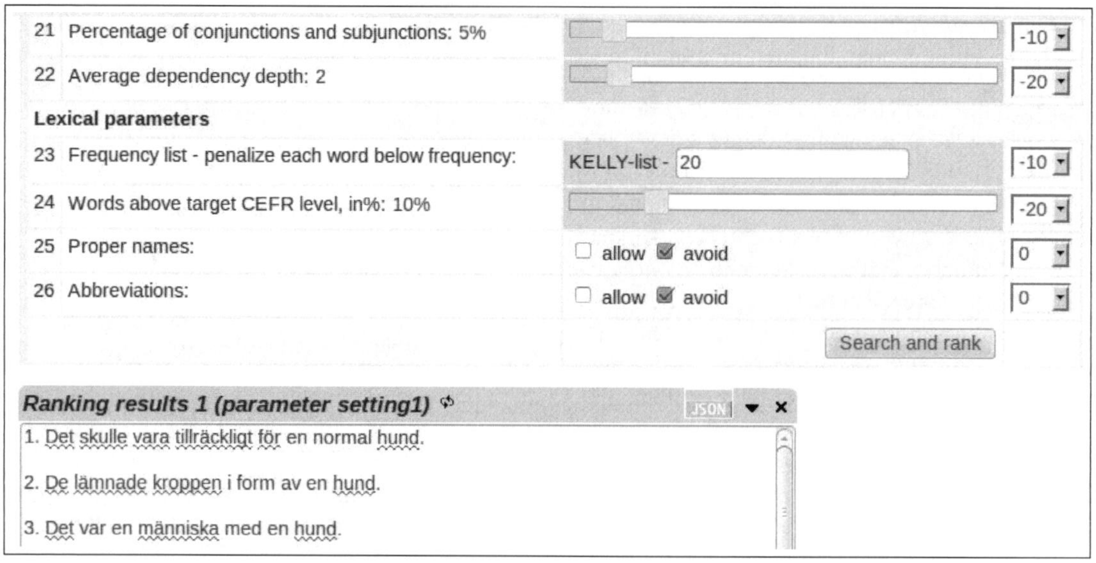

Figure 2: Part of the user interface and example search results.

8 Conclusion

In this study we investigated linguistic factors influencing the sentence-level readability of Swedish from a L2 learning point of view. The main contribution of our work consists of two sentence selection methods and their implementation for identifying sentences from a variety of Swedish corpora which are not only readable, but potentially suitable also as automatically generated exercise items for learners at intermediate (CEFR B1) level and above. We proposed a heuristics-only and a combined selection approach, the latter merging rule-based parameters (targeting mainly the filtering of "undesired" linguistic elements), and machine learning methods for classifying the readability of sentences from L2 learners' perspective. We obtained a classification accuracy of 71% with an SVM classifier which compares well to previously reported results for similar tasks. Our results indicate the success of lexical-morphological and semantic factors over syntactic ones in the L2 context. The most predictive indicators include, besides sentence length, the amount of difficult words in the sentence, adverb variation, nominal pre- and post-modifiers and two semantic criteria, the average number of senses per word and nominal ratio (Table 5). Within a smaller-scale evaluation, about 73% of the sentences selected by our methods were understandable at B1 level, whilst about 60% of the sentences proved to be suitable as exercise items, the heuristics-only approach being slightly preferred by evaluators. Further investigation of the salient properties of exercise items may contribute to the improvement of the current selection approach. The method, as well as most of the parameters and features used, are language independent and could, thus, be applied also to languages other than Swedish, provided that NLP tools performing similarly deep linguistic processing are available. Future additions to the filtering parameters may include aspects of word order, independence from a wider context, valency information and collocations. The optimization of the classifier could also be studied further; different algorithms and additional features could be tested to improve the classification results. The machine learning approach might show improvements in the future with training instances tagged at the sentence level and it can be easily extended, once additional data for other CEFR levels becomes available. Finally, additional evaluations could be carried out to confirm the appropriateness of the sentences ranked by the extended and improved selection method. To indicate the extent to which a sentence is understandable, 4- or 5-point scales may be used, and the employment of exercises instead of a list of sentences to read could also be investigated for verifying the suitability of the examples.

References

Lisa Beinborn, Torsten Zesch, and Iryna Gurevych. 2012. Towards fine-grained readability measures for self-directed language learning. In *Electronic Conference Proceedings*, volume 80, pages 11–19.

Douglas Biber, Susan Conrad, Randi Reppen, Pat Byrd, Marie Helt, Victoria Clark, Viviana Cortes, Eniko Csomay, and Alfredo Urzua. 2004. *Representing language use in the university: Analysis of the TOEFL 2000 spoken and written academic language corpus*. Test of English as a Foreign Language.

Carl Hugo Björnsson. 1968. *Läsbarhet*. Liber.

Lars Borin, Markus Forsberg, and Johan Roxendal. 2012. Korp - the corpus infrastructure of Språkbanken. In *Proceedings of LREC*, pages 474–478.

Lars Borin, Markus Forsberg, and Lennart Lönngren. 2013. SALDO: a touch of yin to WordNet's yang. *Language Resources and Evaluation*, 47(4):1191–1211.

Kevyn Collins-Thompson and James P Callan. 2004. A language modeling approach to predicting reading difficulty. In *HLT-NAACL*, pages 193–200.

Council of Europe. 2001. *Common European Framework of Reference for Languages: Learning, Teaching, Assessment*. Cambridge University Press.

Scott A Crossley, Jerry Greenfield, and Danielle S McNamara. 2008. Assessing text readability using cognitively based indices. *Tesol Quarterly*, 42(3):475–493.

Felice Dell'Orletta, Simonetta Montemagni, and Giulia Venturi. 2011. Read-it: Assessing readability of Italian texts with a view to text simplification. In *Proceedings of the Second Workshop on Speech and Language Processing for Assistive Technologies*, pages 73–83. Association for Computational Linguistics.

Johan Falkenjack, Katarina Heimann Mühlenbock, and Arne Jönsson. 2013. Features indicating readability in Swedish text. In *Proceedings of the 19th Nordic Conference of Computational Linguistics (NODALIDA 2013)*, pages 27–40.

Cecilia Fasth and Anita Kannermark. 1989. *Goda grunder*. Folkuniversitetets Förlag.

Folkuniversitet. 2013. Kurser i svenska. Svenska B1. `http://www.folkuniversitetet.se/Kurser--Utbildningar/Sprakkurser/Svenska_Swedish/Svenska-B1--Swedish-B1/`.

Thomas François and Cédrick Fairon. 2012. An AI readability formula for French as a foreign language. In *Proceedings of the 2012 Joint Conference on Empirical Methods in Natural Language Processing and Computational Natural Language Learning*, pages 466–477. Association for Computational Linguistics.

Arthur C Graesser, Danielle S McNamara, and Jonna M Kulikowich. 2011. Coh-Metrix providing multilevel analyses of text characteristics. *Educational Researcher*, 40(5):223–234.

Michal J. Heilman, Kevyn Collins-Thompson, Jamie Callan, and Maxine Eskenazi. 2007. Combining lexical and grammatical features to improve readability measures for first and second language texts. In *Proceedings of NAACL HLT*, pages 460–467.

Katarina Heimann Mühlenbock. 2013. *I see what you mean*. Ph.D. thesis, University of Gothenburg.

Jocelyn Howard and Jae Major. 2004. Guidelines for designing effective English language teaching materials. In *9th Conference of Pan Pacific Association of Applied Linguistics*.

Tor G Hultman and Margareta Westman. 1977. *Gymnasistsvenska*. Liber.

Milos Husák. 2010. *Automatic retrieval of good dictionary examples*. Bachelor Thesis, Brno.

Adam Kilgarriff, Milos Husák, Katy McAdam, Michael Rundell, and Pavel Rychlý. 2008. GDEX: Automatically finding good dictionary examples in a corpus. In *Proceedings of Euralex*.

Paula Levy Scherrer and Karl Lindemalm. 2009. *Rivstart B1 + B2. Textbok*. Natur och Kultur, Stockholm.

Fabian Pedregosa, Gaël Varoquaux, Alexandre Gramfort, Vincent Michel, Bertrand Thirion, Olivier Grisel, Mathieu Blondel, Peter Prettenhofer, Ron Weiss, Vincent Dubourg, et al. 2011. Scikit-learn: Machine learning in Python. *The Journal of Machine Learning Research*, 12:2825–2830.

Ildikó Pilán, Elena Volodina, and Richard Johansson. 2013. Automatic selection of suitable sentences for language learning exercises. In *20 Years of EUROCALL: Learning from the Past, Looking to the Future. 2013 EUROCALL Conference, 11th to 14th September 2013 Évora, Portugal, Proceedings.*, pages 218–225.

Ildikó Pilán. 2013. *NLP-based Approaches to Sentence Readability for Second Language Learning Purposes*. Master's Thesis, University of Gothenburg. `https://www.academia.edu/6845845/NLP-based_Approaches_to_Sentence_Readability_for_Second_Language_Learning_Purposes`.

Sarah E Schwarm and Mari Ostendorf. 2005. Reading level assessment using support vector machines and statistical language models. In *Proceedings of the 43rd Annual Meeting on Association for Computational Linguistics*, pages 523–530. Association for Computational Linguistics.

Thomas M Segler. 2007. *Investigating the selection of example sentences for unknown target words in ICALL reading texts for L2 German*. PhD Thesis. University of Edinburgh.

Wade Shen, Jennifer Williams, Tamas Marius, and Elizabeth Salesky. 2013. A language-independent approach to automatic text difficulty assessment for second-language learners. In *Proceedings of the 2nd Workshop on Predicting and Improving Text Readability for Target Reader Populations*, pages 30–38. Association for Computational Linguistics.

Ajay Kumar Tanwani, Jamal Afridi, M Zubair Shafiq, and Muddassar Farooq. 2009. Guidelines to select machine learning scheme for classification of biomedical datasets. In *Evolutionary Computation, Machine Learning and Data Mining in Bioinformatics*, pages 128–139. Springer.

Sowmya Vajjala and Detmar Meurers. 2012. On improving the accuracy of readability classification using insights from second language acquisition. In *Proceedings of the Seventh Workshop on Innovative Use of NLP for Building Educational Applications*, pages 163–173. Association for Computational Linguistics.

Sowmya Vajjala and Detmar Meurers. 2014. Assessing the relative reading level of sentence pairs for text simplification. In *Proceedings of the 14th Conference of the European Chapter of the Association for Computational Linguistics (EACL-14)*, Gothenburg, Sweden. Association for Computational Linguistics.

Elena Volodina and Sofie Johansson Kokkinakis. 2013. Compiling a corpus of CEFR-related texts. In *Proceedings of the Language Testing and CEFR conference, Antwerpen, Belgium, May 27-29, 2013*.

Elena Volodina and Sofie Johansson Kokkinakis. 2012. Introducing the Swedish Kelly-list, a new lexical e-resource for Swedish. In *Proceedings of LREC*, pages 1040–1046.

Elena Volodina, Richard Johansson, and Sofie Johansson Kokkinakis. 2012b. Semi-automatic selection of best corpus examples for Swedish: Initial algorithm evaluation. In *Workshop on NLP in Computer-Assisted Language Learning. Proceedings of the SLTC 2012 workshop on NLP for CALL. Linköping Electronic Conference Proceedings*, volume 80, pages 59–70.

Elena Volodina, Dijana Pijetlovic, Ildikó Pilán, and Sofie Johansson Kokkinakis. 2013. Towards a gold standard for Swedish CEFR-based ICALL. In *Proceedings of the Second Workshop on NLP for Computer-Assisted Language Learning. NEALT Proceedings Series 17. Nodalida 2013, Oslo, Norway.*

Author Index